The English Nobility under Edward the Confessor

PETER A. CLARKE

CLARENDON PRESS · OXFORD
1994

Oxford University Press, Walton Street, Oxford OX2 6DP
Oxford New York Toronto
Delhi Bombay Calcutta Madras Karachi
Kuala Lumpur Singapore Hong Kong Tokyo
Nairobi Dar es Salaam Cape Town
Melbourne Auckland Madrid
and associated companies in
Berlin Ibadan

Oxford is a trade mark of Oxford University Press

Published in the United States
by Oxford University Press Inc., New York

British Library Cataloguing in Publication Data
Data available

Library of Congress Cataloging in Publication Data
Clarke, Peter A.
The English nobility under Edward the Confessor / Peter A. Clarke.
p. cm. — (Oxford historical monographs)
Includes bibliographical references and index.
1. Great Britain—History—Edward, the Confessor, 1042–1066. 2. Land tenure—England—History. 3. Nobility—England—History. 4. Anglo-Saxons. I. Title. II. Series.
DA154.8.C57 1994
942.01'9—dc20 93-27129

ISBN 0-19-820442-6

1 3 5 7 9 10 8 6 4 2

Typeset by Best-set Typesetter Ltd., Hong Kong
Printed in Great Britain
on acid-free paper by
Bookcraft (Bath) Ltd.
Midsomer Norton, Avon

For Liz

ACKNOWLEDGEMENTS

I would like to take this opportunity to give my thanks to a number of people who have, directly or indirectly, assisted in the production of this book.

Mr Norman Shead first introduced me to medieval history, and his example encouraged me to continue my studies at university. Dr Patrick Wormald, my tutor at the University of Glasgow, helped to increase my interest and suggested the subject of my research. As I developed my thesis at Oxford, he continued to give me useful advice and comment. My supervisor, Mr James Campbell, provided a great deal of inspiration and practical help whilst I wrote my thesis, and later as I worked on this book. Thanks are also due to my mother and father, for their interest and encouragement.

This book is dedicated to my wife, Liz, to whom I owe my greatest debt. It is quite true to say that without her continuing help and support neither my doctorate nor this book would have been completed.

CONTENTS

LIST OF MAPS AND FIGURES

LIST OF TABLES

ABBREVIATIONS

ASC	*The Anglo-Saxon Chronicle*, trans. G. N. Garmonsway (London, 1972)
BAR	British Archaeological Reports
Carmen	*Carmen de Haestingae Proelio*, ed. C. Martin and H. Muntz, Oxford Medieval Texts (Oxford, 1972)
Chron. Abingdon	*Chronicon Monasterii de Abingdon*, ed. J. Stevenson, Rolls Series (London, 1858)
Chron. Ramsiensis	*Chronica Abbatiae Ramsiensis*, ed. W. D. Macray, Rolls Series (London, 1886)
Chron. St Albans	*Gesta Abbatum Monasterii Sancti Albani*, ed. H. T. Riley, Rolls Series (London, 1867)
DB	*Domesday Book*, Records Commission (London, 1783–1816)
EHD	*English Historical Documents*, gen. ed. D. C. Douglas; i. *100–1042*, ed. D. Whitelock (London, 1955); ii. *1042–1135*, ed. G. W. Greenaway (London, 1953)
EHR	*English Historical Review*
Exon.	Exon. Domesday in DB iv
Florence	*The Chronicle of Florence of Worcester*, trans. T. Forester (London, 1854)
Heming	*Hemingi Chartularium Ecclesiae Wigorniensis*, ed. T. Hearne (Oxford, 1723)
ICC	*Inquisitio comitatus Cantabrigiensis*, ed. N. E. S. A. Hamilton (London, 1876)
Liebermann	F. Liebermann, *Gesetze der Angelsachsen*, i. *Text und Übersetzung* (Halle, 1903)
Liber Eliensis	*Liber Eliensis*, ed. E. O. Blake, Camden Society, 3rd ser., 92 (1962)
Monasticon	*Monasticon Anglicanum*, ed. W. Dugdale (London, 1817–30)
Morris	*Domesday Book: Text and Translation*, gen. ed. J. Morris (Chichester, 1975–86)
Orderic Vitalis	Orderic Vitalis, *Historia Ecclesiastica*, ed. M. Chibnall, Oxford Medieval Texts (Oxford, 1969–80)
Reassessment	P. H. Sawyer (ed.) *Domesday Book: A Reassessment* (London, 1985)
Regesta	*Regesta Regum Anglo-Normannorum*, i. ed. H. W. C. Davis (Oxford, 1913)

Roman de Rou	Wace, *Roman de Rou*, in *Chroniques Anglo-Normandes*, i. ed. F. Michel (Paris, 1836)
S	Sawyer, P. H., *Anglo-Saxon Charters: An Annotated List and Bibliography*, Royal Historical Society Guides and Handbooks, 8 (London, 1968): refs. are to Charter no.
TRE	*Tempore regis Edwardi*
TRHS	*Transactions of the Royal Historical Society*
TRW	*Tempore regis Willhelmi*
VCH	*Victoria County History of England*
Vita Edwardi	*Vita Edwardi Regis*, ed. F. Barlow, Nelson's Medieval Texts (London, 1962)
William of Poitiers	William of Poitiers, *Gesta Guillelmi*, ed. R. Foreville (Paris, 1952)
Williams, 'Land and Power'	'Land and Power in the Eleventh Century: The Estates of Harold Godwineson' in R. A. Brown (ed.), *Proceedings of the Battle Conference on Anglo-Norman Studies, 1981* (Woodbridge, 1982)

1

INTRODUCTION

THE study of the late-Anglo-Saxon aristocracy as a group is possible only because of the survival of a single source: Domesday Book. Other sources for the period which might be expected to shed some light on the landholders in England at this time—in particular narrative sources and charters—give almost no information about laymen other than those who became earls. There is, for example, no large body of private charters from this period. The wills which have survived are interesting in themselves, but are too few in number to establish what general conditions existed. On the other hand the royal charters, although largely concerned with gifts to the Church, are generally witnessed by a number of laymen, who are usually described as '*ministri*'. But in the absence of other information, these charters provide little more than a list of names.[1]

As for the narrative sources, the most important of these is the Anglo-Saxon Chronicle, which hardly ever mentions any laymen other than the earls; the other narrative sources are generally monastic histories which only mention those laymen who have had dealings with the house in question. In fact there are probably more entries concerning the activities of English landowners after the Conquest than there are for the period of Edward the Confessor's reign. For example, Æthelnoth of Kent, whom Domesday records as having been one of the most important of the non-earlish landholders in Kent and elsewhere, is not mentioned in a chronicle before 1066, but appears in Florence of Worcester as one of the hostages taken by William to Normandy in 1067.[2]

On the other hand, in Domesday Book we have a source which covers all England south of the Tees so thoroughly that one chronicler believed that 'not a single hide, nor one virgate . . . not even one

[1] For a summary of the charter and narrative evidence, see Ch. 6.
[2] *Florence*, *sub anno* 1067.

ox nor one cow nor one pig escaped notice'.[3] The details were to be gathered not only for the time of the survey itself, but also, and most importantly for the purposes of this study, for the day on which King Edward died.

Of course, Domesday gives a quite different perspective upon the nobility than would a body of either narrative sources or charters. Narrative sources tend to give evidence in the main on political activities, and on the relationships between laymen and the Church, but information about lay estates is only given incidentally. A collection of charters provides information about individual manors, but usually only at the moment when they enter or leave a particular estate. Charters may also allow us to build up a picture of both the lord's family and his household by examination of the witness lists. Both charters and narrative sources provide information about a particular subject over a long period of time, although evidence for a particular manor or a specific year might be very scant indeed.

In contrast to this, Domesday provides a detailed source which describes the landholding patterns over most of the kingdom for two particular dates. What Domesday was not intended to record, and to which it only occasionally refers, is the long and often complicated history of the descent of a property which might have preceded or followed the date upon which a particular manor was recorded in the survey. Domesday records that the land at Ryhall and Belmesthorpe had been held by Earl Waltheof in the time of King Edward, and by the Countess Judith at the time of the survey. Evidence from a charter shows that these lands had been the subject of a long and frequently altered series of agreements between the family of Waltheof and the Abbot of Peterborough.[4]

Again, the large estates which appear in Domesday Book have the impression of permanence, but this can be quite misleading. Estates could easily be broken up at short notice if the holder died or was outlawed. The great East-Anglian lord, Eadric of Laxfield, was outlawed during Edward's reign, his lands taken into the king's hands and his men required to seek other lords.[5] Domesday Book describes the estate of Ketill Alder as comprising a group of manors worth £50, but luckily we also have a copy of Ketill's will.[6] If this will had been carried out before 1066, the land would have been divided amongst

[3] *ASC* E *sub anno* 1085.
[4] *DB* i, fo. 228; S 1481.
[5] *DB* ii, fos. 313, 342b.
[6] S 1519.

eight different beneficiaries, and it is unlikely that there would have been any indication in Domesday itself that the collection of manors had once formed a single estate. Urk, a follower of Cnut, built up a substantial holding in Dorset during his life, valued at over £60. He and his wife died before 1066, apparently without issue, leaving the land to their foundation of Abbotsbury.[7] Had they had children, or had they survived until 1066, their estate would have been included in Domesday. Indications such as this suggest that, had the Domesday Survey referred to a day other than that on which King Edward died, there would have been significant differences in the make-up of many individual estates.

Nor does Domesday provide very much evidence on family relationships between the great men, or of their political activity during Edward's reign. On the other hand, under ideal conditions Domesday Book could provide all the information concerning the land held by a lord at the end of King Edward's reign, with details of the value of each of the constituent manors and of tenurial relationships. Unfortunately, conditions are rarely ideal, and the information which the *Inquisitio Eliensis* states was collected by the commissioners is often not recorded in full in the Survey itself.[8]

One problem which confronts anyone who attempts to draw statistics from Domesday is the regional variation between the various circuits. Separate groups of commissioners were responsible for each of the seven circuits, and each group tended to record details in a different way, or to include details that others omitted. Whilst some circuits include details of values in 1066, at the time of transfer, and in 1086, circuits IV, V, and VI only include details for 1066 and 1086. Different circuits record woodland by length and breadth, as a number of acres, or by the number of swine that could be pastured there. When considering the patterns of landholding in 1066, there are two important areas where the various circuits differ.

In the first place there are gaps in the record, since Domesday does not always name the man (or men) who held a particular manor '*tempore regis Edwardi*'. In the counties of circuit IV, Oxfordshire, Leicestershire, Northamptonshire, and Warwickshire, the information is very sketchy indeed: in Oxfordshire, for example, about 60 per cent of the entries do not mention a landholder *TRE*, although the problem is not quite so serious in the other three counties.

[7] S 961, S 1063, S 1064. [8] *EHD* ii. 215.

Elsewhere more than 95 per cent of entries include information on the pre-Conquest landowner, but a particular entry might go into varying degrees of detail. In circuits III and VII, ample details are given concerning the commendation of the person who actually held the land. In other circuits no details of such relationships are given, or so few as to suggest that the majority have been omitted (this particular problem is dealt with in detail in Chapter 4).

A potentially more serious problem exists throughout the whole of Domesday: as a general rule, only the first name of a Saxon *antecessor* is given. The stock of first names is not large, and it is often difficult to know whether we are dealing with one man, or with many. However, there are a number of criteria which can be applied to help determine, with a greater or lesser degree of certainty, how many individuals of the same name are involved.

It is sometimes possible to identify an individual who has a particularly uncommon name: for example, all the entries relating to Mærlswein almost certainly refer to a single man. Many other names are used in a limited number of entries: about 90 per cent of all names in Domesday Book occur in less than fifty separate entries. When all the occurrences of a particular name are examined, the geographical location of the manors in question, the use of bynames, and the particular tenant-in-chief who held the land in 1086 can all be used to help identify how many individuals with the same name have been recorded.

In a proportion of entries, bynames are sometimes provided, either in the text of the Exchequer Domesday itself, or in such satellite texts as the Exeter Domesday or the *Inquisitio comitatus Cantabrigiensis*. When a byname is used regularly we can be reasonably certain of identifying most of the land of a particular individual. We can also be sure of distinguishing two men with different bynames. Clearly entries mentioning 'Ulf the son of Tope' and 'Ulf the son of Azor' refer to different men;[9] and we can also be reasonably certain that Godwine Cilt, Godwine Wambestrang, and Godwine Scild are all separate individuals, although all three held land in the same county.[10] On the other hand, it is possible for a particular person to be identified by more than one byname. A prime example of this is the woman called 'Eadgifu Faire' (sometimes rendered 'Eadgifu

[9] *DB* i. 220, 376b.
[10] Morris, Cambridgeshire, nn. 22. 7, 41. 14; *DB* i. 193b.

Pulchra') or at other times 'Eadgifu Dives'.[11] There are other cases of men being given more than one byname. Eadric, normally called 'of Laxfield' (when given a byname at all) seems to have been called 'son of Ingold' in a single entry;[12] and 'Æthelnoth of Kent' was known as 'Æthelnoth Cilt' inside the county itself.[13] At least in the case of these important landholders there are usually sufficient other clues to indicate where one man is known by two names.

The most generally helpful way of distinguishing a landholder *TRE* from others of the same name is by reference to the tenant-in-chief in 1086. In a large number of cases the majority of the land held by a single Saxon lord was passed on to a single tenant-in-chief of William. So if one name appears regularly as the *antecessor* of a particular Norman, then it is likely to represent a single man. For example the holder *TRE* of many of the manors which Aubrey de Vere held in 1086 was named Wulfwine, and although no byname is given it is likely that most, if not all these entries refer to a single man. In one other entry a man is said to have held land from Aubrey's predecessor (*sub antecessore Alberici de Ver*) and again this can be confidently presumed to be the same Wulfwine.[14] William of Warrenne appears to have succeeded to all of the land of a Saxon named Toki,[15] whilst in 1086 Alfred of Marlborough held most of the land held by Karl twenty years earlier.[16] In this last case the name, Karl, is particularly unusual, and this enables us to identify Alfred's predecessor with the man of the same name who held three other pieces of land in the same area.

However it was by no means a golden rule that the estates of King Edward's time were kept intact throughout William's reign. Ælfric Camp had held land in fourteen villages: in 1086 it was divided between Eudo Dapifer, Rober Gernons, Ralph Baignard, and Roger de Ramis.[17] In this case the presence of a distinctive byname allows us to identify Ælfric confidently. Or again, Domesday Book states directly that the land of a very minor Suffolk landholder, Beorhtmær, had been divided amongst no fewer than three men.[18] Domesday

[11] *DB* i. 189b; ii. 284b, 285.
[12] *DB* ii. 299b.
[13] *DB* i. 1, 46.
[14] *DB* i. 199b; ii. 76–7b, 107.
[15] *DB* i. 196, 196b; ii. 157b, 160–70, 398, 398b.
[16] *DB* i. 21b, 22b, 28, 36b, 47b, 63, 70b, 97.
[17] *DB* i. 61b, 196b, 197b, 212; ii. 66, 67b, 69b, 70b, 83, 83b, 403b.
[18] *DB* ii. 423b.

Book does not always provide the information to allow us to make correct identifications. Drogo de Bevere held land which had previously belonged to 'Ulf' in Lincolnshire and Yorkshire, but the will of Ulf the son of Tope suggests that the Yorkshire 'Ulf' was quite different from the man who held land in Lincolnshire; the will also goes on to show that Ulf Tope's son also had land which was held in 1086 by Erneis de Burun and the Archbishop of York.[19]

King William does appear to have appointed certain tenants-in-chief as successors to individual Saxons, but this was not the only method used to distribute lands. There were whole regions of England which were given to an individual lord, on a purely geographical basis: Odo acquired most of Kent; Sussex was divided into geographical Rapes; Shropshire became the fief of Roger of Montgomery, and Cheshire of Hugh d'Avranches. In these areas it is not possible to use the post-Conquest lord as a means of identifying pre-Conquest lords.

Robin Fleming has argued convincingly that the distribution of land to William's followers took place in at least one other way.[20] At some time in William's reign, he began to distribute land to certain followers on a hundredal basis. Men were granted the remaining parts of hundreds of which the king had not previously disposed. So in Yorkshire, the Count of Mortain appears to have been granted the residual land of no fewer than nineteen wapentakes. In these wapentakes the king and the Church held considerable amounts of land, and there were other tenants-in-chief, but in every case, these last appear to have held land inherited from a specific *antecessor*. Robert of Mortain, on the other hand, had a fief in this area made up of the land of more than fifty pre-Conquest landholders.[21] The estate of Thurkill White seems to have been divided as a result of a similar method of land distribution in Herefordshire. Roger Lacy's land in Hereford was based on territorial considerations and included the land of a certain Thurkill. As this was not a particularly common name, it is likely that this is the same man as Thurkill White, the *antecessor* of Hugh Ass elsewhere in the county. Only by a very sophisticated analysis of these hundredal distributions would it be

[19] *DB* i. 231, 236, 324, 324b, 340, 344, 344b, 348b, 358b, 360, 360b; Ulf's will: D. Whitelock, *Anglo-Saxon Wills* (Cambridge, 1930), no. 39.

[20] Fleming, *Kings and Lords in Conquest England* (Cambridge, 1991), Ch. 4.

[21] Ibid. 155–8.

possible to make up any other estates which have been broken up in this way, and this has not been attempted here.

Fleming has assessed the amount of land which was transferred by inheritance from specified important *antecessors* at 10 per cent.[22] At first sight, this figure seems to imply that any attempt to identify nobles from their Norman successors is doomed to failure before it begins. However, as this figure was given to show one aspect of the tenurial revolution which had taken place, and not the possibilities of identifying individuals, there are a number of important considerations. In certain large areas—the counties and rapes given entire to a single tenant-in-chief—it is clear that there is no possibility of using details from 1086 in making such identifications, and they should be excluded. Further, the land of the earls has been included, and this can normally be identified from other information. By excluding these factors, we can say that perhaps a fifth of the remaining secular land was held by the successors of important individual Saxons. Again, this seems low: but in Cambridgeshire, where almost all of the landholders *TRE* can be identified with confidence, only about 30 per cent of the land (excluding that held by the king, his earls, and the Church) was held by landholders whose entire estate was valued at over £40, and only one major demesne estate was divided after the Conquest (see below, Ch. 5). Although it is dangerous to extrapolate from the results of a single county, the findings from Cambridgeshire suggest that, outside the counties where land was transferred wholesale to a single lord, the majority of major landholders can be identified by identifying their successor *TRE*. We can only hope that in those cases where a pre-Conquest estate was divided amongst numbers of Normans, there is other evidence either in Domesday or outside it to prove that fact.

Ann Williams has demonstrated another method by which pre-Conquest estates might be reconstructed, namely by the careful examination of the land held in divided villages.[23] By comparing the holders who divided the villages, and recognizing groups of

[22] Ibid. 112.

[23] A. Williams, 'A Vice-Comital Family in Pre-Conquest Warwickshire', in R. A. Brown (ed.), *Anglo-Norman Studies, XI: Proceedings of the Battle Conference, 1988* (Woodbridge, 1989), 279–92; and 'The King's Nephew: The Family and Career of Ralph, Earl of Hereford', in C. Harper-Bill, C. J. Holdsworth, and J. L. Nelson (eds.) *Studies in Medieval History Presented to R. Allen Brown* (Woodbridge, 1989), 327–42.

landholders who are found together on more than one occasion, it is possible to identify kinship groups. For example, Asgot, Beorhtric, and Edmund were all landholders in a number of counties, with their own distinctive Norman successors—William Leofric, Thurstan fitz Rolf, and Roger Lacy. However, the fact is that these men had divided the villages of Childrey and Coleshill between them. Childrey was a village of 35 hides, and was approximately evenly divided between these men: but Coleshill was divided precisely between the three. Three entries for Coleshill record that each man held 8 hides which were each valued at £7 *TRE* (although after the Conquest the values had changed in the three holdings); a fourth entry states that one hide in Coleshill was held by William Leofric, Thurstan fitz Rolf, and Roger Lacy in 1086, and had been held by three unnamed thegns in 1066. The presumption must be that the three thegns are none other than Asgot, Beorhtric, and Edmund, giving a total of 25 hides valued at £25.[24] This kind of division suggests that three brothers (or at least, close relatives) had recently succeeded to the manor and divided it—had the division been carried out earlier, it is likely that the value of the three holdings would not have remained identical. In this case, the land of the three Saxons has been treated as a single estate, but there are likely to be many other connections which could be made, and which are beyond the scope of this present study.

The evidence given by Domesday for landholding *tempore regis Edwardi* is, according to the Exeter Domesday, for the day that King Edward was alive and dead. Since William was presenting himself as the heir of King Edward, this is exactly what we would expect. However, it is known in a number of instances that the landholder named in Domesday had either died or been outlawed before the beginning of 1066. Earls Godwine, Leofric, and Siweard had all died in the 1050s, and Earl Ælfgar died in the early 1060s, but all these men are recorded as important landholders in Domesday Book.[25] Indeed Godwine, who had died the earliest, was said to have held the most land.

It has been suggested that the lands which Domesday assigns to these men were, in 1066, being held by their widows.[26] This,

[24] *DB* i. 59b, 61, 63, 72b.
[25] See App. I for a list of land held by members of the earlish families.
[26] Williams, 'Land and Power', 177.

however, cannot have been true in every case. In the first place Gytha, Godwine's widow, was named in Domesday as holding land worth £500 in her own right. This made ber exceptionally wealthy, and it is hard to see why she might have been named the holder of some land, while her late husband was named as the holder of other portions. Next, Siweard's wife had predeceased her husband, and so cannot be presumed to have held the land in 1066.

There is some evidence to suggest that the Domesday commissioners were not always assiduous in ensuring that the details that were gathered were accurate for the day on which King Edward died. Tostig was replaced by Morkær as Earl of Northumbria in 1065. However, both are recorded as holding considerable amounts of land within the earldom, although it is likely that Morkær did not gain control of some, at least, of his land until after Tostig's outlawry. One Shropshire entry does describe the situation as it was on the day of Edward's death: a law suit on which the king was to give judgment was postponed due to the illness which led to King Edward's death.[27] But, as the examples of Tostig and Morkær show, not all the entries in Domesday necessarily refer to the same precise date, and inconsistencies clearly did occur. Whatever the reasons behind the naming of men long dead as landholders in 1066, it would be unwise to assume that there was a single explanation for all of them.

We know the approximate dates at which the various earls died, and so are able to show that some of the details of Domesday regarding the situation in Edward's reign are inaccurate. But it is possible that a number of the other lay landholders named by Domesday were also dead in 1066, and that their estates were recorded incompletely. This problem is most acute when Domesday records a number of members of the same family as holding land: for example, Burgeræd and his sons Eadwine and Ulf were all recorded as holding land in Bedfordshire *TRE*.[28] It is at least possible that Burgeræd had died before 1066, and that before his death, his estate had comprised the land which Domesday apportioned among all three men. Taking account of the possible problems arising from this I have chosen, where possible, to treat all the land which was held by two members of the same immediate family as belonging to a single estate.

[27] *DB* i. 252b. [28] See App. II for the lands of these men.

The difficulties listed above have been caused by the lacunae in the information provided by Domesday, but the next problem is caused by the surfeit of data which the survey brought together. Domesday gives not one method of valuing most manors, but three: the number of ploughlands available, the hidage of the manor, and a financial value. All three methods might be used to calculate the overall value of one lord's lands. However, Sally Harvey has shown convincingly that the figure for ploughlands is in fact a fiscal assessment made around 1086–7, and as such would not be appropriate when attempting to assess manorial values before the Conquest.[29]

The hidage of a manor has been used quite frequently as the measure of value of a manor. MacDonald and Snooks have shown that, for Essex at least, there is a relationship between the value of a manor and its assessment in hides. However it is not a direct relationship, as the geld was a regressive tax, and in general it appears that the more resources a manor had, the more beneficial was the hidation. Thus a manor with a value of 10*s*. had an average assessment of 70 acres, or 7 acres per shilling of value. On the other hand a manor worth £5 was assessed at an average of only 2.9 acres per shilling of value.[30] Therefore the total number of hides held by a particular lord does not give a direct assessment of the value of his land.

Moreover, the geld assessment of particular manors could be altered arbitrarily, with no apparent change in the value of the manor to account for the new hidation. This happened at Cold Ashton, Gloucestershire, where there had been five hides but 'by the grant of Kings Edward and William two of them do not geld'.[31] Alternatively, a manor might simply have been favourably assessed in the first instance. Although, as a very broad generalization, a manor of 1 hide was valued at £1, there were striking exceptions. For example, Earl Harold's manor of Torrington, Devon, although assessed at 1¾ hides, was valued at £18.[32] In Cambridgeshire King William reduced the number of hides in Armingford Hundred by 20 per cent. In other hundreds in the same county most manors had their assessment

[29] S. Harvey, 'Taxation and the Ploughland in Domesday Book', in *Reassessment*, 92.

[30] J. MacDonald and G. D. Snooks, 'Were the Tax Assessments of Domesday England Artificial? The Case for Essex', in *Economic History Review*, 2nd ser., 39 (1985).

[31] *DB* i. 165.

[32] *DB* i. 101b.

reduced by an arbitrary amount, while in the remaining hundreds the assessment remained the same.[33] Such reductions could as easily have happened in earlier reigns. In too many cases hidation does not equate directly to the financial values for it to be used as a method of measuring the relative values of different estates.

This leaves the financial value given for each manor, and it is this method of valuation which will be used to compare the overall value of land throughout this study. Exactly what these financial valuations represent is not clear. The most normal term used is *valet* or *valuit*, which implies a value. Very many of the values are in round figures of 20*s*., 50*s*., or £5, and often these valuations reflect the hidage, at the rate of one hide to one pound. In these cases it would appear that such valuations represented a general assessment of 'what will this estate bring in peopled and stocked as it is'.[34] In spite of the fact that these valuations might appear to be as arbitrary as the hidage, MacDonald and Snooks have shown that the values given in Essex (for 1086 at least) do seem to reflect the various resources which were recorded for each manor to a reasonable degree of approximation.[35] Further, where beneficial hidation appears to have taken place, the value better represents the resources which were available: Queen Eadgyth had land in Milverton, Somerset, which was rated at half a virgate, but had land for 16 ploughs and was valued *TRE* at £12.[36] On other occasions, Domesday gives very precise values: Broxton in Cheshire was worth 10*s*. 8*d*. *TRE* and 18*s*. 8*d*. at the time of the Survey;[37] at Skeyton in Norfolk, a freeman had $11\frac{1}{2}$ acres worth 17 pence.[38] Such accurate measures presumably reflect an accumulation of different payments, perhaps with an element of estimation included. Other entries state that a particular manor 'renders' (*reddit*) a certain value, and in these cases the value presumably is the amount of money which the lord received from it. In Buckinghamshire, Upton rendered £21 *TRW*, and £15 before the Conquest.[39] In a few entries, manors were said to have rendered more than they were worth: Fareham (Hants) was valued at £16, but

33 *VCH Cambridgeshire* i. 341–2.
34 F. W. Maitland, *Domesday Book and Beyond* (Cambridge, 1921), 413 n. 3.
35 J. MacDonald and G. D. Snooks, 'The Determinants of Manorial Income in Domesday England: The Case for Essex' in *Journal of Economic History*, 45 (1985).
36 *DB* i. 87.
37 *DB* i. 264b.
38 *DB* ii. 229b.
39 *DB* i. 143b.

was farmed out for £20 '*sed non potest pati*',[40] but such situations are relatively rare, and where they do occur, they almost always refer to the situation in 1086. We can agree with R. Weldon Finn that most of the valuations were not simply arbitrary estimates, but gave a reasonable approximation of the actual value of an estate to its lord.[41]

However, even with this measurement, there are problems which must be mentioned. Whilst in almost every instance some value is given in each entry, in many cases no specific value for the period *TRE* is given, and in these cases the value *TRW* is used instead. Where large areas were devastated, as was the case in Yorkshire and other northern counties, this could result in a significant underestimate of the value of manors in particular areas. Another problem which arises from the use of financial values is that for particular manors, values could vary dramatically through time, particularly as a result of military action. A number of manors in Northamptonshire were waste *TRE*, or had a low valuation, presumably as a result of the Northumbrian rebellion. The Welsh Marches had been quiet since Harold's last incursion into Wales in 1062, but values might not have recovered fully by 1066. When considering estates which include many manors in these areas, we must be aware that the overall value might well be underestimated.

In spite of these difficulties, it must be repeated that in Domesday Book we have a source of information concerning England in the reign of Edward the Confessor which is without parallel, and which illuminates many aspects of the period which would otherwise have remained hidden.

The subject of this study is the lay aristocracy of England in the reign of Edward the Confessor, and these lords will be studied in the main through their estates, as they can be reconstructed from Domesday Book. However, as a certain amount has already been written about the earls, concerning both their estates and their political careers,[42] more emphasis will be placed upon the second rank of the aristocracy who, although holding a significant amount of land, nevertheless received little or no notice from other sources for the reign.

[40] *DB* i. 40b.

[41] R. Weldon Finn, *An Introduction to Domesday Book* (Cambridge, 1961), 223–40 gives a good discussion on the meanings and implications of the various forms of financial valuation.

[42] See App. III for secondary sources concerned with the earls and their families.

2

THE ESTATES OF THE EARLS

THE earls were by far the most prominent group of laymen in England during the reign of Edward the Confessor. This is clear from a reading of the Anglo-Saxon Chronicle for this period; they appear consistently as witnesses to both royal and private charters; and Domesday Book reveals that the earls were also the holders of the greatest lay estates during Edward's reign. The five richest landholders were all earls, and of the twenty greatest lay estates, half were held either by earls or their wives (see Table 2.1). Furthermore, in twenty-six counties the largest lay estate was held by a member of the earlish families (see Fig. 2.1).

During the later years of Edward's reign the earls were drawn from four families. Domesday records the holdings of Earl Godwine (who had died well before 1066), his wife Gytha, and their children Harold, Tostig, Gyrth, Leofwine, and Gunnhilda as being worth just over £5,000. The lands of Leofric's family (including land assigned to Leofric himself, his wife, Earl Ælfgar and his wife, and Ælfgar's sons, Earls Eadwine and Morkær) were valued at £2,400. The other two earlish families were, in comparison, much less significant: Earl Siweard and his son were said to have manors worth £350, whilst land assigned to Earl Ralph, his wife, and son was valued at £170. Both Siweard and Ralph will have held more land when they held office, but both died in the 1050s, leaving young sons to succeed them. It is possible that Waltheof, Siweard's son, had been assigned a small earldom before 1066, but he can hardly have had time to establish himself before the Conquest. According to an entry in Domesday Book, Ralph's son Harold was still under the guardianship of Queen Eadgyth when King Edward died.[1] The figures given above for each family are approximate, and the remainder of the chapter will be spent in examining these estates in more detail, first by

[1] *DB* i. 129b.

TABLE 2.1. Lay estates valued at £100 or more

	Total value (£)	£100s ....2....4...6...8...10..>>..30
Earl Harold:	2,847	**************************>>*
Earl Morkær	960	**********************
Earl Godwine	724	*****************
Earl Ælfgar	714	*****************
Gytha, wife of Godwine	588	**************
Earl Eadwine	588	**************
Beorntric, Ælfgar's son	560	*************
Earl Tostig	492	***********
Asgeir the Staller	448	**********
Ulf Fenisc	394	*********
Eadgifu the Fair	366	*********
Ælfstan of Boscombe	289	******
Earl Leofwine	287	******
Azur	271	******
Æthelnoth of Kent	260	*****
Earl Gyrth	250	*****
Wulfweard White, his wife and son	223	*****
Mærlswein the Sheriff	214	****
Earl Siweard	212	****
Robert fitz Wymarc	204	****
Ralph the Staller	201	****
Eadric of Laxfield	192	****
Wihtgar, Ælfric's son	182	****
Bundi the Staller	182	****
Asgot, Beorhtric, and Edmund	176	****
Family of Earl Ralph	170	***
Eadnoth the Staller and his son	155	***
Toki, Otta's son	151	***
Siweard of Maldon	147	***
Karl	144	***
Eadmær Atre	143	***
Siweard Barn	142	***
Wulfwine (*antec.* Aubrey de Vere)	141	***
Wulfwynn of Creslow	137	***
Cypping	137	***
Earl Waltheof	137	***
Baldwin, Herluin's son	136	***
Leofnoth the son of Osmund	118	***
Wigot of Wallingford	117	***
Azur, Thored's son	116	***
Æthelgyth, wife of Thurstan	111	**
Beorhtmær	109	**
Osweard of Norton	109	**
Askell of Ware	109	**
Beorhtsige Cilt	107	**
Toki (*antec.* William Warenne)	103	**
Beorhtric, man of Queen Eadgyth	101	**
Burgeræd and his sons	100	**
Eadric the Wild	100	**

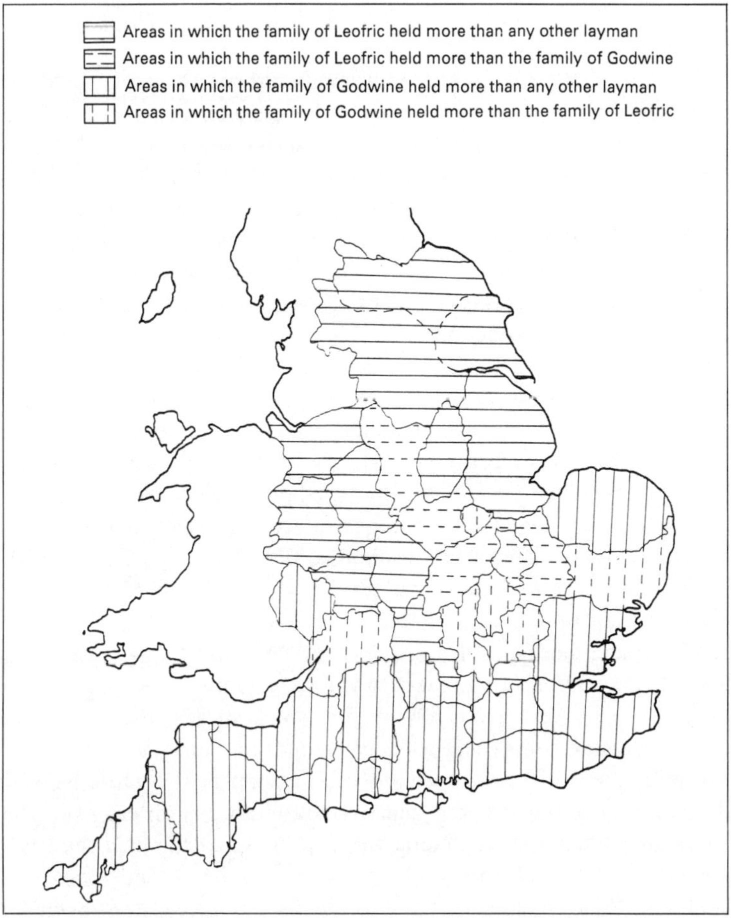

FIG. 2.1. The relative influence of the families of Godwine and Leofric

addressing some general points, and then by looking more closely at the estates of the individuals who comprise this group.

One question which must be considered at the outset is whether the estates of each earlish family should be treated as a whole, or whether the land assigned to different individuals should be treated separately. The majority of other lay landholders must be treated as individuals, as sources rarely provide any information about family connections, and so in order to make reasonable comparisons it might be thought necessary to treat the various members of the earlish families separately.[2]

It is true that the members of a family did not always act together politically. Swein murdered his cousin Beorn, after Beorn and Harold had refused to ask King Edward to revoke Swein's outlawry. Later in the reign, Harold refused to support Tostig during the Northumbrian revolt. This led ultimately to their fighting on different sides at the battle of Stamford Bridge, and the rift between the two brothers formed a major theme of the *Vita Edwardi*.[3] But it is easy to exaggerate these differences. In 1051 Edward felt obliged to outlaw not only Earl Godwine but also his sons, whilst Queen Eadgyth, Godwine's daughter, was sent to a nunnery. As late as 1063 Harold and Tostig led a joint campaign into Wales, which would hardly have been the success it was without a high degree of co-operation between the two brothers. Eadwine and Morkær acted in unison during the Northumbrian Revolt, and fought together at the battle of Fulford. After the Conquest the two brothers acted together when they first submitted to William, then revolted against him. Finally, although Tostig did desert his elder brother, Gyrth and Leofwine died with Harold at Hastings.

There are more positive reasons for choosing to treat the land belonging to different members of the same family as belonging to a single estate. There are a few entries which suggest that there was some confusion concerning which member of a family actually held a particular piece of land. In a number of examples of manors held by the family of Godwine, the geld roll for Wiltshire differs from the Exchequer Domesday in stating which person actually held the land. The texts of the various geld rolls can even be at odds with one another.[4] It is possible that this difficulty is entirely due to errors within the geld rolls, which do have other inconsistencies. However, different parts of a single manor could be held by different family members. Harold held an outlier of his mother's manor of King's Brompton,[5] and both Harold and Gytha were recorded in Domesday as holding outliers of the manor of Laughton, Sussex, which was attributed to Earl Godwine.[6] Gytha was also said to have held a

[2] All but three of the estates considered in Ch. 3 were held by individuals.
[3] e.g. see the poem which ends Ch. 5, book 1 of the *Vita Edwardi*.
[4] R. W. Finn, *Domesday Studies: The Liber Exoniensis* (London, 1964), 117.
[5] *DB* i. 86b, 92.
[6] *DB* i. 19, 21, 22.

number of her manors from her husband.[7] Because different members of the same family could hold manors which were related to one another in various ways, it is quite possible that confusion could have arisen as to the actual holder, not least since the Domesday Survey took place some twenty years after the Conquest.

Another indication that confusion between various members of the same family might have existed is that Domesday attributes large estates to members of the great earlish families who had died long before 1066. It seems likely that land which had been attributed to such men did remain within the family. One of the functions of Domesday appears to have been to ascertain from whom the holder at the time of the Survey had acquired his land. Often Domesday records that a particular manor had or had not belonged to the current tenant's predecessor, which indicates a practical interest in the landholder *TRE*.[8] Given this interest, it would be surprising if extremely outdated information were allowed to be entered if any major changes in ownership had taken place between the death of the recorded landholder and the time of the Conquest.

On occasion, Domesday attributes a manor to someone who had died long before 1066, but other evidence is available to indicate the person who actually held the land on the day of King Edward's death. Where this happens the land always appears to have remained within the dead man's family. The Exeter Domesday mentions a wood which had belonged to Godwine's manor of Frampton, Dorset, whilst the Exchequer Domesday states that Gytha held the manor.[9] In the Domesday account of Colchester, there were three houses which belonged to Shalford, 'which Ælfgifu used to hold'. But in the entry for Shalford itself, Earl Ælfgar (Ælfgifu's husband) was said to have been the holder *TRE*.[10] In Hampshire, Earl Godwine was recorded as holding land at *Allege* in 1066, which was valued with Earl Harold's manor of Bishop's Sutton.[11] A similar example can be shown in Sussex, where Godwine was recorded as holding land which pertained to Harold's manor of Rodmell.[12] In Shropshire, land which

[7] *DB* i. 24, 38b, 39b.

[8] e.g. Geoffrey de Mandeville held Clapham wrongfully, because it did not pertain to Asgeir's land, *DB* i. 36; whilst Aubrey de Vere held land which had not belonged to his predecessor 'in the king's despite', *DB* i. 199b.

[9] *DB* i. 78b, Exon. 28.

[10] *DB* ii. 3b, 106b.

[11] *DB* i. 44b.

[12] *DB* i. 21b, 26.

was assigned to Earl Leofric was valued with a manor which was being held in 1066 by his grandson Eadwine.[13] It is possible that the cases where values were combined or manors assessed together were examples of post-Conquest reorganization. However, as in each case they involve land which had belonged to different members of the same family, one of whom was dead by 1066, it seems probable that in at least some of the examples the land had passed to the wife or son of the deceased landholder before 1066.

These examples suggest that by no means all the land which Domesday assigns to men long dead by 1066 was held by the widows of those men *TRE* (see Ch. 1). This leaves open the question of which of the family members actually did hold the land for which there is no other information. Because in the majority of cases this cannot be resolved, it is best to treat the lands of each family as a whole when comparing them with other estates, and only to separate the lands held by individuals when the estate is being examined in detail.

Another basic question is how far the large estates held by the earls were attached to their office or to what extent their landed wealth was held independently of their position. The difficulties of determining the history of more than a relatively small proportion of the manors of any particular estate makes it impossible to approach this problem by analysing the various dates on which the land had been acquired. However, a number of attempts have been made to identify specifically 'comital' manors, that is, manors which were held by whoever occupied the office of earl. In the words of Maitland: 'The enormous wealth of the house of Godwine seems only explicable by the supposition that the earlships and older ealdormanships had carried with them a title to the enjoyment of wide lands.'[14]

A number of different features have been used to identify these comital manors. The name, first used by Maitland,[15] comes from a heading used in the Exon Domesday account of Somerset.[16] There, a number of manors are described as being '*mansiones de comitatu*'. Round pointed out that these *mansiones* were not simply distinguished by their heading, but had a number of other distinctive features which made them stand out from the 'normal' manor.[17] All the

[13] *DB* i. 254, 259b.
[14] F. W. Maitland, *Domesday Book and Beyond* (Cambridge, 1921), 168.
[15] Ibid.
[16] Exon. 107.
[17] *VCH* Somerset, i. 397.

mansiones de comitatu were valued in terms of the renders which they owed, rather than just the financial value of the manor, and the render was to be paid '*ad numerum*'. So at Dulverton, Domesday states that Harold's manor there '*reddit xi libras et x solidos*'; but of 2 hides attached to Dulverton after 1066, Domesday records the value with the following phrase: '*valet lxiii solidos et ii denarii*'.[18] Also, many of the entries of this group rendered an amount which was some multiple of £1 3*s*. Harold had held six of the *mansiones de comitatu* in Somerset, of which five rendered an amount which was a multiple of 23*s*.[19]

Of these manors, Old Cleeve also shows another feature which had been used to identify the comital manors: to this manor pertained the third penny of five hundreds. The earl had the right to the third penny in each hundred and borough of the counties where he held office, and it is likely that the manors to which this profit pertained were held by the current earl by right of his office. Harold held a number of manors apart form Old Cleeve to which were due the third penny of one or more hundreds. In Devon, the revenue from four hundreds pertained to Moretonhampstead and Mollan,[20] and the third penny from the whole of Dorset was due at Puddletown.[21] Harold also held the manor of Much Cowarne, Herefordshire, to which three hundreds were attached, and Burghill, in the same county, with two hundreds.[22] Gyrth, Earl of East Anglia, held the profits of Lothingland hundred in Suffolk.[23] Eadwine, Earl of Mercia, held the manors of Bloxham and Adderbury,[24] to which the profits of two hundreds were attached. Finally, Earl Waltheof held the manor of Yardley, Northamptonshire, which may have had the third penny of two hundreds attached to it.[25]

A few manors held by earls did not have a financial valuation but were stated to owe a number of night's farm. This was a feature normally associated with manors of the royal demesne, as it was a

[18] *DB* i. 86b.
[19] Dulverton, Old Cleeve, North Curry, Congresbury, and Henstridge. Only Capton (valued at 22*s*. 6*d*.) does not fit the pattern exactly, *DB* i. 86b–87.
[20] *DB* i. 101b.
[21] *DB* i. 75.
[22] *DB* i. 186.
[23] *DB* ii. 283; H. Cam, *Law-Finders and Law-Makers in Medieval Englang* (London, 1962), 170.
[24] *DB* i. 154b.
[25] Cam, *Law-Finders and Law-Makers*, 169.

rent paid in kind, and intended to support the royal court for a specified period of time. In Essex and Suffolk some manors which were valued in this way were said to have been held by earls. It is possible in these cases that this is evidence of royal manors being given to these earls. Earl Ælfgar held a single manor of this sort in Essex, while Harold held five (four in Essex and one in Suffolk) which each owed a number of night's farm.[26] Both Harold and Ælfgar had held Essex and Suffolk as part of the East-Anglian earldom, although at the time of Edward's death, Essex was held by Leofwine, and Suffolk by Gyrth. The fact that Domesday records Harold and Ælfgar as holding these manors may simply be another example of Domesday's inconsistency with regard to the precise date implied by the term *TRE*. But Essex may have been a special case, as there was no royal demesne recorded for the county in 1066, and the case for describing these manors as 'comital' is far from having been proved.

Given that many of the *mansiones de comitatu* of Somerset had a render rather than a value, other manors which had renders recorded might also have been comital. Harold's manors of Swanbourne, Prince's Risborough, and Upton in Buckinghamshire all owed renders of coin '*ad numerum*', as did Edward's demesne manors in the same county.[27] In addition, Harold's three manors were distinguished by the use of a phrase other than the normal '*X tenuit Y*'. In the case of Upton, for example, Domesday states '*Opetune fuit villa Heraldi*'.[28] In Worcestershire, Earl Eadwine received a farm from his manor of Bromsgrove.[29] Up to this point, all the manors which have been identified as being 'comital' in some way are all in the southern half of the country. There is also a group of manors in Yorkshire which can be distinguished by their being valued in multiples of £56, and because many had been held by men who had been Earl of Northumbria at some point in Edward's reign. The manor of Whitby was valued at £112; Falsegrave, Burstwick, Pocklington, Kilnsea, Withernsea, Mappleton, and Hornsea were all worth £56; and the combined value of the manors of Bridlington and Burton Agnes was

[26] Harold's manors were Writtle, Brightlingsea, Newport, and Lawstead in Essex, and Necton in Suffolk. Ælfgar held the manor of Baddow, Essex. *DB* ii. 5, 6, 7, 21b, 235.

[27] *DB* i. 143, 143b.

[28] *DB* i. 143b.

[29] *DB* i. 172.

also £56.[30] It may be a coincidence, but the manor of Bloxham and Adderbury in Oxfordshire, identified above as a comital manor by virtue of the fact that it had the earl's third penny attached, was also valued at £56.

The combined value of these Yorkshire manors was £560, an extremely large amount, and equivalent to the very largest of the non-earlish estates. If they had all been held by the Earl of Northumbria then they would have provided Siweard, Tostig, and Morkær with more land by virtue of their office than they held by any other means. If so, it would confirm Maitland's opinion that the bulk of the earlish estates was made up of comital manors. On the other hand, in the south the comital manors which Harold held only appear to have made up about 10 per cent of his entire estate, and although a number of comital manors may not have been recognized, it does not seem likely that the bulk of Harold's estate came directly through his tenure of comital manors.

Even those manors which have been identified as being comital in origin were not in fact held solely by the earl of the region in which they lay. First, the manors listed under the Somerset heading '*mansiones de comitatu*' include land held by Earl Godwine and all his family, not simply the land of Earl Harold, and manors which had not been held by Harold still rendered amounts of money '*ad numerum*' which were multiples of £1 3*s*. For example, Creech St Michael, which rendered £9 4*s*. (eight times £1 3*s*.) was held by Harold's sister Gunnhildr.[31] King's Brompton, which was also included amongst the *mansiones de comitatu*, and which was held by Gytha *TRE*, was said to have been a royal manor.[32] In fact, the heading '*mansiones de comitatu*' might well refer to post-Conquest organization, rather than to the situation before 1066.

Nor was the third penny of the hundred held exclusively by the local earl. Earl Godwine's wife Gytha, Earl Leofric's wife Godgifu, Robert fitz Wymarc, and Ralph the Staller all held manors which included the profits of hundreds or wapentakes.[33] It is therefore not possible to state with certainty that those manors which did include the third penny in their valuation were being held as comital rather than private manors. Even the '£56 manors' of Yorkshire were not

30 *DB* i. 299, 299b, 305, 323b.
31 *DB* i. 86b.
32 *DB* i. 86b, 92, Exon. 103, 272b.
33 See the list of 'private hundreds' in Cam, *Law-Finders and Law-Makers*, 166–70.

the sole preserve of those men who held the Northumbrian earldom. Earl Eadwine held Gilling, valued at £56,[34] and both he and Earl Harold held a number of manors which combined to be worth some multiple of £56.[35] In all these cases it is possible that these manors had been originally assigned to the local earl, and were then redistributed by that earl to his family or his allies. But if the earl was free to dispose of the comital lands in this way, this would very much weaken the bond between the manors and the office.

Furthermore, if, as has been suggested above, the land assigned to men long dead by 1066 were still in the hands of the same family until much nearer the time of the Conquest, this would imply that any so-called 'comital' manors had remained with the family even where the office itself had been lost. Earl Siweard, who died in 1055, was recorded by Domesday as holding one of the Yorkshire manors valued at £56. If this manor had indeed remained in the hands of Siweard's family, it cannot have passed to the later earls, and so it makes very little sense to regard this manor at least as being comital, even if, as is possible, the land was originally assigned to Siweard by the king on Siweard's accession to the earldom.

It is extremely difficult to separate those manors which may have been assigned specifically to the earl by virtue of his office from those which were held by the earl as a private landholder. While some groups of manors do appear to be in some way distinguishable from the rest, it is never the case that such manors were held exclusively by the earl of the area in question. Some manors might have been given to the earl on accession to the office, and this may well explain why Ælfgar and Harold held manors in East Anglia which appear at one time to have belonged to the royal demesne. But in those examples the earls appear to have received at least a life interest in the manors, as they continued to hold them even after they lost the earldom of Essex. The comital manors, if they can be said to exist at all, seem to have been given to the earls to hold for their life (at least) in spite of the fact that the extent of the earldoms themselves could be quite flexible, and could change from year to year. Moreover, if the *mansiones de comitatu* were indeed comital manors, then the example of Creech St Michael would appear to show that the earls could not be

[34] *DB* i. 309.

[35] Harold held Cleeting and Flamborough (*DB* i. 305, 323b); Eadwine's manors in the county, excluding Gilling and Askam Bryan, combine to a value of £56, *DB* i. 307, 310b, 313, 315, 319.

prevented from disposing of the land to their families. There is very little indeed to distinguish such land from the manors which were held by the earls as private landholders, and so it is impossible to calculate just how much of the earlish estates were indeed held by virtue of the office.

Domesday, then, does not show clearly any manors which might have been attached to the office of earl, and which were transferred with that office to any succeeding earl. On the other hand, many of the manors described above might have been granted by the king to an earl when he first received the office. It would seem probable that Tostig at least would have needed the provision of lands in Northumbria, since his family's main power lay in the south. The royal demesne manors which Harold and Ælfgar held in Essex may also have been granted to them in order to establish their power in the area. It is also possible that much of the land which earls held within their sphere of influence was acquired through the power and influence of the office itself. Earl Harold was named as the beneficiary in two East-Anglian wills which were drawn up whilst he was earl there. One of these granted Harold money, the other a portion of land.[36] The extent of such gains cannot be established from Domesday, which only describes the land held at a particular time, whilst there are too few wills and other lay documents to make it possible to quantify in any way the gains a particular earl might have made during his period of office.

Land could also be acquired by using extra-legal methods. Earls Godwine and Harold seem to have despoiled a number of churches of large amounts of land. Steyning (Sussex), worth £86, had been granted to Fecamp Abbey, but was in Harold's hand *TRE*;[37] Banwell and Congresbury were taken from the Bishop of Wells, and there were many more depredations against other ecclesiastical establishments.[38] Harold even used his own power to enable others to do the same: Æthelnoth Cilt was able to take Merclesham and Hawkhurst from St Martin's, giving only inadequate compensation, 'through the support of Harold'.[39]

[36] Thurstan granted Harold half a mark of gold, while Wulfgyth gave the manor of Fritton to Earl Godwine and Earl Harold. Ketel also granted Harold land at *Moran*, but this may have been after Ælfgar had become Earl of East Anglia. In any case the will was not carried out before the Conquest. None of the family of Godwine held either of these pieces of land *TRE*, according to Domesday. S 1531, S 1535, S 1519.

[37] S 1054, *DB* i. 17.

[38] Fleming, *Kings and Lords*, 84–6 n. 126.

[39] *DB* i. 2.

The estates of each family will now be considered in more detail. Of all the earlish families, that of Earl Godwine, with land and revenues valued at over £5,000, was by far the greatest: its estates even rivalled those of King Edward and his queen, which were worth around £6,000. Domesday assigned land worth a total of £2,846 to Earl Harold, more than half his family's holdings, disregarding for the moment any land which Domesday assigned to Earl Godwine and which may have been in Harold's hands by 1066.[40] Harold held land in all but five counties, although in seven other counties he had less than £20's worth of land. Most of the counties where Harold had little or no land lay in the west Midlands; the one exception to this was, perhaps surprisingly, Kent.[41] Since Godwine was recorded as the greatest lay landholder in that county, it is very possible that Harold had succeeded to much of his father's land there. Harold's main power lay south of the Thames, where 60 per cent of his land lay. He held more land than any other layman (excluding the king) in Surrey, Hampshire, Berkshire, Wiltshire, Dorset, Somerset, Devon, and Cornwall, as well as north of the Thames in Essex and Hertfordshire. In Yorkshire he held about £300's worth of land (some of which might have belonged to Tostig before the rebellion of 1065) and he also had smaller amounts of land in the south Midlands.

Harold's younger brothers were much less well endowed with land. Earl Tostig was recorded in Domesday as holding land valued at £492. Two manors of the royal demesne in Bedfordshire and one in Hertfordshire were specified as having been held by Tostig before his outlawry, and a manor which Tostig had held in Oxfordshire was in Earl Eadwine's hands in 1066. The figure of £492 for Tostig's estate is probably an underestimate. It is quite likely that Domesday failed to note all the cases where land which had been held by Tostig was transferred to another holder between Tostig's departure from England and King Edward's death, for example some at least of Harold's land in Yorkshire, mentioned above. Of the land which we know Tostig held, £132's worth lay in Yorkshire and almost £140's worth in Hampshire. The remainder was spread around the Midlands, with a few outlying manors in the south and west.

Gyrth Earl of East Anglia, held land to the value of £250, of which £160's worth lay in Norfolk, Suffolk, Cambridgeshire, and Bedford-

[40] See 'Lands of Earl Harold in 1066', Map 181, in D. Hill, *An Atlas of Anglo-Saxon England* (Oxford, 1981), 103.

[41] For the details of manors on the earlish estates, see App. I.

shire. He held land worth a few pounds in several other counties, but in Sussex his manors were valued at £67. Leofwine, whose earldom lay in the south-east, held £60's worth in the counties of Kent and Middlesex, and a further £40's worth in both Essex and Buckinghamshire. Apart form £20's worth of land elsewhere in his earldom, the remainder of his estate (worth £287 in total) was found in Dorset and Devon. Harold's sister Gunnhildr had two manors worth £22 in all in Somerset, and in the same county Harold's son Godwine held two much smaller manors worth just £5.

Gytha, the widow of Earl Godwine, was recorded as holding land valued at £588. All of it lay to the south of the Thames, but it was concentrated largely in Wiltshire, Somerset, and Devon. Earl Godwine himself was recorded as holding manors worth £723, mainly in Sussex and Kent, and his lands in those two counties made him the richest recorded lay landholder there. Godwine also had a few manors in Hampshire and Surrey, as well as a single manor in Worcestershire. It is not possible to determine the descent of Godwine's manors after his death, with the exception of the few examples mantioned earlier in this chapter.

An interesting point concerning the distribution of the family's land is that the estates of the younger sons—Tostig, Gyrth, and Leofwine—appear to have been geographically discrete. As might be expected, each of these men held land both in their own earldom, and in the counties south of the Thames where their father had held his power base. Tostig's manors in the south lay mainly in Hampshire, but Gyrth had just a single manor there valued at £7, and Leofwine had none. Conversely, Leofwine held land in Kent worth £60 while the two other brothers held no land there, while Gyrth had land worth £67 in Sussex, although Tostig and Leofwine each had only one small manor. These three brothers appear to have been provided with family land in geographically separate areas. Yet Harold's manors extended into each of these counties, and even within his brothers' own earldoms, Harold tended to be the dominant landholder. In Hertfordshire, Buckinghamshire, and Essex, Harold held more than Leofwine, whilst in Suffolk he held more than Gyrth, and in Yorkshire more than twice the amount of land assigned to Tostig. The family of Godwine was by far the most powerful landed group in England at the end of Edward's reign, and within the family, Harold's position was predominant.

The next of the great families was that of Leofric of Mercia. At the end of Edward's reign Leofric's two grandsons, Eadwine and Morkær, were earls of Mercia and Northumbria respectively.[42] Eadwine's lands lay mainly in the west Midlands, and he was recorded as the richest lay landholder in Warwickshire, Cheshire, and Shropshire. He also had land worth £115 in Yorkshire, a single manor worth £56 in Yorkshire, and another in Lincolnshire worth £24. In total Eadwine's land was worth £610. His younger brother Morkær held a larger estate, with land worth half as much again—£970. Almost two-thirds of this land lay in Yorkshire, but Morkær was also the richest individual lay landholder in Lincolnshire, and held £150 of land elsewhere in his brother's earldom of Mercia. In Yorkshire £336 was accounted for by just six manors which belonged to the '£56' group discussed above. In Lincolnshire, there is some doubt as to the actual status of £37 10*s*. which Domesday states was held by Earl Morkær.[43] This land is mentioned in a will made by Ulf Tope's son which can be dated between the Conquest and 1069. The land was said in the will to have belonged to Ulf, and was distributed without reference to the earl, some of it being given to the Church. There would seem to be two possible explanations: that Ulf had held the land as Morkær's dependant before 1066, or that he had acquired the land from Morkær some time after Edward's death. The latter explanation seems to be the more acceptable in view of an entry in the *clamores* relating to Lincolnshire. The land in question was held in 1086 by Drogo de Bevere, the successor of Ulf Tope's son. The claim disputes Drogo's right to hold this land which, it is said, had belonged to Morkær *TRE*.[44] If Ulf had held the land before 1066 then Drogo, his successor, could have held it without dispute in 1086. But if Ulf had acquired the land after Edward's death, then Drogo would have had no such claim, although he might have taken control of the land at the same time as he was given the other parts of Ulf's estate. If this explanation is correct, then Morkær had sold his land at some point after Edward's death, and this might have been necessary to raise money to cover the earl's expenses during the battles against Harald Hardrada, or to enable Morkær to 'buy back' his lands from King William.[45]

[42] See 'Land of the Leofric Family', Map 182, in Hill, *Atlas of Anglo-Saxon England*, 104.

[43] These figures have been included as part of Morkær's estate in the figures given in Apps. I and II.

[44] *DB* i. 377b.

[45] *ASC* E *sub anno* 1066: 'Men payed him [William] tribute, and gave him hostages, and redeemed their land from him.'

Domesday also records land as being held by Earls Leofric and Ælfgar, in spite of the fact that Leofric had died in 1057 and Ælfgar some time in the 1060s. Leofric's land was confined to two Shropshire manors, of which one was worth £21 and the other was valued with one of Eadwine's manors in the same county. Earl Ælfgar's recorded estate was much larger than that assigned to his father, being valued at £714, and was more widespread than those of his two sons. Ælfgar had the largest recorded lay estate in Staffordshire, and had considerable amounts of land in Derbyshire and Warwickshire. In Cambridgeshire and Huntingdonshire he held almost £100, and only slightly less in Oxfordshire and Buckinghamshire. In East Anglia and Essex his manors were worth £126, and in Middlesex Ælfgar had two large manors, worth £120, which made him the largest lay landholder in that county. Some of Ælfgar's wealth in the east may have resulted from his having been Earl of East Anglia, but he was a significant figure in the county before he took over that office. Whilst Harold was still Earl of East Anglia, Ælfgar was cited as a witness to Thurstan's will in the county of Essex, which shows his influence there. At some point in the reign Ælfgar reduced his landholding in Norfolk, selling Hemsby (valued at £26),[46] and Beighton (valued at £6).[47] There may have been other sales which Domesday fails to record, but it is not possible to say when these sales took place.

There have been some doubts as to whether Ælfgar's land would still have been in the hands of Leofric's family by 1066. Davies suggest that 'the manors in question may have passed to his successor, or to anyone else the King chose'.[48] However, as pointed out earlier, where the history of these lands between the death of the recorded holder and 1066 can be established, they always appear to have remained in the family. It seems best to assume that most if not all of the land did indeed pass to Ælfgar's wife or sons, even if we do not know who precisely held the land on the day of Edward's death.

The widows of Leofric and Ælfgar both had quite large estates in their own right. Godgifu had land worth £111 in Worcestershire, Warwickshire, Staffordshire, and Shropshire. In addition, a single manor which she held in Nottinghamshire (Newark, valued at £50) made her the richest lay landholder in that county. Ælfgifu, the widow of Ælfgar, had land worth £65, and it lay close to the land of her husband, particularly in Suffolk and Essex.

[46] *DB* ii. 195. [47] *DB* ii. 194b.

[48] R. H. Davies, 'The Lands of Harold, Son of Godwine, and their Distribution by William I', MA Diss. (Cardiff, 1967).

There are two striking differences between the estates of the families of Godwine and Leofric: the value of the land involved, and its distribution. In fact, these two aspects are not unconnected. Figure 2.1 shows the relative power of the families within each county, whilst Figure 2.2 shows the relative wealth of each county, calculated by determining the total value of each county relative to its recorded population. The west Midlands, where the main power of the house of Leofric lay, was the poorest area in the country, whilst the south, the stronghold of Godwine's clan, was the richest. With the exception of Yorkshire, the sixteen counties with the highest value per head all lie south of a line running from Bristol to the Wash. The poorest counties are Shropshire, Staffordshire, and Derbyshire, which were the heart of the Mercian earldom. That Yorkshire is the exception to this rule is likely to be due to inaccuracies in the survey of that county. Many settlements were described as waste, and although a value for 1066 is given, no population is recorded. The result is that the population was undervalued, artificially inflating the calculated value per head. The family of Godwine may well have had more influence nationally by virtue of the wealth which accrued from its land, but it would be a mistake to think that the Mercian earls were not as influential in the areas where their land was concentrated as Godwine and his sons were south of the Thames.

The other two earlish families which Domesday mentions were not in the same class as either of the two dealt with above. Earl Siweard, who had been Earl of Northumbria until 1055, had land recorded in his name which was valued at £212.

This comprised the manor of Whitby, worth over £100, two other large manors in Yorkshire, and a smaller manor in Derbyshire. His son, Waltheof, had an estate valued at £136, which was more scattered than that of his father. It lay in nine counties, from Essex and Middlesex in the south to Derbyshire, Rutland, and Yorkshire in the north.

The last of the earlish families was also the least, as far as land recorded in Domesday was concerned. Ralph, a nephew of King Edward, and Earl of Hereford before his death in the 1050s, was recorded as holding £85's worth of land. The land lay mainly in the counties of Gloucester and Leicester, but included single manors in Berkshire, Northampton, and Warwick. He had rights of *sac* and *soc* in Lincolnshire, but he was not recorded as holding land there, and nor were his wife or son. Ralph's wife Gytha, who also died before

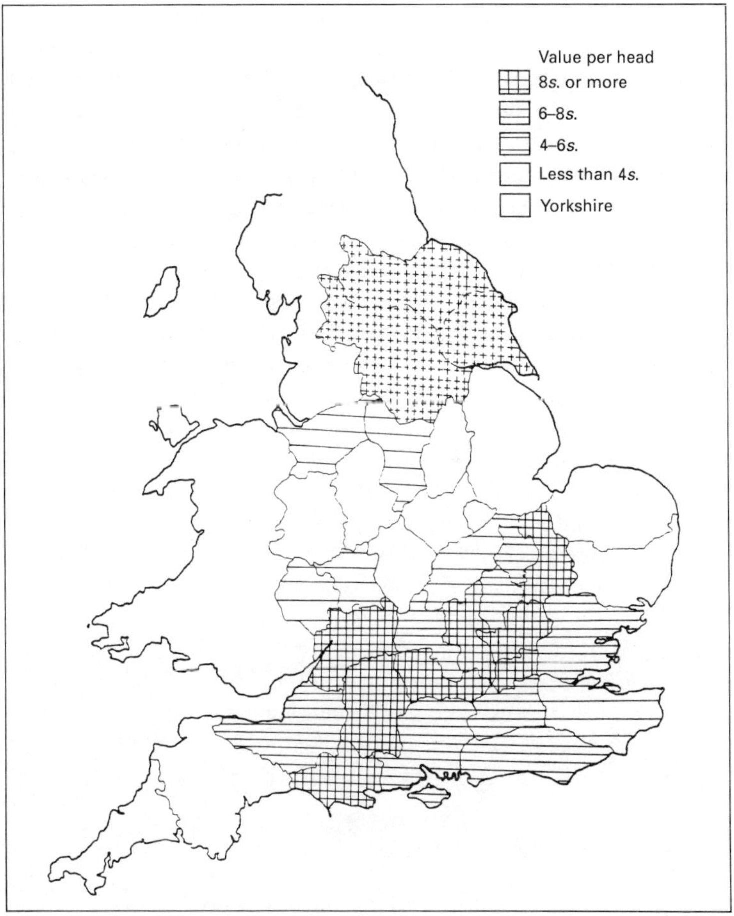

FIG. 2.2. Value per head of counties *TRE*

1066, had land worth £55 in Buckinghamshire and Northamptonshire. Ann Williams has suggested that Gytha was connected to the family of Burgeræd, who had an estate valued at £100 in Bedfordshire, Buckinghamshire, and Northamptonshire.[49] This is based on the fact that Gytha and the family of Burgeræd had shared interests in a number of the same villages in the east Midlands. This connec-

[49] 'The King's Nephew: The Family and Career of Ralph, Earl of Hereford', in C. Harper-Bill, C. J. Holdsworth, and J. L. Nelson (eds.), *Studies in Medieval History Presented to R. Allen Brown* (Woodbridge, 1989), 327–42.

tion is important in Williams's argument that Ralph's earldom was based primarily on the east Midlands, and that a large portion of his wealth was acquired through his marriage into a powerful Midlands family. The only surviving member of the family was their son Harold, who was still a minor at the time of King Edward's death. He was said to have three manors, of which one lay in Middlesex, another in Warwickshire, and the third in Worcestershire. By 1086 he had inherited his father's manors in Warwickshire and Gloucestershire. The terms used might allow that he had received them before the Conquest, but this is by no means certain.[50] What Domesday does say is that his guardian, Queen Eadgyth, held Harold's Middlesex manor on his behalf.[51] Any land which Ralph held in Herefordshire when he was earl there had been lost by the family in 1066, and it is possible that Harold Godwinesson, who succeeded to Ralph as earl also succeeded to much of his land.

[50] *DB* i. 169, 244.
[51] *DB* i. 129b.

3

THE LARGEST NON-EARLISH ESTATES

THIS chapter will include a discussion of all those estates which Domesday Book values *TRE* at £40 or more. Above this figure, most landowners can be identified with a fair degree of reliability, and their estates given a relatively accurate evaluation, but as estates get smaller, the relative accuracy of the figures involved is reduced. Identification of the lesser landholders is not as easy as that of greater lords. Bynames are given less frequently for poor men than for the wealthy, and in many cases a Norman succeeded to land which had been held by many different Englishmen before the Conquest.[1] It is therefore not easy to discover how many individuals are being mentioned in a given location. This in turn means that there is a greater chance of attributing a particular manor to the wrong individual, and because the overall values being dealt with are small, every mistake has a great effect on the value of the estate being calculated.

The lower limit of this study—£40—has no precise significance. There is no qualitative difference between the estate held by Dunna, which was valued at £40, and that of Thorgils, a Kentish thegn with land worth £39.[2] There is a gradual transition in value between the largest estates of this group, such as those belonging to Beorhtric, Ælfgar's son, or Asgeir the Staller, and those of very minor thegns who had a few pounds' worth of land. All gradations between these two extremes can be found throughout Domesday Book, and no true break-point in the series can be found. However, the limit of £40 was not chosen entirely at random. The *Liber Eliensis* differentiates between *proceres* and lesser thegns by stating that the former held more than 40 hides of land, and formed a separate class above those thegns

[1] See R. Mortimer, 'The Beginnings of the House of Clare', in R. A. Brown (ed.), *Proceedings of the Battle Conference on Anglo-Norman Studies, 1980* (Woodbridge, 1981).

[2] *DB* i. 1, 7, 8, 10, 13, 31b.

TABLE 3.1. Non-earlish lay estates valued at £40 or more

	Total value (£)	£100s ....1....2....3....4....5....6
Beorhtric, Ælfgar's son	560	********************************
Asgeir the Staller	448	*************************
Ulf Fenisc	394	***********************
Eadgifu the Fair	366	*********************
Ælfstan of Boscombe	289	****************
Azur	271	***************
Æthelnoth of Kent	260	***************
Wulfweard White, his wife and son	223	*************
Mærlswein the Sheriff	214	************
Robert fitz Wymarc	204	***********
Ralph the Staller	201	***********
Eadric of Laxfield	192	***********
Wihtgar, Ælfric's son	182	**********
Bundi the Staller	182	**********
Asgot, Beorhtric, and Edmund	176	**********
Eadnoth the Staller and his son	155	*********
Toki, Otta's son	151	********
Siweard of Maldon	147	********
Karl	144	********
Eadmær Atre	143	********
Siweard Barn	142	********
Wulfwine (*antec.* Aubrey de Vere)	141	********
Wulfwynn of Creslow	137	*******
Cypping	137	*******
Baldwin, Herluin's son	136	*******
Leofnoth the son of Osmund	118	*******
Wigot of Wallingford	117	*******
Azur, Thored's son	116	*******
Æthelgyth, wife of Thurstan	111	*******
Beorhtmær	109	******
Osweard of Norton	109	******
Askell of Ware	109	******
Beorhtsige Cilt	107	******
Toki (*antec.* William Warenne)	103	******
Beorhtric, man of Queen Eadgyth	101	******
Burgeræd and his sons	100	******
Eadric the Wild	100	******
Wulfmær of Eaton	99	******
Wulfgifu of Betteslau	98	******
Tonni	93	******
Eadweard Cilt	93	******
Æthelfrith and Ælmar	90	*****
Leofnoth and Leofric	80	****
Ingeware	79	****
Ælfric Camp	77	****
Toli the Dane	75	****

TABLE 3.1. (*cont.*)

	Total value (£)	£100s ....1....2....3....4....5....6
Godwine the priest	73	****
Guthmund	73	****
Siweard Grossus	72	****
Earnesige	70	****
Thorkell White and his wife	69	***
Normann	68	***
Æthelric, Mærgeat's son	68	***
Ordwulf	67	***
Azur, Toti's son	66	***
Eadric of Elmham	66	***
Sigeræd of Chilham	66	***
Æthelwig (*antec.* Alfred of Spain)	65	***
Æthelmar Melc	63	***
Eadric (*antec.* Arnulf of Hesdin)	63	***
Ælfric, Goding's son	61	***
Ælfweald	60	***
Engelric	60	***
Hrolf, Sceldeware's son	59	***
Thorgautr Lag	59	***
Ulf (*antec.* Robert de Tosny)	57	***
Saxi	54	***
'Ælfwine', Sheriff of Gloucester	54	***
Spirites the priest	54	***
Osmund	53	***
Gauti, Earl Harold's housecarl	50	***
Tope's family	50	***
Orm (*antec.* Hugh fitz Baldric)	50	***
Æthelsige (*antec.* Walter of Douai)	49	***
Thorkell (*antec.* Countess Judith)	49	***
Asbiorn Bigga	49	***
Bundi (*antec.* Hugh de Montfort)	49	***
Ælfweald of Stevington	47	**
Ketill Alder	46	**
Stori (*antec.* Ivo Taillebois)	46	**
Æthelstan, Godram's son	45	**
Godric the Sheriff	45	**
Siweard (*antec.* Baldwin of Exeter)	45	**
Beorhtric (*antec.* Odo fitz Gamelin)	43	**
Godwine (*antec.* Eudo Dapifer)	42	**
John the Dane	42	**
Oswulf, Frane's son	42	**
Osfrith	41	**
Dunna (*antec.* Osbern Giffard)	41	**
Godwine and Azur	40	**

who held less than 40 hides.[3] The passage in question stated that marriage to the daughter of a *procere* was only allowed to one of the same class. There is also some additional information supporting the existence of such a class.[4] This study uses financial value rather than hidage as a measure of the value of an estate,[5] so it is not possible to establish an exact correspondence between the *proceres* and the holders of the large estates listed. But since on average throughout the country 1 hide or 1 carucate was valued at almost exactly £1, the men holding estates worth £40 or more will tend to coincide with those who held at least 40 hides. So although no distinction can be discovered in Domesday Book to mark a difference between the larger and smaller estates, there is good reason to believe that a social distinction nevertheless did exist.

Excluding the land held by the royal or earlish families, eighty-eight estates were valued in Domesday at £40 or more *TRE*, and details of each of these estates can be found in Appendix II. Table 3.1 lists these estates, with those of the earls in Figure 2.1 for comparison. The largest of the non-earlish estates was valued at £559, and there were ten more worth between £200 and £450. Of the remainder, twenty-six were valued at more than £100, and fifty-one were worth less. Before looking at these estates as a group, a few examples will be examined in more detail.

Ulf Fenisc held the third largest of the non-earlish lay estates, valued at £394. The origin of his byname is obscure, and two alternative derivations have been given: first, that he came from Fjon, in Denmark; or alternatively, that it means 'from the Fens'. Certainly, his estate was concentrated around the fenland counties, although it extended into a total of eleven counties. In Lincolnshire, Ulf had sixteen manors, worth a total of almost £190, including the substantial manors of Folkingham (£50), Barton upon Humber (£39 16*s*.), and Bardney (£20), and five other manors valued at £10 each. In Yorkshire he held Aldborough (£40) as well as six other manors which

[3] *Liber Eliensis*, book 2, cap. 97.

[4] *Liber Eliensis*, 424 n. 9. It is perhaps significant that 40 hides is equivalent to the land of 8 thegns, and (if the customs of East Anglia were similar to those of Berkshire) the lord would have been required to send 8 men when the king summoned his army. The heriot of an earl, as recorded in Cnut's laws, provided equipment for 8 men (although admittedly, only 4 were to be fully equipped). Given that the status of the thegn depended on landholding, the status of *eorl* in the law codes may have embraced more than those men who actually held office. *DB* i. 56b; II Cnut 71, in F. Liebermann, *Die Gesetze der Angelsachsen*, i (Aalen, 1903).

[5] See Ch. 1 for the reasons for choosing financial value rather than geld assessment.

brought the value of his land in the county to £88 in total, while his lands in Nottinghamshire were worth £45. In these three counties, Ulf was included in the list of those who held *sac* and *soc* in the county, and in Nottinghamshire he was one of three landholders who retained the third penny from profits of justice which were received from his lands: the others who received this benefit were the Archbishop of York, and Godgifu, the widow of Earl Leofric. Elsewhere, Ulf had single manors in the counties of Buckingham, Oxford, Huntingdon, Bedford, Northampton, Derby, and Rutland, which were valued between £4 and £17 each; while in Cambridge, Ulf had land valued at £2 10*s*. in three villages. In addition, Ulf had a single house in Lincoln, and eighteen burgesses in Huntingdon. Ulf's successor in 1086 was Gilbert of Ghent, who held almost all of Ulf's lands except for those in Yorkshire, which were given to Drogo de la Beuvrière.

Askell of Ware held an estate worth almost £110 in Hertfordshire and Bedfordshire. In Hertfordshire he held the single manor of Ware, valued at £50, from which he took his name. Across the border in Bedfordshire, he was named as the holder in nine entries, from Stotfold (£20) to Wyboston (2*s*.) which were worth £58 12*s*. in total. Askell was also recorded as being the lord of a relatively large number of men. At Pelham (Herts.) two thegns, the men of Askell, held £10 of land; another of his men, Wulfmær, held £1 10*s*. in Wallington (Herts.); and two of Askell's sokemen held land worth 28*s*. in Henlow (Beds.). These and various other men of Askell held a total of £24 5*s*.' worth of land. Askell's main successor after the Conquest was Hugh Beauchamp, and his lands in Bedfordshire included the land of a considerable number of sokemen who had no specified lord. It is quite possible that some or most of these men—whose land was worth approximately £50 altogether—had been the men of Askell before the Conquest. By 1086 Askell's lands had been divided between Hugh Beauchamp, Hugh de Grandmesnil, who held Ware, and Adelzina, the wife of Ralph Taillesbois. In fact, the whole of Askell's land had probably been granted by William to Ralph Taillesbois. Ralph held a number of lands in Bedfordshire '*pro excambio de Wares*', and so it would appear that he had given Ware to Hugh de Grandmesnil in return for these Bedfordshire manors.[6]

[6] *DB* i. 212b, 213b, 214, 218; also J. H. Round 'Introduction to the Hertfordshire Domesday', in *VCH Hertfordshire*, 283–4.

Ralph died before 1086, and his lands were divided between his wife, Azelina (as her marriage portion) and Hugh Beauchamp.

The last estate which will be described in detail is that of Osfrith, a West Country thegn, who held land in seventeen villages in Devon and Cornwall. His estates was worth just over £40 in total, and his largest manor of Okehampton was valued at £10; but only one of his other holdings (Penpont, Devon) was worth as much as £5, and the remaining fifteen were all valued at between 10*s*. and £3. Osfrith lost most of his Devon manors to Baldwine the sheriff, but in contrast retained all his Cornish land, albeit under the Count of Mortain.

Of the thirty-seven estates worth more than £100, only three lay mainly to the north of a line running between the Wash and the Severn, whilst another four included land on both sides of the line. Only nine out of fifty-one estates worth between £40 and £100 lay in the north. In part, this bias can be accounted for by the factors which were described in Chapter 2, and in particular the difference in the value of land between north and south, but there is at least one other reason which must be mentioned. It is very likely that many men who held land in Yorkshire also held land in the areas which Domesday failed to cover—Northumberland, Cumberland, and Lancashire. Because this area was not covered in the Survey, a number of landholders who did hold more than £40 did not have their estate fully recorded in Domesday, and so cannot be included in the list. Whilst it is not possible to quantify the likely effect of this lack of evidence, it is probably not very important. The number of wealthy landholders recorded by Domesday north of the Wash–Severn line is small, and the addition of a few more counties—and those not the wealthiest in England—would be unlikely to have a great effect.

It is possible to make other useful comparisons between these estates, for example, the distribution of manors within individual estates. On different estates, manors were often distributed in very different ways. Even among quite large estates, there were a few which were concentrated into a very confined area. Of these, the largest belonged to Eadric of Laxfield.[7] He had land worth £230 which lay in thirty-three different villages, all of which lay within thirty-six miles of Laxfield, Suffolk, which was itself one of Eadric's largest manors. Slightly to the south of Eadric's estate, in south-west Suffolk and north-west Essex the estates held by Wihtgar, Ælfric's

[7] The details of all the manors with estates valued at over £40 are given in App. II.

son, and Siweard of Maldon were also restricted to a small area, although both were valued at over £140. All the land of Wulfwine, the predecessor of Aubrey de Vere, was situated entirely in south-west Cambridgeshire and north Essex. In the south of England, seventeen of Cypping's manors lay in the valleys of the Itchen and the Test, although he also had two manors on the Isle of Wight. Beorhtric the man of Eadgyth (whose land was valued at £100) held all but one of his manors within a fifteen-mile radius from the centre of his estate, while the exception lay just thirty miles away from the centre.

Other estates, which could still not be described as scattered, were distributed over a rather larger area. The manors of Eadgifu the Fair lay mainly in Cambridgeshire, but she also held land in Suffolk, Essex, and Hertfordshire. Beorhtmær's estate was distributed throughout Devon and Cornwall. The majority of Asgeir the Staller's land lay in Essex, Middlesex, and Berkshire, but he also held a few manors in Suffolk, Hertfordshire, Buckinghamshire, Oxfordshire, Northamptonshire, and Warwickshire, making a fairly extended estate, even if most of the land lay in a contiguous group of counties.

Some estates had more than one nucleus. The best example of this is the estate of Mærlswein, the Sheriff of Lincoln. He had land worth £90 in Lincolnshire and Yorkshire, and further land worth £120 in the West Country. Eadmær Atre and Ælfstan of Boscombe both held land in western counties as well as in Buckinghamshire, Hertfordshire, and Bedfordshire. Siweard Barn had four manors in Berkshire, three in north Lincolnshire, and a larger concentration which lay in and around Derbyshire.

In other cases the estate was so scattered as to have no identifiable centre. Wulfweard White had thirty manors in twelve different counties, and even if outliers in Kent and Lincolnshire are ignored, 120 miles separated the next most distant manors of his estate. Wulfwynn of Creslow held nine manors, which were spread across England from Dorset to Hertfordshire.

Finally, a number of estates which could be fitted into any of the above categories might also include one or two outlying manors. Ralph the Staller's estate was confined to Norfolk and Lincolnshire, with the single exception of his manor at Tybesta in Cornwall. Although there is no conclusive evidence, it is possible that this manor was acquired as a staging post on journeys to and from Brittany, the home of Ralph's family. Karl, who held most of his land

TABLE 3.2. Average value of manors held by major landholders

	Total value (£)	No. of manors	Average value of manors £ 1 1 2 1...5...0..5..0
Beorhtric, Ælfgar's son	560	42	***********
Asgeir the Staller	448	38	**********
Ulf Fenisc	394	42	********
Eadgifu the Fair	366	39	********
Ælfstan of Boscombe	289	43	*****
Azur	271	38	******
Æthelnoth of Kent	260	16	**************
Wulfweard White, his wife and son	223	30	*******
Mærlswein the Sheriff	214	48	******
Robert fitz Wymarc	204	26	*******
Ralph the Staller	201	19	*********
Eadric of Laxfield	192	34	*****
Wihtgar, Ælfric's son	182	12	*************
Bundi the Staller	182	19	********
Asgot, Beorhtric, and Edmund	176	22	*******
Eadnoth the Staller and his son	155	45	***
Toki, Otta's son	151	21	******
Siweard of Maldon	147	17	*******
Karl	144	22	******
Eadmær Atre	143	25	*****
Siweard Barn	142	21	******
Wulfwine (*antec.* Aubrey de Vere)	141	17	*******
Wulfwynn of Creslow	137	9	*************
Cypping	137	19	*******
Baldwin, Herluin's son	136	28	*****
Leofnoth the son of Osmund	118	30	***
Wigot of Wallingford	117	17	******
Azur, Thored's son	116	8	************
Æthelgyth, wife of Thurstan	111	20	*****
Beorhtmær	109	34	***
Osweard of Norton	109	20	*****
Askell of Ware	109	10	**********
Beorhtsige Cilt	107	10	**********
Toki (*antec.* William Warenne)	103	23	****
Beorhtric, man of Queen Eadgyth	101	10	*********
Burgeræd and his sons	100	28	***
Eadric the Wild	100	34	***
Wulfmær of Eaton	99	16	*****
Wulfgifu of Betteslau	98	16	*****
Tonni	93	15	*****
Eadweard Cilt	93	14	******
Æthelfrith and Ælmar	90	11	*******
Leofnoth and Leofric	80	28	**
Ingeware	79	10	*******
Ælfric Camp	77	14	*****

TABLE 3.2. (*cont.*)

	Total value (£)	No. of manors	Average value of manors £ 1 1 2 1...5...0..5..0
Toli the Dane	75	13	******
Godwine the priest	73	5	*************
Guthmund	73	13	******
Siweard Grossus	72	24	***
Earnesige	70	9	*******
Thorkell White and his wife	69	21	***
Normann	68	12	*****
Æthelric, Mærgeat's son	68	22	***
Ordwulf	67	17	****
Azur, Toti's son	66	12	*****
Eadric of Elmham	66	5	***********
Sigeræd of Chilham	66	6	**********
Æthelwig (*antec.* Alfred of Spain)	65	24	**
Æthelmar Melc	63	10	*****
Eadric (*antec.* Arnulf of Hesdin)	63	13	*****
Ælfric, Goding's son	61	12	*****
Ælfweald	60	8	*******
Engelric	60	7	********
Hrolf, Sceldeware's son	59	25	**
Thorgautr Lag	59	11	*****
Ulf (*antec.* Robert de Tosny)	57	7	*******
Saxi	54	5	**********
'Ælfwine', Sheriff of Gloucester	54	12	****
Spirites the priest	54	11	*****
Osmund	53	8	******
Gauti, Earl Harold's housecarl	50	8	******
Tope's family	50	29	**
Orm (*antec.* Hugh fitz Baldric)	50	12	****
Æthelsige (*antec.* Walter of Douai)	49	13	***
Thorkell (*antec.* Countess Judith)	49	8	******
Asbiorn Bigga	49	8	******
Bundi (*antec.* Hugh de Montfort)	49	14	***
Ælfweald of Stevington	47	6	*******
Ketill Alder	46	15	***
Stori (*antec.* Ivo Taillebois)	46	3	**************
Æthelstan, Godram's son	45	15	***
Godric the Sheriff	45	10	****
Siweard (*antec.* Baldwin of Exeter)	45	6	*******
Beorhtric (*antec.* Odo fitz Gamelin)	43	7	******
Godwine (*antec.* Eudo Dapifer)	42	5	*******
John the Dane	42	5	*******
Oswulf, Frane's son	42	10	****
Osfrith	41	17	**
Dunna (*antec.* Osbern Giffard)	41	8	****
Godwine and Azur	40	4	*********

in Wiltshire, also had one substantial manor which lay in Surrey. The outliers to the estate of Wulfweard White have been mentioned in the previous paragraph.

It is possible to discern differences in the average value of manors within different estates, and to a certain extent, to correlate the different average values with different types of distribution (see Table 3.2). Before this is demonstrated, one particular feature of the evidence must be pointed out. In general, the larger the estate as a whole, the greater the average value of manors within that estate. This is mainly because the larger estates usually included a few extremely large manors. Beorhtric, Ælfgar's son, held Tewkesbury and Thornbury (Gloucestershire), valued at £100 and £50 respectively, as well as six other manors worth over £20. Karl, whose estate was worth less than a third of Beorhtric's, had just two manors worth over £20. The average value of Beorhtric's manors was £13 6*s*.; the average value of Karl's was just £7 4*s*. Æthelstan, Godram's son, with land worth £45, had manors with an average value of £2 16*s*.

But within this general pattern there are a large number of exceptions. There are examples of large estates made up of a great number of small manors, whilst at the other end of the scale there were smaller estates made up of just a few manors. In some cases the estates which have a smaller average value per manor than might have been expected are those which have more than one centre. The average value of Mærlswein's manors was definitely smaller than those of estates of similar size (see Table 3.2). But if the two groups of manors (those in the north of England and those in the West Country) are treated as separate estates (and therefore relatively smaller) the average value of the manors which make up each of the two portions is closer to what we might expect. The average value of the estates of Ælfstan of Boscombe, Eadmær Atre, and Siweard Barn, all of which had more than one centre, were also all lower than the norm.

The cases where values are higher than would have been predicted from the overall value of the estate fall into two different groups. A number of the concentrated estates have high average values per manor. This is true of the estates held by Beorhtric, Eadgyth's man, and Wihtgar, Ælfric's son, which both have particularly high values. The estates of Wulfwine, Siweard of Maldon, and Cypping, whilst not so exceptional, are still above average.

The two most scattered estates worth more than £40, those held by Wulfwynn of Creslow and Azur, Thored's son, are both made up of a small number of large manors which had an average value of more than £15 in each case. This is perhaps twice the figure that would be normal for estates of a similar size. There are some exceptions to the general rules mentioned above. The manors held by Eadric of Laxfield were concentrated in a small area, but the average value of each manor was quite low, and he did not hold a single manor valued at more than £15. Whilst the average value of Siweard Barn's manors was low, each of the manors in the isolated group in Berkshire has a high value, and taken alone would exceed the expected average value. In spite of these exceptions, the observations can, if used carefully, give some clues as to the probable history of the estates in question. We will return to this matter after considering other sources which can shed light on the history of estates in this period.

Whilst Domesday gives fairly precise details about the composition of the larger estates which existed towards the end of Edward's reign, it rarely gives evidence regarding their history, or even regarding the history of individual manors. Other sources for the history of lay estates must be examined for such information, and while these cannot be compared in volume to the data from Domesday Book, they can provide some general indication about the acquisition and disposal of land. Also, since more is known about the history of ecclesiastical estates, it is possible to compare these with the lay estates in order to try to infer something about the latter.

The family of Beorhtric, Ælfgar's son, seems to have been quite important from at least the end of the tenth century, and it is also relatively well documented. One source suggests that Beorhtric was a descendant of Edward the Elder, and if this is true then the family was probably well established from the beginning of the tenth century.[8] Beorhtric's grandfather Æthelweard founded the abbey of Cranbourne, Dorset, and attached to it the priory of St Mary's, Tewkesbury. It can hardly be a coincidence that Æthelweard's grandson held important manors in both Cranbourne and Tewkesbury, and it seems probable that they had been in the family since Æthelweard's day. There is no information about the land held by Beorhtric's father, Ælfgar Mæw. However, he was of

[8] *Chronica monasterii de Tewkesburye*, in *Monasticon*, ii. 60.

some importance, as he witnessed a number of Ethelred's charters. In 1016 he defected with Eadric Streona to join Cnut.[9] We do not know whether Ælfgar returned with Eadric to give his support to Edmund later that year, or if he continued to support Cnut. Whatever he did, his son was acting as a prominent witness to both royal and private charters at the beginning of Edward's reign,[10] and was presumably holding much of the land which Domesday recorded him as having on the day King Edward died.

The history of Æthelgyth's estate is also documented to a certain extent. Her land lay in Norfolk, Suffolk, and Essex and was inherited almost entirely from her husband Thurstan.[11] Thurstan had received at least some of the land in his estate from his father, Lustwine, although in a will recorded in the *Liber Eliensis*, much of the land which Thurstan himself bequeathed was supposed to have been granted to the abbey.[12] It is possible that the will as preserved by the abbey had omitted to record the fact that some or all of these manors were to remain in the hands of the family for one or more lives after the death of Lustwine. In any case the will of Lustwine as recorded in the *Liber Eliensis* only listed land which was to be granted to Ely. It is probable that other manors which were held by Thurstan when he made his will had also been held by his father, and that these were omitted as irrelevant when the monks copied the will into the *Liber Eliensis*. While nothing is known of Lustwine's origin, his wife was of distinguished descent, since she was the granddaughter of Ealdorman Brythnoth, who died at Maldon. On the female side at least, Thurstan's family was long established, and it is quite probable that some of the land which was held *TRE* by Æthelgyth had belonged earlier in the century to an ealdorman's estate.

In a number of instances, although nothing is known of the history of the actual land recorded in Domesday, it is possible to demonstrate that the men who held the land belonged to families which had been well established in earlier reigns. Eadric the Wild held all his

[9] Ælfgar witnesses S 890, S 893, S 902, S 906. See S. Keynes, *The Diplomas of King Ethelred 'the Unready'* (Cambridge, 1980), 209, 227 n., and *Florence*, *sub anno* 1016.

[10] He is probably to be identified with the Beorhtric who witnesses S 993 and S 994, dated 1042. See Ch. 6.

[11] S 1531.

[12] Lustwine's will is recorded in the *Liber Eliensis*, book 2, ch. 89. Other transactions involving the family are to be found in chs. 62, 63, 64, 67, and 68.

land in Shropshire, and he was the nephew of Eadric Streona, an ealdorman in Ethelred's reign.[13]

Ælfric, the father of the Suffolk thegn Wihtgar, was related to a Midlands thegn, Æthelwine Niger, who was himself a fairly substantial landholder.[14] Ælfric had also been an important officer of Queen Emma's, and had administered the eight and a half hundreds of Thingoe on her behalf.[15] It is possible that Ælfric had been given some of his land by Queen Emma, although there is only circumstantial evidence to suggest this. Ælfric was said to have given a great deal of land to the Church. His largest manor, Clare (valued at £40) was held by his son Wihtgar *TRE*, but it was due to be given to St Edmund's on his death following an agreement made by Ælfric. Long Melford, worth £20, had been given by Ælfric to the Abbey, and Wihtgar retained no rights there.[16] Assuming that Ælfric held all the manors which Domesday recorded as being held by his son, this means that 30 per cent of his estate had been passed on to the Church, an extremely large amount considering that Ælfric had a son to provide for, as well as other relations. One possible explanation is that the manors in question had been given to Ælfric by Emma on condition that they were passed on to St Edmund's either on his death or that of his son. This would be similar to the agreement which was made between Emma and Wulfweard White concerning Hayling Island, in Wiltshire. Emma granted half to St Peter's, Winchester, and half to Wulfweard for his life only, after which the whole was to be held by the Church.[17] Ælfric was also related to a woman named Leofgifu, a substantial landholder in the area. In her will she bequeathed an estate comprising land in fourteen locations in East Anglia,[18] and to Ælfric she left land at Bramford, near Ipswich. Although Ælfric was not recorded as holding the manor of Bramford *TRE*, he was in possession of a church and land listed in Ipswich which the sheriff claimed was attached to the royal manor of Bramford.[19] Why the sheriff was claiming this land is unclear, but it was

[13] *Florence*, *sub anno* 1067.

[14] *Chron. Ramsiensis*, 169–70. Ælfric also witnessed a grant by Æthelwine to St Albans between 1042 and 1049 (S 1228).

[15] S 1078.

[16] *Pinchbeck Register*, ed. Lord Francis Hervey (London, 1925), ii. 290.

[17] S 1476.

[18] S 1521.

[19] D. Whitelock, *Anglo-Saxon Wills* (Cambridge, 1930), 188.

perhaps connected with the fact that Ælfric had been the man of Queen Emma.

There were a number of substantial estates which were held by men who were, or who may have been, foreigners by birth. Toli the Dane and John the Dane both had substantial estates in the south-west. Earnesige, whose estate lay mainly in Gloucestershire, was the son of a Danish father and an English mother.[20] Thorkell the White was another Dane who married an English wife, Leofflæd, and both had been active in the reign of Cnut, as well as being recorded as landholders at the time of King Edward's death.[21] Ulf 'Fenisc' held a great deal of land, principally in Lincolnshire and Nottinghamshire, with some manors further south. Nothing definite is known of his background, but his name may indicate that he was of Scandinavian origin.[22] It is possible that Ulf came to England either with Cnut, or perhaps in the path of relatives who had themselves accompanied Cnut. Even if this were so, Ulf's estate might have been of some antiquity by 1066, as he could have gained his wealth by marrying into a wealthy English family. On the other hand, it might have been created after the defeat of Ethelred II and Edmund, as a reward for one of Cnut's supporters. Asgeir the Staller was the grandson of Tofig the Proud, one of Cnut's more important thegns. As such, much of the land which Asgeir held in 1066 may have descended from land acquired by Tofig after Cnut's conquest.

Three men who were almost certainly of French descent held quite large estates in England in 1066. Robert fitz Wymarc was said to be a kinsman of King Edward, and he may have come to England when Edward returned from his time in exile.[23] Ralph the Staller was said to have been born in Norfolk[24] but his name is not English. The reference to Ralph being an Englishman may well be mistaken, as it was made after the Conquest and might merely have been made because Ralph had been established in England before William's arrival. At any event, both Ralph and Robert are known to have received land from King Edward himself. Robert fitz Wymarc was

[20] A. Williams, '"Cockles amongst the wheat": Danes and English in the Western Midlands in the First Half of the Eleventh Century', in *Midlands History*, 11 (1986), 14.

[21] S 1462, S 1469.

[22] G. Tengvik, *Old English By-Names* (1938), 135.

[23] *Vita Edwardi*, 76.

[24] *ASC* D *sub anno* 1075.

given the manor of Bromfield, Shropshire, after it had been forfeited to the Crown when Spirites the Priest was outlawed;[25] and Ralph the Staller held two manors which had belonged to the royal demesne in Norfolk.[26] Finally, Baldwin, who held land worth £136 in seven counties, was the son of Herluin. This Herluin was an associate of Bishop Beorhteah of Worcester, who went with the bishop when he escorted Cnut's daughter, Gunnhild, to her marriage with Henry, the son of Emperor Conrad II, and who held land at Lyppard from the bishop. Baldwin appears to have retained this land, and held it under Hugh de Grandmesnil in 1086, as part of the fief of the Bishop of Worcester.[27] Further, Baldwin leased Weston on Avon from Worcester, and is described as the steward of Beorhteah's successor at Worcester, Ealdred.[28] Domesday does state in some of Baldwin's entries that he had held the land 'from King Edward',[29] but this formula does not appear to refer to a particularly close relationship between king and landholder (see below, Chapter 4). On the other hand, an Oxfordshire entry refers to 2½ hides which King Edward gave to '*S. Petro de Westmon. et Balduino suo filiolo*', and it is possible that Baldwin, Herluin's son, was the godson of King Edward.[30]

Other important landholders had names of Scandinavian origin: Ulf, Thorgautr, and Ketill. By themselves the names cannot prove that the man belonged to a foreign family. Earl Ælfgar, whose family was of long-established English stock, gave Eadwine his elder son an English name, but his younger son, Morkær, a Scandinavian one. Of the four sons of Earl Godwine, three had Scandinavian names, although in this case Godwine had a Scandinavian wife. Clearly the forename alone cannot be used to indicate the nationality of a landholder, as names of Scandinavian origin were clearly in fashion during Edward's reign. Even Earl Ralph named his own son Harold.

As well as the information which can be gained about estates as a whole, or the history of families which held such land, there is also a certain amount of detailed evidence which can be used to demonstrate general trends in the transfer of land towards either the consolidation or dissolution of estates.

25 *DB* i. 252b.
26 Sporle and Swaffham: *DB* ii. 119, 144.
27 *DB* i. 174, *Heming*, 267.
28 S 1407.
29 Such as Sulham where '*Balduin tenuit de R. Edwardo*', *DB* i. 61b.
30 *DB* i. 154b.

Domesday itself records a small number of separate land transfers which took place before the Conquest. Among these is Edward's grant of Bromfield to Robert fitz Wymarc, mentioned above. In this case the manor lay far from the main part of Robert's estate (which was mainly in the east), and in spite of the conditions of tenure, Robert gave the land to a relative, presumably in preference to alienating land closer to the heart of his estate. The manors given by the king to Ralph the Staller lay on the edge of Ralph's estate, since Ralph had only a small proportion of his other land in Norfolk, while the remainder lay in Lincolnshire.

Earl Godwine bought the manor of Woodchester from a man named Azur.[31] It is possible that the vendor was the same man who held a considerable amount of land in Sussex and the south-east. If this were so, then Azur may have been deliberately ridding himself of an outlying manor which would have been awkward to administer. On the earl's part, it is said that he was obliged to make the purchase, since his wife refused to stay at Berkeley. Godwine was said to have acquired this last manor after the dissolution of the nunnery there.

Asgeir the Staller was recorded as giving the manor of Leighs (Essex) to Earl Harold.[32] It is possible that this was indeed a gift, but it is equally likely that the land was sold to Harold. Domesday Book often uses the word 'gift' when money changed hands. In this case, Asgeir was disposing of land which lay within his circle of influence, as he had a lot of land in Essex and adjacent counties. Harold did not hold the manor himself, but gave (or sold) it to his man Skalpi.

Although there are a number of surviving royal diplomas granted by Edward in favour of laymen, only one can be shown to have been given to a man who was recorded in Domesday as holding a large estate. This was the grant of Sevington, Wiltshire, to Ælfstan of Boscombe.[33] This manor lay at the heart of Ælfstan's estate in 1066, but it is not clear whether its acquisition was a deliberate attempt to increase the amount of land which Ælfstan held in his area of influence, or whether it had been given entirely on Edward's own initiative.

The method of land acquisition most commonly recorded in Domesday was the leasing of land from the Church. The details of such leases are dealt with in the next chapter, but at this point what is important is the location of the leased land with respect to the

[31] *DB* i. 164. [32] *DB* ii. 59. [33] S 999.

remainder of the estate. In many instances, laymen leased land which lay close to other manors in the estate. Ælfstan of Boscombe leased land worth £12 in three different villages from the Abbot of Malmesbury and the Bishop of Salisbury. All three villages lay close to other manors which Ælfstan held in Wiltshire. Cypping's manors of Otterbourne, Headbourne Worthy, and Swampton (all in Hampshire) were leased from the Bishop and Old Minster of Winchester, and all three lay close to the rest of Cypping's land. Wulfweard White had a particularly scattered estate, but this did not prevent him from consolidating locally. He received a life interest in half the manor of Hayling Island, and proceeded to buy a life lease of the remainder from the Old Minster at Winchester.[34] Wulfwynn of Creslow also held a scattered estate, but the manor of Great Gaddesden which she leased from St Alban's lay within a few miles of her manor of Creslow, from which she took her name.

In a few instances land which was leased lay on the edge or outside the main area of the lessee's estate. Beorhtric, Ælfgar's son, leased land from the Bishop of Worcester which lay on the northern extremity of Beorhtric's estate.[35] The manor of Clapham, Bedfordshire, which was leased by Beorhtric, the man of Queen Eadgyth, lay outside the very restricted area where the remainder of Beorhtric's manors lay. It is possible that in these examples there was no land closer to the centre of the estate which could be leased, but in any case they remain exceptions, and on the whole when manors were leased they either lay within the main body of the estate or represented some sort of local consolidation.

We can be quite sure that the most frequent cause of change of ownership of land was the death of its holder. Nothing illustrates the limitations of Domesday Book more than the fact that this aspect of land transfer is almost never mentioned in relation to the circumstances of 1066. However, a number of wills or portions of wills survive and these can be used in conjunction with the static picture presented by Domesday Book to illustrate how inheritance affected the distribution of estates.

Three wills which refer directly to estates recorded in Domesday Book have survived. These are the will of Thurstan[36] (the husband of

[34] S 1476.
[35] The terms of this lease were disputed in 1086, and this is discussed in Ch. 4.
[36] S 1531.

the East-Anglian landholder Æthelgyth), the will of Ketill Alder[37] (another East Anglian, whose will had not been carried out by the time of the Conquest), and the will of Ulf and Madselin[38] (which was drawn up some time between 1066 and 1069). In addition a number of wills which were made by members of Ketill's family are also of interest.[39] In all these wills there were many beneficiaries. These included members of the testator's family, various churches, and important men in the area, the latter presumably being included to secure their support in ensuring that the terms of the will were actually implemented.

Of the nine manors which were mentioned in Ketill's will, one manor was to be given to Christchurch, and one to Ketill's lord, Archbishop Stigand, whilst a third was to go to St Edmund's after the deaths of both Ketill and his daughter Ælfgifu. Ketill's brother Godric was to receive four manors, and by an arrangement with two of his sisters, land was to go to the women if they outlived Ketill. If he survived them then he would be given the manors which the sisters had held. The last manor was to be given to Earl Harold.

Thurstan's will bequeathed sixteen manors, and an indeterminate amount of land in Norfolk. The Norfolk land was all to go to his wife Æthelgyth, as her marriage portion, and she was also to receive six other manors elsewhere, of which three were to pass to the Church after her death. Three more manors were to go directly to Ely or St Edmund's. Three other beneficiaries were each to receive a single manor, while a priest and two chaplains were granted a single manor between the three of them. The last manor was to be sold, and from the proceeds Thurstan's heriot was to be paid, and gifts given to Stigand (Bishop of East Anglia at the time the will was drawn up) and the then Earl of East Anglia, Harold, amongst others.

The will of Ulf and Madselin was made after the Conquest, prior to their going on pilgrimage to Jerusalem. The largest group of manors—five in all—was to go to the Archbishop of York. In fact, Ulf had actually sold two of these manors to the archbishop, and the other three had been mortgaged, in order to finance the pilgrimage. Of the remaining land, five manors were given to five different religious houses, and another five were distributed between Ulf's mother, brother, and two other kinsmen. Two manors were to be

[37] S 1519.
[38] D. Whitelock, *Anglo-Saxon Wills* (Cambridge 1930), no. 39.
[39] S 1516, S 1535.

given to Ingemund, a man whose relationship to Ulf and Madselin is unknown; and again, one manor was to be sold, and the proceeds used for good works.

The wills of wealthier landholders in Edward's reign have not survived. Earl Godwine's wife and sons all held land in the south of England, irrespective of where the sons later held their earldoms. The likelihood is that much of the land which they held, at least in the south, had been given to them in Godwine's will. Harold received the largest portion, to judge from the amount which he held in 1066, but Gytha and Harold's younger brothers were well provided for. The main impression provided by this distribution, as with the extant wills, is that estates tended to be dispersed on the death of the holder.

In two respects, the trend towards the dispersal of estates is more apparent than real. In the first place, although gifts of land and money to lay people outside the family were often included in a will, they were not normally very great when compared to the size of the whole estate. Ketill Alder's mother, Aldgyth, bequeathed a total of nine manors to seven different beneficiaries. But of these seven, five were her children, while the remaining two—Earls Godwine and Harold—received a single manor between them. Of the four lay beneficiaries in the will of Ulf and Madselin, only one was not specifically described as being a kinsman of Ulf, whilst amongst the bequests to monasteries was one manor to Peterborough's abbot, Brand, who was himself related to Ulf.

In wills of this period much land is given, not to members of the testator's family, but to the Church. Close examination suggests, however, that these extensive grants were not always carried out. In practice, land granted to the Church in this way might be leased back immediately, or might never have been given to the Church in the first place. The *Liber Eliensis* records a part of the will of Lustwine, Thurstan's father, in which ten manors were granted to Ely.[40] Of these, two appear to have been given to the abbey on Lustwine's death, but seven more were held by Thurstan, and were mentioned in his will. Two of these seven manors were bequeathed by Thurstan to Ely, and it is possible that Thurstan had leased these manors for life. But a third was granted by Thurstan to Christchurch, implying that Thurstan had the power, if not the right, to bestow the land as

[40] *Liber Eliensis*, book 2, cap. 89.

he pleased, while the remaining four were bequeathed to lay people. The tenth manor granted by Lustwine to Ely was not recorded in Thurstan's will, and was held in 1066 by two men, according to Domesday. Æthelgyth did not continue to hold any of the manors which her husband had granted directly to the Church, but was, according to Domesday, in possession of Pentlow and Ashdon in 1066, which were the two manors that her father-in-law had supposedly given to Ely. Clearly Lustwine's family did not abandon all interest in the land which he had given to the Abbey of Ely, and although this is a very dramatic example, there are many other cases of relatives preventing the alienation of land to the Church. Godgifu, the wife of Earl Siweard, granted two manors to Peterborough on her death, which took place before 1055. In fact, the land remained in the hands of her family until at least 1086 (see Ch. 4).

The *Liber Eliensis* provides a number of instances of relations trying to prevent bequests to the abbey taking effect, although these depredations tended to have taken place in the late tenth and early part of the eleventh centuries.[41] The Chronicle of Ramsey provides an example from Edward's reign. Æthelwine Niger had bequeathed land to Ramsey abbey, but this grant was opposed by his kinsman Ælfric, the father of the Suffolk thegn Wihtgar. Ælfric must have had a reasonable chance of making good his claim to the land, since the abbot thought it prudent to give the king the gift of a horse to ensure a beneficial decision.[42] Other examples of men taking land from the Church by force—such as the claim by Ely that Asgeir the Staller had taken High Easter from them by force and had later agreed to return it after his death—might actually be indicative of a family member attempting to stop land being alienated to the Church. In any event it seems likely that the family did not necessarily lose the use of land which a layman left to the Church, whether it was leased back from the Church, or whether the land was never actually given to the Church in the first place.

Having said all this, there was a degree of loss of land to any estate bequeathed in this way, whether the land was given to more or less distant kinsmen, passed to the Church, or simply sold to realize cash for heriot or charitable gifts. In addition, an estate might be divided among a number of family members. There are indications that when

[41] *Liber Eliensis*, book 2, caps. 11, 24, 34. Throughout, the need to secure the agreement of relatives for a gift or sale is evident.

[42] *Chron. Ramsiensis*, 169–70.

a will was being compiled, consideration was given to keeping part or parts of the estate in geographically compact blocks. In Chapter 2 it was suggested that Godwine's sons had received land from their father in distinct areas. When Thurstan made his will he intended that Æthelgyth should only receive six of the sixteen manors which lay outside Norfolk. Four of these manors formed a compact group in north-west Essex, while the fifth lay a few miles across the border in Suffolk; the sixth lay halfway between this concentration and Æthelgyth's manors in Norfolk (see Fig. 3.1). The manors which

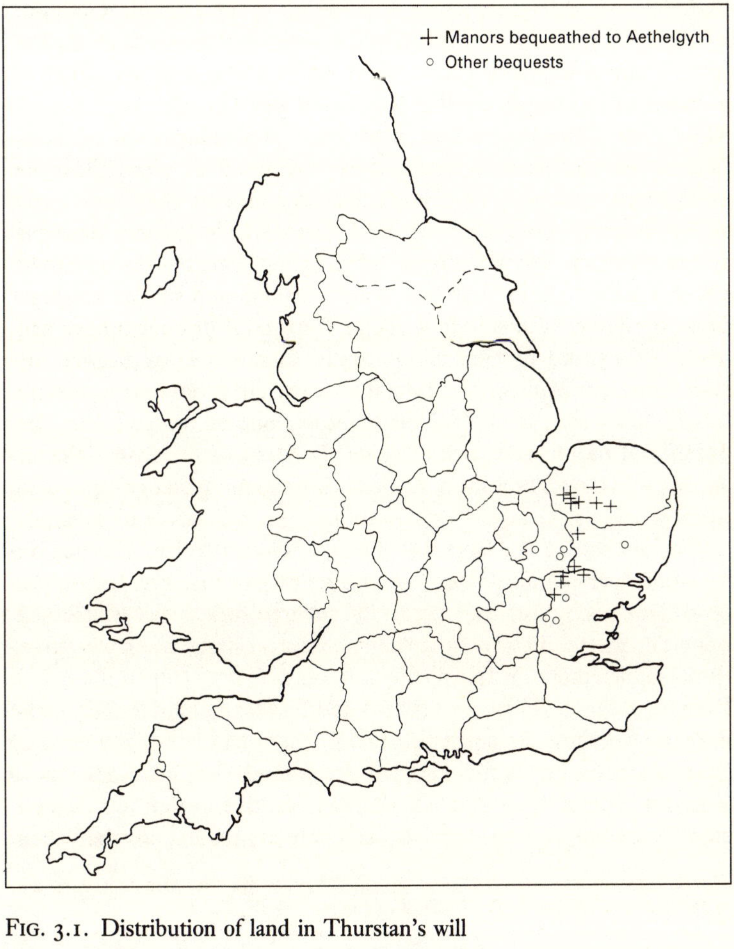

FIG. 3.1. Distribution of land in Thurstan's will

Thurstan granted away from the estate comprised all his land in Cambridgeshire, a single manor in the centre of Suffolk, and manors which lay to the south of Æthelgyth's land in Essex. In short, Thurstan appears to have kept a certain degree of geographical integrity to the estate which he left his wife, and the evidence suggests that Earl Godwine also had such considerations in mind when he provided for his various sons.

The *antecessores* of Roger Arundel, Æthelfrith, and Ælmar, may well have been brothers. Apart from sharing the same successor, each held land in Dorset and Somerset, with Æthelfrith's being assessed at 55 hides, and Ælmar's at $54\frac{1}{2}$. Together, they held the large estate of Piddletrenthide as two manors from King Edward, but they were not free to take it to another lord. As it was held in 1086 by St Peter's, Winchester, it is possible that the manor had been left to Æthelfrith and Ælmar for their lives only, after which the manor was to go to the Church. Assuming that the manors of Æthelfrith and Ælmar had originally formed a single estate, the manner of its division is quite striking. Six of the manors lay in the west of Dorset and Somerset, and four in the east, with only a single manor lying between these two groups. Æthelfrith held all the eastern manors and the least valuable of those in the west. Ælmar held the remainder of those in the west, while the central manor, Piddletrenthide, was divided between the men. Two principles appear to have controlled the division of this estate: first, that Æthelfrith and Ælmar should receive the same number of hides; and secondly, that the estates which they inherited should be as geographically distinct as was compatible with the first principle.

While much of the land that was lost to an estate on the death of its owner went to the Church, a smaller proportion of it also went to other landlords, and the receipt of such bequests was probably an important factor in the expansion of some estates as it was in the dispersal of others. Ælfric, Wihtgar's son, was bequeathed the land in Bramford,[43] and Ælfric also considered that he had a right to some of the land which his kinsman Æthelwine Niger had left to Ramsey.[44] If he had succeeded in this claim Ælfric would have acquired land in Bedfordshire. Ælfric's son, also Wihtgar, held land in a very compact area in the south-west of Suffolk and the north of Essex. Bramford

[43] S 1521; Whitelock, *Anglo-Saxon Wills*, 188.
[44] See S 1228 and *Chron. Ramsiensis*, 169–70.

lay outside this area, in the centre of Suffolk, and it is possible that some of the land was alienated when Ælfric died, although Wihtgar did retain some land which the sheriff claimed was attached to the manor of Bramford. However for a period Ælfric's estate had increased in its geographical extent, and had he succeeded in his claims to Æthelwine's land, it would have been enlarged even further. It would only take a few such acquisitions to alter an estate from being very compact to being reasonably widespread. In fact, the estate which Ælfric passed to his son was more compact still, since Long Melford, on the periphery of Wihtgar's area of influence, was passed to the Church. What we know of the history of Ælfric's estate suggests that there was a cycle of accumulation and reduction in the amount of land in the estate, as land was bought or inherited, or lost, either by sale or through dispersal on the death of the owner. This cycle probably also affected the composition of other estates. Whilst land was acquired close to the main body of the estate where possible, other land might be inherited some distance away. When the time came to sell land, or dispose of it by will, it was the peripheral estates which were most likely to be alienated, leaving the central core intact. The relative balance between the acquisition of land and its loss could result in an estate growing and becoming more scattered, if more land was acquired than lost; or conversely the estate might shrink to a small number of manors in a concentrated area if losses exceeded gains.

There is rather more information concerning the history of the estates held by the great abbeys of England, and some very general comparisons can be made between the distribution of land in these estates, and the distribution of land held by laymen. There are at least two important differences between the ecclesiastical and the lay landholder which must be remembered. Religious houses held land in the first instance to provide for their own monks, who lived in a fixed location. This would provide an incentive for a religious house to consolidate its land in the immediate vicinity of the monastery itself. A lay landholder, on the other hand, could move from manor to manor, enjoying the produce at source, and did not have the same incentive to build up a particularly compact group of manors. A more important difference is that ecclesiastical estates did not suffer the regular dispersal of land which followed the death of a lay lord. Some manors were leased out for a number of generations, but always with the intention that they be recovered eventually—and usually at a profit. Even land which had been stolen by force could be recovered, as happened when Asgeir the Staller deprived Ely of High Easter, but later came to an agreement with the monks that it be returned to them on his death.[45] Thus the great abbeys could look forward to a gradual accumulation of land, which would rarely be checked, whilst lay estates were subject to regular reductions in size. However the example of Burton Abbey, below, shows that even a religious house could lose a large amount of its endowment, so this difference may not have been so important as it appears at first sight.

Bearing these points in mind, it is still possible to draw some useful parallels between ecclesiastical and lay estates. The older and more established abbeys conform to the expected picture. Bury St Edmunds and Glastonbury both held large estates which centred around the monasteries themselves, and were restricted to a relatively small area. Ely's land was rather more widespread. A large amount of land was held in Cambridgeshire, close to the abbey itself, but there was also a considerable amount of land in East Anglia and Essex. The land in these latter areas comprised, in the main, gifts which were given by the family of Ealdorman Beorhtnoth of East Anglia.

Burton was a smaller abbey than the three previously mentioned, and was founded rather later. Wulfric Spot donated land in seven counties from Lincolnshire to Gloucestershire to his foundation.[46] A very large proportion of these lands had been lost by 1066, but with only two exceptions the manors which had been lost were situated more than ten miles from the abbey. Burton had also managed to acquire some manors which were not included in Wulfric's will, and all of these new acquisitions lay within ten miles of Burton itself. In one case the abbey exchanged its two manors in Gloucestershire for Rolleston, Staffordshire, which was just four miles from the abbey.[47] A number of manors which Wulfric had granted to the abbey were in the hands of Earl Leofric's family in 1066. This family had itself been important benefactors of Burton, and it is possible that some of the land which the family held had been acquired by way of exchanges between the family and the monks.[48] Other land may have been lost through the disfavour into which Wulfric's family fell later in

45 *Liber Eliensis*, book 2, cap. 6.
46 S 1536.
47 S 920.
48 Of the land in Wulfric's will which was given to Burton, Godgifu held Cauldon and Cotwalton, and had leased Appleby Magna (*DB* i. 248b, 273); Earl Ælfgar held Newton Solney (*DB* i. 272b); Eadwine held Longford and Stirchley; his brother

Ethelred's reign, if this disfavour extended to the family foundation. It is also quite possible that the terms of the will were never fully carried out, and that some of the manors left in the will never found their way into Burton's hands. Nevertheless, it is clear that following the initial grant by Wulfric, the abbey consistently acquired land close by, and in at least one proven case this was at the expense of manors which lay much further away. As a result the estate held by the abbey *TRE* was smaller but much more compact than the original land bequeathed by Wulfric.

Westminster Abbey had its lands greatly extended during Edward's reign, largely as a result of royal patronage. It also differed from most of the other English abbeys of the period by having its manors spread over a wide area. Westminster did hold a large number of manors in Middlesex, Hertfordshire, and Essex, fairly close to the abbey itself, but it also held a relatively small number of highly valued manors in nine other counties, as far north as Staffordshire. Since the estate was not an old one, the forces which acted towards the consolidation of lands closer to the centre of the estate had not had a chance to have much effect. It would appear that for ecclesiastical estates at least, the pattern of distribution of land within an estate is a good indicator of its maturity, with a compact distribution indicating a well established estate, and a more scattered pattern with a small number of highly valued manors indicating a much younger one.

Using the information which we have concerning the transfer of land and the distribution of ecclesiastical estates, the different types of distribution amongst lay estates can now be re-examined, to see what, if anything, can be inferred about their history. There are strong indications, both from the distribution of land within the estate, and from other evidence, that a small number of the larger estates recorded in Domesday had not been long in existence by 1066. The best example of this is the holding of Robert fitz Wymarc. Robert, although of French descent, was related to King Edward, and he appears to have been close to the king, at least at the end of Edward's life, as he was present at Edward's death-bed along with Harold and Stigand.[49] Robert's estate consisted of a number of

Morkær had Sutton Maddock (*DB* i. 259). A number of manors which the family held in 1066 were in the abbey's hands in 1086: Godgifu's manor of Branston, Staffs. (*DB* i. 247b); Ælfgar's manor of Coton in the Elms, Derbys. (*DB* i. 273); and Austrey, which Domesday notes had been given to Burton by Earl Leofric (*DB* i. 239).

[49] *Vita Edwardi*, 75.

manors in Suffolk and Essex (where Robert may have been sheriff; his son, Swein, certainly was after 1066), but he also had manors in Huntingdonshire, Somerset, Herefordshire, and Shropshire. In its scattered nature, Robert's estate is reminiscent of the newly enlarged estate of Westminster. Since Robert was a newcomer to the kingdom it is reasonable to suggest that his estate was a new creation, which had not existed before Edward's reign. In one case at least we know that Robert received land directly from the king,[50] and it is probable that other manors were also held as the result of Edward's generosity. John the Dane (presumably a relatively new arrival to the country) had just five manors in Dorset, Somerset, and Gloucestershire, three of which were worth £10 or more.

Two other men who may have been new arrivals in England were Ulf Fenisc and Ralph the Staller. The Anglo-Saxon Chronicle claimed that Ralph the Staller was English, but married to a Breton,[51] but most scholars have discounted this possibility; it seems likely that in fact it was Ralph who was the Breton, and there is good evidence that his wife was English.[52] Their estates, in contrast to that of Robert, were not particularly dispersed, and it does not seem likely that either was a new creation in Edward's reign. Both Ulf and Ralph held large amounts of land in the east, although Ralph's estate did have an outlier in Cornwall. Ralph would have had good reason to acquire this himself (see above). Between the two of them, Ulf and Ralph held 10 per cent by value of the land in the county of Lincolnshire as well as land in other counties around the Fens. If both estates had been created in Edward's reign this would imply a massive upheaval had taken place in the landholding patterns of eastern England, and it is hard to see how this could have happened without some mention of it appearing in other sources. It is more probable that the estates held by Ralph and Ulf had been built up over a number of generations. This is not to say that neither man was a new arrival; they may have been able to marry into the existing landholding families, or might have been provided with the land of outlawed men.

[50] *DB* i. 252b.

[51] *ASC* D, E *sub anno* 1075.

[52] F. Barlow, *Edward the Confessor* (London, 1970), 165; F. M. Stenton, *Anglo-Saxon England* (Oxford, 1947), 420, and G. H. White, 'The Earldom of Norfolk', in H. A. Doubleday and H. de Walden (eds.) *The Complete Peerage*, ix (London, 1936), 568–71.

A tentative identification is possible for Ralph's wife. In the Little Domesday, reference is made both to Godwine the uncle of Earl Ralph, and to Ælfsige his nephew.[53] Whether the earl in question was Ralph the Staller, or his son Ralph the Gæl, it is clear that these men had English relatives, and these can only have been acquired by marriage. Since the younger Ralph married the daughter of Roger, Earl of Hereford,[54] Ralph the Staller must have married an English wife. As to her identity, there are a number of indications (although no direct statement) which point towards Eadgifu the Fair. First, Count Alan was the main successor to both of these great lords. However, in Norfolk and Suffolk, Godric the Steward administered a number of manors as part of the royal demesne, and these manors had been held by both Earl Ralph and by Eadgifu the Fair.[55] Godric also held the manor of Exning of Cambridgeshire, the largest of Eadgifu's manors in that county, and also the location of Earl Ralph's marriage feast.[56] Ralph the Staller's estate was divided between the counties of Norfolk and Lincoln, with the Fens between them. By far the largest part of Eadgifu's land lay in Cambridgeshire, although it extended into East Anglia and Hertfordshire. Together, these two estates form a much more coherent whole (see Fig. 3.2). A further possible connection is Ælfsige the nephew of Earl Ralph. Land valued at around £10 was held in Suffolk by Ælfsige and free men commended to him.[57] In the counties of Cambridgeshire and Hertfordshire, a man named Ælfsige held land valued at £12 as the man of Eadgifu, and $1\frac{1}{2}$ hides of this land lay in Exning: it is possible that these two men were one and the same. If the estates of Eadgifu and Ralph were combined, they would have a value of £570, equal to the largest of the non-earlish estates, that of Beorhtric, Ælfgar's son. As there is no definite evidence to connect the two lords (Ralph might have acquired his interests in Eadgifu's manors after 1066, and the identification of Ælfsige is uncertain) the estates have been considered separately in all the analysis presented here: but the prospect of their being connected is an intriguing one.

The estates belonging to Wulfwynn of Creslow, Azur, Thored's son, and Wulfweard White were all more scattered than those of

[53] *DB* ii. 127b, 131, 262, 324.
[54] *ASC* E *sub anno* 1075.
[55] *DB* ii. 117b, 119b, 128b, 286.
[56] *Florence, sub anno* 1075.
[57] *DB* ii. 324, 322, 437, 444b.

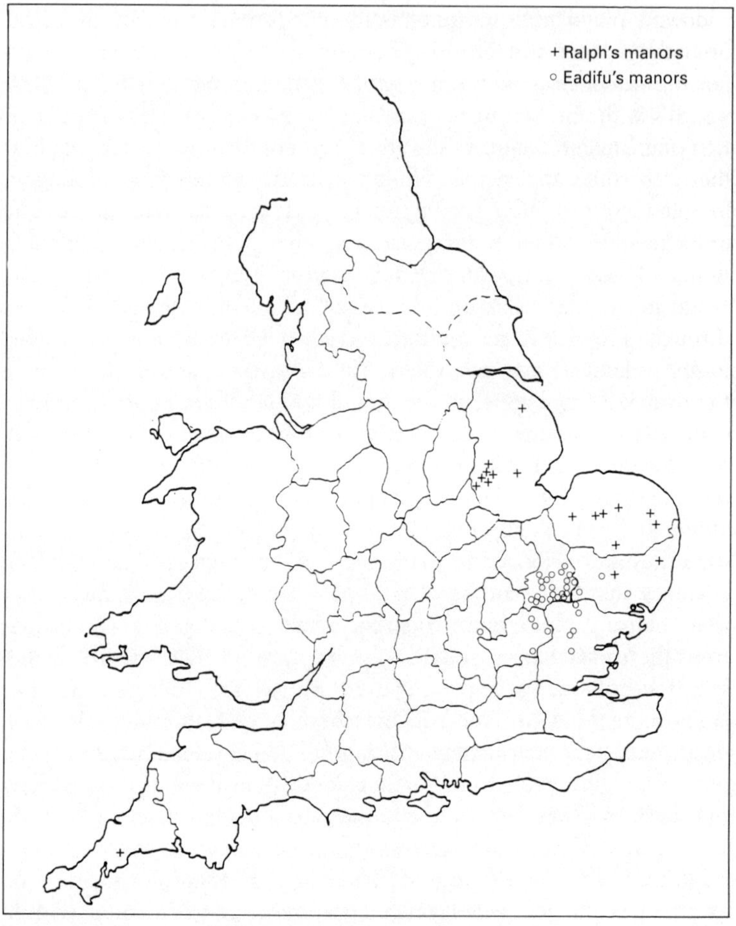

FIG. 3.2. Estates of Ralph the Staller and Eadgifu the Fair

Robert fitz Wymarc or the Abbey of Westminster. Given the tendency noted above for landholders to consolidate their manors into more compact areas, it is probable that some or all of these three estates had been created shortly before 1066. Of the three, only Wulfweard White can be shown to have been associated with the Crown in any way. He was a beneficiary of Queen Emma's will, and, at least after the Conquest, witnessed charters given by Eadgyth, King Edward's widow.[58] Wulfweard may have been given some of his land by either or both of these women, but the only case for which there is supporting evidence is the Domesday entry for Hayling Island.[59] Wulfweard's wife and son were recorded in Domesday as having land in Buckinghamshire, and Wulfweard himself held two small manors there. It would appear that Wulfweard had been a minor landholder in that county before coming into the Queen's service. There is, unfortunately, no basis for speculating how Wulfwynn of Creslow or Azur, Thored's son, acquired their land.

Earlier in this chapter it was suggested that estates would go through a cycle of accumulating land at times of prosperity, and losing peripheral manors in more difficult times and on the death of the owner. Where accumulation was more rapid, an estate would become more widespread, but if more land was being lost the tendency would be for a compact group of estates to be retained. There are a few examples of pre-Conquest estates which support this suggestion, although as ever, evidence is rather thin. The largest of the non-earlish estates belonged to Beorhtric, Ælfgar's son, and there is good evidence that his estate had been in existence for more than seventy years before the Conquest. Beorhtric himself had witnessed charters from the early 1040s (see Ch. 6), so it is quite probable that he had held the bulk of his land for the full period of Edward's reign. His lands, as recorded in Domesday Book, were quite widely spread, and this would tend to suggest that more land has been accumulated during the twenty years before the Conquest than was lost. Asgeir the Staller also appears to have been active from the beginning of the 1040s, and his estate was also quite widespread.[60]

Although Eadric of Laxfield also held a substantial estate, it was extremely compact, and lay almost entirely in the eastern half of Suffolk, with only a small proportion of the estate in the rest of Suffolk and in Norfolk. Unlike Beorhtric and Asgeir, Eadric had not

[58] S 1476 records Emma's gift. In Domesday Wulfweard was said to have held it from Queen Eadgyth. After the Conquest Wulfweard's daughter married Eadgyth's steward (*VCH Buckinghamshire*, i. 274–5), and Wulfweard witnessed two of Eadgyth's charters (*Regesta*, i. no. 23; *Calendar of Manuscripts of the Dean and Chapter of Wells*, Historical MSS Commission Reports (1907), i. 434.

[59] *DB* i. 43b.

[60] Asgeir was the addressee of a writ dated 1042–4 (S 1119), and appears on 2 spurious charters dated 1043 and 1044 (S 1000 and S 1002). However the main bulk of his attestations occur later in the reign, and if the writ is discounted, Asgeir may only have held his estate from a later date.

held his land without interruption from 1042 until 1066. Sometime in Edward's reign, and perhaps when Harold was earl in East Anglia (1043–51, 1052–3), Eadric was exiled, his land was seized by the Crown, and his men forced to take other lords. Eadric was allowed to return at some point before 1066, and his lands were returned to him. His men were free to return to his lordship, provided the new lord gave permission.[61] It may be that following this hiatus Eadric did not recover all his lands, but only the nucleus of an estate which had been larger. Another possibility is that Eadric was forced to sell some of his land on his return, perhaps to pay fines or other debts which he had incurred. It is possible too that Eadric's estate had always been confined to a small area. However, that would be unusual in the light of what we know of the land market at the time, and since we do know of a reason why Eadric's estate might have been subject to a potentially considerable reduction in size, it seems fair to suggest that this is in fact what occurred. Similar informed guesswork suggests that those estates which had more than one nucleus were the result of two separate estates being merged into one, as a result of either marriage or a bequest from one member of an extended family to another. The fact that separate groups of manors were once independent of each other is indicated by the particularly low average value per manor throughout the estate as a whole. They come closer to the expected values when the two distinct parts of the estate are treated separately (see above). Having said this, there is no evidence to show, for example, that the estate of Mærlswein had been brought together during his lifetime or at an earlier period.

The general impression which the sources give is of a quite lively movement of land between different estates. Although some, and perhaps many, of the estates recorded *TRE* had been in existence for some considerable time before Edward's reign, others were of more recent origin. These new estates could include three or four of the thirty-two valued at over £100. Other estates were reduced in size, or eliminated altogether. If Eadric of Laxfield had died in exile, instead of being allowed to return, then nothing would have been known of the great estate in East Anglia. For all the information which Domesday gives about England 'in the time of King Edward', the picture is static. We must remember that in fact the details of landholding, if not the general pattern, were subject to constant change.

[61] *DB* ii. 313.

4

DEPENDENT TENURE AND RELATIONSHIPS *TRE*

THE majority of entries in Domesday Book give no more details about the tenure of land *TRE* than the name of the Saxon who is said to have held it at that time. For Great Tew (Oxon.) the entry reads: '*Alnod Chentisc tenuit*',[1] while the entry for old Swinford (Worcs.) says only '*Uluuinus tenuit*'.[2] However, for a sizeable minority of entries more information is provided, either concerning the holder or the manner in which the land was held. Achi was said to have held Romsley (Worcs.) '*libere*'.[3] Asgeir the Staller held Ivinghoe Aston '*in dominio*'.[4] Other entries suggest more complex tenurial arrangements. Beorhtric, Ælfgar's son, held 1 hide at Bushley (Worcs.) '*de episcopo*'.[5] At Hexton (Herts.) 1 hide was held by '*Alric homo Asgari Stalr. Vendere potuit*'.[6] In Cambridgeshire, Grimbold held Quy under (*sub*) Eadgifu the Fair, and did not have the right to sell his land without the consent of his lord.[7] In Surrey, Osmund held 15 hides '*de rege Edwardo*'.[8] This chapter will cover the various forms of tenure implied by these formulas, and attempt to build up a picture of the dependent relationships which existed in England at the time of the Conquest.

The distribution of entries which give more than just the name of the holder *TRE* is not even throughout the country. The great majority of references to dependent relationships are recorded in circuits I, III, V (particularly the counties of Worcestershire, Gloucestershire, and Herefordshire) and VII. In other circuits, any dependent relationships which are recorded involve laymen leasing land from the Church.

In the counties of Circuit I, and in Worcestershire, Herefordshire, and Gloucestershire (the southern counties of Circuit V), the usual

[1] *DB* i. 155b. [2] *DB* i. 177.
[3] *DB* i. 239. [4] *DB* i. 149b.
[5] *DB* i. 173. [6] *DB* i. 140.
[7] *DB* i. 190b. [8] *DB* i. 34b.

formula used to denote dependent relationships was '*X tenuit de Y*'. At Sakenham '*Brictuuinus tenuit de Azor*',[9] while at Kingston both Azur and Gunnhildr held land '*de Heraldo*'.[10] Only the greatest of the lay landholders in these counties are recorded as having dependants. In Sussex, £251 was recorded as being held from various lay lords, excluding the king (for reasons given later in this chapter). Of this land, all but £6 14*s*. was held either from members of the family of Earl Godwine, or from Azur, the next most wealthy lay lord in the county. In the southern counties, even very important landholders might themselves hold land from another lord. Gytha the wife of Godwine held £8 worth of land in Mundham (Sussex) and £57 worth in Over Wallop and Wroxhall (Hants) from her husband. A number of men held land from Azur, but he himself held land valued at £48 from Earl Harold.

In Circuit III and in Essex, a variety of formulas are used. Land is sometimes said to have been held from (*de*) or under (*sub*) another, but the most common formula referring to dependant relationships simply says that the holder of a piece of land was the man of another lord. Asgeir the Staller held land throughout this region, and of seventy-two entries where Asgeir is referred to as superior, sixty-seven use some variant of '*X homo Asgari tenuit*'. Within these counties, it is generally only the most important landholders who have dependent men. The earls, Asgeir the Staller, Eadgifu the Fair, and other major landholders such as Robert fitz Wymarc had many men. But even a lord such as Toki, who had land valued at £102, had only a single group of sokemen who were described as his men; and altogether the land of the sokemen was valued at less than £1.

In Norfolk and Suffolk (but almost nowhere else) men are described as being commended to one or more lords. Even quite unimportant landholders usually had a few free men commended to them. For example Wicolf, whose own land was valued at £2 4*s*., had the commendation of twelve freemen. Wicolf was himself commended to a man named Toli.[11] Wihtgar, Ælfric's son, a major landholder in the south-west of Suffolk had men commended to him whose land was valued at £60 in total.[12] Another feature which appears to be unique to East-Anglian commendation is that a number of freemen

[9] *DB* i. 28b.
[10] Ibid.
[11] *DB* ii. 238, 421b.
[12] See App. II.

were commended to more than one lord: outside East Anglia no dependants appear to have had more than one lay lord.

The large number of commended freemen in East Anglia is paralleled to some extent by the sokemen of Cambridgeshire and Hertfordshire. But whereas the lords of East-Anglian commended men could range from great lords down to freemen with only a few acres of lands themselves, the lords of sokemen outside East Anglia were almost without exception relatively powerful men (see end of Ch. 4 and Ch. 5). The difference might be caused by the fact that Norfolk and Suffolk, with Essex, made up a separate circuit, and one which was never put into the less detailed format of the Great Domesday. But this argument does not take into account the fact that Essex does not have anything like the same number of recorded freemen as the other two counties in the Little Domesday, and, as elsewhere in England, the lords of men all held significant amounts of land themselves. Furthermore, in the west of Suffolk there were a number of sokemen, and like their neighbours in Cambridgeshire, they tended to be commended to relatively important men such as Wihtgar, the dominant landholder in the area. All this tends to suggest that East-Anglian commendation included some quite different elements from dependent relationships recorded in the rest of the country, and because of this East-Anglian commendation will be dealt with at the end of the chapter.

In Circuits II, III, and VI, and in the northern half of Circuit V, the only tenurial relationship which was mentioned with any regularity was the lease of land by laymen from the Church. It seems extremely unlikely that half England had dependent relationships while the remainder did not. It is more probable that the difference in the record is another example of the variations which occur in the thoroughness of the Survey from county to county. In the same way that *servi* are not recorded in a number of counties, although we know from other sources that they were present,[13] the omission of the details of dependent relationships from so many counties is a fault of the source we have, not an indication of geographical differences which actually existed. This is best illustrated by examining entries on either side of the border between Buckinghamshire and Oxfordshire. On the Buckinghamshire side there were many instances of men who

[13] See H. C. Darby, *Domesday Geography of Eastern England* (Cambridge, 1971), 330–1.

had others as their lord. But on the other side of the border no such relationships are mentioned. To take just one example, both Wulfric and Beorhtric held land on both counties, and their lands had passed to the same Norman by 1086. In Buckinghamshire all the entries which mention Wulfric state that he was the man of Beorhtric, but the relationship is not mentioned in the Oxfordshire entries.[14] The law codes allow for lesser thegns (as distinguished from king's thegns) in Mercia and the Danelaw as well as in Wessex.[15] This further reinforces the view that dependent relationships were common throughout the country, and not, as the evidence of Domesday implies, restricted to certain areas.

The types of dependent relationship involving the major landholders which are recorded by Domesday and other sources can be broadly divided into three groups: those involving the lord's relationship with the king; those involving his relations with the Church; and relationships between two laymen. A large number of landholders, from the most minor to the greatest, were described in Domesday as holding all or some of their land from King Edward. A freeman called Godric had two manors in Sussex, worth £1 8*s*., and in both entries he was said to have held the land '*de rege Edwardo*'.[16] At the other extreme, Earl Harold was said to hold the manor of Chigwell, Essex, in the same fashion.[17] No indication is given in any entries that the king necessarily had any specific rights over land which was held in this way. In one entry, Godric, Sheriff of Berkshire, held land '*de rege Edwardo*' which had been royal demesne, and which had later been given to Godric.[18] But the same formula is not used in other instances where land was granted by the king to other men. Neither was a special formula used by Domesday when referring to Sevington, Wiltshire, which had been granted to Ælfstan of Boscombe by royal diploma,[19] nor when referring to two manors which had been granted from the royal demesne to Ralph the Staller.[20]

Indeed, in one instance at least the expression is used when the king appears to have had no particular rights over the land. Cypping held Headbourne Worthy (Hants) '*de rege Edwardo*', but a subsequent note stated that the land had in fact been leased from St Peter's,

[14] *DB* i. 150, 159.
[15] *Leis Willhelmi*, 20. 2; II Cnut 71 in Liebermann, i. 356–9, 506–7.
[16] *DB* i. 27, 27b. [17] *DB* ii. 90b.
[18] *DB* i. 60b. [19] *DB* i. 71b; S 999.
[20] *DB* ii. 119, 144.

Winchester, for a period of three lives.[21] In this case the formula seems to have been used to emphasize the fact that the Church only had the right of reversion at the end of the agreement. This would have supported the claim of Cypping's successor, Ralph Mortimer, to the land, against the claim of St Peter's for its return. In this instance at least the statement that Cypping held his land from the king can have meant only that he was responsible for the obligations which lay upon the manor—geld, fyrd duty, and work on fortifications and bridges.

Furthermore, it seems to have been a general rule that men did not have more than one lord.[22] The exception to this is that a number of men who held land from, or were the men of, another lord are often stated to have held some of their land '*de rege Edwardo*'. Eadric of Alham held one manor from Asbiorn Bigga, and the rest of his estate from the king.[23] Wulfweard White was generally described as the man of Queen Eadgyth, and yet held land from the king in Kent and Berkshire.[24] The apparent problem of these men (and these men only) having two lords disappears if it is presumed that the phrase '*tenuit de rege Edwardo*' merely signifies that the land was not being held under any other lord. This would be a natural phrase for a Norman to use after the Conquest, when all land which was not held from another lord was indeed held from the king.

The evidence all suggests that no special relationship is implied when an entry records that land was held from the king *TRE*. It can mean no more than that the holder owed the normal obligations of the land to the king. This must have been true for the far more numerous cases where no mention of the king is made, as well as those for which the formula is used.

A large number of dependent relationships mentioned in Domesday involved the leasing of land from the Church. Sixteen landholders with more than £40 of land held at least some—valued at between £2 and £36—which was due to revert to the Church. Fortunately quite a lot is known about the terms of such agreements from other sources, and Domesday itself sometimes records the details of the lease. For example, a certain Wulfwine held 4 hides of land at Selly Oak

[21] *DB* i. 46b.

[22] There were exceptions in East Anglia which are dealt with at the end of this chapter.

[23] *DB* i. 9b, 11–12, 13b.

[24] *DB* i. 62b.

(Worcs.), and the Domesday entry for the manor includes the following: '*Hoc manerium emit eisdem Wluuinus TRE de episcopo Cestrensi et aetatem trium hominum*'.[25] The entry goes on to state that when Wulfwine fell ill, he gathered together his wife, his son, the Bishop of Lichfield, and others to declare that he wished the agreement to last only until the death of his wife, after which the land was to return to the Bishop of Chester. The lease is typical of many of the period, because of three features: the lease was bought by the lessee; the original period of the agreement was a set number of lives; and the terms of the agreement were altered at a later date.

Wulfweard White bought the lease of half the manor of Hayling Island (Hants) for an unspecified sum.[26] In Suffolk, Beorn bought 50 acres from St Edmund's, which was to revert to the abbey on his death.[27] Ælfweald bought 5 hides from the Abbot of Cerne, and again the land was to revert to the Church on the death of the purchaser.[28]

In other instances, Domesday states that land was held from a bishop or abbot, and was to return on the death of the holder, but there is no mention of a purchase. Eadgifu the Fair held Norton (Suffolk), which belonged to the demesne of St Edmund, and it was to return to the abbey on her death.[29] Asgeir the Staller held 30 hides in Buckinghamshire from Christ Church, Canterbury. He was not allowed to sell the land away from Christ Church, but no details are provided as to how the land had been acquired, or whether the land was to revert to the Church on Asgeir's death.[30] But in both of these cases, as in many others, it is likely that the holder had arranged to lease the land for a set period. Domesday Book gives only limited information about Godric the Sheriff's tenure of Fyfield, Berkshire: '*Godricus tenuit de abbatiae et non potuit ire quolibet cum ista terre*'.[31] But the Abingdon Chronicle states that the land was held by Godric on a lease for three lives, showing that on occasion Domesday was quite capable of omitting such information.[32]

Where Domesday does mention reversion to the Church, it is possible that in some cases there was no lease. Instead, Domesday might be recording the fact that a gift had been made to the Church, which was to take effect on the death of the holder, or one of his

[25] *DB* i. 177.
[26] *DB* i. 43b; S 1476, and Ch. 3.
[27] *DB* ii. 373.
[28] *DB* i. 96b.
[29] *DB* ii. 286.
[30] *DB* i. 143b.
[31] *DB* i. 60b.
[32] *Chron. Abingdon*, i. 484, 491.

family. Ælfric, Wihtgar's son, gave the manor of Clare to the Church, but the gift was only to take effect after the death of both Ælfric and his son. In this case the details are given in Domesday,[33] but it is possible that in other more abbreviated entries the right of reversion refers to this kind of arrangement, rather than to a lease. But Domesday does not always give information about the reversionary interests which might in fact exist. For example, the will of Thurstan stated that land in Wimbish (Essex) and Shouldham (Norfolk) should be given to the Church after the deaths of both Thurstan and his wife Æthelgyth. However Domesday, while naming Æthelgyth as the holder, makes no mention of the Church's rights in these manors.[34]

Leases could be paid for by a lump sum, as described above, or through a variety of other methods of payment. Leofgifu, a freewoman in Suffolk, held half a carucate from Holy Trinity. This was to return to that church on Leofgifu's death, along with other land which Leofgifu held in the same village.[35] Guthmund leased land from his brother, the Abbot of Ely, and payment for this may have been Guthmund's own manor of Bensted, in Essex, to be given to the abbey at the end of the lease. Domesday recorded that a number of manors were held by Guthmund from Ely, but does not mention Bensted amongst them.[36] But the *Liber Eliensis* (which has a good account of the lease) claimed that Bensted was included in the land which Guthmund had leased from the abbey.[37] In the account given by the *Liber Eliensis* no mention is made of the payment which Guthmund must have made for the lease. If Guthmund agreed to give Bensted to Ely after his death, this might have appeared to be a rather weaker claim to the land than if the manor had originally belonged to Ely. The monks of Ely needed a good claim to all the land which had been involved in Guthmund's lease because all the manors (along with the remainder of Guthmund's own land) passed into the hands of Hugh de Montfort after the Conquest.

Rent was sometimes payable during the course of a lease. Sometimes this might be a nominal sum paid in addition to a large initial payment, but on other occasions it could be quite substantial. A widow named Tova paid 3 marks of gold for the lease of *Cyrictuna* from St Albans. In addition to this sum she had to pay a sextar of honey each year as recognition of the monks' right of reversion.[38]

33 *DB* ii. 389b.
34 *DB* ii. 69b, 250b; S 1531.
35 *DB* ii. 372b.
36 *DB* ii. 54, 406, 408, 410b.
37 *Liber Eliensis*, book 2, cap. 97.
38 *Chron. St Albans*, 39.

Stigand leased the large manor of Tidenham from Bath, for which he paid an initial sum of 10 gold marks and 20 pounds of silver. Each year he also had to pay a mark of gold and fish from the weirs to the abbot.[39] For the lease of a manor from Ely, Stigand paid a food rent to the abbey.[40] As a last example Azur paid 1 pound a year, as well as giving service, for the lease of land from St Mary's, Pershore, which was valued at £2 10*s*.[41]

Not all leases were entered into freely on the part of the Church. Asgeir the Staller held High Easter, but it was to return to Ely on his death. However, this agreement was the result of a settlement between Asgeir and the abbey, after (as the abbot claimed) Asgeir had taken the manor by force. The only way that the monks could ensure the eventual return of the land was to recognize Asgeir's current tenancy.[42]

The king himself may have had some influence on the arrangement of leases of Church property. Edward gave Bromfield (Salop) to Robert fitz Wymarc, which was to be held '*sicut canonici*'.[43] This phrase apparently implied a restriction upon Robert's power to alienate the land from St Mary's, Bromfield. When Robert gave the land to a relative, the Church appealed to the king. This case was probably somewhat unusual, in that St Mary's may have been a royal college, and in any case, the land in question had belonged to Spirites the Priest, and had been forfeited to the Crown when Spirites was outlawed. But whatever the circumstances it does show that the Church was not always entirely free to do as it chose with its own property.

Another case where the king may have been involved was the lease of land from the Bishop of Worcester to Wulfgeat, for a period of three lives.[44] There is nothing unusual in the terms of this lease, with the exception of a note at the end. This states that King Edward had reduced the assessment on the land from its original value to 1 hide, and this reduction was to last for the period of the lease. The fact that the reduction in the geld was to last for the period of the lease shows that the reduction was not a coincidence, and it may indicate

[39] S 1426.
[40] R. V. Lennard, *Rural England 1086–1135* (Oxford, 1959), 169.
[41] *DB* i. 175.
[42] *DB* ii. 60; *Liber Eliensis*, book 2, cap. 96.
[43] *DB* i. 252b.
[44] S 1409.

that royal influence helped secure the lease for Wulfgeat. Heming recorded at least one instance where Earl Leofric compelled Prior Æthelwine to grant land to Simund the Dane. In this case Simund was obliged to do military service on behalf of the Church.[45]

Leases always appear to have been arranged to run for a limited number of lives, between one and three. Many of the examples above illustrate the use of such a period. But in spite of the regularity with which this limitation is recorded, in many cases the period initially agreed was changed at a later date. The example of Wulfwine's lease from the Bishop of Chester, given above, is an example of a reduction in the original length of the lease. It was more common however, for leases to be extended beyond the period specified in the original agreement. The *Liber Eliensis* stated that when Guthmund first leased land from his brother Wulfwine, the Abbot of Ely, the agreement was only to last as long as both brothers lived. But when Wulfwine died, Guthmund was able to rearrange the lease with his brother's successor, and so the land remained in Guthmund's hands until the Conquest.[46]

Information survives regarding a long series of agreements concerning the manors of Ryhall and Belmesthorpe.[47] Godgifu, the wife of Earl Siweard, promised to give both manors to Peterborough Abbey on her death. But when she did die, Siweard made his own agreement with the abbey, so that he kept both manors until his own death. This was not the end of the matter. Waltheof, Siweard's son, did give Belmesthorpe to the abbey, but paid 5 marks in order to be allowed to keep Ryhall until his death. But Waltheof did not lose all interest in Belmesthorpe, for during the disruption which followed the Conquest, Waltheof took the manor from Peterborough by force. He later agreed to return both manors after his own death. All this information is found outside Domesday. In the Survey, no details are recorded other than the fact that Waltheof had held both manors *TRE*, and his widow, Judith, held them in 1086.[48] So even in 1086 the land had not passed to Peterborough, although whether Judith had come to a new agreement with Abbot Brand, or whether she held the land by force, we do not know.

In this connection it might be remembered that land which had been promised to the Church in a will often remained within the

45 *Heming*, i. 264–5; *DB* i. 174.
46 *Liber Eliensis*, book 2, cap. 97.
47 S 1481.
48 *DB* i. 228.

donor's family. In such cases the descendants may have held on to the land by force, but it is equally possible that the relatives arranged for a series of leases which allowed them to keep the land in return for some form of payment. The example of Ryhall and Belmesthorpe shows that these two courses might not be mutually exclusive.

In some cases where land was leased, the lessee was said to have had to do service in return for the land. This was particularly common in Worcestershire where a large number of leases have survived. In some Domesday entries, service is specifically mentioned. At Oddingley, '*Turchil tenuit et inde episcopo servivit*';[49] and at Ditchford, '*Aluuardus tenuit et servitum reddidit*'.[50] But Worcester was not typical in this respect. In a few instances elsewhere, service was mentioned in connection with leased land. Siweard of Maldon held Tollesbury (Essex) from the Abbot of Barking, for an unspecified service.[51] Eadric held 2 carucates of land from St Benet of Holme, for which service was due.[52] But these examples are rare, and Worcester stands almost alone in this respect. Indeed, there was a tradition of lands leased in return for service which went back at least as far as Bishop Oswald in the tenth century.

Worcester was also unusual in that it was able to keep hold of most of the land which had been leased to laymen before the Conquest, whereas in most other cases the Church lost such land. The evidence suggests that Worcester's success was precisely because the lessee owed service for the land. Two examples support this view, the first of which concerns the lease of Bushley (Worcs.) to Beorhtric, Ælfgar's son. This was one of the few portions of leased land which the Bishop of Worcester had lost by 1086, although he still claimed it, maintaining that Beorhtric had done service for the land and paid to Worcester those dues which normally went to the king.[53] On the other hand, the entry for this manor in the royal demesne (where much of Beorhtric's land lay in 1086) stated that Beorhtric had bought the land outright, and owed no service for it to any man.[54] The implication is that, had service been due, the bishop's claim to Bushey would have been successful.

The example of Siweard of Maldon's land, leased from the Abbot of Barking, also suggests that the question of service was critical in determining whether or not leased land could be recovered after

[49] *DB* i. 173b. [50] *DB* i. 173.
[51] *DB* ii. 18b. [52] *DB* ii. 219b.
[53] *DB* i. 173. [54] *DB* i. 180b.

1066. In 1086, Siweard's successor, Rannulf Peverel, held Tollesbury from Barking Abbey, in return for the same services which Siweard had performed.[55] On the other hand, the land which Siweard had leased from Ely at Rettendon, where no service was specified, was held in 1086 by Rannulf directly from the king, in spite of Ely's claims to the land.[56]

Again, after the Conquest some men who held land from Worcester nevertheless commended themselves to Æthelwig, Abbot of Evesham. Walter de Cerissy, Æthelwig's successor, claimed that the land of these men belonged to Evesham. However, Worcester claimed land at Bengeworth and Hampton on the grounds that these estates had owed customary services to Worcester,[57] although the Abbot of Evesham appears to have continued to hold this land in 1086.[58]

In most other instances land which appears to have been leased from the Church before 1066 was held by laymen from the king in 1086. All the land which Guthmund had leased from Ely was being held by Hugh de Montfort in 1086.[59] Miles Crispin succeeded to all the manors of Beorhtric the man of Queen Eadgyth, including the manor of Clapham, which Beorhtric had leased from Ramsey.[60] Toki leased two manors from Ely *TRE*, which were both held by his successor in 1086. In none of these cases was any mention made of service which was due from the lessee.[61] But St Benet of Holme did retain Honing, which had been leased to Eadric, and service had been due on this land.[62]

The contrast between the way in which leased land was treated when service accrued to it, and when it did not, shows that the Normans at least distinguished between the two. Where no service was due, the land was considered to have been held directly by the lessee; where service was due, it was treated as if it had been held by the lessor. It is true that this interpretation enabled the barons to increase their own holdings at the cost of the Church; but since they might have claimed all land held through a lease, the fact that they did not emphasizes the distinction that was made. Where no service

55 *DB* ii. 18b. 56 *DB* ii. 75.

57 E. Mason, 'Change and Continuity in Eleventh Century Mercia', in R. A. Brown (ed.), *Anglo-Norman Studies, VIII: Proceedings of the Battle Conference, 1985* (Woodbridge, 1986).

58 *DB* i. 174, 175f. The Abbot of Evesham may have held the land from Worcester, but this is by no means clear.

59 *DB* ii. 406, 408, 410b. 60 *DB* i. 212.

61 *DB* i. 196b. 62 *DB* ii. 219b.

was due to the lessor, the lessee took over all the rights and obligations of the land, leaving the lessor only with the right of reversion, and in some cases, the payment of rent.

When Guthmund leased land from St Etheldreda, he did so in order to raise his personal status. The *Liber Eliensis* states that Guthmund aspired to the ranks of the *proceres*, who were distinguished by holding more than 40 hides of land.[63] Domesday records that Guthmund had 36 hides of his own land (which was not due to revert to Ely) and he leased a further 13 hides from the abbey, bringing his total holding substantially above the limit mentioned. What is most important for our current purposes is that Guthmund's status was raised by his holding the land, whether leased or not: for the period of the agreement, the land was Guthmund's own, even to the extent of improving his status.

In the entry for Headbourne Worthy, which Cypping had leased for three lives, the thegn was said to have held it '*de rege Edwardo*'.[64] Use of this formula emphasized the fact that St Peter's, Winchester's only right to the land was the right of reversion: until the end of the agreement Cypping held the land with no responsibility to anyone but the king. It appears that, although land held by lease could be subject to a number of different conditions, the lessor retained nothing but the right of reversion of the land. On occasions rent was due, and more rarely, the lessee had to perform regular service. But for the most part, leased land was in every way the land of the lessee, until the specified period of lives had run its term.

Throughout the history of Anglo-Saxon England, a strong emphasis was placed upon the relationship between a man and his temporal lord. In the Penitential of Archbishop Theodore, a penance of forty days was required for the man who killed in order to avenge the death of his lord, while seven years' penance were required if a man killed in order to avenge the death of a kinsman.[65] The laws of Alfred include a number of sections concerning the respective rights and duties of a lord and his men, whilst Æthelstan required that every man should have his lord.[66] In his 'Sermon of the Wolf to the

[63] *Liber Eliensis*, book 2, cap. 97.

[64] *DB* i. 46b.

[65] *Councils and Ecclesiastical Documents Relating to Great Britain and Ireland*, ed. A. W. Hadden and W. Stubbs (Oxford, 1871), iii. 180.

[66] Laws of Alfred, 4.2, 42.5, 42.6; II Æthelstan 2 in Liebermann, i. 50–1, 76–7, 151–3.

English', Wulfstan dealt at some length with the evils of men who betray their lord (although he seems to have meant the betrayal of the king in particular).[67] The duties of the lord are again mentioned in the laws of Ethelred and Cnut.[68] It is therefore not surprising that Domesday furnishes a large number of dependent relationships between laymen.

A number of different terms are used to record dependent relationships. In the south of England, in Kent, Sussex, and Hampshire, and in the counties of Gloucestershire, Herefordshire, and Worcestershire, Domesday normally states that land was held by one man from another, where any details are given at all. At Cokeham (Sussex), '*Brismaer tenuit de Azor*', and at Wilmington in the same county Ælfnoth, Wulfnoth, and Wulfstan all held land '*de Goduino*'.[69]

In Cambridgeshire, Huntingdonshire, Hertfordshire, Buckinghamshire, and Essex, a wider variety of formulas are used. Sometimes, the same formula that is used in the southern counties appears: at Hazelhanger (Herts.) it is said, '*Hanc terram tenuit Leflet de Stigando archiepiscopo*'.[70] Beorhtric held High Wycombe (Bucks.) from Queen Eadgyth,[71] and Merewin held land in Haslingfield (Cambs.) from (*de*) Eadgifu the Fair.[72] But on other occasions land was said to have been held by one person under (*sub*) another. At Papworth (Cambs.), '*Goda tenuit sub Edeva*',[73] and at Barrington, in the same county, '*Edzi tenuit sub Roberto filio Wymarci*'.[74] The wife of Wulfweard White held land worth £7 at Worminghall (Bucks.) under Queen Eadgyth.[75] The most common of all the formulas used in the counties of Circuit III was '*X homo Y tenuit*'. In the entry for Wymondley (Herts.), Domesday declares that '*Hoc manerium tenuit Suuen homo Heraldi*'.[76] At Wallington, also in Hertfordshire, land was held *TRE* by one '*Wluuar homo Anschil de Wares*'.[77] An entry concerning 3 virgates in Bradwell (Berks.) stated that *TRE*, '*Hanc terram tenuit Aluuard homo Goding*',[78] and 1 hide in Swavesey (Cambs.) was held by '*Lefsi homo Wallef comitis*'.[79]

At first sight these formulas seem to imply rather different things,

[67] *EHD* i. 854–7.
[68] III Ethelred 4; II Cnut 13.1, 22.2, 30.7, 31; Liebermann, i. 228–9, 316–17, 324–5, 334–5.
[69] *DB* i. 21b, 29. [70] *DB* i. 134b. [71] *DB* i. 149.
[72] *DB* i. 194b. [73] *DB* i. 195.
[74] *DB* i. 200b. [75] *DB* i. 145.
[76] *DB* i. 140b. [77] *DB* i. 141b.
[78] *DB* i. 148b. [79] *DB* i. 197.

and it might be suggested that they refer to different types of relationship. In particular, the two formulas '*X tenuit de Y*' and '*X tenuit sub Y*' imply a lordship over land, whilst the third, '*X homo Y tenuit*', seems to emphasize lordship over the man rather than over his possessions. Maitland detected a difference even between the first two forms: 'We catch a subtle shade of difference between the two prepositions: *sub* lays stress on the lord's power . . . whilst *de* imports a theory about the origin of the tenure.'[80] In particular, the term *de* is used to refer to the relationship between a tenant-in-chief and his subtenants in 1086. This could be used to suggest that, when Domesday uses this particular formula for the period *TRE*, it implies that some form of feudal tenure had already been established, at least in certain areas.

There is important evidence against attaching weight to the apparent distinctions between these formulas. For many Cambridgeshire hundreds, the Domesday Book folios are paralleled for at least some of the county by the *Inquisitio comitatus Cantabrigiensis* (which was drawn up at the same time as the Domesday Survey, although the exact relationship is uncertain). They differ in format: Domesday is organized by tenant-in-chief, whilst the *ICC* is arranged geographically, by hundreds and villages. The two surveys, despite being differently arranged, provide much the same information, although the *ICC* often provides extra details, including more frequent use of bynames and information regarding livestock. In both surveys all three different formulas are used, but when the two accounts are compared, the two entries referring to the same dependent relationship often use different terms.

Table 4.1 shows a number of examples where the *ICC* and Domesday Book use different formulas to describe the same entry. In Cambridgeshire at least, the compilers of these two documents used the various formulas interchangeably. The different terms were presumably considered to be equivalent, and so it is not possible to state that the different formulas found in other parts of Domesday refer definitely to specific types of bond between lord and man. This is not to say that there was only one type of dependent relationship between lay landholders *TRE*, merely that the different terms used by the compilers of the Survey cannot be used to distinguish between them.

[80] F. W. Maitland, *Domesday Book and Beyond* (Cambridge, 1921), 154.

TABLE 4.1. A comparison of formulas used in equivalent entries of Domesday and the ICC

Vill	Domesday Book	ICC
Camps	*Lefsi sub comite Heraldo* *DB* i. 196b	*Lefsi tenuit de comite Heraldo* *ICC* p. 29
Foxton	*Sigar tenuit sub Asgar* *DB* i. 197	*Sigar tenuit de Asgaro* *ICC* p. 45
Pampisford	*Almarus tenuit sub Eddeva* *DB* i. 194b	*tenuit Almarus homo Eddive* *ICC* p. 37
Babraham	*unus homo Guert comitis* *DB* i. 202	*tenuit Lemmarus de Gurdo comite* *ICC* p. 96
Badlingham	*tenuit Ormar sub Eddeva* *DB* i. 195b	*tenuit Ormar homo Eddive* *ICC* p. 2
Soham	*tenuit Alsi sub Eddiva* *DB* i. 195b	*tenuit Alsi homo Eddive* *ICC* p. 7
Shepreth	*tenuit Sigarus de Asgaro* *DB* i. 197	*tenuit Sigar homo Asgaro* *ICC* p. 54
Guilden Morden	*tenuit Godwinus de Asgaro* *DB* i. 197	*tenuit Godwin Wambestrang homo Asgaro* *ICC* p. 76

Why did this confusion of terms arise, and which of the various formulas is the most descriptive of the relationships being described? No definite answer can be given, but the confusion probably arose because the commissioners who carried out the Domesday Survey were not well informed about the details of Saxon dependent tenure. Where such relationships were mentioned, they may automatically have been assumed to be similar to the relationship between tenant and lord in 1086. The word used throughout Cambridgeshire (and most of the rest of England) to express the fact that land was held by a tenant at the time of the survey was '*de*'. For example, in Sussex: '*Goisfridus tenet de comite* CONTONE'[81] and '*Hugi tenet de Willelmo* ROTINGEDENE'.[82] It would be perfectly natural for the commissioners (or their scribes) to use this formula when referring to the situation in 1066, even if it was, in fact, a quite anachronistic term. Where different formulas are used in Domesday, 'A the man of B' is by far the most common. It is possible that this was the form of words which was used by the English jurors when describing the situation

[81] *DB* i. 24.
[82] *DB* i. 26b.

which pertained before the Conquest. If this is the case then it is significant that the formula appears to describe a personal relationship: as will be seen later, most of the dependent relationships recorded in Domesday between two laymen did not imply that the land of the man was under any form of control from his lord.

A very few of the greatest landholders were said in some entries to have been the man of, or to have held their land from, a lord other than the king. Gytha, the wife of Earl Godwine, held some of her land from her husband.[83] Azur, the shadowy Sussex lord, held six manors from either Earl Godwine or Earl Harold.[84] In almost every entry which relates to the Midlands thegn Beorhtric, he is described as being the man, or the thegn, of Queen Eadgyth.[85] Of the eighty-eight landholders listed in Table 3.1, eighteen were said in at least one entry to have had another layman as their lord. Of these eighteen, six had over £100's worth of land. As well as Gytha, Azur, and Beorhtric, Cypping had two manors from Earl Harold,[86] Baldwin, Herluin's son, was the man of Archbishop Stigand, and Wulfweard White was the man of Queen Eadgyth. Of the remaining twelve, seven were the men of Earl Harold, two more the men of Queen Eadgyth, and one the man of Archbishop Stigand. The remaining two men, Eadric of Alham and Sigeræd of Cilleham, held some of their land from Asbiorn Bigga, who himself had land worth just £49.

Table 4.2 summarizes the evidence of Domesday Book concerning dependent landholders *TRE*. It shows the value of land in each entry where the land was said to have been held from, under or by the men of the greater landholders. Because of the sporadic nature of the Domesday record of such relationships, such a diagram must be treated with the greatest of care. To take a single example: Ulf Fenisc was said to have been the lord of very few men, in spite of his large estate. However, most of his land lay in Yorkshire, Lincolnshire, and Nottinghamshire, where dependent relationships were not generally recorded, and we cannot guess at the number of Ulf's dependents in these counties who have been omitted. Table 4.3 shows the data in a rather different way. Only those lords who held at least half their land in counties which recorded dependency have been included, and the amount of land held by dependent men is shown as a proportion of the total land held directly by the lord.

[83] *DB* i. 24, 38b, 39b. [84] *DB* i. 21b, 27b–28b.
[85] *DB* i. 136b, 149, 150, 150b. [86] *DB* i. 46b.

Table 4.2 shows as a general trend just what we would expect: the more land a man held himself, the more dependent men he was likely to attract. Table 4.3 shows that even in areas where dependent tenure was recorded, a number of wealthy landholders had relatively few men under them, while some of the less wealthy lords, such as Ælfric, Goding's son, and Askell of Ware, had attracted a relatively large proportion of dependents.

On the whole, the most powerful lord in any particular area was able to build up the largest number of commended men, while other lords in the same area would have few, if any commended men, unless they were of equal stature nationally. Where no lord dominated an area, many men with relatively small estates were able to acquire at least some dependent men. Eadgifu the Fair, Asgeir the Staller, Eadric of Laxfield, and Wihtgar, Ælfric's son, all had more or less concentrated estates. In the areas where they held most of their land, they were often the most prominent lay lord by a considerable margin, and all of these lords had a considerable number of dependents. By way of a contrast, the estate of Æthelnoth Cilt was quite scattered. He was not particularly prominent in any one area, and this might be the reason why he did not attract many followers. But Azur had a concentrated estate in Sussex, and had very few men under him, relative to the value of his estate. It may be that, because his land was in the centre of the powerbase of the house of Godwine, Azur was overshadowed. Wulfwine and Toki both had valuable land concentrated in Cambridgeshire and Essex, but perhaps because their estates lay between those of Eadgifu the Fair to the north and Asgeir the Staller to the south, they too had few dependent men of their own. Another factor which may have limited Azur's influence is that he (like Cypping, who also had few dependents) held some of his land from Earl Harold. The fact that Azur and Cypping were themselves dependent on a lord may have stopped other free men from commending themselves to either of them. On the other hand, Beorhtric, the thegn of Queen Eadgyth, did have a number of dependent men. This would suggest that while having another man as a lord might be a contributory factor in limiting the number of men who were commended to a particular lord, it was not a decisive one.

At the other end of the scale, Burgeræd, Askell of Ware, and Ælfric, Goding's son, had a larger proportion of dependents than had many lords with larger estates. They all held most of their land in Buckinghamshire and Hertfordshire, where no other single lord held

TABLE 4.2. Value of land held by dependent men of the lords

	Value of land held		
	By lord (£)	From or by men (£)	£10s .....4.....8....12....16....20..>>.140
Family of Earl Godwine	5,187	1,430	*************************************
Family of Earl Leofric	2,470	172	************************
Beorhtric, Ælfgar's son	560	31	****
Asgeir the Staller	448	206	****************************
Ulf Fenisc	394	3	*
Eadgifu the Fair	366	160	***********************
Family of Earl Siweard	348	84	***********
Ælfstan of Boscombe	289	3	*
Azur	271	8	*
Æthelnoth of Kent	260	20	***
Wulfweard White, his wife and son	223	7	*
Mærlswein the Sheriff	214	—	
Robert fitz Wymarc	204	35	****
Ralph the Staller	201	3	*
Eadric of Laxfield	192	225	*******************************
Wihtgar, Ælfric's son	182	103	**************
Bundi the Staller	182	5	*
Asgot, Beorhtric, and Edmund	176	—	
Family of Earl Ralph	170	2	*

Eadnoth the Staller and his son	155	—	
Toki, Otta's son	151	—	
Siweard of Maldon	147	6	*
Karl	144	—	
Eadmær Atre	143	1	*
Siweard Barn	142	—	
Wulfwine (*antec.* Aubrey de Vere)	141	1	*
Wulfwynn of Creslow	137	2	*
Cypping	137	—	
Baldwin, Herluin's son	136	4	*
Leofnoth the son of Osmund	118	5	*
Wigot of Wallingford	117	6	*
Azur, Thored's son	116	—	
Æthelgyth, wife of Thurstan	111	5	*
Beorhtmær	109	—	
Osweard of Norton	109	1	*
Askell of Ware	109	24	***
Beorhtsige Cilt	107	4	*
Toki (*antec.* William Warenne)	103	1	*
Beorhtric, man of Queen Eadgyth	101	22	***
Burgeræd and his sons	100	30	****
Eadric the Wild	100	—	
Wulfmær of Eaton	99	9	*
Wulfgifu of Betteslau	98	—	
Tonni	93	—	
Eadweard Cilt	93	2	*
Æthelfrith and Ælmar	90	—	

TABLE 4.2. (*cont.*)

	Value of land held		
	By lord (£)	From or by men (£)	£10s .....4.....8....12....16....20..>>.140
Leofnoth and Leofric	80	—	
Ingeware	79	4	*
Ælfric Camp	77	—	
Toli the Dane	75	—	
Godwine the Priest	73	—	
Guthmund	73	19	***
Siweard Grossus	72	—	
Earnesige	70	—	
Thorkell White and his wife	69	—	
Normann	68	—	
Æthelric, Mærgeat's son	68	—	
Ordwulf	67	1	*
Azur, Toti's son	66	7	*
Eadric of Elmham	66	—	
Sigeræd of Chilham	66	—	
Æthelwig (*antec.* Alfred of Spain)	65	—	
Æthelmar Melc	63	—	
Eadric (*antec.* Arnulf of Hesdin)	63	—	
Ælfric, Goding's son	61	19	***

Ælfweald	60	—	
Engelric	60	7	*
Hrolf, Sceldeware's son	59	—	
Thorgautr Lag	59	—	
Ulf (*antec.* Robert de Tosny)	57	3	*
Saxi	54	—	
'Ælfwine', Sheriff of Gloucester	54	—	
Spirites the priest	54	—	
Osmund	53	—	
Gauti, Earl Harold's housecarl	50	—	
Tope's family	50	—	
Orm (*antec.* Hugh fitz Baldric)	50	—	
Æthelsige (*antec.* Walter of Douai)	49	—	
Thorkell (*antec.* Countess Judith)	49	—	
Asbiorn Bigga	49	4	*
Bundi (*antec.* Hugh de Montfort)	49	—	
Ælfweald of Stevington	47	2	*
Ketill Alder	46	2	*
Stori (*antec.* Ivo Taillebois)	46	—	
Æthelstan, Godram's son	45	—	
Godric the Sheriff	45	4	*
Siweard (*antec.* Baldwin of Exeter)	45	—	
Beorhtric (*antec.* Odo fitz Gamelin)	43	—	
Godwine (*antec.* Eudo Dapifer)	42	—	
John the Dane	42	—	
Oswulf, Frane's son	42	—	
Osfrith	41	—	
Dunna (*antec.* Osbern Giffard)	41	—	
Godwine and Azur	40	—	

TABLE 4.3. Value of land held by dependent men as a proportion of their lord's estate

	Value of land held		
	By lord (£)	From or by men (£)	As % of land held directly by lord
			10 20 30 40 50 60 70 80 90 100 110 120
Family of Earl Godwine	5,187	1,430	*******
Asgeir the Staller	448	206	***********
Eadgifu the Fair	366	160	************
Family of Earl Siweard	348	84	******
Azur	271	8	*
Æthelnoth of Kent	260	20	*
Robert fitz Wymarc	204	35	***
Ralph the Staller	201	3	*
Eadric of Laxfield	192	225	***********************************
Wihtgar, Ælfric's son	182	103	*****************
Siweard of Maldon	147	6	*
Wulfwine (*antec.* Aubrey de Vere)	141	1	*
Cypping	137	—	
Leofnoth the son of Osmund	118	5	*
Azur, Thored's son	116	—	
Æthelgyth, wife of Thurstan	111	5	*
Osweard of Norton	109	1	*

Askell of Ware	109	24	******
Toki (*antec.* William Warenne)	103	1	*
Beorhtric, man of Queen Eadgyth	101	22	*****
Burgeræd and his sons	100	30	********
Wulfmær of Eaton	99	9	**
Eadweard Cilt	93	2	*
Ingeware	79	4	*
Ælfric Camp	77	—	
Godwine the priest	73	—	
Guthmund	73	19	******
Normann	68	—	
Azur, Toti's son	66	7	**
Eadric of Elmham	66	—	
Sigeræd of Chilham	66	—	
Æthelmar Melc	63	—	
Ælfric, Goding's son	61	19	********
Engelric	60	7	***
Ulf (*antec.* Robert de Tosny)	57	3	*
Thorkell (*antec.* Countess Judith)	49	—	
Asbiorn Bigga	49	4	*
Bundi (*antec.* Hugh de Montfort)	49	—	
Ælfweald of Stevington	47	2	*
Ketill Alder	46	2	*
Godric the Sheriff	45	4	**
Godwine (*antec.* Eudo Dapifer)	42	—	
Oswulf, Frane's son	42	—	

a particularly large amount of land. Instead, there were a number of local thegns, such as Askell and Ælfric, along with greater landholders such as Earl Harold and Asgeir the Staller. Both Harold and Asgeir did have a number of men in the two counties, but the presence of these important lords was not so significant as to prevent lesser thegns from accumulating their own commended men—as happened elsewhere. Beorhtric also held his land in this area, and it may be that, because he had land worth over £100, and because there was no great lord in the area, he was able to hold commended men in spite of himself being Queen Eadgyth's man.

In some cases dependent men had lords who themselves had no land at all in the county. In Cambridgeshire, Asgeir the Staller, Earl Waltheof, and Robert fitz Wymarc all had numbers of commended men, although none of these lords had any manors of their own in the county. It may be that these dependent men needed a lord who could not be easily overawed by the major lay landholder in the county, Eadgifu the Fair, and sought other major landholders from adjacent counties in order to escape from her influence. This question is further considered in Chapter Five.

The first volume of Domesday Book records no definite examples of one man holding land from two or more lay lords, or being the man of more than one layman (Little Domesday does provide examples from East Anglia, which will be dealt with at the end of this chapter). In Cambridgeshire, Sigar held land in six villages. In each entry he was described as holding the land from or under Asgeir, or as being Asgeir's man. In the same county, Godwine Cilt always appears as the dependent of Eadgifu the Fair. In Sussex, there were three entries where Beorhtmær held land from Azur.[87] At first sight, Azur himself was an exception to this rule, since he held land from both Earl Godwine and Earl Harold. Rather than see this as a unique exception, it is simpler to presume that Azur was Godwine's man until the death of the latter, after which time he became Harold's man. P. H. Sawyer suggested that contrary to this view, many Saxons had more than a single lord. He gives the example of Code, a minor landholder in Lincolnshire, whom Sawyer suggests had more than one lord.[88] Because his land was divided amongst three different men in 1086, Sawyer states that this proves that Code was the man of

[87] *DB* i. 26b, 28b, 29.

[88] P. H. Sawyer, '1066–1086: A Tenurial Revolution?', in *Reassessment*, 83.

three different lords. That this need not have been the case is suggested by the example of the Suffolk landholder Beorhtmær, who, like Code, also held a small amount of land which by 1086 had been divided amongst three different Normans.[89] He was not described as having been the man of any lord other than the king *TRE*. As the Suffolk folios mention dependent relationships very frequently, it seems unlikely that they would have been omitted in every entry which relates to Beorhtmær, while a note in the text makes it clear that we are indeed dealing with a single tenant *TRE*.[90] If Beorhtmær's land could be divided (as was that of at least some of the greater landholders—see Ch. 7) then so could the estate of Code: evidence for multiple lordships should be drawn from those counties where dependent relationships were recorded, rather than counties where the information was omitted.

Whilst men do not appear to have had more than a single lay lord, laymen could and did hold land on lease from one or more ecclesiastical establishment, and such a tenant of the Church could also have a lay lord. Beorhtric the man of Queen Eadgyth held a manor worth £12 from Ramsey Abbey.[91] Cypping was recorded as holding some of his manors from Earl Harold, but he also leased two manors from the Bishop and Old Minster of Winchester.[92] Siweard of Maldon held land from the abbeys of Barking and Ely.[93] There would seem to have been a qualitative difference between the relationship of lessor and lessee, and between a lord and his man. A man might lease land from several sources, but he had a single lord.

No single source provides a detailed account of the rights and duties involved in the relationship between lord and man in England before the Conquest. In particular, it is not clear whether lordship was being exercised primarily over the man himself, or over his land. In the east Midlands at least, the most common formula used to express lordship was that 'X the man of Y held this land'. This form of words does not imply that the lord had any rights over the land, and there is evidence to support the view that, in the majority of the cases recorded in Domesday, lordship was primarily a personal rather than a tenurial relationship. Thus Domesday often states that a man could give or sell his land without the permission of his lord. Thorbern held land at Orwell (Cambs.) under Eadgifu the Fair, and the entry

[89] *DB* ii. 424, 424b, 429. [90] *DB* ii. 424.
[91] *DB* i. 212. [92] *DB* i. 46b. [93] *DB* ii. 18b–19.

ends '*et recedere potuit ab ea*'.[94] At Croydon in the same county, Godgifu the 'man' of Eadgifu had the freedom to sell her land without her lord's consent.[95] At Munden, in Hertfordshire, a certain Leofwine, the man of Earl Harold, held the land '*et vendere potuit*'.[96] The information that land could (or could not) be sold or otherwise disposed of without the lord's permission is provided most commonly in the counties of Circuit III, and, where it was recorded, it was much more common for a man to have the freedom to sell than not. Of forty-nine entries referring to the men of Asgeir the Staller, his men had the freedom to sell in thirty-eight cases, and in a further three entries no information was given.[97]

A specific example of a thegn who appears to have been able to dispose of his lands freely, at least on his death, is provided by the will of Ketill Alder.[98] In Domesday Book Ketill is described as being Archbishop Stigand's thegn, in the entry for Walsingham, and as holding Hainford under Stigand.[99] Both lands are mentioned in the will which Ketill made prior to going on a journey to Rome. Walsingham was left to his sister Gode, and Hainford to his brother Godric. No mention is made of Stigand concerning these grants, and there was certainly no suggestion that Stigand had any rights over these manors. However, Ketill did give Stigand another manor, and made provision for the payment of his heriot to Stigand, so it is clear that the archbishop remained Ketill's lord at the time the will was drawn up. In spite of the entries in Domesday, Stigand's lordship over Ketill was not in respect of the two lands where it was recorded; rather it was a personal relationship in which lordship over land does not appear to have played any significant part.

The law tract known as the *Gethynctho* recognized that a lord might have amongst his men someone who himself held 5 hides (or more) of land, upon which the man himself (and not the lord) discharged the king's dues.[100] It is made clear that the lord who had such a thegn as his man had more rights than a lord who did not (see below). Ketill was no doubt such a thegn, holding his own land but

[94] *DB* i. 194b.
[95] *DB* i. 194.
[96] *DB* i. 139.
[97] In Ch. 5 this point is covered in more detail, for the county of Cambridge.
[98] S 1519.
[99] *DB* ii. 243b, 254.
[100] *Gethynctho* 3, in Liebermann, i. 456–7.

being the man of Archbishop Stigand. In Cnut's second code of laws such men were described as median thegns, and according to the *Leis Willhelmi* such thegns paid their heriot to their lord rather than directly to the king.[101]

Although in the majority of cases the lord appears to have had few, if any, rights over the land of his men, this was by no means true in every instance. In Ashwell (Herts.) Uhtred held half a hide of land '*sub Roberto filio Wimarch. Non potuit vendere praeter eius licentiam*'.[102] Godwine Cilt was the man of Eadgifu the Fair, and held land worth £18 in Cambridgeshire. He was not able to sell or give any of it away without the permission of his lord.[103] Eadnoth the Staller had 2 hides of land at Drayton (Berks.) which he held '*de Heraldo et non potuit ire quolibet*'.[104] The Domesday account of the manor of Tewkesbury ends: '*Hoc manerium tenuit Brictric filius Algar T.R.E. et has subscriptas terras aliorum teinorum ipso tempore in sua potestate habuit.*' There follow six entries involving 35 hides of land, held by between six and eleven men (the number is uncertain as some of the men are not named). Some of these are described as thegns, although others were merely '*villani*'. At the end of these entries we are told: '*Qui T.R.E. has terras tenebat et se et terras suas sub Brictrici potestate submiserunt*'.[105] In combination, these entries suggest that Beorhtric had power over both the men and their land, and that this was the result of a voluntary act on the part of the men themselves. It is quite possible that Beorhtric had applied pressure to some of these men in order to force their submission, but the implication is that the final decision lay with the dependents rather than with their superior. Unfortunately this example is unique, but it is possible that some such act of voluntary submission lies behind other instances where Domesday notes that a subordinate man had to seek his lord's permission before alienating his land.

The *Abingdon Chronicle* gives a specific example of a man who needed the permission of his lord before he could donate his land to the Church. A certain Thorkell is said to have done homage to the abbot for his land at Kingston, and he did this with the witness and consent of Earl Harold.[106] The terms used suggest Norman rather than Saxon practice, and it is probable that Thorkell had either

101 II Cnut 71; *Leis Willhelmi*, 20.2 in Liebermann, i. 356–9, 506–7.
102 *DB* i. 141b. 103 *DB* i. 193b, 195b. 104 *DB* i. 60.
105 *DB* i. 163b.
106 *Chron. Abingdon*, i. 484.

promised to give the land to Abingdon on his death, or that the land was involved in some arrangement whereby Thorkell leased land from the abbot. Certainly Thorkell was in possession of the land at the time of the Battle of Hastings, where he died, since the Norman sheriff seized Kingston as part of Thorkell's forfeited estate. Whatever the exact relationship between Thorkell and the abbot, there is no reason to introduce Harold into the story, unless he was Thorkell's lord, and Harold's consent was necessary to legitimize the gift.

For the most part men who could not sell their land freely were poor men. Uhtred, mentioned above, had just half a hide, and in Cambridgeshire seven sokemen who had land worth just £1 in total needed Eadgifu's permission before they might sell it. Godwine Cilt, with land worth £18, was an exception, and Eadnoth the Staller was an even greater one. Men being unable to sell their land without permission from their lord is reminiscent of leases of Church property, where Domesday often states that the land could not be separated from the Church.[107] It is possible that in some cases, then, where a layman could not sell land without a lay lord's permission, that land had been leased too. This would be an attractive explanation for the one entry where Eadnoth the Staller was said to hold land that he could not sell without the permission of Earl Harold.[108] If this one entry referred to a lease, it would help to explain why none of the remaining twelve entries refer to Eadnoth's relationship with Harold, and would also allow us to separate Eadnoth (whose estate was valued at £64, and whose son had a further £90's worth of land) from belonging to the same class as the impoverished Cambridgeshire sokemen just described.

However, there are definite differences between Church leases and many of the cases where land could not be sold without the permission of a lay lord. In the first place it should be repeated that a dependent man had but a single lay lord, although he might lease land from more than one ecclesiastical lord. Secondly, a man who leased land from the Church always appears to have had land of his own which was freely held. But those men who needed their lord's permission before selling their land generally needed that permission in every instance. In all the entries referring to Godwine Cilt, he is described

[107] e.g. the land which Guthmund leased from Ely: *DB* ii. 406, 408, 410b, and *Liber Eliensis*, book 2, cap. 97; or the manor leased by Godric from Abingdon: *DB* i. 60b, and *Chron. Abingdon*, i. 484, 491.

[108] *DB* i. 60.

as needing Eadgifu's consent to sell. Swein, who was described as the man of Asgeir in three Buckinghamshire entries, could not sell any of his land.[109] Where a man had the freedom to sell any of his land, he appears to have had that freedom in every case—this was certainly true of Sigar, the man of Asgeir the Staller,[110] and Goda, the 'man' of Earl Ælfgar.[111] Information about ability to sell is not always given, but in Cambridgeshire, where it does appear for most entries, there are no examples of a man who required his lord's consent before he sold some of his land being free to sell the remainder.

The freedom to dispose of land without reference to their lord clearly separated two different groups of dependent men. It is possible that when one man took another as his lord, he had the choice as to whether he also gave his land into the power of that lord. Presumably there was some extra benefit to the man who brought his land to a lord, but unfortunately there is no evidence on this point. It is also possible that, since it was the poorer men who lost the freedom to sell, they were forced to buy the protection of a lord with their land, whilst wealthier men were considered more of an asset, and would be welcomed into a lord's following. Equally, a lord would have found it easier to force a poor man into giving up rights over his land, if the relationship were not entirely voluntary. In Bedfordshire, Domesday preserves a post-Conquest example of a man changing his lord.[112] Augi had been a man of Askell of Ware, who was free to go with his land to another lord. Through a writ of King William, he was commended to Ralph Taillebois. On Ralph's death, he declared himself to be the man of William Warenne, and William held the land at the time of the Survey. The first transfer of commendation, by writ, may demonstrate one aspect of the transfer of power following the Conquest, although it is reminiscent of the writ of King Edward, which gave Ælfric Modercope permission to give his commendation to the Abbots of Ely and Bury St Edmunds.[113] However, the transfer of commendation on the death of Ralph Taillebois would seem to be a good example of the way in which a man might exercise the freedom of choosing a lord, and was probably quite common. In another case where we know that lordship changed, Viking, who had

[109] *DB* i. 149b.
[110] *DB* i. 197.
[111] *DB* i. 193, 193b, 197b.
[112] *DB* i. 211b.
[113] S 1081.

been the servant (*knihte*) of Thurstan, had been left $1\frac{1}{2}$ hides by his lord.[114] By 1066, Thurstan was dead, and Viking was the man of Earl Harold, and was unable to dipose of his lands freely.[115]

The usual basis for any dependent relationship is the protection of the inferior party in return for services of various types provided to the superior. Both elements—protection and service—were present in dependent relationships in England before 1066.

Although it is not mentioned in law codes of the late tenth and early eleventh centuries, earlier codes do state that if an offence were made against a man, it was to be considered also as an offence against the lord.[116] Both men would be owed compensation, and this would ensure the support of the lord in getting a settlement of the offence. There was also presumably the element of deterrence when a man had an important lord, because that lord would have more resources with which to seek redress. The greater the lord, the greater the deterrent effect, and this goes far to explain why only the most powerful landholders gathered a significant following. Domesday provides one example of a lord becoming involved in a dispute which concerned his man. Brungar was the man of Robert fitz Wymarc, and when stolen horses were found in Brungar's possession, Robert was present at his trial. Unfortunately it is not clear whether Robert was there to defend his man, or to divide the profits of justice with the bishop, who held *sac* and *soc*.[117] The laws also held that a lord was to some degree responsible for the actions of his men. The lord was obliged to ensure that any of his men who were to answer charges before a hundred or county court appeared on the day appointed.[118] If they did not appear, the lord paid a fine to the king. In this way the lord was involved not only in securing justice for his men, but also in controlling their actions, or at least ensuring that his men answered for their actions.

In return for the protection which a lord provided for his men, his followers must have provided services to their lord, but again, it is difficult to ascertain precise details of such services. In the tenth-century Hundred Ordinance, the only valid reason for missing a session of the hundred court was being prevented by the summons

114 S 1531.
115 *ICC* 109b.
116 Ine 21, in Liebermann, i. 98–9.
117 *DB* ii. 401b.
118 II Cnut 31, in Liebermann, i. 334–7.

of one's lord.[119] The reasons for such a summons are not enumerated in the Ordinance or elsewhere, but some are implied by other sources. A lord would presumably call upon two of his own men to support the defendant in a legal case. The passage in the *Gethynctho* cited above provides some examples of the type of service which a man of substance might do for his lord. A man could be expected to attend his lord when the lord went to the royal court. If he was of sufficient status—that is, if he held at least 5 hides of land upon which he performed the general obligations—the dependent might go to the king's court on his lord's behalf, and even initiate legal actions for his lord.

There is certain evidence to show that dependent men owed military service to their lord, if not the full extent of that service. In the first place, while the earls and king's thegns gave their heriot to the king himself, lesser thegns gave their heriot to their immediate lord. This is stated in the unofficial collection of customs known as the *Leis Willhelme*,[120] and is supported in the evidence of the later Anglo-Saxon wills.[121] The will of only one lesser thegn, Ketill Alder, has survived.[122] In this will a heriot comprising weapons to fully equip a single warrior (a sword, spear, shield, helmet, and byrnie, with a single harnessed horse) was to be given to Ketill's lord, Stigand. Since the heriot of the lesser thegn was sufficient to arm a single man, it might be suggested that the service expected of him was purely personal. Although this might have been true when the custom of leaving weapons to one's lord started, by the late eleventh century things may well have been different. The heriot of an earl could equip just eight men, but these lords could clearly field many times more armed men than the level of heriot implies. Earl Godwine gave a ship and 120 well-armed men to King Edward on his coronation.[123] Ketill Alder, with land valued at £45, could certainly have armed at least a small retinue.

The laws of Cnut describe the punishments due to a man who deserted his lord whilst on campaign. Such a man was to lose his life; any bookland he held was forfeit to the king; and any *lænland* to his

[119] Hundred Ordinance 2.1, in Liebermann, i. 192–3.

[120] *Leis Willhelmi*, 20.2, in Liebermann, i. 506–7.

[121] See N. Brooks, 'Arms, Status and Warfare in Late Saxon England', in D. Hill (ed.), *Ethelred the Unready* (British Archaeological Reports no. 59, 1978).

[122] S 1519.

[123] *Vita Edwardi*, 13–14.

lord.[124] Equally, a man who fell by his lord's side in battle was deemed to be quit of his heriot.[125] Such legislation seems to make it clear that men were expected to attend their lords on campaign, and to fight beside them in battle.

The customs of Worcester and Berkshire, as recorded in Domesday,[126] distinguish between two classes of men who were expected to attend the king when he went on campaign. The first group were men who had rights of jurisdiction and alienation over their land, and these men received a personal summons to join the *fyrd*. If they did not attend, they were liable to forfeit all their lands to the king. The features which marked the second group were that they had lords between themselves and the king, and it was the lord's responsibility to ensure that they, or a substitute, attended the muster. Failure to attend for this second group resulted in a fine of 40*s*. or 50*s*., which was paid to the lord if a substitute was arranged, otherwise it was paid to the king. R. Abels has stated that this second group comprised those men who 'held their tenures by loan from a lord other than the king . . . or under his [the lord's] seignury'.[127] However, we should not fall into the trap of imagining that this group included all those men who owed their commendation, and their heriot, to a lord other than the king. Earlier in this chapter it was shown that the majority of dependent men had the right to dispose of their land without their lord's permission, and had to discharge the king's obligations on that land. Such men would have belonged to the group which received a personal summons to attend the king's expeditions, and may well have been responsible for the attendance of other men.

The dependent men mentioned in the Worcester and Berkshire customs were far inferior to the commended men just described. If we accept that the Berkshire custom requiring one soldier to attend from each 5 hides of land was current across the country (allowing for relatively minor variations across the country due to regional differences in tenurial practice),[128] then a lord who held 50 or 100 hides in his own right would presumably have to provide ten or

[124] II Cnut 77.

[125] II Cnut 78.

[126] *DB* i. 56, 172.

[127] R. Abels: 'Bookland and Fyrd Service in Late Anglo-Saxon England', in Brown (ed.), *Anglo-Norman Studies* VII, 1984 (1985), 11.

[128] Ibid.; and N. Hooper, 'Anglo-Saxon Warfare on the Eve of the Conquest: A Brief Survey' in R. A. Brown (ed.), *Proceedings of the Battle Conference on Anglo-Norman Studies, 1978* (Woodbridge, 1979), 88.

twenty armed men for the fyrd. It is these soldiers who comprise the dependent men mentioned in Domesday as attending the muster under their lord. The lord was free to choose how to make up this group, and they are likely to have been lesser men, perhaps holding some land from their lord, but perhaps also members of the lord's household. The Abbot of Peterborough, for example, appears (from admittedly late evidence) to have placed the burden of fyrd service on a restricted number of vills in the abbey's estate.[129] Worcester leased land out to men who were to perform military service on behalf of the bishop.[130] The men of the Abbots of Bury St Edmunds and Abingdon who fought and died at Hastings held land which could not be alienated from those abbeys,[131] and was probably held on terms similar to the Worcester leases. Abels also speaks of two documents, one of which describes the dues from the Bishop of Winchester's manor of Taunton (including the obligation of certain tenants to perform military service), and the other the distribution of obligation for the ship fyrd within the manors of the Bishop of London.[132] In all the above cases, the men who were to do the service were tenants on land which could not be separated from their lords. In no case is there evidence of a man, commended to a lord (whether lay or ecclesiastical) who held his land freely and who did military service on behalf of his lord.

Lay lords probably maintained greater or lesser military households, similar to the housecarls of Tostig who were killed at the start of the revolt of Northumbria in 1065.[133] Domesday Book refers to the housecarls of a number of earls.[134]

Thus a lord could expect support in arms from two groups of dependents: those who held their own land, and whose ties to the lord were personal; and those who were more directly dependent upon their lord for either their land or a place in his household. This dichotomy helps to illuminate one of the events which took place during the struggle between Edward the Confessor and Godwine during 1051. The earl had gathered his men together at an early stage, but Edward is said to have weakened Godwine's army by

[129] See C. W. Hollister, *Anglo-Saxon Military Institutions* (Oxford, 1962), 83–4.

[130] S 1368, and comments in R. Abels, *Lordship and Military Obligation in Anglo-Saxon England* (London, 1988), 152–3.

[131] *Chron. Abingdon* ii. 3; *EHD* ii. 464.

[132] Abels, *Lordship and Military Obligation*, 157–9.

[133] *ASC* C, D *sub anno* 1065.

[134] Abels, *Lordship and Military Obligation*, 160 n. 98.

calling on the fyrd. By doing this, the king obliged many thegns who were commended to Godwine, but who held land in their own right, to join the royal army, or to forfeit their land. Since no overt split had taken place between the king and the earl, thegns not answering the royal summons would have had to commit themselves absolutely to their lord, and might have suffered even if the major figures had eventually made their peace. The desertion of these relatively important men from Godwine's force must have weakened him considerably, although he would still have had the troops called directly from his own land. In spite of the fact that a large number of men were dependent upon the great lords, it would appear that King Edward was still able to command their loyalty, in 1051 at least.

So far, discussion of the nature of dependent relationships in East Anglia has been avoided, because such relationships appear to have been rather different from those recorded elsewhere. In the first place, Norfolk and Suffolk are the only counties where the term '*commendatio*' is used frequently, and indeed it is found (usually in an abbreviated form) on almost every page. In other counties the term was used in only a few entries, if at all. The difference in terminology could be the result of regional variations, but there are other, more important factors which mark East-Anglian commendation as a quite distinct form of relationship from those already examined. In the first place, nearly every man with a few pounds of land in East Anglia had some other freemen commended to him. Great lords like Eadric of Laxfield, Wihtgar the son of Ælfric, and the Abbot of Bury St Edmunds had considerable numbers of men commended to them. Acolf, a thegn with land worth just £4 in two villages, had nineteen freemen commended to him.[135] Morewine, a freeman himself commended half to Ely and half to Eadric of Laxfield, held just 42 acres of land, while fourteen freemen commended to him held 40 acres.[136]

The other major difference between dependent relationships in East Anglia and elsewhere in England is illustrated by the example of Morewine: the commendation of one man could be divided between two lords. This is quite different to the situation in other parts of the country. Eadric Grim was said to have been half commended to Eadric of Laxfield, and half to Bury St Edmunds.[137] Another freeman was described as being half commended to Beorhtmær and half to

[135] *DB* ii. 354b, 436b.
[136] *DB* ii. 324b.
[137] *DB* ii. 293b.

Stanmar.[138] In a few instances commendation was split into unequal fractions. Ælfric was one-sixth commended to Eadric of Laxfield, and five-sixths to Aki.[139] Another man, Alwin, was one-sixth commended to an unnamed man who was himself commended to Eadric of Laxfield, and for the remaining five-sixths was commended to Saxo.[140] However, in spite of the division of lordship into sixths, there do not appear to have been any examples of a man being commended to more than two lords.

A writ survives in which Edward the Confessor permitted Ælfric Modercope to take as his lord both the Abbot of St Edmunds and the Abbot of Ely.[141] In view of the fact that outside East Anglia no man had two lords, it is no coincidence that Ælfric was a landholder in Norfolk. In spite of the fact that a single man might be commended to two lords, this does not necessarily mean that the relationship was based upon land tenure. The division of lordship is expressed in terms of exact fractions (most often two halves) and it is not possible that men would regularly hold exactly half their land from each lord.

At Loudham in Suffolk, Morewine had held 40 acres of land and fourteen men were commended to him. Morewine was half commended to Eadric of Laxfield and half to Ely. Robert Malet, as Eadric's successor, claimed all Morewine's land, but Ely claimed that they were owed 20 acres and seven freemen because of the half commendation which the abbey held.[142] It seems unlikely that Morewine had held an equal amount of land from each lord. A more probable explanation is that this settlement was a result of a post-Conquest practice whereby the land of a lord's men was often given to the lord's successor. When the lordship of a man was divided, then his land was also divided.

In spite of this there was an intimate connection between commendation and the land. Many freemen held land in the same village as the man to whom they were commended. In Chilton (near Sudbury, Suffolk) Godwine, Alfer's son, held 2 carucates, and three freemen who were commended to Godwine also held land there.[143] At Great Fakenham, in the same county, the thegn Æthelstan had 5

[138] *DB* ii. 424.
[139] *DB* ii. 309.
[140] *DB* ii. 376b.
[141] S 1081.
[142] *DB* ii. 324b, 388.
[143] *DB* ii. 304.

carucates, and six and a half sokemen were attached to the manor. As well as these men there were twenty other freemen who were commended to Æthelstan.[144] In Yoxford, Norman held 100 acres, and five freemen who were commended to him also held land there.[145]

Many of the so-called '*libere homines*' do not appear to have been free to choose their lord. At Occold, Guthmund leased £3's worth of land from Ely (see Fig. 4.1). In the same village were eight freemen who were (according to Domesday Book) commended to Guthmund, and who held land worth 10*s*. as part of the manor.[146] It is probable that these men had been commended to Ely until the arrangement of the lease, and that their commendation was transferred along with the land. More details are provided by a gift from Thurstan to Bury. Thurstan granted the abbey the manor of Culford, and included Ixworth Thorpe and Wordwell in the gift.[147] According to Domesday, the last two villages were entirely inhabited by freemen, so Thurstan's gift presumably included the land held by his commended men. The Domesday entry goes on to say that the inhabitants of the two villages were free to sell their land, but the commendation and services due from it (which were owed to Culford) were reserved to the abbey. The most probable interpretation of this is that whoever held the land at Ixworth Thorpe and Wordwell owed commendation and service to whoever held the manor of Culford.

The fact that some men were obliged to give their commendation to a particular lord depending on the land they held explains to some extent the differences between dependent relationships in East Anglia and those elsewhere. If a man could choose his lord, then he might expect better support and protection from a wealthy and important man than from a minor local landholder. But in East Anglia at least it appears that men were obliged to give their commendation to whichever manor the land they held pertained to, no matter to whom the manor pertained. And if a man held land in two or more places, it would be possible for him to owe commendation to two different lords.

However, other commended men did have more freedom in choosing their lord, as is shown by the example of Eadric of Laxfield's outlawry. When Eadric was outlawed his men were obliged to seek other lords, and we know that at least some did so.[148] On Eadric's

[144] *DB* ii. 420b. [145] *DB* ii. 333. [146] *DB* ii. 410b.
[147] S 1225; *DB* ii. 364, 366b, 367b. [148] *DB* ii. 310b.

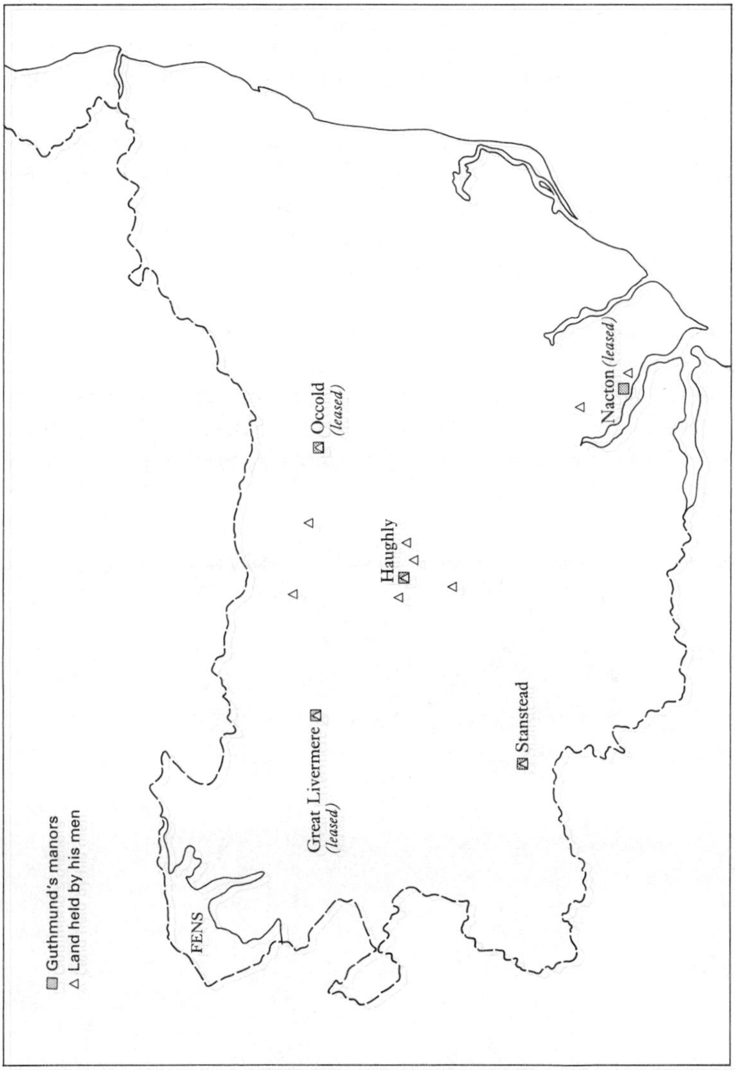

FIG. 4.1. Guthmund's land and men in Suffolk

return, Edward gave a writ allowing these men to return to Eadric's lordship if they chose to do so, and if their new lords agreed. In many cases the men must have returned, because by 1066 Eadric had very many men commended to him. Some will have returned because, like the freemen described below, they owed commendation to the holder of a particular manor, and when the manor was returned to Eadric, they would have come under his lordship automatically. But at least some men had a certain degree of choice as to whether they returned to Eadric's commendation. One of Eadric's men before the outlawry became the man of Norman, and remained Norman's man after Eadric's return,[149] and in other cases it was disputed whether or not a man had returned to his original lord.[150]

Where a man did have freedom to choose his lord, it is likely that the relationship between man and lord was not dissimilar to that elsewhere in England. It is the existence of a second group of men in the Domesday record, who were tied to a particular lord through the tenure of land, which makes East Anglia different. It is unfortunate that the Domesday text only rarely allows us to distinguish between the two types of tenure.

[149] *DB* ii. 342: Godric the Priest, who held 7 acres of land.
[150] *DB* ii. 310b, 313.

5

THE COUNTY OF CAMBRIDGE, *TRE*

It is now proposed to examine the relationship between the greater landholders and lesser men in some detail in a single county—Cambridgeshire. There are good reasons for choosing this particular county. First, the text of the Exchequer Domesday is supplemented as a source for the county by two satellite texts: the *Inquisitio Eliensis* (*IE*) and the *Inquisition comitatus Cantabrigiensis* (*ICC*). The first of these documents is connected with the Domesday survey of the lands of Ely Abbey, and so does not provide more than a few sidelights on the lay lords of Cambridgeshire. The second source, the *ICC*, covers all landholders (with the notable exception of the Crown) over an area of about two-thirds of the county. It lists its information by village and hundred rather than by tenant-in-chief, and although clearly linked to the Exchequer text, it nevertheless provides a useful amount of additional detail (see Ch. 4). In particular, the *ICC* often names lesser men and their lords, while the Exchequer Domesday merely lists a number of freemen or sokemen. For example, at Dullingham, the primary text merely mentions 'three sokemen' whilst the *ICC* gives their names and the names of their lords: Horulf, the man of Eadgifu the Fair, Ælfstan, the man of Ordgar, and Viking, the man of Earl Harold.[1] This, with the additional information about bynames, makes the identification of lesser landholders much easier than would otherwise be the case.

Furthermore, the Exchequer text itself is particularly informative concerning Cambridgeshire *TRE*. In almost all the entries the name of the landholder is given, and where apppropriate, the name of the tenant's lord. It is only in a relatively small number of entries that the *ICC* is needed to supply extra details on dependent relationships.

[1] *DB* i. 195b, *ICC* 18.

This allows some degree of confidence that the great majority of such relationships have been recorded in one or other of the texts.

A final reason for choosing Cambridge is its convenient size: whilst it is not too large (a recorded population of 4,800 in Domesday Book), it is geographically diverse. The two northernmost hundreds were almost entirely fenland, and the only inhabited land comprised the islands which rose out of the marsh. In the south and east of the county the edge of the brecklands rises to some 400 feet. There were also low hills on the western boundary of the county, and between these two areas of high ground lay the valleys of the Cam and the Bourne.[2]

In Cambridgeshire before the Conquest, Domesday records that there were seventy-four landholders with land valued at £1 or more. Of these, three were worth over £100, and thirteen were worth between £20 and £100. The value of the entire county was put at £2,100 on the day King Edward died. The greatest of the Cambridgeshire estates at this time was held by the abbey of Ely, and was worth some £300. Almost the whole of the two fenland hundreds was held by the abbey, with the exception of a few hides of land and some fishing rights held by the abbeys of Ramsey and St Mary of Chatteris. This block of land comprised about half Ely's estate, by value. In addition, Ely had various manors spread throughout the mainland of the shire, which together were valued at about £150. Altogether Ely had about forty manors, of which the largest was worth £30 on its own. Another nine were valued at between £10 and £20. There were a number of other ecclesiastical estates in the country, all of which were much smaller than that of Ely. Ramsey Abbey had eight manors, worth £84 in total; the Bishops of Winchester and Dorchester each had four manors worth a total of £31 and £27 respectively. Crowland's three manors were worth £15; the land of Chatteris, £10; and the single manor held by Thorney, £7. In all, ecclesiastical landholders held over 20 per cent of the county, by value.

By far the largest of the lay estates was held by Eadgifu the Fair, or as she was called elsewhere in Domesday Book, Eadgifu the Rich.[3] Her lands in Cambridgeshire were worth £216, about three-fifths of all her land in England. The remainder of her estate lay in adjacent

[2] H. C. Darby, *Domesday Geography of Eastern England*, 3rd edn. (Cambridge, 1971), 264–7.

[3] *DB* ii. 285.

counties. Within the county she had twenty-two manors, which were spread evenly across the mainland of the county: no lay lords held land in the two hundreds of Ely, unless they were the men of the abbot. Half the value of her estate was to be found in just four manors: Exning (valued at £56 alone), Bassingbourne, Swavesey, and Linton. Last of the three estates worth over £100 was that of the Crown. Edward had nine manors in the county, with an overall value of £107. However six of the manors rendered additional dues in corn, malt, and honey, which had been commuted by 1086 to a monetary payment of £93 10*s*. in all. Thus the value of the royal estate *TRE* (if income in kind is added to the cash value of other manors) probably approximated to that of Eadgifu.

Amongst those who held lesser amounts of land in Cambridgeshire were ten whose lands throughout the kingdom were valued at £40 or more. Domesday states that three earls held land in the county: Ælfgar, Harold, and Gyrth, whose manors were valued in total at £58, £37, and £24 respectively. Unfortunately it is not clear in which earldom the county lay between 1042 and 1066. A large number of men in the county were commended to Earl Ælfgar, and more will be said of this later. Ælfgar's influence was extensive throughout the county, and it is possible that this influence was acquired during a period in which the shire was in his earldom, but whether it was part of the Mercian or the East-Anglian earldom cannot be determined. A fourth earl, Waltheof, held no land in the county, although a number of other minor landholders were commended to him. Of the remaining lay estates in Cambridgeshire, the largest, valued at £67, was held by Wulfwine, the predecessor of Aubrey de Vere. Wulfwine's eight manors lay in the south-east of the county, and he had other land, worth slightly more, nearby in Essex. Of his land in Cambridgeshire, his largest manor, Silverley, was worth £20, and the remainder between £2 and £10. Toki, the predecessor of William Warenne, had £38 of land in the county, and both Wulfmær of Eaton and Ælfric Camp had manors worth £20 in total. All three held less than half their total estate in Cambridgeshire: Toki's land was worth £102 altogether, Wulfmær's £100, and Ælfric Camp's £55. Their other manors all lay in nearby areas, and their land in and around Cambridge must have made them men of consequence in the county.

Of the greater landholders who held part of their estate in Cambridgeshire, there were three who only had a few pounds' worth in the county. Ulf Fenisc had a total estate worth £300, mostly in counties surrounding the Fens. In Cambridge Ulf had land in just three villages, worth £2 10*s*. Ingware, a thegn with a total of £70's worth of land, had just £2 of it in the county. Finally, Ulf, King Edward's housecarl, had a single manor in Duxford, valued at £8, and land in the adjoining counties worth £57.

Only two of the estates worth over £20 in Cambridgeshire were held by people whose total estate was worth under £40. The first of these landholders was Ælfsi Squitrebil, whose single manor in Cambridgeshire was worth £24. Five miles away in Essex, he held the manor of Newnham, valued at £11, and may also have held land worth 30*s*. at Elvedon, in north-west Suffolk. Domesday described Ælfsi as one of King Edward's thegns. All his land had passed to Eustace of Boulogne by the time of the Survey.[4] The second of these estates was held by a woman called Goda; it lay in six villages, and was worth a total of £26 13*s*. 4*d*. Two of her manors, Shingay (valued at £14) and Meldreth (worth £8) made up the largest part of her estate. In every entry Goda is said to have held her land from or under Earl Ælfgar, or in one entry, to have been commended (*commendata*) to him.[5] In every entry except those relating to Shingay and its appurtenances it was declared that Goda could dispose of her land without Ælfgar's permission. In the case of Shingay, no details are given, but since all a single person's land was generally treated in the same way (see Ch. 4) it is likely that Goda was equally free to dispose of Shingay as well. Goda probably did not hold any land outside Cambridgeshire, although it is just possible that she could be identified with Goda, the woman of Queen Eadgyth, who held half a hide of land in Broadfield, Hertfordshire. This land was held in 1086 by Earl Roger, who had succeeded to all Goda's land in Cambridgeshire.[6]

Of those whose land in Cambridgeshire was worth less than £20, a few had no other lord than the king. Blacuin the Sheriff had land in six villages worth a total of £15;[7] Judichael, the king's huntsman, held three small portions of land worth £6 15*s*. altogether;[8] and Herulf, a thegn of King Edward, had land valued at £11 10*s*. in Duxford and

[4] *DB* i. 196; *DB* ii. 34, 303.
[5] *DB* i. 193, 193b.
[6] *DB* i. 137b.
[7] *DB* i. 190, 201, 201b.
[8] *DB* i. 193.

Trumpington.[9] None of these men appear to have held land outside the county.

But the majority of landholders with less than £20 of land were said to have been dependents on one or another of the greater lords. Godwine Cilt, who had the manor of Fulbourn (worth £15) as well as other land valued at £4, was the man of Eadgifu the Fair, and was not free to dispose of his land without her permission.[10] Ordmær, another of Eadgifu's men, held land worth a total of £15, but in contrast to Godwine, Ordmær was free to grant this land where he would, without reference to his lord.[11] Ordnoth was one of Robert fitz Wymarc's men, who held land worth £5 in Papworth, which he could dispose of freely.[12] As a last example of a man commended to another lord, Sigar, the steward of Asgeir the Staller, had land in six villages in the county, worth a total of £18 13*s*. In each entry Sigar is described as either holding his land under Asgeir, or as being Asgeir's man.[13]

As well as the dependent men who held land worth more than £1, Domesday also records a large number of sokemen in this county, who generally held land valued at £1 or less. Some, like Eadwine, a sokeman of Eadgifu the Fair, were free to give or sell their land; but the three sokemen of Earl Gyrth at Shelford did not have the same privilege.[14] In many cases Domesday records that sokemen had to provide a certain amount of cartage or escort duty to the sheriff. Eadwine paid 8*d*. or provided one cartage if the king came into the county. At Swaffham three sokemen, who held their land under Eadgifu and could not sell without her permission, had to provide three escorts to the sheriff. Godwine Cilt had two sokemen at Weston Colville, of whom one provided cartage and the other performed escort duty.[15] However these duties were not mentioned for every sokeman, so it is possible that these do not constitute the distinguishing mark of the sokeman. In other instances, men who were not described as sokemen were said to have owed such duties. Toki, the predecessor of William Warenne, was said to have owed cartage

[9] *DB* i. 196.
[10] *DB* i. 193b, 195b.
[11] *DB* i. 195b.
[12] *DB* i. 199b.
[13] *DB* i. 197.
[14] *DB* i. 195b, 198.
[15] *DB* i. 196b.

for his land at West Wratting, although he was far wealthier than any sokeman.[16] It is possible, however, that in this case the service was performed by a sokeman who was omitted from the Survey and who was dependent upon Toki.

Some 600 sokemen are recorded in Cambridgeshire. It would appear that the majority were free to sell their land without their lord's permission, but in many cases information about their status is not given. It may be that the exceptions where sokemen were free to sell were recorded whilst the normal situation, where a sokeman could not dispose of his land, went unremarked. Around 250 sokemen were men of King Edward. Of the others, Ely had 150 sokemen of whom the majority were not free to sell; Eadgifu the Fair had 100 sokemen, of whom a third were not free to sell their land; Earl Ælfgar had sixty sokemen. Only three other laymen—Ulf Fenisc, Earl Waltheof, and Earl Harold—had more than ten sokemen in the county. Eadgifu was the lord of twenty other men and women other than the sokemen. These ranged from Godwine Cilt, whose land was worth £19 and who could not sell without permission, through men like Colswein, with £6 in four villages, which could be sold without consent, to Grim, with land worth 10*s*. in Stetchworth, who was not free to sell. In all, the land held by Eadgifu's various dependants was valued at about £120. Of this land £34 was held by several men and sokemen who were not free to sell. If all the land of Eadgifu's dependants is added to her own land, the total is about one-sixth of the county.

Of the lay lords of Cambridgeshire, Earl Ælfgar had attracted the next largest group of followers. Ælfgar was the lord of ten landholders who between them held land worth about £40, as well as his sixty sokemen with land worth about £50. The most important of Ælfgar's dependants was Goda, whose land, valued at £26, could be sold without the permission of her lord. Only £4's worth of the land of Ælfgar's dependants could not be freely sold. Earl Harold had barely a dozen sokemen and four other dependants in the county. Between them their land was worth less than £25. Eight of the sokemen, with land worth less than 30*s*. in all, could not depart without Harold's permission, but the remaining dependants were free to dispose of their land. Wulfwine, who held the largest lay estate in the county after Eadgifu and Ælfgar had just two sokemen, who were

[16] Ibid.

not free to sell their land, valued at only 6*s*. 8*d*. Toki, the predecessor of William Warenne, who held as much land as Harold did in the county, had no recorded dependents at all. In contrast, Ulf Fenisc, whose land in Cambridge was reckoned at less than 5 hides, had in addition sixteen sokemen with land worth £3.

Clearly, the number of dependent men was not directly related to the amount of land which a man held in the county. This is emphasized by the fact that three men who held no land at all in Cambridgeshire nevertheless had a significant number of dependent men in the county. Earl Waltheof was the lord of fifteen sokemen and ten other commended men, who held between them land worth £50. Of this, all but £5 could be sold without his consent. The nine men and six sokemen of Asgeir the Staller again held land worth about £50 in total, of which Sigar, Asgeir's steward, held £19's worth. Finally, Robert fitz Wymarc had seven sokemen and seven others with land worth £17 in the county. None of the men of Asgeir or Robert needed their lord's permission to sell.

It would appear that lords of local importance such as Wulfwine and Toki were unable to attract dependent landholders to any significant extent. Rather, it was those lords of national importance, who also held land in or close to Cambridgeshire, who were able to accumulate large numbers of dependent men. Eadgifu was the holder of one of the largest estates in England, as well as having the largest lay estate in the county. Earl Ælfgar may have acquired his dependants whilst he was earl of the county, and it is posssible that Waltheof held the county as part of an earldom at the very end of Edward's reign. Asgeir the Staller had no land in the county, but the heart of his large estate lay close by, in Essex and Hertfordshire. Robert fitz Wymarc, who was close to the king (see Ch. 6), may have been sheriff in Essex, as his son was in William's reign, and he held land in Bedfordshire. In spite of Earl Harold's influence throughout the south of England, he does not appear to have had sufficient power in the east Midlands to become a significant lord in Cambridgeshire.

In comparing landholding patterns before the Conquest with the situation in 1086, it is possible to demonstrate a certain amount of continuity, in terms of the continued existence of quite a number of pre-Conquest estates with little change other than the actual lord. When the minor landholders are considered, there is even some continuity in actual personnel. But there are also certain basic differences between the two periods, and this balance between continuity and change will now be examined.

One important difference between 1066 and 1086 was that in the intervening period the value of the county as a whole had declined by about 13 per cent. There was also a systematic reduction of the hidation of a number of Cambridgeshire hundreds, which amounted to an overall reduction of 8 per cent in the number of hides in the county.[17] It is possible that the reduction in hidage and value followed damage caused during the Conquest and subsequent rebellions—particularly the actions of Hereward the Wake which centred around the Fens. But there are uncertainties about this hypothesis, as it is normal to find manors described as 'waste' in areas which were damaged by war. In Sussex, along the path taken by William's army, there is a noticeable drop in values, and a number of manors were declared to be waste. In Yorkshire, following the harrying of the north which followed the rebellion of 1070, a very high proportion of settlements were waste in 1086. But in Cambridgeshire no single manor was described as being waste. The causes of the decline in values must therefore remain somewhat obscure.

Domesday records that William had forty-three tenants-in-chief in Cambridgeshire in 1086, as well as land in demesne worth £270. Of the lay tenants-in-chief the greatest was Count Alan of Brittany, whose land was valued at just over £300. The only other lay estate worth over £100 was that of Picot, Sheriff of Cambridge, who had land worth £137. Eleven more tenants-in-chief had land valued between £20 and £75, leaving eighteen more lay tenants with less than £20's worth of land.

Often an individual's estate *TRE* passed substantially unaltered into the hands of a single Norman successor. All of Wulfwine's manors passed to Aubrey de Vere. In three entries Aubrey was stated to hold land which had not been held by either Wulfwine or his men. In two of these entries, Aubrey was said to have held the land 'in the King's despite',[18] because Aubrey's predecessor had not held the land. The third entry concerned land which had been held by a priest, the man of Eadgifu the Fair, and Count Alan declared that he should have the land, not Aubrey.[19] Apart from Exning (admittedly the largest of

[17] *VCH Cambridgeshire*, i. 342.
[18] *DB* i. 199b.
[19] *DB* i. 199b.

Eadgifu's manors) Count Alan succeeded to all the manors of Eadgifu herself, as well as the land held by the greater part of her dependants. All King Edward's demesne manors were held by King William in 1086; and as a last example, all Toki's manors in the county passed to William Warenne, who held just one other manor in the county.

A final group of estates which remained largely unaltered were those held by the Church. Whilst Ely claimed to have been deprived of quite large amounts of land since the Conquest, the larger part of its estate remained intact. Some demesne land which had been leased (such as Weston Colville and Trumpington, which had been leased to Toki[20]) was lost, but the rest of the land which had been lost to the abbey by 1086 had been held by men or sokemen of Ely. The other major ecclesiastical estates—those belonging to the abbeys of Ramsey and Crowland, and the bishoprics of Winchester and Dorchester—were also in the main unaltered, although a number of Ramsey's sokemen were in the hands of other lords by 1086.

Not all the Saxon estates remained intact. The land of Ælfric Camp was divided between Robert Gernons and Eudo Dapifer in 1086, and these two tenants-in-chief, along with other men, succeeded to Ælfric's land in other counties. Of Earl Harold's four manors in Cambridge, one was held in the royal demesne in 1086, another was held by Walter Giffard, while the remaining two were in the hands of the Countess Judith. Earl Ælfgar's manors were divided between the King, William of Warenne, the Canons of Bayeux, and the Abbey of St Wandrille. However, it may be that the lands of the earls were subject to special treatment; and it is certainly true that in the large majority of cases in Cambridgeshire the lands of one pre-Conquest tenant passed largely intact to a single successor. In this, Ælfric Camp is one of relatively few exceptions.

The land held by men of a particular lord in 1066 was not always held by the successor to that lord in 1086. It is true that Count Alan held the land of most of Eadgifu's men, but this is something of an exception. Throughout most of England Geoffrey de Mandeville succeeded to the demesne manors of Asgeir the Staller. Asgeir, as we have seen, had no land in Cambridgeshire, although a number of his men did. Geoffrey succeeded to the land of three of these men, but five other tenants-in-chief also held the land of one or another of Asgeir's men. The land of men who had been commended to Robert

20 *DB* i. 196b.

fitz Wymarc was divided amongst Earl Roger, Eudo Dapifer, Eustace of Huntingdon, Picot of Cambridge, and Hardwin of Scales. Aubrey de Vere succeeded to all Wulfwine's manors, but half a virgate of land held in 1066 by Wulfwine's man Leodmær was, in 1086, being held by Hardwin of Scales.

Even although groups of dependants might be split up, it was still normal for all the land of a single dependent man to be held by a single tenant-in-chief after the Conquest. Sigar, the man of Asgeir, had held six manors *TRE*, all of which were being held by Geoffrey de Mandeville in 1086. Countess Judith succeeded to both the manors of Godwine Scild, who had been the man of Earl Waltheof. Earl Roger succeeded to all of Goda's manors, whilst Hardwin of Scales held both plots of land which had been held by Estred in Edward's reign. Both Estred and Goda had been commended to Earl Ælfgar.

Although most of the Saxon estates remained intact, this does not mean that landholding patterns at the highest level remained unaltered during the twenty years which followed the Conquest, as a number of tenants-in-chief acquired the land of a number of different *antecessores*. Count Eustace held land which had belonged to three of King Edward's thegns, namely Aelfsi, Herulf, and Ingware, as well as land which had belonged to Archbishop Stigand and three sokemen, of whom two had been the men of King Edward, and one of Asgeir the Staller. Both Hardwin of Scales and Picot of Cambridge held estates which were largely made up of land which had been held by the sokemen of many different pre-Conquest lords. As a final example, Eudo Dapifer's land in Cambridge had been held before the Conquest by Ælfric Camp, Wulfmær of Eaton, Earl Gyrth, and the men of Waltheof and Robert fitz Wymarc. The concentration of the land of a number of Saxons into the hands of a single tenant-in-chief is shown by the fact that whereas in 1066 there were seventy-four estates with land valued at £1 or more, at the time of the Domesday Survey there were just forty-four tenants-in-chief in the county. This represents a major break in continuity, and this will be examined further in the final chapter.

The most obvious difference between the landholders *TRE* and those of 1086 is that none of the lay tenants-in-chief at the time of the Survey were English. None of the major Saxon landholders had survived the intervening twenty years with any of their Cambridgeshire manors intact, nor do they appear to have been able to pass on any of their land to English successors. However, a number of minor landholders did survive with some or all of their land, and a number of these were also named as jurors in the *ICC* and *IE*. In Armingford Hundred Colswein and his son Ælfmar were jurors. Colswein continued to hold all the land which had been his before 1066 (worth a total of £3 15*s*.). Before the Conquest he had been one of Eadgifu's men, and in 1086 he was a vassal of Eadgifu's successor, Count Alan. His son Ælfmar may well be identified with Ælfmar of Bourne, who continued to hold land worth £11 from Count Alan in 1086. He had lost one piece of land worth 30*s*., but had gained another (worth slightly less) which had been held by Godgifu, who had been commended to Eadgifu, in 1066.[21]

Ordmær of Badlingham continued to hold the smaller of his two manors in 1086 as the man of Count Alan, although the greater of the two manors had been given to one of Count Alan's foreign vassals.[22] Sigar, the steward of Asgeir the Staller, also survived with a portion of his land, as the vassal of Geoffrey de Mandeville, and like Ordmær was one of the jurors named in the *Inquisitio Eliensis*.[23] Ordnoth, one-time man of Robert fitz Wymarc, continued to hold half his manor of Papworth from Eustace of Huntingdon in 1086, although the other half was held by another of Eustace's men, Walter.[24] Two other jurors, Huscarl of Swaffham and Thorbern of Orwell, also held land before the Conquest.[25] But although these men were apparently active at the time of the Survey, they too must have been in very straitened circumstances, as Domesday does not list them as holding any land at all in 1086, either as tenants or as subtenants.

Many of the more minor landholders and sokemen must have survived the change of lordship, and in a few instances Domesday states this explicitly. At Steeple Morden the seven sokemen who held slightly less than a hide of land before the Conquest were still there at the time of the Survey.[26] But such men were little more than *villani* themselves, and the only examples of landholders of any importance who did survive have been listed above. The level of

[21] *ICC* 51, 98; *DB* i. 194–5b.
[22] *ICC* 1, 97; *DB* i. 195b.
[23] *ICC* 43, 98; *DB* i. 197.
[24] *DB* i. 199b.
[25] *ICC* 12, 68, 98, 99; *DB* i. 194b, 195b.
[26] *DB* i. 195b; *ICC* 18.

continuity of personnel of rank in Cambridgeshire was low indeed, amounting to half a dozen of more than sixty lay landholders who held land worth more than £1 on the day King Edward was alive and dead. When these few men are considered against the number of foreign subtenants who held land from tenants-in-chief in 1086, it is hard to see them as more than archaic survivals, soon to disappear entirely under a flood of men of foreign descent.

Mention of the subtenants in 1086 brings up another difference between Saxon and Norman patterns of lordship in Cambridgeshire. Almost all the major Norman tenants-in-chief had given a substantial proportion of their land (anything between a fifth and a third of their total holding) to be held by subtenants. In spite of the use of phrases to describe pre-Conquest tenure such as '*Godwin tenuit de Eddevae*', the commended men of 1066 cannot be equated with the subtenants of 1086, since in the majority of cases Saxon dependent men appear to have been free to dispose of their land as they wished. In addition they had but a single lord, whereas in 1086 a man might hold land from a number of different tenants-in-chief—and might, indeed, be a tenant-in-chief himself. Picot the Sheriff had an extensive personal fief, but in addition held land from Count Alan, Robert Gernon, Eudo Dapifer, Guy de Raimbeaucourt, Peter de Valonges, William fitz Ansculf, and the Countess Judith. There is another important difference between the dependent men of 1066 and those of post-Conquest England. All the more important tenants-in-chief of 1086 had given land to subtenants, so all had a body of men dependent upon them. But as we have seen above, by no means all of even the more important lords of 1066 had any significant number of commended men; only those lords with more than simply local influence were able to attract and hold dependent men. Moreover, it was possible for some Saxon lords with no demesne land in the county to have dependent men in Cambridgeshire; whereas all the Norman estates worth more than £20 included at least some demesne land. Only a few lords, each with just one or two small manors, had all their land held by subtenants, but this was a clear attempt at rationalizing extended estates.

The effect of this was that power appears to have been concentrated in fewer hands during Edward's reign than in William's. Under William there were fourteen lay estates worth more than £20, whilst under Edward there were just ten. Of these ten only half were of sufficient status to be able to attract a large number of commended men. In the final chapter, the question of what changes were brought about in the whole of the kingdom will be considered in more detail; but the next chapter will examine such evidence as there is concerning the careers and activities of the major landholders of England before the Conquest.

6

THE LANDHOLDERS AND THE KINGDOM IN THE TIME OF KING EDWARD

THE men identified in earlier chapters as holding the larger lay estates in England on the eve of the Conquest were presumably involved to some extent in the political life of the kingdom. For information on that life we have to look to sources other than Domesday Book. Quite a lot is known concerning the greatest lay landholders—the earls and their immediate families. The narrative sources provide many references to different members of the families of Godwine, Leofric, and Siweard, and they also appear prominently among the witnesses to both royal and private charters. The activities of this group during Edward's reign has been thoroughly covered in the literature and will not be considered here.[1] Instead, this chapter will be concerned with the remaining major lay landholders, as identified in Chapter 3 (see Fig. 3.1).

The narrative sources provide almost no information about the activities of these men before the Conquest. The various texts of the *Anglo-Saxon Chronicle* provide the most important sources for the political history of Edward's reign, and while they mention the activities of the King and earls at length, other laymen are almost entirely ignored. Often there is an exception to a rule: in this case it is the career of Osgod Clappa, a royal staller who was outlawed, and who later attacked the east coast of England with a number of ships which he recruited in Flanders. The threat he posed must have remained significant, since both the C and D versions of the *ASC* recorded his death in 1054.[2] Osgod, understandably enough, does not appear as a landholder in the Domesday Book. Apart from these references, there is almost no other mention made in the *ASC* of

[1] See App. III: Secondary literature concerning Edward's earls.
[2] *ASC* D, E, *sub anno* 1047, 1049, 1054.

laymen other than the earls. Ælfnoth the Sheriff was noted as one of the casualties when the new Bishop of Hereford led his men against the Welsh,[3] and Osbern Pentecost and 'Robert' (perhaps Robert fitz Wymarc) were noted as holding castles in England in 1052.[4] This exhausts the *Chronicle*'s references to laymen other than the earls between 1042 and 1066.

Another important source for the period is 'Florence of Worcester', who often includes information in addition to that provided by the *ASC*. Florence mentions three Frenchmen who were allowed to remain in England following the return of Earl Godwine and his sons in 1052,[5] and a number of Northumbrian nobles who were involved in the rebellion of 1065—Gammall Bearn, Gloniarn son of Heardulf, and Dunstan son of Æthelnoth.[6] None of these men can be identified with men who held more than £40 of land *TRE*, but they each held around £10 of land in Yorkshire.[7] Their land may have been worth rather more than that in 1066, as many of the Yorkshire entries do not give a value *TRE* because the land was laid waste as a result of the harrying of the North in 1070; and in any case these men probably held land further to the north, in areas not included in the Domesday Survey.

Later sources provide a few glimpses of pre-Conquest events, although these sources are not necessarily reliable. In the *Roman de Rou* of Wace there is a story about Beorhtric, Ælfgar's son, the richest of the non-earlish landholders.[8] Beorhtric was said to have been to Flanders on an embassy, where he refused the hand of Matilda, the count's daughter. Matilda later married William of Normandy, and when William conquered England, Matilda persuaded him to arrest Beorhtric in revenge for the slight which Beorhtric had done her. William then divided Beorhtric's land between his wife and Robert fitz Haimon.

There are some incidental facts in the story which seem to support its validity. Beorhtric was said to have been arrested '*a Hanleye, a sun maner*', and Beorhtric did indeed hold land at Hanley Castle, Worcestershire. Matilda did succeed to much of Beorhtric's land.

[3] *ASC* D, E, *sub anno* 1056.
[4] *ASC* E *sub anno* 1052.
[5] *Florence, sub anno* 1052.
[6] *Florence, sub anno* 1065.
[7] Gammall: *DB* i. 301b, 321b–322, 326b–327; Gloniarn: *DB* i. 301, 311, 315b, 320; Dunstan: *DB* i. 315, 317b–318.
[8] *Roman de Rou*, 73.

However, not all of Wace's details were correct, as Robert fitz Haimon only received his portion of the land from William Rufus after Matilda's death. This suggests that Wace had some information concerning the extent of Beorhtric's estate, and its descent to various Norman lords. Armed with this information, Wace could very easily have invented the site of Beorhtric's arrest, so even this piece of information cannot be used to verify the story. In these circumstances, it is not possible to place great weight on the story, and it may be that it was fabricated to explain why Matilda received those particular lands. On the other hand, Beorhtric was an important man who witnessed Edward's charters from early in the reign[9]—certainly before 1049 when William sought Matilda's hand. It is quite conceivable that Beorhtric could have acted as an ambasssador for Edward; and given the fact that Edward had been to Flanders during his exile, and that raiders often attacked England from bases in Flanders, it is entirely likely that Edward did send an embassy there early in his reign. All we can say with respect to Wace's story is that it is entirely possible.

A second anecdote is recorded in the *Carmen de Haestingae Proelio*. A certain Ansgardus, who had been wounded in the service of his country (perhaps at Hastings, but equally it could have been at one of the earlier engagements fought in England in 1066) was said to have taken charge of the defence of London after the death of Harold.[10] William offered Ansgardus control of the country if he acknowledged William as king and surrendered the city to him. It is most likely that Ansgardus should be identified with Asgeir the Staller. Such an offer of power would only be reasonable if the man in questioin was already in a position of considerable influence. With the destruction of Harold and his brothers, Asgeir was by far the most important layman in the south-east. Asgeir is known to have died in captivity, which proves that he survived the fighting of 1066, at least for a time.[11] Although the precise details of William's negotiations with Asgeir seem somewhat far-fetched, it is likely that Asgeir was involved in the defence of London, possibly by right of his office. Asgeir was the addressee of a writ concerning the city, and although the writ was a forgery, it suggests that there was a tradition that Asgeir had some role in the administration of the city.[12] This sug-

[9] See below, p. 133. [10] *Carmen*, lines 681 ff.
[11] *Liber Eliensis*, book 2, cap. 96. [12] S 1119.

gestion is reinforced by the fact that Asgeir's successor, Geoffrey de Mandeville, was acting as portreeve of London in 1067,[13] suggesting that he had succeeded not only to Asgeir's lands, but to his offices as well. As in the case of Wace, the full details of the story might not be accepted, but there may well be a basis in fact.

It might be thought that the lack of references to the political activities of even the greatest of the non-earlish landholders implies that they were either inactive or ineffectual throughout the reign. On the other hand, many thegns attended the king at his court, some appearing on a regular basis (see below). Those who attended regularly would presumably have been in a position to make their views known to the king. It also seems improbable that these men would have remained inactive during the upheavals of 1051 and 1052, whilst others must have been involved in the uprising of 1065—if only when the earls consulted their dependent men, as they presumably did, as the king consulted his earls. But with the exception of the leaders of the Northumbrian revolt named by Florence, nothing is known of how these nobles acted during Edward's reign.

Domesday Book is the only source which records the outlawry of Eadric of Laxfield. Eadric was one of the greatest landholders of England after the earls, and in East Anglia no lay lord had an estate to rival his. In spite of this the only thing that is known is that Eadric was exiled in Edward's reign, and later allowed to return.[14] The event is mentioned in Domesday because of the complications which arose from these upheavals, and which were still taking effect after Eadric's land had been distributed amongst the Normans. When Eadric was outlawed, his men had to seek other lords. At least one of them becam the man of Earl Harold, so this suggests that Eadric was not outlawed at the same time as Godwine's family was sent into exile.[15] One possibility is that Eadric was involved with Osgod Clappa, who was outlawed early in the reign. Osgod was an East-Anglian landholder, and a man of some importance, although the extent of his lands is not known. It may be that Eadric and Osgod were related, and that some of the land held by Eadric in 1066 had been held by Osgod earlier in the reign. Whilst there is no direct

[13] D. A. E. Pelteret, *Catalogue of English Post-Conquest Vernacular Documents* (Woodbridge, 1990), no. 5.
[14] *DB* ii. 313, 342b.
[15] *DB* ii. 313.

proof of this, there is some circumstantial evidence to support it. First, Harold was earl of East Anglia when Osgod was outlawed, and at least one of Eadric's men took Harold as his lord after Eadric was outlawed.[16] Furthermore, if Eadric had been outlawed alone, this would have been a major event, and we would expect some notice to have been taken of it in other sources. But if Eadric's outlawry had been connected with that of Osgod, it might have been omitted as an unnecessary detail by the chroniclers who recorded Osgod's rebellion. Using the same argument, it is possible to suggest that Eadric might have been involved in one of the two occasions on which Earl Ælfgar was driven out of the kingdom, especially since the first took place when Ælfgar was Earl of East Anglia. There is no evidence to prove conclusively which, if any, of these occasions saw Eadric in exile.

Ironically, more information survives concerning the careers of the major Saxon lords after the death of King Edward than for the many years of Edward's reign. Quite a number of the major landholders before 1066 are mentioned in the chronicles of William's reign, even in the *Anglo-Saxon Chronicle.*

Robert fitz Wymarc, a relative of King Edward, was present (with Harold, Eadgyth, and Archbishop Stigand) at the old king's deathbed.[17] When William landed, Robert went to attempt to dissuade the duke from joining battle with King Harold.[18] It is likely that Robert stayed with Duke William, in spite of the fact that his advice was ignored, and in 1086 Robert's son Swein held much of the land which his father had held in Edward's reign. Robert was the only man who is known to have gone over to William before Harold's death. Godric the Sheriff was killed at Hastings whilst fighting for Harold,[19] and Asgeir the Staller may have been wounded there.[20] As suggested above, Asgeir may have died of his wounds shortly after the battle.[21]

Quite a number of important lords made an early submission to William following the Battle of Hastings. Siweard Grossus and Eadric the Wild, both Shropshire landholders, submitted to the Conqueror

16 Ibid.
17 *Vita Edwardi*, 76.
18 *William of Poitiers*, book 2, p. 10.
19 *Chron. Abingdon*, ii. 484.
20 See above, pp. 114–15.
21 *Liber Eliensis*, book 2, cap. 96.

at the same time as Earls Eadwine and Morkær.[22] This appears to have been an example of the important men of a region acting together in a crisis.[23] When William left England soon after his coronation, he took with him a number of important hostages. Along with Edgar the Ætheling, the surviving earls, and Archbishop Stigand, William took at least one other member of the Saxon nobility—Æthelnoth Cilt, a major landholder in Kent and elsewhere in England.[24] Other men who submitted were not taken hostage, but allowed to keep posts of responsibility which they had held before the Conquest. Mærlswein was addressed as Sheriff of Lincolnshire in a writ dated 1067.[25] In Somerset, Eadnoth the Staller, who had been Harold's man in 1066, died defending the coast against the attacks of Harold's sons and their Irish allies.[26] Hearding, the son of Eadnoth, continued to hold land worth £24 in 1086, and appears to have been closely associated with another man who survived the Conquest, Wulfweard White. Together they witnessed a number of documents after the Conquest, including two which were issued from Queen Eadgyth's court,[27] and another recording the dues owed to the Bishop of Winchester from his manor of Taunton.[28] Hearding is also recorded as selling a slave named Leoffleda to a certain Wulfweard for 5*s*., and the purchaser may well have been identical with Wulfweard White.[29] It is possible that William took hostages from among the families of these men, and Toki, the son of Wigot of Wallingford, was killed in the battle of Gerberoi, fighting at William's side.

Not all who first submitted to William remained loyal to him. One of the first to revolt was Eadric the Wild. Eadric followed the example of Earl Ælfgar in a previous reign, and allied with the Welsh in order to raid the English border. Like Ælfgar, Eadric was eventually reconciled with his king, and Eadric accompanied William on his expedition to Scotland in 1072. Eadric's byname, '*Silvaticus*', may well have been acquired as a result of his participation in the early

[22] Orderic Vitalis, ii. 194.

[23] However, since they are named by Orderic Vitalis, a native of Shropshire, men from many other areas may have been there as well, and Eadric and Siweard named because they were known to Orderic.

[24] *Florence, sub anno* 1067.

[25] *Regesta*, i. no. 8.

[26] *ASC* D *sub anno* 1067.

[27] *Regesta* i. no. 23, and *VCH Somerset*, i. 399 f.

[28] Pelteret, *Catalogue*, no. 144.

[29] Ibid. no. 107.

resistance to the Conqueror.[30] Mærlswein fled to Scotland some time in 1067, in spite of having remained in office as sheriff after William's coronation. Two years later Mærlswein participated in Malcolm's invasion of England, but nothing is known of his later career.[31] Siweard Barn took part in the revolt made famous by Hereward the Wake.[32] Siweard Barn's end is not clear, for while Florence of Worcester states that he was imprisoned, and released only when King William lay on his deathbed, Simeon of Durham says that he escaped to live in King Malcolm's court. It is even possible that he ended his days in the service of the Byzantine Emperor.[33]

The reasons why these men revolted against the rule of the Conqueror are unknown, but the fate of those who remained at peace with the new king might well point the way. Hearding the son of Eadnoth did comparatively well, holding on to land worth £24, although before 1066 he and his father had an estate valued at £150. Others did much less well. Siweard the Fat lived until at least the time of the Survey, and apparently was not implicated in any of the risings against the Normans. The estate which he had held freely beforee 1066 was put at £100 by Domesday, but in 1086 he held land worth less than £2, as a vassal of Earl Roger. Wulfweard White was another Englishman who does not appear to have been involved in any of the rebellions which took place after the Conquest, and he died shortly before the Survey. His estate *TRE* was worth £170, but in 1086 his wife held a single manor worth just £3, whilst his son-in-law, Ælfsi, held a second of Wulfweard's manors. If the experience of these men was typical, and there is no reason to believe that it was not, it may be that the English nobles did not lose their land because they rebelled against the king, but rather revolted because their lands were being taken from them. If this were the case it might go some way to explaining the piecemeal nature of the English uprisings, as men doubtless refrained from breaking with

30 *ASC* D *sub anno* 1067, and *Florence*, *sub anno* 1070, 1072. See also S. Reynolds, 'Eadric "Silvaticus" and the English Resistance', in *Bulletin of the Institute of Historical Research*, 54 (1981).

31 *ASC* D *sub anno* 1067, 1069.

32 Hereward was not recorded in Domesday as a prominent landholder, although it is possible that he was related to one of the more important families of pre-Conquest England.

33 *Florence*, *sub anno* 1067; J. Godfrey, 'The Defeated Anglo-Saxons Take Service with the Eastern Emperor', in R. A. Brown (ed.), *Proceedings of the Battle Conference on Anglo-Norman Studies, 1978* (Woodbridge, 1979), 69 nn.

William until the threat to their own lands became apparent. Ironically the uncoordinated nature of the rebellions contributed greatly to their downfall.

Just as there is little direct narrative evidence concerning the activities of the greater landholders in England during Edward's reign, there is also very little evidence to demonstrate family relationships amongst the nobility, and between them, the higher clergy, and the king. A few of the greater landholders are described as being related to King Edward. Both Robert fitz Wymarc and Wigot of Wallingford are described as being the king's kinsmen, but no details of their relationship are given.[34] Beorhtric, Ælfgar's son, and Eadric the Wild could also claim a distant kinship. Eadric's uncle, Eadric Streona, had married one of Edward's half-sisters,[35] whilst Beorhtric's grandfather was said to have been a descendant of Edward the Elder.[36] Siweard the Fat, whose land lay mainly in Shropshire, was said by both Domesday Book and the *Ecclesiastical History* of Orderic Vitalis to have been related to Edward the Confessor.[37]

It is very probable that many of the greater landholders were related by marriage to one another, but there are few documented examples. Ælfric Wihtgar's son was a kinsman of Æthelwine Niger, a landholder in the east Midlands. Ælfric witnessed a grant by Æthelwine to St Albans, and later disputed the terms of Æthelwine's will, which he claimed did not have the consent of Æthelwine's kinsmen.[38] The *Liber Eliensis* states that the daughter of one of the *proceres* (those who held more than 40 hides) could only marry another of the same class.[39] This is mentioned when Guthmund was forced to acquire land by lease before being allowed to marry the daughter of a certain wealthy man. Whilst the situation might not have been so formal as the *Liber Eliensis* implies (where the restriction is an absolute one) it does seem to suggest that, as we would expect, intermarriage between rich landholding families was the rule rather than the exception. One of the most interesting possibilities for further research in identifying connections between various land-

[34] *Vita Edwardi*, 76; S 1148.
[35] *Florence, sub anno* 1067.
[36] *Chronica de Tewkesburye*, in *Monasticon*, ii. 60.
[37] *DB* i. 180; Orderic Vitalis, ii. 194.
[38] *Chron. Ramsiensis*, 169–70; S 1228.
[39] *Liber Eliensis*, book 2, cap. 97.

holding families stems from the work of Ann Williams, who has identified a probable link between Gytha, the wife of Earl Ralph of Hereford, and the family of Burgeræd, a major east-Midlands family, on the grounds that they and their men held land in the same villages.[40]

There are examples of English landholders who married foreigners. Eadgifu the Fair probably married a Breton, Ralph, who was a staller in Edward's court. Ralph's son held land in Brittany as well as becoming Earl of Norfolk under King William.[41] Ælfweard, a wealthy man who cannot be identified with any of the landholders recorded in Domesday, married one of Queen Eadgyth's waiting women, called Matilda.[42] Her name suggests that she was not English, whilst the fact that she was one of the queen's ladies-in-waiting suggests that she was from a good family. Finally, there is Wace's story concerning Beorhtric, Ælfgar's son, who was offered the hand of the daughter of the Count of Flanders. Whilst the story may not have been true, it shows that Beorhtric, as an important English noble, could have been considered to have been worthy of such a match.

It is to be expected that senior members of the clergy will have been drawn from the families of major landholders, and in a number of instances such relationships can be demonstrated. Guthmund was the brother of the Abbot of Ely,[43] and indeed Abbot Wulfric was criticized by the author of the *Liber Eliensis* for having leased land to his brother.[44] Ulf and Haldein, landholders in Lincolnshire, were kinsmen of Brand, who became Abbot of Peterborough in 1066. Leofric, who was made abbot of a number of religious houses in the Midlands including Coventry and Peterborough, was the nephew of Earl Leofric.[45] Although little is known about the families of particular bishops in Edward's reign, it is likely that both the abbots and royal priests, who formed the greatest part of those Englishmen who were raised to the episcopate, were made up largely of men from the wealthier families.[46] Leofgar of Hereford was said to have worn the

[40] A. Williams 'The Family and Career of Ralph, Earl of Hereford', in C. Harper-Bill, C. J. Holdsworth, and J. L. Nelson (eds.), *Studies in Medieval History Presented to R. Allen Brown* (Woodbridge, 1989), 327–42.

[41] See Ch. 3 nn. 54–62.

[42] *Heming*, i. 253.

[43] *Liber Eliensis*, book 2, cap. 97.

[44] See above, p. 67.

[45] F. Barlow, *The English Church 1000–1066* (London, 1979), 57.

[46] Ibid. 47, 63.

moustache of a warrior after he was made bishop.[47] This may be a clue that he came from a rich family, but we have no details of his background. A kinsman of Earl Godwine was a monk at Canterbury, and was chosen by the chapter to become archbishop in 1050, although King Edward overruled the election.[48] On the other hand, about half the bishops raised during Edward's reign came from abroad, so they at least cannot have been related to the English nobility.

Whether physically related or not, the lay lords had considerable dealings with the Church. Many leased ecclesiastical land (see Ch. 3), and others made donations or *post-obitum* gifts. Mærlswein, a major landholder in the north and west, was listed among the *festermen* or sureties of the Archbishop of York.[49] Siweard of Maldon gave fifteen ornate documents to the Abbey of Ely.[50] Ælfric the son of Wihtgar founded a college of secular canons which after the Conquest became the house of Stoke-by-Clare, endowing his foundation with a number of churches, as well as tithes and land throughout the area in which his own lands lay.[51] Ulf Fenisc built a church at his manor of Aldborough (Yorks.), and his action was recorded in an inscription upon a sundial,[52] while Earl Odda dedicated a chapel at Deerhurst in Gloucestershire, following the death of his brother Ælfric. Siweard the Fat had what was described after 1066 as 'a small wooden church' built in Shropshire.[53] As this description was made after the Conquest, and was meant to compare with Earl Roger's new foundation on the same spot, it may be that Siweard's church building was more substantial than the phrase suggests. In Surrey, John Blair has demonstrated that churches tended to be found on the larger estates of important landholders, such as Earl Godwine and his sons, Azur, Osweard of Norton, and Beorhtsige Cilt: and in fact there are quite a number of churches on these manors which show, to a greater or lesser extent, surviving late-Saxon fabric.[54] The

47 *ASC* D *sub anno* 1056.
48 *Vita Edwardi*, 17–19.
49 W. H. Stephenson, 'Yorkshire Surveys and Other Documents of the Eleventh Century', *EHR* 27 (1912).
50 *Liber Eliensis*, book 2, cap. 50.
51 C. Harper-Bill and R. Mortimer (eds.), *Stoke by Clare Chartulary* (Woodbridge, 1982), no. 70.
52 E. Okasha, *A Handbook of Anglo-Saxon Non-Runic Inscriptions* (Cambridge, 1971), 147.
53 Orderic Vitalis, iii. 142.
54 J. Blair, *Early Medieval Surrey* (Stroud, 1991), 115–19.

minster church of Christ Church, Hampshire, recorded an agreement with a relatively minor thegn, Ælfric Parva, by which a priest from the minster would perform services at the church which Ælfric built at his manor of Milford. The mother church's position was protected—for example, although there was to be a burial ground at Milford, all those who could afford it were to be buried at Christ Church—but Ælfric's own position was recognized: the priest was not to start his services before Ælfric arrived, and the priest would accompany the thegn when he attended the hundred court.[55]

In addition to the evidence of the chronicles, there is a reasonable body of documentary evidence for the reign of Edward the Confessor, including royal writs, diplomas, and private charters and agreements. Laymen were often mentioned in these documents as witnesses as well as participants (either recipients or donors) in the gifts which were described. There are two main problems with this group of sources. The first difficulty is a bias in the distribution of documentary evidence. The majority of the documents (and especially the royal diplomas) were written in the early part of Edward's reign. Moreover, while documentary evidence is quite common for some areas, in other regions there are few documents from even the early part of the reign. Furthermore, the majority of documents refer to grants and agreements in which at least one party is an ecclesiastical landholder. A separate problem is the difficulty of identifying the laymen named in the documents with the landholders mentioned in Domesday Book.

The majority of Edward's diplomas date from the first half of his reign. Since Domesday ostensibly recorded only those landholders who held their estates at the very end of Edward's life, at least some of the landholders recorded in the Survey as holding their estates 'on the day King Edward was alive and dead' may not have inherited their estates until the 1060s. Such men would probably not appear as witnesses in earlier documents, while the small number of later charters cannot be taken as a representative sample. The diplomas also suffer from a geographical bias, and the majority of them refer to land in the south and west of England. The regular appearance of

[55] P. H. Hase, 'The Mother Churches of Hampshire', in J. Blair (ed.), *Minsters and Parish Churches in Transition, 950–1200* (Oxford, 1988), 54–6; Richard Dennis has identified Ælfric Parva as being a reasonably substantial thegn in the county, whose kin together made up one of the more important lay landholding groups in the county (unpublished research towards a D.Phil., Oxford).

West-Country thegns might suggest that they dominated the court. In fact the preponderance of nobles from that region is more than likely owing to the fact that the grants which they witnessed were mostly located in the counties in which they held their land. Diplomas from every region usually included a few thegns local to the area where the grant was made, as well as major landholders from all parts of the kingdom.

In private charters, the Christian names of witnesses are often distinguished by bynames, and it is often possible to identify these men with landholders named by Domesday. 'Beorhtric the son of Ælfgar' is named as a witness on three of the Bishop of Worcester's leases.[56] Without doubt this man can be identified with the great Gloucestershire landholder of the same name, who incidentally also leased land from Worcester. In a bequest by Thurstan (the husband of Æthelgyth, who held an estate in East Anglia *TRE*) seven out of the eight lay witnesses are distingushed with a title or in some other way.[57] However, authentic royal charters, almost without exception, do not add bynames, and lay witnesses are either described as being earls or *ministri*. This makes identification very uncertain, especially where the name is a common one. For example, '*Eadric minister*' witnesses one surviving royal charter.[58] It is not possible to say whether this man should be identified with Eadric of Laxfield, Eadric the Wild, Eadric of Alham, Eadric the predecessor of Arnulf of Hesdin, or with some other Eadric, who was not recorded in Domesday as a singnificant landholder. It is also difficult to decide whether or not a number of attestations on different charters refer to a single man, or whether two or more are represented. For these reasons, in the discussion which follows, the identification of known landholders with particular witnesses will only be made if there is a strong reason for so doing. This will lead to an underestimate of the number of major landholders who are represented among the witnesses, but means that those identifications which are made will be relatively reliable.

Having stated the problems, it should be said that the royal charters and other documents do provide evidence concerning the officers of the royal court, and of some other men who, if they held no specific office, still seem to have witnessed royal documents on a regular basis.

[56] S 1406, S 1408, S 1409.
[57] S 1530. [58] S 1028.

It cannot be proved beyond doubt that the witness lists of royal diplomas give evidence of the presence at court of the men named. However, there are features in the composition of the documents which make it likely. In the first place, many prominent men, both ecclesiastical and lay, are mentioned. It might be thought that these lists could have been drawn up without reference to attendance at court, but this is improbable. If the lists were created as lists of important personages, we would expect a certain amount of consistency. For example, while all the earls do appear regularly as witnesses, it is only rarely that all witness a single document; and on some diplomas only one or two are mentioned.[59] Some abbots appear frequently, while others only rarely witnessed royal documents. This is true even if the abbey were an important one: Earnwig of Peterborough only witnessed one diploma in the ten years during which he held office.[60] This pattern suggests that the witness lists refer to men who were actually present, rather than to those whom the compiler felt it was prudent to name as guarantors to a particular gift.

The witnesses to royal charters represent at least a number of those who were present at Edward's court, and in particular some of the more important lords from around the kingdom. This is in contrast even to those private documents which the king attested. Whereas royal diplomas all tended to include men who did not necessarily hold land in the area concerned, the witnesses to private charters—even when the king himself acted as a witness—all tended to be local lords. Edward witnessed three charters which were issued by the Bishop of Worcester. The only earls to witness these grants were Leofric, Ælfgar, and Odda, all men of influence in the immediate area; whereas the Earls of Wessex and Northumbria were omitted in each case. The thegns, where they can be indentified, were all men from Worcestershire and Gloucestershire. They included Beorhtric, Ælfgar's son, as well as less important men such as Wagen, Owine, and Ceolmær.[61] All these thegns also appear on charters issued by the bishop which King Edward did not witness.[62]

Some private charters emphasize the local aspect of the grant even

[59] S 1013, S 1029, S 1059, S 1060.

[60] Earnwig was abbot from 1042 to 1052, when most of Edward's charters were issued. See T. J. Oleson, *The Witanegemot in the Reign of Edward the Confessor* (Oxford, 1955), 124.

[61] S 1405, S 1406, S 1408.

[62] S 1407, S 1409.

more strongly. A number include a formula stating that the grant was witnessed by all the thegns of the shire. This was true, for example, of a lease of land by Bishop Ealdred to Æthelstan the Fat.[63] The witness list of a grant by Thurstan included 'all the thegns of Essex'.[64] In another document, Thurstan bequeathed land in a number of counties to various recipients. The witnesses to this complex document were divided into groups, with different men acting as witnesses for different shires.[65] It is at least possible that such charters were presented at the shire court, in order to publicize a gift or settlement. Thurstan's will, involving land in various counties, would need to have been presented in each relevant shire court for acceptance. This would help to explain the contrast in the make-up of witness lists to royal charters, which, it is suggested, were witnessed by the members of the royal court.

Eight men are described in various sources as stallers, who officiated at Edward's court. These were Ælfstan, Osgod Clappa, Leofing, Asgeir, Ralph, Bundi, Robert fitz Wymarc, and Eadnoth. This group can be divided into two, since the first three men only witnessed documents during the first half of the reign, while the last four only came to prominence after 1050. Asgeir alone appears to have spanned the entire reign. Most of these men witnessed a number of royal diplomas. Ælfstan appeared as a witness to fifteen royal charters,[66] and Osgod to fourteen.[67] Leofing only witnessed two surviving charters.[68] None of the later stallers can match the attestations of Ælfstan or Osgod. Asgeir witnessed only six remaining authentic charters, although he does appear on many spurious ones.[69] Ralph also witnessed six diplomas.[70] Robert was a witness on four occasions,[71] and Bundi on two.[72] Eadnoth was only named as a witness on two forged diplomas.[73] Many more charters were issued

[63] S 1406.
[64] S 1530.
[65] S 1531.
[66] S 993, S 994, S 999, S 1001, S 1003, S 1004, S 1006, S 1007, S 1008, S 1010, S 1012, S 1013, S 1044.
[67] S 993, S 994, S 999, S 1001, S 1003, S 1004, S 1006, S 1007, S 1008, S 1010, S 1012, S 1013, S 1016, S 1044.
[68] S 999, S 1003.
[69] S 1028, S 1029, S 1031, S 1033, S 1034, S 1060.
[70] S 1021, S 1028, S 1029, S 1031, S 1033, S 1034.
[71] S 1028, S 1031, S 1033, S 1034.
[72] S 1033, S 1034.
[73] S 1041, S 1046.

in the first half of the reign than in the second, and this helps to explain why Ælfstan and Osgod appear on very many more charters than do the later stallers. It is clear that as a group, the stallers made up a significant proportion of the total number of lay witnesses to Edward's diplomas.

Apart from Leofing, who is known only through his appearance as a witness to documents, we know that all the other stallers were men of some substance. All of the later group of stallers are named in Domesday as holding estates worth more than £100, providing that Eadnoth's land is taken to include that of his son, Hearding. Of the earlier stallers, Osgod Clappa was wealthy enough to be able to raise a small fleet, even when in exile in Flanders. Osgod's exile in 1046 explains why he witnessed no charters after this date. But Ælfstan presents a slight problem of identification. In 1043 'Ælfstan my minister' was granted land in Sevington, Wiltshire, by King Edward.[74] According to Domesday, the land was held *TRE* by Ælfstan of Boscombe. It is reasonable to suggest that Ælfstan of Boscombe was the original recipient of the grant, and also that we should identify Ælfstan with the staller who witnessed so many of Edward's early grants. However, this leaves open the question of why, if Ælfstan did survive until 1066, he did not continue to witness later charters. There are a number of possibilities. Ælfstan, like Earl Godwine, might have died in the 1050s, and have been included only because of Domesday's inconsistency in applying a date for the term '*tempore regis Edwardi*'. A second possibility is that Ælfstan stopped attending court, but continued to hold his estate. He may have fallen from favour during the crisis of 1051–2, since Ælfstan witnessed no documents after this time; or he may have been disabled in some way which prevented his attendance. Finally, he might have died, and been succeeded by a man who bore the same name. As similar names tended to be used within the same family, this possibility would at least suggest that the two men were fairly closely related, if not actually father and son. Ælfstan of Boscombe's estate was valued at over £200, and most of the possibilities listed above suggest that Ælfstan the Staller (if he was not indeed the same man as the holder of Sevington *TRE*) was at least related, and probably held an estate of similar size.

Each of the stallers tended to hold land in a different area of the

[74] S 999.

country. The main part of Asgeir's estate lay in Essex, Buckinghamshire, Hertfordshire, and Middlesex. Ralph's land lay in Lincolnshire and Norfolk. Ælfstan held land in the West Country, with some manors in Hertfordshire and Bedfordshire. The land of Eadnoth and his son Hearding was also to be found in the West Country, although Hearding also held land in Leicestershire. Immediately after the Conquest, Eadnoth defended Devon against Harold's sons, suggesting that his sphere of authority did indeed lie in that area, so it is possible that Eadnoth replaced Ælfstan later in the reign of King Edward.

In a recent study of the stallers of Edward's reign, Mack considered that the stallers' duties outside the court involved maintaining the king's personal interests outside Wessex.[75] They must each have had their own regional concerns, if only by virtue of the areas in which they held their own land, but they were not restricted to witnessing diplomas concerning those areas: for example, Ælfstan witnessed diplomas concerning land in Kent and Oxfordshire.[76] Asgeir witnessed two which involved land in Devon and Somerset.[77] Five of the six charters witnessed by Ralph dealt with land far from his own estate.[78] In addition Ælfstan, Asgeir, and Ralph all witnessed at least one charter which concerned land in a county where they themselves held a number of manors.

The duties of the stallers cannot be closely defined. Judging from the number of diplomas which they witness, most of them appear to have been in regular attendance at the king's court. The Waltham charter, a forgery purporting to date from 1062, gives more precise titles to the men we know to have been stallers.[79] Asgeir was '*regiae procurator aulae*'; Bundi was '*regis palatinus*'; Leofing was described as the king's steward;[80] Ralph was '*regis aulicus*'; Robert fitz Wymarc was described as the king's kinsman, but was afforded no title. These men we know from other sources to have been stallers. Three other men were given titles: Azur, like Leofing, was described as being a royal steward; Wigot was '*regis picerna*'; and Godwine the queen's

[75] K. Mack, 'The Stallers: Administrative Innovation in the Reign of King Edward the Confessor', in *Journal of Medieval History* (1986).

[76] S 1001, S 1044.

[77] S 1033, S 1034.

[78] Ralph witnessed diplomas concerned with Hertfordshire, Oxfordshire, and the West Country. S 1021, S 1028, S 1031, S 1033, S 1034.

[79] S 1036.

[80] '*Regis dapifer*'.

steward. The witness named Azur could easily have been one of the two major landholders of that name; Wigot, a most unusual name, certainly refers to Wigot of Wallingford. The remaining twelve laymen were described as princes, and included Ælfstan and Dodda amongst their number.

The witness list of the Waltham charter cannot be a copy of a single authentic list. It includes Leofing, Ælfstan, and Dodda who only witnessed authentic charters from the first half of the reign. On the other hand the list also includes Asgeir and Robert, who only witnessed later diplomas. Since most of the names included in the list do occur on authentic charters (albeit from different parts of the reign) it seems likely that the person who compiled the witness list copied the names from two or more authentic charters. Because so many of the stallers are given titles, it is tempting to think that the detailed offices assigned to them might have had some basis in fact. However it seems more probable that the twelfth-century compiler of the document, knowing that the men had been officers in Edward's court, chose to add some detail to this and made up the titles. The forger gave the bulk of the lay witnesses the title '*princeps*'. If he was indeed copying from original witness lists (and the names suggest he was) he deliberately gave them this inflated title in place of the more staid '*minister*', which is normally rendered in later copies as '*miles*'. This suggests that the writer was prepared to elaborate upon the original material, and it is likely he also did so concerning the leading men on the list. There is therefore no reason to suggest that the forger had information concerning precise details about their activities. The Waltham charter must, unfortunately, be put aside as no more than an interesting forgery.

Two more major landholders may have played a different part in the country's administration from that taken by the stallers. Azur the son of Toti, and Ulf the predecessor of Robert de Tosny, were described by Domesday Book as being King Edward's housecarls.[81] Both were wealthy men in their own right: Azur had an estate valued at £73, and Ulf's manors were worth £62 in total. A number of other men were said in Domesday Book to have been housecarls, but none were as wealthy as these two. It seems probable that if Ulf and Azur were not actually in command of King Edward's household troops, they were at least leaders within his guard.

[81] Azur: *DB* i. 130b, 152b; Ulf: *DB* i. 149.

Edward's freedom of action might well have been restricted if part of his household troops were under the command of some established member of the English nobility, rather than someone who owed his position entirely to the king. There are indications that both Ulf and Azur had newly created estates, and may have been 'new men' raised up by Edward. Ulf had three manors in Gloucestershire, two in Suffolk, and one each in Cambridgeshire and Buckinghamshire. Azur's estate, although not quite so scattered, included manors in Warwickshire, Buckinghamshire, and Middlesex. In both estates the average value of the manors was over £6. These characteristics—a small number of highly valued, widely scattered manors—have been shown in Chapter 3 to have been features of newly created estates, rather than long established ones. As both Ulf and Azur have Scandinavian names, it is tempting to suggest that they came to England from across the North Sea, and made their career as successful warriors. There is no evidence that Edward gave land to either Ulf or Azur, but he did reward other housecarls. The regalian rights to a portion of sea-shore were granted to Urk.[82] Richard fitz Scrob, a Norman whom Edward established on the Welsh border, and who must have received some gifts of land from the king, was addressed as '*mine huscarl*'.[83] If these men were given gifts by the king, it is reasonable to suggest that Ulf and Azur received the bulk of their estate from the same source.

An Azur witnessed four authentic charters of King Edward. Three are dated 1044 or earlier, while Azur also occurs as a witness to some of the diplomas issued by Cnut.[84] In each case the man is simply given the title 'minister'. The man witnessing these early diplomas may well have died soon after 1044; at any rate it is likely that he was no longer present at court, and it is improbable that he survived to be recorded as a landholder *TRE*. The final attestation by Azur occurred in a charter dated 1069. There is nothing to indicate whether the man referred to was indeed the housecarl of that name, the Sussex lord, or some other thegn. Ulf the housecarl probably did not witness any of the surviving authentic charters.

In late-Saxon England, another group of men (apart from the stallers and other officers of the king) could claim a degree of 'closeness' to the monarch, namely, the king's thegns. In Cnut's laws,

[82] S 1004, S 1063.
[83] S 1157.
[84] S 993, S 1003, S 1028, S 1044.

the lesser thegn owed a heriot of equipment for a single fully armed warrior, which was to be given to his immediate lord; but the king's thegn owed equipment for four men, and an earl for eight, and both were to be given to the king,[85] while cases concerning a king's thegn were reserved to the king; and they were required to pay larger fines for certain misdemeanours than were other men.[86] The king's thegn also held judicial authority in his own lands, through the possession of *sac* and *soc* over their land, as well as other rights. *Sac* and *soc* conferred upon the thegn the right to try the majority of crimes which concerned the lord's men or land (excluding a number of particularly serious crimes), and to receive the share of the profits of such cases which would normally go to the king. A large number of those lords who held land worth more than £40 must have been king's thegns. Although Domesday often refers to men as '*teignus regis Edwardi*', this form does not necessarily identify those who held the status of king's thegn as defined by the law codes. Ketill Alder was a lesser thegn, whose heriot of a single set of arms was to be given to his lord, Stigand, and yet in Suffolk he was described as King Edward's thegn.[87]

Reid identified tenure of *sac* and *soc* as the main means of distinguishing the king's thegn from lesser thegns,[88] and in four of the counties of northern England, Domesday provides a list of those who held *sac* and *soc* in the county in King Edward's reign.[89] Although many of the names on these lists can be identified with major landholders, others are men of lesser importance (to judge by the size of the estate assigned to them elsewhere in Domesday), whilst others do not appear to be recorded elsewhere in the Survey. D. Roffe has suggested that those who do not appear as landholders in their own right may have had commended men in the county, over whose land the lord had *sac* and *soc*.[90] While this is possible, in at least some of the cases cited it seems unlikely. Ulf Fenisc probably did hold land in Yorkshire, although his successor in other counties, Gilbert de Ghent, had just a single manor in Yorkshire which had been held

[85] II Cnut 71.
[86] See R. R. Reid, 'Barony and Thegnage', in *EHR* 35 (1920) 170–2, for a fuller description of the rights and dues of a king's thegn.
[87] S 1471; *DB* i. 416b.
[88] Reid, 'Barony and Thegnage', 171, 173–4.
[89] *DB* i. 280b (Derbys. and Notts.); 298b (Yorks.); 337 (Lincs.).
[90] D. Roffe, 'From Thegnage to Barony', in *Anglo-Norman Studies*, 12 (1989), 166.

by Karl *TRE*.[91] Drogo de Bevrere held a very concentrated estate in Yorkshire, which included land worth over £80 assigned to Ulf *TRE*.[92] This included two substantial manors at Aldbrough and Beeford (valued at £40 and £20 respectively). Such large manors are likely to have been held by a man of substance, and one who would have held *sac* and *soc*.[93] Ulf Fenisc is the only man with that personal name who held *sac* and *soc* in Yorkshire, which makes the identification of the *antecessores* of Drogo and Gilbert highly probable. Presumably the foundation of Drogo's concentrated fiefdom took precedence over Gilbert's claim to the land of his predecessor in other counties. The case of Azur, son of Sualeva, is somewhat different. Azur appears to have been Robert Malet's predecessor in both Nottinghamshire and Lincolnshire. Azur held only a single manor, valued at £3, in Nottinghamshire, according to Domesday. Robert Malet's land in Lincolnshire is stated in the main text to have been held *TRE* by a certain Godwine.[94] However, in the *clamores*, Robert claimed some of this land through his predecessor Azur.[95] Roffe suggests that this proves that Godwine held his land under Azur,[96] but it seems unlikely that a man with a single small manor would have authority over another whose land was valued at £37. A more convincing explanation would be that Godwine was the father of Azur, and recorded in Domesday as the holder of that land in much the same way that Domesday records the earl of the same name in other counties. This argument is supported by the fact that Robert the Bursar succeeded to the land of Siweard and his sons, Aki and Vigeleikr. Some of this land was assigned to the father *TRE* in the main text of Domesday,[97] including soke at Coningsby; but Robert claimed land in the same village through Aki, his *antecessor*.[98]

[91] *DB* i. 326.

[92] *DB* i. 324, 324b.

[93] e.g. Heming, who had land worth just under £40 in total, nevertheless had *sac* and *soc* in Lincs. and Notts. His land comprised two highly valued manors (Branston, £20, and Granby, £12), as well as a third worth £6 (*DB* i. 289, 337, 361). Barthi, a Lincs. thegn, had land worth about £30, of which £20 came from a single manor, New Sleaford (*DB* i. 344b).

[94] *DB* i. 368.

[95] *DB* i. 377.

[96] Roffe, 'From Thegnage to Barony', in Marjorie Chibnall (ed.) *Anglo-Norman-Studies XII: Proceedings of the Battle Conference, 1989* (Woodbridge, 1990), 166.

[97] *DB* i. 363b.

[98] *DB* i. 375b. Again, Roffe uses this as an example of Aki being Siweard's lord, but this can hardly be the case, since the list of holders of *sac* and *soc* names Siweard as Aki's father: 'From Thegnage to Barony', 166; *DB* i. 363.

Fyach may equally well have been the predecessor (or perhaps the successor) of another landholder who was recorded in Domesday. Finally, in the main text and in the *clamores* of Lincolnshire, reference is made to a number of men who held *sac* and *soc* who were not listed earlier. At Stow St Mary, Eadgifu had three houses with *sac* and *soc*;[99] Grimketill had *sac* and *soc* over his land until the year King Edward died;[100] and Wulfgrim had *sac* and *soc* over his village of Laughton.[101] Yet none of these lords appeared on the list of those who held *sac* and *soc* in the county.

In spite of these problems, the majority of landholders whose estates were valued at more than £40 appear on the list of those who also held *sac* and *soc*. In Lincolnshire, twelve lords who held large estates had these rights: Ulf Fenisc, Mærlswein, Thorgautr Lag, Toki son of Otta, Stori, Ralph the Staller, Siweard Barn, Hrolf son of Sceldeware, Azur son of Sualeva, Athelric son of Mærgeat, Æthelstan son of Godram, and Wulfweard White all appear on the list; whilst only Eadweard Cilt (total estate of £92, of which £14's worth was in Lincolnshire) and Tonni (who had £60's worth of his total estate of £93 in the county) do not. Even those who were absent from the list may have had the rights of *sac* and *soc*, since we know that the lists do not necessarily conform to the details recorded in the main text of Domesday. The fact that such a large proportion of the greater lords who held land in Lincolnshire were also king's thegns gives good reason to suppose that most of the other great landholders had the same status. Elsewhere, information on the possession of *sac* and *soc* is much less well recorded, but it does occur. In Kent, Æthelnoth Cilt had *sac* and *soc* in the whole county, Asbiorn Bigga had the same rights in Canterbury, and a number of men, including Beorhtsige Cilt and Osweard of Norton, only in the western hundreds of Kent.[102] Burgeræd held his lands in Northamptonshire with *sac* and *soc*, although his lands in other counties were not so distinguished.[103] On the other hand, just thirteen of the greater landholders listed in Appendix II were described as the man of, or the thegn of, or holding land from, another lord, out of ninety landholders, and this tends to support the suggestion that the large majority of these men were indeed thegns 'nigh to the king' as Cnut's laws describe some of the thegns of the Danelaw.[104] These various distinctions all

[99] *DB* i. 363. [100] *DB* i. 376.
[101] *DB* i. 367, 376b. [102] *DB* i. 1, 1b, 2.
[103] *DB* i. 220b. [104] II Cnut 71.

indicate that the king's thegns were indeed close to the king: their heriot went directly to the king; they received dues that would otherwise be the king's; and the king had the right to justice over them. As such, we should expect that they attended the king at his court.

The witness lists of Edward's diplomas suggest that quite a varied group of thegns was present at Edward's court, in addition to the stallers. Some individuals were very frequent witnesses, but even they can be difficult to identify. 'Beorhtric' occurs as a witness on twenty authentic charters issued between 1042 and 1061. Usually he is given the title 'minister', but he also occurs on lists described as '*nobilis*' or '*consilarius*'.[105] In no single charter do two men with this name act as witnesses. This encourages the belief that most, if not all, of the attestations are made by a single person. There are two possible candidates for this witness amongst the landholders recorded in Domesday Book. Beorhtric the son of Ælfgar had a particularly large estate, and this might well have prompted a clerk to use the unusual title '*nobilis*'. We would expect such an important man to be present at court at least some of the time. The second possible candidate is Beorhtric the man of Queen Eadgyth. He had an estate worth £100, and since he was associated with the queen, he might also have been regularly at court. Little is known of this Beorhtric, but as a man of Queen Eadgyth he may not have come to court before her marriage in 1045. On the other hand, Beorhtric, Ælfgar's son, was active as a witness to private charters by 1042,[106] and so this makes him an altogether more probable candidate.

Other men witnessed royal charters much less frequently than did the stallers, or the somewhat elusive Beorhtric. Mærlswein can be easily identified in diplomas as in Domesday Book because of his unusual name. He held large amounts of land in the North and in the West Country, but he witnessed only two charters.[107] These dealt with grants in Lincolnshire to Peterborough Abbey. Oswulf, Frane's son, may also have witnessed two charters.[108] However Oswulf's name is not so uncommon, so the identification is less certain. Æthelsige (who had land in Devon and Somerset worth £49) and Everwacer (whose land in the same area was only worth £20[109]) both witnessed a charter of 1061 concerning land in Somerset[110] but do not appear on any other charters. Æthelstan, Godram's son, a

[105] S 1003, S 1021, S 1027, S 1034. [106] S 1406.
[107] S 1029, S 1060. [108] S 1010, S 1019.
[109] *DB* i. 96b, 97b, 98, 107b. [110] S 1034.

Lincolnshire landholder, also witnessed a single charter, this time in favour of Peterborough.[111] Where a man was an infrequent witness, he normally only attested to diplomas concerned with counties where he himself held land. This is certainly true of Mærlswein, Æthelsige, and Everwacer in the examples above. On the other hand, Oswulf's land lay in the Midlands, while the charters he witnessed lay in the West Country, so there can have been no firm rule on when such lesser landholders might act as witnesses.

Domesday Book records a number of men who had substantial estates, but who did not appear as witnesses on any royal diplomas. Ælfric, Wihtgar's son, Cypping, and Wigot of Wallingford do not appear on the witness list of any authentic royal charters. All of these men held land valued at over £100. Eadric of Laxfield can have witnessed at most a single surviving charter, and there is no certainty that it was not some other Eadric who was recorded even on that one. Some of these men may have been present at court, although they did not act as witnesses for any of the charters that have survived. As we have seen earlier, many of the witnesses to royal charters were thegns local to the area of the grant: it may be that other thegns, although present at court, were not called to act as witnesses. Eadric of Laxfield and Ælfric, Wihtgar's son, were both East-Anglian landholders, and none of the surviving charters involve land in that region. Cypping, on the other hand, was one of the most important lords in Hampshire, and although there are a number of surviving diplomas which concern land in the county, Cypping witnessed none of them. It may be that Cypping only came into his estate at the end of Edward's reign, when diplomas were granted.

It would appear from all this that the lay witnesses to Edward's diplomas can be divided into two groups. The first comprised the stallers, with a few other prominent men such as Beorhtric, who attested frequently. All these men were wealthy in their own right. The second group acted as witnesses much less frequently. This is a much larger and more disparate group. It includes some men of national importance, such as Mærlswein, and others such as Everwacer, who held a limited amount of land in a confined area. A third group, who never acted as witnesses, can also be identified. The members of the first group were clearly at court on a regular basis, otherwise they could not have acted as witnesses with such frequency.

[111] S 1059.

It is possible that members of the other two groups were also present regularly, but this does not seem very likely. Mærlswein did not witness any of the many diplomas which concerned land in the West Country, although he had considerable estates there. If he had been present when the diplomas were being issued, he would surely have been considered to be a suitable witness.

Three men who held substantial estates 'in the time of King Edward' are described as sheriffs in one or more of the Domesday entries which refer to them or their land. Godric held land worth a total of £44. Three-quarters of it lay in Berkshire, and most entries refer to him as '*Godricus vicecomes*'.[112] Osweard of Norton had land worth £108 in the south-east, and in one entry he too is described as being a sheriff.[113] Both Godric and Osweard received royal writs addressed to them, Godric in respect of land in Berkshire,[114] while Osweard received two writs concerning land in Kent.[115] The third wealthy pre-Conquest sheriff mentioned in Domesday was Mærlswein, who appears to have been Sheriff of Lincolnshire, where he held a large portion of his estate.[116] It is possible that Mærlswein was a sheriff under King Edward, but it is possible that he was given the office by Harold in 1066. After the Battle of Stamford Bridge, Harold was said to have left the north of England in Mærlswein's charge, and this might have included making him Sheriff of Lincolnshire. Only one Domesday entry refers to Mærlswein having held this office. This entry concerns a man who was outlawed 'in the year King Edward died', and it is possible that this circumlocution was used to refer to the fact that it had been King Harold who declared the man to be an outlaw.

Three other men, all stallers, may have been sheriffs as well. Although there is no direct statement that they held the office, they were all addressed in writs in the position normally reserved for the sheriff. Asgeir the Staller was addressed in writs concerning London, Middlesex, and Hertfordshire.[117] Eadnoth was addressed in a writ sent to Hampshire,[118] while Robert fitz Wymarc was one of the addressees of a writ confirming a bequest of land in Essex.[119] There is indirect supporting evidence that Robert and Asgeir were sheriffs

112 *DB* i. 57b–58, 60b, 144, 149, 152, 213.
113 *DB* i. 2b. 114 S 1066.
115 S 1090, S 1092. 116 *DB* i. 376.
117 S 1119, S 1135, S 1142.
118 S 1129. 119 S 1128.

from William's reign. Robert's son Swein was Sheriff of Essex in William's reign, and he may have succeeded to the position after his father's death, as he succeeded to Robert's land in that county. Asgeir's successor was Geoffrey de Mandeville, and Geoffrey was made Sheriff of London and Middlesex, and it is plausible to suggest that he gained the offices as well as the lands by virtue of being Asgeir's successor. However, F. E. Harmer doubts that these men ever held the office of sheriff, because nowhere were they actually given the title.[120] However, in each case the staller was named after the bishop and the earl. Where writs were concerned with more than one county (for example, the confirmation of the election of an abbot) a general address was written to '*ealle mine biscops und eorls und gerefas*',[121] showing that the third addressee of a writ was the king's reeve for the county. As all the men in question were also stallers, it is conceivable that, where a title was given at all, that of staller was preferred over that of sheriff, presumably because it had more prestige.

Although all the stallers who can be identified had large estates, a large number of sheriffs appear to have held relatively little land. Two men who held land in Cambridgeshire *TRE* were called 'sheriff', but neither held land worth more than £15.[122] Wada, Sheriff of Devon, had an estate worth £20,[123] while the sheriff of the large counties of Norfolk and Suffolk, Toli, also had just £20's worth of land.[124] The fact that these minor landholders could hold the office of sheriff, along with men of national importance, suggests that it may have been a rather less important or desirable office than that of staller. With one exception, all the sheriffs identified held a substantial proportion of their land in the counties in which they held office. Three-quarters of Godric's land lay in Berkshire; and over half of Osweard's land lay in Kent. Robert fitz Wymarc, Sheriff of Essex, held land worth £100 there. About half Wada's land lay in Devon and the remainder in Somerset, while all Toli's land lay in East Anglia. The single exception to the rule was Eadnoth the Staller. Although he was the addressee of a writ to Hampshire, his land lay further west, in Wiltshire, Berkshire, and Gloucestershire.

120 F. E. Harmer, *Anglo-Saxon Writs* (Manchester, 1952), 51.
121 e.g. see S 1071, S 1072, S 1088.
122 Ordgar: *DB* i. 197, 200; Blacuin: *DB* i. 199.
123 S 1161; *DB* i. 74, 80b, 84, 92, 105, 105b.
124 S 1078, S 1080, S 1083, S 1084, S 1085; *DB* ii. 211b, 230, 230b, 232, 264, 334b, 402, 432b.

The duties of sheriff have been studied elsewhere,[125] but a recapitulation of the main points will demonstrate the wide range of duties which must have served to spread the influence of a powerful sheriff throughout the county. The sheriff's main function involved the administration of the royal demesne. In Gloucestershire, Ælfwine the Sheriff paid a farm for three manors of the royal demesne.[126] In each case the arrangements seem to have been somewhat unusual. At upper Clopton the sheriff had to render whatever the manor produced; but at Dymock and Lower Slaughter the sheriff himself determined the amount of the farm. It is possible that Ælfwine had farmed other royal manors. Domesday does not mention any other examples, but the three cases above might have been picked out because they were exceptions. Some sheriffs took advantage of their involvement with the royal demesne. The best recorded example of this is Godric, Sheriff of Berkshire. He established a pasture for his own horses on the king's demesne land,[127] and appropriated another hide which he ploughed for his own profit.[128] At Shalbourne half a hide was put outside the royal demesne 'in the time of Godric the sheriff'.[129] When Edward gave Godric part of the manor of Woolhampton (perhaps at farm) Godric took another virgate for which he had no authority.[130]

As well as administering the king's land, the sheriff also played an important role in the two main arms of government, justice and defence. In a summary of the customs of Worcester, Domesday mentions '*pacem vero regis quam vicecomes dat*'.[131] At Wallingford, the customs stated that if a man broke into the city at night, he had to pay his fine to the king and not to the sheriff, implying that fines for other misdemeanours were paid to the sheriff.[132] The sheriff also played a role in defence. The customs of Shrewsbury state that the sheriff had the power to organize and lead military expeditions into Wales. Any man failing to accompany him paid a fine of 40*s*.[133] Ælfnoth, Sheriff of Hereford, was killed on Bishop Leofgar's ill-fated expedition in 1056.[134] Godric the Sheriff of Berkshire was killed at Hastings.[135] It is likely that both Ælfnoth and Godric were leading levies from their shires when they were killed.[136]

[125] W. A. Morris, *The Medieval English Sheriff to 1300* (Manchester, 1927).
[126] *DB* i. 162b, 163, 164. [127] *DB* i. 57b. [128] *DB* i. 57b.
[129] *DB* i. 57b. [130] *DB* i. 60b. [131] *DB* i. 172. [132] *DB* i. 56b.
[133] *DB* i. 252. [134] *ASC* D, E, *sub anno* 1056. [135] *Chron. Abingdon*, i. 484, 491.
[136] C. W. Hollister, *Anglo-Saxon Military Institutions on the Eve of the Norman Conquest* (Oxford, 1962).

Because of his various duties, the sheriff must have had influence throughout the shire. He was in a good position to make a profit from his office, from the profits of justice and the land which he farmed, or by taking advantage of his privileged position as Godric did. The possibility of such financial benefit would help to explain why such important men as Asgeir, Robert fitz Wymarc, and Mærlswein became sheriffs. Even Godric, who was by no means as wealthy as these other men, was at least one of the wealthiest men in Berkshire, where he was sheriff. However, if the offices were so desirable that powerful men sought them, it is not easy to explain why in other counties men of much more slender means came to hold office. Richard fitz Scrob, who held a small amount of land in Shropshire and Herefordshire, was sheriff of the latter county.[137] Richard, a Norman who had been placed on the Welsh March by Edward, had presumably been given the office by the king both to consolidate his own position and to allow him to control the defence of the county. But Devon, Somerset, Cambridgeshire, and East Anglia all had sheriffs who held no more than £20's worth of land.

Both Essex, where Robert fitz Wymarc was sheriff, and Hertfordshire, where Asgeir held office, had little or no royal demesne. In contrast there were extensive royal manors in Devon and Somerset. One explanation might be that the king was not prepared to allow powerful men to administer large amounts of royal demesne, since they might be able to alienate large portions of it. In Berkshire, where both the king and the sheriff held large amounts of land, there were frequent complaints in Domesday about Godric's invasions of royal land. In addition, where there was a large amount of royal land, the burdens of office would presumably have been heavier, as more administration would have been required. Men who had important holdings on their own account might have been unwilling to take on additional duties.

There are exceptions to the rule that the wealth of the sheriff was in inverse proportion to the amount of demesne land in the county. There was not a great deal of royal demesne land in East Anglia, but the sheriff, Toli, was relatively poor. Why did a more powerful local figure such as Ælfric, Wihtgar's son, not aspire to the office? Perhaps the wide extent of the counties, and the large number of independent

137 S 1157. Richard is addressed as '*mine huscarl*' rather than as a sheriff, but in the position that a sheriff would be expected.

free men in the area, meant that there was a considerable burden of work placed on this sheriff. But in Hampshire King Edward had a large number of valuable manors, yet the sheriff there was Eadnoth the Staller, and there is no good explanation for this exception. For the moment it is not possible to explain why in some counties the sheriff might be of national importance, while in others he was of much more moderate means. However, we might notice that the variation in the wealth of sheriffs was not confined to Anglo-Saxon England, but was also a feature of the reign of William I.[138]

The evidence from royal charters and from other sources suggests that many thegns of all ranks were involved in local government, or attended the king's court, and were presumably given some opportunity to give their advice and opinions to the king and his earls. The fact that many men were involved in the political life of the kingdom in normal times suggests that at least some of them must have played some role in the main crises of the period: but there is no account of the extent of their influence. Given that the families of Earls Godwine and Leofric were so much more wealthy than those of any other lay lords, it is likely that, unless they were united on one side or the other, only the most powerful of the non-earlish lords, such as Asgeir or Beorhtric, Ælfgar's son, can have had much personal influence.

One final word should be said about a group of landholders who appear to have been excluded from any formal role in local or national government. Women did hold large estates *TRE*, for instance, Eadgifu the Fair, who had land worth over £300, or Æthelgyth, the widow of Thurstan, whose estate had descended from ealdorman Beorhtnoth in the tenth century. As landholders, they were capable of initiating and defending cases concerning their land. In a dispute between Wynflæd and Leofwine in the late tenth century, Wynflæd's oath was supported by both men and women;[139] Edwine disputed the ownership of a manor with his mother, who declared in open court that it would descend instead to Leoflæd.[140] But they do not appear as witnesses to royal or private charters, nor do they appear to have held any administrative office. Any influence they might have held must have stemmed from the extent of their estates, or through

[138] J. Green, 'The Sheriffs of William the Conqueror', in R. A. Brown (ed.), *Anglo-Norman Studies*, V: *Proceedings of the Battle Conference, 1982* (Woodbridge, 1983).

[139] S 1454.

[140] S 1462.

family connections. The status of women was higher before the Conquest than after it, but we must recognize that (with the exception of the queen) they were excluded from any official part in government, and considered to be very much the inferior sex.

7

PRE-CONQUEST CONDITIONS COMPARED WITH THOSE ON THE CONTINENT: A SKETCH

A COMPARISON of English conditions with those on the Continent could be extremely important in further illuminating conditions on either side of the Channel, but it is beyond the scope of this book to do more than indicate below some of the major areas of comparison.

The nobility of England at the end of the Anglo-Saxon period seems to be similar in a number of ways to that of Germany at the end of the Millennium. It has been pointed out, for example, that whilst from the eleventh century it is possible to trace the descent of well-defined families of German nobles, before that time the nobility 'had been composed of large groups, linked by descent . . . but very loosely organized'.[1] The difficulty of tracing family trees for even the wealthiest of the pre-Conquest landholders suggests that the English nobility may have formed a similar, somewhat ill-defined group as existed in Germany at a slightly earlier period. One of the methods used to build up family trees in Germany has been by studying the names of people remembered in the prayers of monks which were recorded in *liber memoriales*.[2] The repetition of sequences of particular names, or of elements within these names, is taken to indicate that the groups represent particular kindreds. This suggests the possibility that in England too, personal nomenclature may provide a means of tracing family relationships. As von Feilitzen has pointed out, 'variation and repetition was evidently to some extent still practised in the eleventh century'.[3] Ælfric, the son of Wihtgar, named his

[1] L. Genicot, 'Recent Research on the Medieval Nobility', in T. Reuter (ed.), *The Medieval Nobility* (Amsterdam, 1978), 27.

[2] K. Schmid, 'The Structure of the Nobility in the Earlier Middle Ages', ibid. 37 ff.

[3] O. von Feilitzen, *The Pre-Conquest Personal Names of Domesday Book* (Uppsala, 1937), 31–2. See also W. G. Searle, *Onomasticon Anglo-Saxonicum* (Cambridge, 1897), xiii–xiv.

own son Wihtgar;[4] Earl Harold named a son after his father;[5] and the relations of Æthelstan 'Half-King' included his grandfather Æthelwulf, his father Æthelfrith, two brothers Æthelsige and Æthelwold, sons named Æthelsige and Æthelwine, and a grandson named Æthelweard.[6] But this is only half the story, and particularly in the eleventh century a change seems to have taken place. Godwine gave his three eldest sons Scandinavian names, and there was a definite fashion towards such names during and after Cnut's reign. Æthelric Bigga, a Kentish thegn who witnessed a number of documents in the reign of Edward the Confessor, was the father of Asbiorn,[7] who held land *TRE*, and Earl Ralph named his son and heir Harold. Even where English names were retained, families did not necessarily reuse the same names or even the same elements: the largest lay estate after those of the earls was that of Beorhtric, whose father was Ælfgar and whose grandfather was named Æthelweard. In short, by the reign of Edward the Confessor, it would certainly be unwise to use name elements as the only indicator of membership of a particular kinship group. On the other hand, where there is supporting information, this practice can be useful. In a church in Stratfield Mortimer there was an inscription naming a certain Æthelweard, son of Cypping, who is presumed to be the ealdorman of the some name who was ealdorman of Hampshire at the end of the tenth century.[8] Given that Cypping is an unusual name, and that a wealthy thegn named Cypping held Stratfield Mortimer in 1066, it is reasonable to presume that Cypping is at least of the same extended family as the ealdorman, if not a direct descendant.

The Continental nobility was differentiated from lesser landholders by legal distinctions, and the possession of judicial authority.[9] In late Saxon England, the earls and the king's thegns both had separate legal rights and duties, and held their own courts. In Cnut's laws, the lesser thegn owed a heriot of equipment for a single fully armed warrior, which was to be given to his immediate lord; but the king's thegn owed equipment for four men, and an earl for eight, and both were to be given to the king,[10] while cases concerning a king's thegn

[4] *DB* ii. 389.
[5] *Florence, sub anno* 1068.
[6] R. Fleming, *Kings and Lords in Conquest England* (Cambridge, 1991), 24, fig. 2.1.
[7] S 1400, S 1471, S 1473, S 1502.
[8] *VCH* Berkshire, i. 248.
[9] Genicot 'Recent Research on the Medieval Nobility', 21–2.
[10] II Cnut 71.

were reserved to the king; and they were required to pay larger fines for certain misdemeanours than were other men.[11] The king's thegn also held judicial authority in his own lands, through the possession of *sac* and *soc* over their land, as well as other rights. *Sac* and *soc* conferred upon the thegn the right to try the majority of crimes which concerned the lord's men or land, the profits of which cases would normally go to the king. It seems likely that the majority of men who held land worth more than £40 held rights of *sac* and *soc* (see Ch. 6).

The concept of *konigsnahe* is often referred to in the study of the German aristocracy of the period. 'Those closest to the crown were endowed with lands, privileges, offices and titles. They were entrusted with the leadership of armies and with governmental tasks of all kinds which brought them power and honour throughout the kingdom.'[12] Indeed, the kings actively strengthened their friends, relations, and allies to such an extent that with each new king the top rank of the nobility changed dramtically.[13] Fleming has shown that, at the start of the reign of Ethelred II, such a group of nobles, related to the king and to each other, dominated the ranks of the ealdormen. However, this group was all but destroyed in the later years of Ethelred's reign and during that of Cnut.[14] When Edward returned to England in 1041, he had been in exile for over twenty-five years, and had no power base at all in the country. As king, Edward clearly attempted to build up a group of men who owed their position entirely to him. Robert fitz Wymarc and Ralph, Earl of Hereford, were both related to the king.[15] The full extent of Earl Ralph's lands cannot be assessed, but they are likely to have been fairly extensive: in spite of the fact that Ralph had died in 1057, he (or his family) were still recorded as having land worth £170. Robert fitz Wymarc was holding land worth around £200 on the day King Edward died. In addition, it is reasonable to suggest that the estate of Ralph the Staller, which

[11] See R. R. Reid, 'Barony and Thegnage', in *EHR* 35 (1920), 170–2, for a fuller description of the rights and dues of a king's thegn.

[12] G. Tellenbach, 'From the Carolingian Imperial Nobility to the German Estates of Imperial Princes', in Reuter (ed.), *The Medieval Nobility* (Amsterdam, 1978), 207.

[13] K. Schmid, 'The Structure of the Nobility in the Earlier Middle Ages', ibid. 50, 54.

[14] Fleming, *Kings and Lords*, fig. 2.1, lists the connections and alliances between the various ealdormen and the king, and see ch. 2 *passim*.

[15] Ralph was the son of Edward's sister, Goda, and Drogo, Count of Mantes; Robert's precise relationship with Edward is unknown but he was close enough to the king to be present at Edward's deathbed (see F. Barlow, *Edward the Confessor* (London, 1970), 163 n. 1, and 247).

included land provided from the royal fisc, was built up through the king's generosity and influence, and it was similar in size to that of Robert.[16] The fact that Edward was unable to build up a group which could rival even the second of the earlish families demonstrates the power of those families, and the relative weakness of Edward's position when he received the crown.[17] In fact, one of Edward's earliest acts was to marry the daughter of Earl Godwine, presumably in an attempt to link the powerful earl to the interests of the new king, while most of the witnesses to the diplomas which Edward issued in the first years of his reign had also witnessed the documents of Cnut and his sons. It may be significant that Earl Ralph and Ralph the Staller only appear as witnesses to English documents (both royal and private) from 1050, while the earliest document in which Robert fitz Wymarc occurs was a writ of 1052–3.[18] Edward may have been unable to build up his own party in court before that date, and it is an interesting comment on the results of the crisis of 1051–2 that the promotion of these particular Frenchmen did not end with the return of Earl Godwine and his sons, and they continued to be present at court throughout the reign.[19] Earl Ralph himself may have been among the allies of Earl Godwine and his family. Ralph named his son Harold, and this boy was under the guardianship of Queen Eadgyth, Earl Harold's sister, in 1066.[20]

A number of Englishmen were related to the king, but their fortunes appear to have been mixed. Wigot of Wallingford was addressed in a writ as '*my dear kinsman*', and instructed to transfer a manor in Oxfordshire into the possession of the Abbot of Westminster,[21] suggesting that he had some authority in that area. Wigot's lands were widely spread, and although he had seventeen manors, they

[16] Ralph the Staller's manors at Sporle and Swaffham in Norfolk had both belonged to the demesne, and been given to Ralph by King Edward (*DB* i. 119, 144). Robert fitz Wymarc was given at least some of the land which had reverted to the crown after Spirites the Priest was banished (*DB* i. 252).

[17] Earl Leofric's family was assigned land valued at £2,500 in 1066 (see App. I), while the sum of the estates held by Earl Ralph, Ralph the Staller, and Robert fitz Wymarc was under £600.

[18] Earl Ralph witnessed three charters issued in 1050 (S 1020, S 1021, S 1022); Ralph the Staller witnessed one in the same year (S 1021); and Robert fitz Wymarc first appears as an addressee on a writ of 1052–3 (S 1128).

[19] Earl Ralph died in 1057, but Ralph the Staller and Robert fitz Wymarc both witnessed documents into the 1060s (Ralph: S 1028, S 1029, S 1031, S 1033, S 1034, S 1476, S 1478; Robert: S 1028, S 1031, S 1033, S 1034).

[20] *DB* i. 129b.

[21] S 1148.

were spread amongst eight counties, and it is possible that some of these were received from the king. Such a scattered estate may be a sign that it had recently been increased in size. He does not appear as a witness on any authentic diplomas, but the forged Waltham charter describes him as *regis picerna*.[22] Other kinsmen do not appear to have been favoured by King Edward: the Shropshire thegns Eadric the Wild and Siweard the Fat were both related to the king,[23] but it is unlikely that either witnessed any of Edward's diplomas,[24] and there is no evidence that either benefited from their relationship with the king.

An important question is that of aristocratic inheritance, since it was the largest single method of land transfer, and it affects the manner in which estates could be built up or reduced. In France, primogeniture became more and more common throughout the eleventh century, although this was perhaps more true in the central and southern parts of France than it was in the north. Lambert of Wattrelos, a Flemish clergyman who wrote in the twelfth century, gave details of his genealogy, extending back over a hundred years.[25] Lambert's family had been well off in the early eleventh century, but in spite of a number of good marriages, the patrimony of his father and grandfather had been broken up to provide for the members of a large family (Lambert himself was one of ten). Norman inheritance practices were not fixed by the time of the Conquest. Whilst in some cases a single son might inherit the bulk of his father's land, it was more common for at least two sons to be given a significant portion of land. Of the four sons of Giroie, the eldest received his father's own inheritance, while William, the next in age, was given those lands which his father has acquired in his own lifetime. The remaining sons received only minor bequests.[26] Ralph Taisson divided his land between two sons, resulting in the churches of Fontenay and a wood

[22] S 1036.

[23] Siweard is described in Domesday as Edward's kinsman (*DB* i. 180b), as he is by Orderic Vitalis, ii. 194; Eadric the Wild was the nephew of Eadric Streona (*Florence, sub anno* 1067), and Streona had married Edith, one of Ethelred II's daughters by his first marriage.

[24] One authentic charter is witnessed by Siweard minister (S 1004), and Eadric minister witnesses another (S 1028) but both are common names, and there is nothing to identify these witnesses with the Shropshire thegns of those names.

[25] F. Vercauteren, 'A Kindred in Northern France', in Reuter (ed.), '*Medieval Nobility*', 27.

[26] D. Bates, *Normandy before 1066* (London, 1982), 118.

being divided between them.[27] In Germany, *co-hereditas* was the usual custom in the eleventh century. Such practices did not necessarily lead to a division of estates, but, as Karl Leyser described 'if it was not checked by a high rate of mortality, could lead to a progressive fragmentation of a great fortune. It could also shift possessions from kin to kin or at least bring about a continuous re-distribution of wealth within an important family.'[28]

The evidence from pre-Conquest England is not sufficient to demonstrate a uniform practice in the matter of inheritance, but the indications are that a lord's land was normally divided amongst a number of beneficiaries within the kindred of the legatee. Domesday Book records many manors which were held by several thegns. In a number of cases, it is clear that these men were in fact brothers who had jointly inherited from their fathers. The Lincolnshire *clamores* record that the three brothers Harold, Guthfrithr, and Ælfric divided their father's land equally and jointly (*aequaliter et pariliter*), although the soke was divided between only the first two brothers.[29] Elsewhere in the same county, four brothers divided their father's estate, and the military service which was due was provided by each brother in turn.[30] In other cases, Domesday states that the manor was being held *in paragio*. On the Isle of Wight, Ælfric and Wislac held their land in this manner, as did a number of other king's thegns.[31] In Stratfield Mortimer (Berks.) two thegns, Cypping and Edwin *tenuerent in paragio*.[32] It should be noted that such joint inheritance did not necessarily mean that the land in question could not be divided amongst its holders: whilst in some cases the joint heirs might live and hold the land together, on other occasions they partitioned their inheritance.[33] The division of an estate did not necessarily mean that each son inherited equally: the example of the sons of Godwine, where Harold was pre-eminent, is sufficient to demonstrate that. But significant amounts of land were being held by the younger brothers; and in any case, it is impossible to determine how much of Harold's

[27] Ibid. 118–19.

[28] K. Leyser, 'The German Aristocracy from the Ninth to the Early Twelfth Century: A Historical and Cultural Sketch', in *Medieval Germany and its Neighbours, 900–1250* (London, 1982), 173.

[29] *DB* i. 375.

[30] *DB* i. 375b.

[31] *DB* i. 54.

[32] *DB* i. 62b.

[33] F. Pollock and F. W. Maitland, *The History of English Law* (Cambridge, 1968), ii. 253–4.

lands were acquired as a result of his own activity, rather than inherited from his father. Tostig, Gyrth, and Leofwine all held considerable amounts of land in Kent, Sussex, and Hampshire, close to the original source of Godwine's power, and this suggests that original family lands may have been divided more equally than those which Godwine had acquired later (and it is impossible, of course, to identify how much of Harold's land had been inherited from his father, and how much had been acquired from other sources). But as many of the extant wills of later Anglo-Saxon England demonstrate, land was also bequeathed amongst brothers, nephews, and the wider kinsfolk of the testator.[34] Leofgifu left land to her daughter, to her brother-in-law, and two men described as kinsmen, as well as a number of other beneficiaries;[35] the wills of Thurstan, Edwin, and Ketel both describe 'partnerships' in which the survivor of two brothers was to succeed to specified estates;[36] Leofwine son of Wulfstan left land to his aunt.[37]

Landholding in central and southern France in the eleventh century appears to have followed a different pattern from that which we have seen in England. In France, the land which the Capetian kings held themselves, or was held by those vassals over whom the king had effective power, was restricted to a relatively small portion of the kingdom. Similarly, the land of the counts lay each within their own *pagus*. The king might attempt to enforce his will on a county, but it could be exceedingly difficult to achieve a successful outcome. Robert the Pious fought for thirteen years to establish his own son as Duke of Burgundy against the claims of the late Duke's son-in-law.[38] As the eleventh century progressed, the power of some or many of the counts within their own counties was being restricted as castellans, once agents, achieved virtual independence from their sometime lords. In Macon, about half a dozen castellans controlled large areas of the county, and the count does not appear to have been able to enforce his will upon them after *circa* 1019. The castellans of Maine and Poitou also grew in power relative to their immediate lords.[39]

[34] J. C. Holt, 'Feudal Society and the Family in early Medieval England I', *TRHS* 32 (1982), 195–8.

[35] S 1521.

[36] S 1516, S 1519, S 1531.

[37] S 1522.

[38] R. Fawtier, *The Capetian Kings of France* (London, 1960), 61.

[39] J. Lemarignier, 'Political and Monastic Structures in France at the End of the Tenth and the Beginning of the Eleventh Century', in F. L. Cheyette (ed.), *Lordship and Community in Medieval Europe* (New York, 1968), 104–7.

One of the most significant sources of power for the castellans lay in their fortifications. From these they were able to defy their lords, and around them they built up their lands. They might hold land of the count, of the Church, or of another castellan, but the important fact was that the nominal lord was in no position to enforce their lordship. In Anjou, Normandy, and Flanders, the counts and dukes were able to retain power over their vassals, but only after considerable struggles.[40] Throughout most of France, the pattern of landholding was of greater or smaller areas, controlled from these same castles. Powerful churches, such as Cluny, acquired immunities and were themselves able to build up regions in which they were the dominant landholder. The main landholding pattern was therefore of compact regions in which a single lord was dominant, and where even the greatest of the lords, and to an extent, the king himself, held little or no power outside a geographically limited area.

These powerful lordships did not simply comprise land held in demesne, but also the land of lesser men who were drawn into the orbit of the local lord. Duby has shown that in the Maconnais, whilst the ties which bound the castellans to the Count of Macon were extremely weak, the castellans had sufficient local power to control their own vassals, the *milites*: 'They carried their homage to the nearest castle or sanctuary. At the end of the eleventh century all the knights of surrounding villages were thus attached to the master of a fortress.'[41]

The circumstances in France contrast with those of England. There, the king held land in all but three of the counties recorded in Domesday Book; furthermore, although many of the important landholders held the rights of *sac* and *soc* over their own lands (and thereby holding what would otherwise be the king's rights of justice) they still owed suit to the wapentake court,[42] providing the king with an interest in the administration of justice throughout his kingdom. The earls, too, had widespread interests, both as officials and landholders. They profited from the administration of justice throughout their earldoms, in so far as they were owed the third penny of justice, even where the king's rights were in the hands of his thegns. In Nottinghamshire, while the majority of the important lay landholders

[40] Ibid., 106–7.

[41] G. Duby, 'The Nobility in Eleventh and Twelfth Century Maconnais', in F. L. Cheyette (ed.), *Lordship and Community in Medieval Europe* (New York, 1968), 142.

[42] D. Roffe, 'From Thegnage to Barony', 158.

had *sac* and *soc* over their own lands, the third penny from such justice as they administered was still owed to the earl: only one layman, Ulf Fenisc, had the right to keep that portion for himself.[43] The lands of the family of Godwine were spread as widely as those of the king; and the family of Earl Leofric held land from Middlesex to North Yorkshire. They were indeed very powerful within particular counties: Earl Eadwine held land worth £134 in Cheshire, or about a third of the value of the county as a whole, and neither the king nor the other earls held a significant amount of land there. In most counties, however, even where one family was the major holder, there were others who could act to balance that power. In Sussex, the family of Godwine were by far the largest landholders with a combined estate worth over £850, or one-quarter of the value of the county as a whole. However, while the Godwines were by far the largest landholders in the county, they were not the only major powers there: the royal demesne (including the land of the queen) in that county was valued at over £400, while Azur held land worth £170. Moreover, the widespread nature of the estates of the earls gave them an interest in the country as a whole, rather than in a single region. This interest is reflected in the witness lists of the royal diplomas, which were regularly witnessed by many of the earls. Of the diplomas recorded by Oleson as being either authentic or doubtful, the earls averaged between three and four attestations per diploma,[44] implying frequent attendance at court by the majority of earls during their period of office.

Even those below the rank of earl who held land worth over £100 tended to have an estate which was spread over a number of counties. On average, these estates were spread over six shires: Bundi the Staller held manors in ten counties worth £180, and the land of Burgeræd and his sons lay in four counties. A few of the lesser lords may have held an estate which was sufficiently concentrated to dominate the region in which they held land: Eadric of Laxfield in eastern Suffolk is perhaps the best example—but he was an exception. Eadric was also unusual in attracting a great number of commended men in the area in which his land lay. As is made clear in Chapter 4, men of national importance could attract the commendation even in counties in which they held little or no land.

[43] *DB* i. 280b.

[44] T. J. Oleson, *The Witenagemot in the Reign of Edward the Confessor* (Oxford, 1955), App. P.

Conversely, even a lord such as Wulfwine, the *antecessor* of Aubrey de Vere, who held a major estate concentrated on the border of Cambridgeshire and Essex, had almost no commended men listed in Domesday, and this in the part of the country where they were most assiduously recorded. On the other hand, a man such as Asgeir the Staller had the commendation of men in Cambridgeshire although he himself held no land there.

A further difference between England and France in the first half of the eleventh century is in the matter of lordship. Throughout society in France it was common for men to have more than one lord. Count Eudes II of Blois was a vassal of the Count of Sens; Fulk Nerra of Anjou was a vassal of the Duke of Aquitaine: and both were the vassals of the Kings of France. Castellans and even *milites* soon became the vassals of more than one lord. In return for their homage, vassals received a heritable fief, and this could and did result in a man inheriting fiefs which were held from different lords. Multiple lordship was so common by the end of the eleventh century that Duby considered that all the knights of the Maconnais held fiefs from more than one lord.[45] Indeed, the appearance of liege lordship in several areas of France by the middle of the eleventh century was an attempt to control the problems that multiple allegiances could cause,[46] and it is a good indication of the widespread nature of this phenomenon. England, in this respect, seems more like Germany, where multiple lordship had not made any headway in the eleventh century.[47]

One of the main differences between the nobility of England before the Conquest and that on the Continent was the absence of castles in England. A few small castles, such as Ewias Harold, may have been built in England before the Conquest, but these all appear to be attributable to Norman incomers rather than native English lords.[48] Excavations at Goltho in Lincolnshire do indicate that the halls of even a relatively minor thegn might be fortified, but the ditch and palisade there were not built on a great scale.[49] The royal lodge

[45] G. Duby, 'The Nobility', 144.

[46] M. Bloch, *Feudal Society* (London, 1978), i. 214–15.

[47] F. Ganshof, referred to by Lemarignier, 'Political and Monastic Structures', 108 n. 55.

[48] R. Allen Brown, *The Origins of English feudalism* (London, 1973), 74–5.

[49] G. Beresford, 'Goltho Manor, Lincolnshire: The Buildings and their Surrounding Defences', in R. A. Brown (ed.), *Anglo-Norman Studies, XI: Proceedings of the Battle Conference, 1981* (Woodbridge, 1982), 13–36.

at Cheddar had no significant defences.[50] King William had to construct a castle in London, although Edward had regularly been in residence there.[51] Defences at South Cadbury were refurbished during the turbulent period of Ethelred's reign, but this was a royal mint and centre of local defence,[52] not a private castle.

The presence of castles has been taken by many, including R. Allen Brown for example, to have been one of the prerequisites for a 'feudal society'.[53] When discussing the possible absence of feudalism in pre-Conquest England, the lack of castles is probably the evidence upon which there would be most agreement. It is therefore worth considering what effects this lack had upon England. Castles had two primary functions: first, they were defensive, enabling their defenders to withstand a very much stronger force. Capturing castles was a time-consuming business. Secondly, they provided a firm base from which the local area could be controlled. The absence of private defences in England directly affected any conflict between the king and his subjects. Whereas in France or Germany a rebellion might drag on for years, as a number of castles had to be reduced before the power of the rebels was broken, events happened much faster in England. Earls and major landholders were forced into exile, and if, as happened on several occasions, they were able to return through the use of force, at least the disputes were ended without extensive warfare. Orderic Vitalis attributed the speed of the Norman Conquest to the small number of castles in the kingdom.[54]

Because there were no private castles, the only way in which a noble might defy the king in the face of a royal army would be by fighting a pitched battle. This would be for all sides a costly undertaking, but more importantly, it was an extremely risky strategy: even William the Conqueror avoided fighting battles where possible.[55] To quite a large extent the absence of private castles and the lack of

[50] P. Rahtz, *The Saxon and Medieval Palaces at Cheddar*, British Archaeological Reports 65 (1979), 57–60.

[51] Oleson lists eleven occasions at which Edward may have consulted his witan whilst present in London: *Witenagemot*, 70–1.

[52] L. Alcock, *By South Cadbury is that Camelot*... (London, 1972), 194–201.

[53] Brown, *Origins of English Feudalism*, 30–1.

[54] Orderic Vitalis, *The Ecclesiastical History*, ed. M. Chibnall (Oxford, 1969), book 4, *c.*1125, ii. 218.

[55] J. Gillingham, 'William the Bastard at War', in C. Harper-Bill, C. J. Holdsworth, and J. L. Nelson (eds.), *Studies in Medieval History Presented to R. Allen Brown* (Woodbridge, 1989), 144–58.

complete control over whole regions by earlish families can explain the way in which the events of 1051–2 (and also the subsequent exile of Earl Ælfgar) occurred. In 1051, Edward succeeded in gaining the support of the Earls of Leofric, Siweard, and Ralph against Godwine and his sons: no battle was fought in Gloucestershire because 'it would be great folly if they joined battle'.[56] By calling up the host, King Edward deprived Godwine of the support of those of his commended men who were also king's thegns—had they refused to go to the king, they would have put their own lands in jeopardy of being seized. As his strength waned, Godwine must have seen that he had no possibility of standing up to the King, and he fled abroad. However, when Godwine returned, he had little to lose and everything to gain by fighting a battle, assuming that he brought sufficient forces to be a credible threat. Knowing that, the king (or at least, his supporters) will have been more inclined to come to a peaceful settlement.

The second function of castles, that of dominating the surrounding countryside, enabled French castellans to build up compact lordships where it was not possible for the writ of their superiors to run. Such lordships simply did not exist in pre-Conquest England. The absence of castles in England prevented the local lords from having a central seat of power from which they could reach out to dominate the locality, safe from the power of the king or other lords. There were other factors which helped prevent the creation of geographically compact lordships which were free to act independently of superior lords: the presence of royal demesne in most of the counties, and of royal officers, the sheriffs, in each shire, meant that the king was not excluded from any region; and the tradition of inheritances divided amongst the family slowed down the establishment of such compact estates: but had there been castles in the country, these factors might not have been enough.

[56] *ASC* D *sub anno* 1051.

8

CHANGES IN TENURIAL PATTERNS BETWEEN 1066 AND 1086

THE question of how much change was wrought on England by the Norman Conquest is one which has been the subject of much controversy. This is especially true when tenurial patterns and practices are considered. At first sight Domesday shows a complete tenurial revolution, with a total replacement of the major landholders of 1066, but signs of continuity do exist. More than one recent paper has questioned whether any revolution took place at all.[1] In this concluding section the evidence from earlier chapters will be used to see what changes in tenurial patterns took place, and how far a 'tenurial revolution' can be substantiated.

R. R. Reid and David Roffe have pointed out that there was a significant level of continuity between the Saxon and Norman concerning the rights which the landholders had as members of the nobility.[2] The argument that Norman tenants-in-chief assumed the legal rights of their *antecessores*—*sac* and *soc* and other rights and duties relating to their closeness to the king—is entirely convincing. Nor should it be surprising: after all, it is an oft-repeated fact that the conquerors took over much of the law and administration of the kingdom intact, altering it rather than replacing native customs wholesale with those of Normandy. This makes it all the more likely that the legal position of the barons would be firmly based on those of their predecessors, the king's thegns.

Both Roffe and Sawyer also argue that the structure of post-Conquest estates owed much more to that of pre-Conquest England than is generally believed to have been the case, and that the major

[1] P. H. Sawyer, '1066–1086: A Tenurial Revolution?' in *Reassessment*, and D. Roffe, 'From Thegnage to Barony', in M. Chibnall *Anglo-Norman Studies, XII: Proceedings of the Battle Conference, 1989* (Woodbridge, 1990).

[2] Roffe, 'From Thegnage to Barony', 158–9; R. R. Reid, '*Thegnage and Barony*', in *EHR* 35 (1920).

change was that of personnel.[3] This is a much more difficult argument to sustain. The continuity of individual estates is by no means as straightforward as is suggested by these articles; the relationship between the nobility and their dependants was quite different; and between the reigns of Edward and William there was a significant change in the structure of the nobility as a whole.

In the majority of cases, the estates of the nobles examined in Chapter 3 had passed almost entirely into the hands of a single tenant-in-chief by 1086. The most prominent of the non-earlish estates were typical in this respect. The lands of Beorhtric, Ælfgar's son, were given to Queen Matilda (although following her death they went into the royal demesne and some of Beorhtric's manors were distributed piecemeal[4]). Asgeir the Staller's manors made up the bulk of Geoffrey de Mandeville's fief. Count Alan held almost all the land which had been held *TRE* by Eadgifu the Fair, with only two significant exceptions.[5] William of Eu succeeded to most of Ælfstan of Boscombe's estate. Of the remaining Saxons who had held estates valued at over £200, the lands of Æthelnoth Cilt, Ulf Fenisc, Eadric of Laxfield, and Mærlswein also passed almost wholly into the hands of a single successor. The only two estates worth over £200 which were divided amongst a number of successors had belonged to Azur and Wulfweard White, and there were clear reasons for these exceptions, which will be dealt with later.

In some respects, the example of Asgeir the Staller's lands is a prime example of the transfer of an entire estate from one man to another as a result of the Conquest. In 1086 Geoffrey de Mandeville had land worth £770, of which more than three-quarters had been held in 1066 by either Asgeir or his dependents.[6] Of the remainder of Geoffrey's estate, some of his land might have been held by Asgeir's men, in counties where such relationships were not recorded. A few of Geoffrey's manors had been acquired through exchanges.[7] Geoffrey also held land worth about £10 in Suffolk which had been held in 1066 by Haldein, and it is possible that Geoffrey was declared

[3] Sawyer '1066–1086: A Tenurial Revolution?', 83; Roffe, 'From Thegnage to Barony', 167 ff.

[4] *DB* i. 83, 166b.

[5] Norton (Suffolk) and Exning (Cambs.), which passed into the hands of Godric, Sheriff of Norfolk. *DB* i. 189; *DB* ii. 286.

[6] *DB* i. 36, 62, 129b, 135, 135b, 139–40, 149b, 159b, 160, 197, 227, 227b, 243b; *DB* ii. 57b–62b, 411–13.

[7] *DB* ii. 57b, 59, 412.

to be Haldein's successor as well as Asgeir's. However, Domesday specifically states that Haldein's manors (along with other manors held by Geoffrey in 1086) had not belonged to Asgeir's fee.[8] Although Geoffrey held all the manors which Asgeir had held directly, quite a lot of land which had been held by Asgeir's men was held in 1086 by other tenants-in-chief. Land worth about £40 was held by the Bishop of London, Odo of Bayeux, and Count Eustace, amongst others.[9] Some of this land may originally have been given to Geoffrey, only to have left his fief before 1086 through the exchanges mentioned earlier; the ownership of other land was in dispute. The land of Godith, one of Asgeir's dependents, had been bought after 1066 by the Bishop of London with William's permission.[10] In this particular case, Geoffrey had seized the land, although the bishop claimed it, but he may have been unable to take possession of other land which had been disposed of between 1066 and the time that Geoffrey was granted Asgeir's land. In spite of these changes, the fief held by Geoffrey de Mandeville in 1086 was still recognizable as that held by Asgeir the Staller and his men. Geoffrey even sought the offices which Asgeir had held as sheriff of Hertfordshire and London. The changes which had taken place between 1066 and 1086 were no more than might have been expected as a result of the normal land market.

However, such a simple transition between the Saxon and Norman tenant of a single estate was not very common. In many more cases a single tenant-in-chief had more than one important Saxon *antecessor*. Whilst Count Alan succeeded to most of the land which had belonged to Eadgifu the Fair and her men, this accounted for only about half of his fief. Another £150's worth of Alan's land, mostly in Lincolnshire, had been held by Ralph the Staller, and the various manors which made up the honour of Richmond had been held by many different men *TRE*.[11] Gilbert of Ghent had both Ulf Fenisc and Tonni as his *antecessores*, as well as a number of lesser men.[12] Henry of Ferrers succeeded to the land of three important Saxon lords: Bondi the Staller, Godric the Sheriff, and Siweard Bearn. In

[8] *DB* i. 36; *DB* ii. 57b, 411.
[9] *DB* i. 133b–134b, 137, 137b, 196.
[10] *DB* i. 140.
[11] *DB* i. 309, for Yorks., and *DB* i. 347 for Lincs.
[12] *DB* i. 62, 149b, 159b, 197–b, 207, 215, 227b, 236, 243b, 277b, 290b, 293b, 326, 354b–356.

addition, Henry held land in Derbyshire and Staffordshire which had belonged to a number of others.[13]

The result of this accumulation of lands by William's tenants-in-chief was that in 1086 larger estates were more common. Whereas in 1066 there had been only thirty-seven estates (including those of the earls) which were valued at over £100, eighty-one lay tenants-in-chief held as much land in England at the time of the Survey. There were forty-five Norman lords whose estate was worth over £200, whilst there had been only fourteen Saxon estates worth as much.[14]

The estates created by William were not all made up using existing Saxon estates as building blocks. In the first place, a number of Saxon estates were split into two or more parts. The land which had been held by Edward's earls was fragmented to a great extent. Much of the land lay within the royal demesne in 1086, and the increase in value of the crown's land—from about £6,000 in 1066 to £10,000 under William—was not the least significant of the changes in tenurial patterns which took place after Edward's death. But a large number of manors which had been held by the earls were transferred into the hands of many different tenants-in-chief.[15] In Berkshire Harold had held eleven manors. Of these, seven were held by the king, while Earl Hugh, Ralph fitz Seigfreid, Ælfsi of Farringdon, and Battle Abbey each held a single manor.[16] In Wiltshire the land of Earl Harold was divided between five tenants-in-chief,[17] and the lands of other earls across the country were similarly broken up.

Some other Saxon lords had their estates divided amongst a number of successors. The land of Wigot of Wallingford was divided between Miles Crispin and Robert d'Oilly. In this case the land may have been assigned to Robert originally, and only divided when Robert's daughter married Miles.[18] In Essex and East Anglia the estate of Ketill was split between Rannulf Peverel, William d'Ecouis, Rainald fitz Ivo, and Peter de Valonges.[19] But for the existence of

[13] *DB* i. 60–b, 72, 151, 157b, 169, 185, 225, 233–b, 242, 248b, 274–6, 291b, 353b; *DB* ii. 56b.

[14] Table 3.1 lists the amount of land held by men *TRE*; for the situation *TRW* see W. J. Corbett, 'The Development of the Duchy of Normandy, and the Norman Conquest of England', *Cambridge Medieval History* (Cambridge, 1926), v. ch. 15.

[15] R. H. Davies, 'The Lands of Harold, Son of Godwine, and their Distribution by William I', MA diss. (Cardiff, 1967), *passim.*

[16] *DB* i. 57–60, 62b, 63b.

[17] *DB* i. 64b, 65, 69, 71, 71b, 72b, 74b.

[18] *VCH* Oxford, i. 383.

[19] *DB* ii. 75b, 223, 230b, 233–4, 243b, 254, 254b, 416b; S 1519.

Ketill's will, these various manors might not have been identified as belonging to a single estate. Arnulf of Hesdin held the largest portion of Wulfweard White's estate, but his other manors were divided amongst six other lords.[20] Wulfweard survived the Conquest, and lived almost to the time of the Survey. It may be that Wulfweard lost many of his manors piecemeal during his lifetime, and only held the rump of estate at the time of his death: this would have been the portion which was assigned to Arnulf.[21]

The actual number of estates divided in this way seems to have been relatively small. In part this may be an illusion, caused by the methods used to identify Saxon landholders. Saxon lords can often be identified simply because they had one main successor: it is precisely those estates which had been divided amongst more than one successor which are likely to have been omitted from the lists produced. As noted in the Introduction, however, this is not likely to be a very serious problem, and, in any case, is likely to affect identification of the smaller estates rather than the larger ones. A much greater change in landholding patterns was caused by William's attempts to defend his kingdom. To do this, entire areas of land in critical regions were granted to a single lord. Odo of Bayeux held most of Kent from his half-brother; Shropshire was almost entirely granted to Earl Roger; and Cheshire was held by Earl Hugh. Sussex was divided into a number of rapes held by the Counts of Mortain and Eu, Earl Roger, William of Braose, and William of Warenne. The scattered Saxon estates in these areas were replaced by a small number of extremely large lordships. One of the effects of this in Sussex was to break up the estate of Azur, the greatest Sussex landholder after the family of Earl Godwine, among a number of different lords.[22]

Elsewhere William established castellries which also formed geographically compact estates. In the West Country the Breton Judhæl was granted the honour of Totnes; whilst the honour of Tutbury, held by Henry of Ferrers, controlled an area across the border between Staffordshire and Derbyshire. In Yorkshire a number of similar castellries were formed, including Count Alan's honour of Richmond. Where these compact honours were set up, scant notice

[20] *DB* i. 1b, 9, 11b, 43b, 62b, 63, 66, 70, 73, 82, 87, 129–30b, 169, 212, 337, 367b.

[21] For Wulfweard's survival see Ch. 6.

[22] *DB* i. 19b, 21, 21b, 22b, 23, 24b–25b, 26b–29.

was taken of the previous Saxon tenants. Geoffrey Alselin succeeded to most of the land held by Toki son of Otta, and claimed some land which had belonged to Toki and which was held by Henry of Ferrers. However, Henry continued to hold the land in 1086, for the apparent reason that it lay within the boundary of the honour of Tutbury.[23] The introduction of these compact honours definitely brought a new element into the landholding patterns of eleventh-century England. This is rather ironic, as one feature which has long been considered to be characteristic of Norman settlement is the scattered nature of many baronial fiefs.[24] As we have seen, many Saxon estates were also spread across a number of counties: what the Saxons did not have were whole counties controlled by a lord other than the king.

Finally, we might note the existence in 1086 of some quite substantial estates which appear to owe their origin neither to the establishment of a castellry nor to the acquisition of the lands of one or more particular Saxons. Rather, these fiefs comprised a little land from many different pre-Conquest estates. Picot the Sheriff and Hardwin of Scales both had estates made up of land which had been held by many different Englishmen, and very frequently the sokemen or other dependents of various Saxon lords. In addition both held the land of many sokemen whose lord had been King Edward. Both estates were substantial, with Picot holding land worth £130 in Cambridgeshire, and Hardwin holding a similar amount split between Cambridgeshire and Hertfordshire.[25] Sawyer suggests that the men whom Arnulf of Hesdin had succeeded in Wiltshire had been the men of a single lord, and a similar argument has been made regarding the estate of Roger de Bully in Nottinghamshire and Yorkshire, which was also made up of the land of a large number of different individuals.[26] However, neither Arnulf nor Roger had a single prominent *antecessor*, and as has been shown earlier, only men who themselves held large estates attracted many dependents. It therefore seems likely that Arnulf's estate was made up in the same way as that of Picot and Hardwin, and there may have been many more of this sort. It is

[23] *DB* i. 274b.

[24] e.g. Sawyer points out that pre-Conquest estates were as widely scattered as post-Conquest fiefs, but makes no mention of the compact honours created by William: Sawyer, '1066–1086: A Tenurial Revolution?', 85.

[25] *DB* i. 200b–201b.

[26] Sawyer '1066–1086: A Tenurial Revolution?', 83, and Roffe, 'From Thegnage to Barony', 169.

interesting to note that both Hardwin and Picot were sheriffs, and their authority within their respective counties may have allowed them to build up their fiefs through private enterprise, rather than through the direct grant of the king.

Another element of continuity which has been suggested is that the patterns of post-Conquest demesne and tenancies were largely determined by whether the land in question had been held by the *antecessor* of the tenant-in-chief or by his men. Sawyer quotes the examples of Geoffrey de Mandeville and Aubrey de Vere in Essex.[27] But although in Essex most of Geoffrey's, and all Aubrey's, demesne manors had been held directly by their respective predecessors, this is by no means the full story. Whilst Geoffrey had retained the largest of Asgeir's demesne manors, he had distributed the smaller manors which Asgeir himself had held, amongst his own vassals. In Buckinghamshire, Geoffrey gave the one manor which Asgeir had held there to his man Germund, whilst retaining in demesne three manors which had been held in 1066 by Asgeir's man Swein. Geoffrey also kept in demesne a manor which had been held by Queen Eadgyth.[28] Three of the four manors kept by Geoffrey were valued at more than the one granted to Germund, so it may be more true to suggest that the principle which governed Geoffrey's distribution of manors to his men was the absolute value of those manors, rather than the tenant *TRE*. In fact only half Geoffrey's demesne manors throughout England had been held directly by Asgeir, whilst half the forty or so manors which Asgeir had held directly were in the hands of Geoffrey's vassals in 1086. The proportion of demesne land to tenant land in Geoffrey's estate was similar to the proportion between the land held by Asgeir and the land held by Asgeir's dependents, but there was no great continuity between the land held in demesne by both Asgeir and Geoffrey.

Asgeir was one of the relatively few Englishmen to have a considerable proportion of commended or dependent men. Many other relatively important lords (judged by the extent of their estates) had few or no dependent men recorded by Domesday Book, in spite of holding considerable amounts of land in areas where such relationships were recorded. Aubrey de Vere's predecessor Wulfwine was such a man. He held land worth £141 in Cambridgeshire and Essex,

[27] Sawyer, '1066–1086: A Tenurial Revolution?', 83.
[28] *DB* i. 149b.

but Wulfwine's men had land worth just 2 marks, which could not be sold without Wulfwine's permission.[29] His successor, Aubrey, did keep a number of manors in demesne, but nevertheless used land which had been held by Wulfwine to enfeoff his own men. In Cambridgeshire, Aubrey succeeded to eight manors which had belonged to Wulfwine, as well as a small portion of land which had been held by Wulfwine's man Godwine. In addition Aubrey held three pieces of land which had not belonged to Wulfwine or his men. Of these various manors, Aubrey kept four of Wulfwine's, and part of a fifth. Aubrey also kept in his own hands the land of one of the king's sokemen. The remaining land was distributed amongst five of Aubrey's vassals.[30] Clearly, both Aubrey and Geoffrey changed the nature of the estate to which they succeeded by granting out large portions of the original core estate to their vassals, whilst bringing into demesne land which had not previously been there.

In general, the more important of William's tenants-in-chief appear to have kept up to two-thirds of their land in demesne, and used the remainder to enfeoff their men. Out of an estate valued at £770, Geoffrey de Mandeville had land worth £540 in demesne. Henry of Ferrers gave about 35 per cent of his land to his vassals. Sometimes the proportion held by subtenants was much greater: 60 per cent of William Peverel's estate (valued at £240 in all) was held by William's men. Tenants-in-chief holding medium-sized estates also tended to grant out a large proportion of their estates to subtenants: Picot, Sheriff of Cambridge, had land worth about £130, of which just less than half was held in demesne. Some of the lesser tenants-in-chief, such as Nigel Medicus (with £40 of land) had no subtenants, but this was not particularly common. Roger de Ramis, with land worth £50 in demesne, did have land worth £12 held from him by twelve different men.[31]

In short, whilst Domesday shows that in 1086 all significant tenants-in-chief had some proportion of their land held by subtenants, this was not true for the period before the Conquest. In the first place, the dependent men of pre-Conquest England did not usually hold their land from their lord (see Chapter 4). Secondly, Domesday records a number of important landholders who had not been able to

[29] *DB* i. 198, 199b.
[30] *DB* i. 199b.
[31] *DB* i. 130b; *DB* ii. 82b–83b, 263, 263b, 421b–423b.

attract a significant number of dependent men. It might be argued that commended men were not recorded for lords such as Wulfwine simply because the returns from their successor's fee did not mention them. However, no additional men commended to Wulfwine are recorded in the *ICC* either. As the *ICC* was produced on a regional, rather than a fee-by-fee basis, it seems likely that there were, indeed, almost no men under Wulfwine's commendation. There is a further reason for trusting Domesday's record. Where a pre-Conquest lord had a significant number of men commended to him, it was extremely rare for all of these dependents to be under the Saxon's Norman successor. Even although Count Alan inherited almost all of Eadgifu's land, and that of most of her men, nevertheless Picot the Sheriff, John fitz Waleran, Jocelyn the Breton, and Richard fitz Gilbert[32] (amongst others) held the land of at least some of her men. A single one of Wulfwine's men, Leodmær (a *villanus* who had land worth just 5*s*.), was under the lordship of Hardwin of Scales in 1086:[33] but this cannot be taken to suggest that much of the land assigned both in Domesday and the *ICC* to Wulfwine had in fact been held by his men. As for Toki, both arguments are equally valid; further, in Bedfordshire, Toki's successor William of Warenne recorded dependent relationships, so it is at least less likely that they would have been omitted in Cambridgeshire.[34]

It would appear that most of the post-Conquest tenants-in-chief in England had a number of landed tenants who could be called upon for support during a crisis. These men were bound to their lord because they held their land from him. Before 1066 only the most important nobles had such a body of landed supporters, and the ties binding man to lord were of a quite different nature, in some ways weaker, but in others actually stronger. Most pre-Conquest dependent men were free to take their commendation, and their land, to another lord, which presumably meant that their lords had to be more considerate in the treatment of their men. On the other hand, the pre-Conquest bond was a personal one, and a man at any one time generally had only a single lay lord to whom he owed his obligations. On the other hand, a Norman tenant might hold land

32 *DB* i. 152, 196b, 200b, 201, 201b.
33 *DB* i. 198.
34 In the return for William's land in Beds., Domesday records Augi, the man of Askell of Ware; Black, the man of Augi; and Godric, the man of the sheriff. *DB* i. 211b.

from more than one tenant-in-chief; indeed, like Picot the Sheriff, might be both tenant-in-chief and the tenant of various other lords simultaneously.

The difference in the relationship between lord and man has a bearing upon the change in the relative power of individuals at the very top of the lay hierarchy. King Edward's demesne lands were worth about £6,000, including the land of Queen Eadgyth. The family of Godwine had lands worth £5,000, and the family of Earl Leofric about half as much. The next richest layman was Beorhtric, Ælfgar's son, but his lands were worth only £560. There were just four other estates worth more than £300. In 1086, the value of the royal demesne had increased to £10,000. The estates of the king's two half-brothers were worth about £5,000 in total. Another nine lords, William fitz Osbern, Roger of Montgomery, William of Warenne, Count Alan, Earl Hugh of Chester, Eustace of Boulogne, Richard of Clare, the Bishop of Coutance, and Geoffrey de Mandeville all had estates worth more than £750. A further ten lords had estates worth more than £400. Because there were so many men of wealth and power at the top of society, and because the king himself had acquired so much extra wealth, the power of any individual or small group could be more easily curtailed if they rebelled against the king. Before the Conquest the wealth of the earlish families had been much closer to that of King Edward, whilst there were very few lords who had even the same order of wealth as the earls. Moreover, the power of the few lords at the top, and in particular the earls, was strengthened by the fact that they alone attracted the commendation of a significant number of thegns, whilst the administrative duties of the earls must also have increased their influence throughout their various earldoms.

Given this difference in the structure of the landholding classes, it is much easier to see why William was able to defeat all the rebellions which took place during his reign, even when the most powerful men in the kingdom were involved. Unless a very large number of men conspired against England, the King alone would have considerably more resources than the rebel, and this would be increased by the adherence of loyal tenants-in-chief. In contrast to this picture, the earls in the reign of Edward the Confessor appear to have had the power to act independently of the crown. The family of Earl Godwine was exiled in 1051, but was able to force its return the following year. Earl Ælfgar was twice exiled and each time was able to raise enough support to force his way back into England. The independence of the earlish families is emphasized by the fact that they were able to make marriage alliances even with Edward's enemies. Tostig married the half-sister of Baldwin of Flanders, who gave help to outlaws from England, whilst Ælfgar's daughter was married to the Welsh prince Gruffydd.[35]

In the Introduction it was noted that the narrative sources of Edward's reign pay almost no attention to the actions of laymen other than those who held the title of earl. The evidence of Domesday Book suggests that this was not a simple bias on the part of the chroniclers, but a reflection of the power of the earls relative to both the crown, of whom they were largely independent, and the lesser nobility whose wealth and influence was of a lesser order.

35 *Vita Edwardi*, 24–5; Orderic Vitalis, ii. 138, 216.

APPENDIX I

Lands Assigned to the Earls

The figures in these appendices are abstracted from Domesday. Wherever possible I have translated Domesday place-names to their modern equivalents, generally using H. C. Darby and G. R. Versey, *Domesday Gazetteer* (Cambridge, 1975). Where no identification has been made, the place-names are italicized. The values of entries held by the men of, or from, a lord have been placed in brackets to differentiate them from those which Domesday records as being held directly by the lord.

The order of entries is by county, following the order of Domesday Book; within each county, items held directly followed by items held from the lord; within that sequence, in the order in which entries are found in Domesday.

LAND ASSIGNED TO EARL GODWINE

Ref. (fos.)	Location	Value £	s.	d.	Notes
vol. i	*Kent*				
1	Dover	6	0	0	The third penny of the burgh
5b	Stoke	8	1	8	The Bishop of Rochester claimed this manor *TRE*, because Earl Godwine bought it from two men who held it from the bishop, and they did not inform the bishop of this sale. The bishop held the manor in 1086
8b	Hoo	60	0	0	
9b	Folkestone	110	0	0	
12	Fordwich	1	13	8	The earl's third penny from the burgh
14	Westerham	30	0	0	Earl Godwine held it from King Edward
	Boughton Aluph	20	0	0	
7	Laybourne	(8	0	0)	Thurgils held it from King Edward

Ref. (fos.)	Location	Value £	s.	d.	Notes
7b	Fairbourne	(4	0	0)	Alwin held it from Earl Godwine
	Shelborough	(1	0	0)	Alwin held it from Earl Godwine
8	Boughton Malherbe	(8	0	0)	Alwin held it from Earl Godwine
	Broomfield	(4	0	0)	Alwin held it from Earl Godwine
	Harbiton	(3	0	0)	Ælfric held it from Earl Godwine
9	Henhurst	(1	0	0)	Godwine held it from Earl Godwine
10	Stalisfield	(3	0	0)	Thurgils held it from Earl Godwine
11	Romney	(5	0	0)	Alsige held it from Earl Godwine
13	South Ashford	(1	5	0)	Thurgils held it from Earl Godwine
	Eastbridge	(10	0	0)	Alsige held it from Earl Godwine
	Sussex				
16	Bosham	40	0	0	
	Rotherfield	16	0	0	
18	Hooe	25	0	0	
19b	*Evebentone*	0	12	0	
20	Higham	5	0	0	
21	Tilton	3	10	0	Godwine held it from King Edward
	Tilton		17	0	Godwine held it from King Edward
	Willingdon	60	0	0	
21b	Hartfield Hundred	2	0	0	
	Frog Firle	3	0	0	
22	Laughton	15	0	0	
22b	Sheffield	5	0	0	*Godwin tenuit de rege Edwardo in alodium*
	Barkham	1	0	0	*Godwin comes tenuit de rege Edwardo sicut alodium*
	Maresfield	4	0	0	
23	Singleton	89	0	0	

Land to Earl Godwine (*cont.*):

Ref. (fos.)	Location	Value £	s.	d.	Notes
23b	Westbourne	30	0	0	Valued at 36 hides but only pays geld for 12
24	Stoughton	40	0	0	Valued at 36 hides but only pays geld for 15
	Marden	2	0	0	*Godwin tenuit in alodium*
24b	Angmering	2	0	0	
25	Climping	20	0	0	
	Climping	20	0	0	
27	Hurstpierpoint	36	0	0	
28b	Offington	1	6	8	It did not pay geld
29	Hoecourt	4	0	0	This land lay in the manor of Hurstpierpoint
17b	Uckham	(1	0	0)	Wulfbold held it from Earl Godwine
19b	Udimore	(7	0	0)	Algar held it from Earl Godwine
	Lidham	(1	0	0)	Leofræd held it from Earl Godwine
	Fairlight Hundred	(5	0	0)	Wulfmær held it from Earl Godwine
21	Ratton	(6	0	0)	Wulfhun held it from Earl Godwine
21b	Wilmington	(13	0	0)	A total of 14 hides: Alnoth had 8, Wulfnoth 4, and Wulfstan 2. All three held from King Edward
	Taring Neville	(8	0	0)	Azur held it from Earl Godwine
	Frog Firle	(1	10	0)	Hemming held it from Earl Godwine
23	Lavant	(8	0	0)	Alward held it from Earl Godwine
	Treyford	(5	0	0)	Ælfhard held it from Earl Godwine
	Chithurst	(2	0	0)	Almar held it from Earl Godwine
	Stedham	(15	0	0)	Eadgifu held it from Earl Godwine
23b	Buddington	(1	10	0)	Eadwine held it from Earl Godwine

Ref. (fos.)	Location	Value £	s.	d.	Notes
	Selham	(4	0	0)	Cuthwulf held it from Earl Godwine
	Todham	(2	0	0)	Wulfnoth held it from Earl Godwine
24	Compton (nr. Harting)	(8	0	0)	Asbiorn held it from Earl Godwine
	Mundham	(8	0	0)	Gytha *comitissa* held it from Earl Godwine
	West Itchenor	(1	0	0)	Leofwine held it from Earl Godwine
25b	Binsted	(1	0	0)	Heorowulf held it from Earl Godwine
	Binsted Hundred	(2	0	0)	Asgautr held it from Earl Godwine
	Binsted Hundred		(10	0)	Two Englishmen held it from Earl Godwine
	Binsted Hundred		(2	6)	Asgautr held it from Earl Godwine
	West Hampnett	(3	0	0)	Two freemen held it from Earl Godwine
26	Orleswick	(1	10	0)	Seven *alodiarii* held it from Earl Godwine
26b	Rottingdean	(2	0	0)	Hemming held it from Earl Godwine
	Brighton	(8	12	0)	Beorhtric held it from Earl Godwine
	Truleigh	(4	0	0)	Bædling held it from Earl Godwine
27	Poynings	(12	0	0)	Cola held it from Earl Godwine, because Godwine had given it to him. It never paid geld
	Saddlescombe	(15	0	0)	Godwine the priest held it from Earl Godwine
	Plumpton	(25	0	0)	Godwine the priest held it from Earl Godwine
27b	Barcombe	(12	0	0)	Azur held it from Earl Godwine
28	Wiston	(12	0	0)	Azur held it from Earl Godwine
	Chancton	(4	0	0)	Essocher held it from Earl Godwine

Land to Earl Godwine (*cont.*):

Ref. (fos.)	Location	Value £	s.	d.	Notes
28b	Applesham	(6	0	0)	Leofwine held it from Earl Godwine
	Worthing	(5	0	0)	Seven *alodiarii* held it from Earl Godwine
	Heene	(2	0	0)	Leofræd held it from Earl Godwine
	Chancton		(11	0)	Werun held it from Earl Godwine
29	Dankton	(3	12	0)	Auti held it from Earl Godwine
	Ashington	(1	10	0)	Two *alodiarii* held it from Earl Godwine
	Washington		(10	0)	Eadwine held it from Earl Godwine
	Eaton	(1	0	0)	Thurgot held it from Earl Godwine
	Surrey				
32	Southwark				The Earl had the third part of the income from the waterway where the ships were moored
36	Witley	15	0	0	
	Hampshire				
44b	Headley	8	6	8	
	Chalton	56	0	0	
38	Soberton	(3	0	0)	Leofman held it from Earl Godwine, but could not sell
38b	Over Wallop	(30	0	0)	Gytha *comitissa* held it from Earl Godwine
39b	Wolverton (IOW)		(10	0)	Eadgifu held it from Earl Godwine
	Wroxhall	(27	0	0)	Gytha *comitissa* held it from Earl Godwine
44	Funtley	(2	0	0)	Wulfweard held it from Earl Godwine, but he could not sell it
44b	Sunwood	(4	0	0)	Tunbi held it from Earl Godwine
	Hambledon	(1	0	0)	Edward held it from Earl Godwine but he could not sell

Ref. (fos.)	Location	Value £	s.	d.	Notes
45b	Buckland	(3	0	0)	Alweard held it from Earl Godwine *in alodium*
46b	Copnor	(3	0	0)	Tofi held it from Earl Godwine, but he could not sell
	Sutton Scotney	(6	0	0)	Tovi held it from Earl Godwine
49	Funtley	(4	0	0)	Thuri held it from Earl Godwine
49b	Sutton Scotney	(6	0	0)	Alweard held it from Earl Godwine
53	Bronchurch (IOW)	(1	10	0)	Ælfstan held it from Earl Godwine *in alodium*
	Wiltshire				
72b	Ugford	(1	10	0)	Earl Godwine siezed this land from St Mary's, Wilton, but it was recovered by Eadnoth
	Gloucestershire				
164	Woodchester	(7	0	0)	Earl Godwine bought this land from Azur and gave it to Gytha, his wife
	Worcestershire				
176b	Wychbold	(14	0	0)	
	Herefordshire				
186	Pembridge	(16	0	0)	The Canons of St Guthlac say that Godwine and his son Harold seized it unjustly

LAND ASSIGNED TO EARL HAROLD

vol. i	*Kent*				
6b	Greenwich	(4	0	0)	
6	Maplecombe	(3	0	0)	Wulfstan held it under Earl Harold
6b	Horton Kirby	(4	0	0)	Alweard held it under Earl Harold
9	Oakleigh	(2	0	0)	Hunnefr held it from Earl Harold

Land to Earl Harold (*cont.*):

Ref. (fos.)	Location	Value £	s.	d.	Notes
	Sussex				
17	Steyning	86	0	0	
18b	Crowhurst	8	0	0	
	Whatlington	2	10	0	
19	Tilton		5	0	
	Ripe		5	0	
	Ripe		4	0	
	Ripe	1	0	0	
21	Compton (West Firle)				This manor was valued with Laughton, a manor assigned to Earl Godwine
21b	*Wildene*	3	0	0	
	Parrock	2	12	0	Harold seized this manor from St John's
22	Ripe	12	0	0	
	Bogelie		15	0	
25b	Eastergate	4	0	0	
26	Rodmell	60	0	0	
	Patcham	50	0	0	
27	Fulking	2	10	0	
28	Findon	28	0	0	
	Tottingdon	6	0	0	
26	Lewes	13	0	0	This is half the value of the burgh: the King had the other half
21b	Rotherbridge Hundred		(10	0)	Thurkill held it from Earl Harold
28b	Shermanbury	(1	4	0)	Azur held it from Earl Harold
	Kingston by Sea	(15	0	0)	Azur held it from Earl Harold
	Kingston by Sea	(7	0	0)	Gunnhildr held it from Earl Harold
	Durrington	(2	0	0)	Wulfweard held it from Earl Harold
	Wantley	(2	0	0)	Beorhtmær held it from Azur, and Azur from Earl Harold
29	Cokeham	(2	15	0)	Grene held it from Earl Harold
	Surrey				
30	Bermondsey	15	0	0	
	Merton	25	0	0	

Ref. (fos.)	Location	Value £	s.	d.	Notes
30b	Gomshall	15	0	0	
32	Pyrford	12	0	0	Before Harold took this manor, it answered for 18 hides, afterwards for only 16, but no royal writ permitting this was ever seen
	Battersea	80	0	0	
34	Limpsfield	20	0	0	
	Ham (in Croydon)		9	0	
36b	Wotton	8	0	0	
31b	Peckham	(1	10	0)	Ælflet held it from Earl Harold
	Copthorne Hundred	(1	0	0)	Leofric held it freely from Earl Harold
	Copthorne Hundred	(1	0	0)	Elmar held it from Earl Harold and could sell
32	Ashstead	(10	0	0)	Thorgils held it from Earl Harold
	Ditton	(4	0	0)	Leofgar held it from Earl Harold, and gave service to him, but Leofgar could sell the land
34	Lambeth	(5	0	0)	The Canons of Waltham held it from Earl Harold
35b	Tadworth	(5	0	0)	Godtovi held it from Earl Harold
	Bookham	(2	10	0)	Godtovi held it from Earl Harold
36b	Wisley	(2	0	0)	Oswold held it from Earl Harold
	Hampshire				
38	Odiham	50	0	0	
38b	Over Wallop	20	0	0	
39	Quarley	12	0	0	
	Kern (IOW)	1	5	0	
	Heasley (IOW)	8	0	0	
44b	Bishop's Sutton	50	0	0	
	Preston Candover	(10	0	0)	Ælfric held it from Earl Harold *in alodium*
	Newtimber	(1	10	0)	Sigeræd held it from Earl Harold

Land to Earl Harold (*cont.*):

Ref. (fos.)	Location	Value £	s.	d.	Notes
45b	Brockhampton	(2	0	0)	Sigeræd held it from Earl Harold but he could not sell
46b	South Tidworth	(10	0	0)	Cuthwulf held it from Earl Harold *in alodium*
47	Silchester	(5	0	0)	Cypping held it from Earl Harold *in alodium*
	Ashe	(7	0	0)	Ælwacre held it from Earl Harold
	Berkshire				
57	Finchampstead	8	0	0	
57b	Great Farringdon	16	0	0	
	Great Coxwell	8	0	0	
	Steventon	25	0	0	
	Little Coxwell	16	0	0	
58	Aldermaston	20	10	0	
	Littleworth	30	0	0	
59b	Brightwalton	10	0	0	
60	Buscot	20	0	0	
62b	Clewer	7	0	0	
63b	*Liercote*	4	0	0	
58	Wokefield				Valued with Aldermaston. Beorhtweald held it by the gift of Earl Harold
	White Waltham	(3	0	0)	Wulfwine the Canon held it from Earl Harold; it pertained to the church of Waltham
59	Chilton				Blæchemann held it from Earl Harold *in alodium* and could sell
60	Drayton	(2	10	0)	Eadnoth held it from Earl Harold but he could not sell
	Wiltshire				
64b	Bath	5	0	0	
65	Compton	12	0	0	
	Melksham	111	11	0	
	Netheravon	40	0	0	
	Collingburne Ducis	40	0	0	
	Bromham	20	0	0	

Ref. (fos.)	Location	Value £	s.	d.	Notes
69	Allington (nr. Amesbury)	3	0	0	Unjustly seized from the church of Amesbury
	Allington (nr. Amesbury)				Not valued, but assessed at 4 hides
71	Chilton Foliat	1	10	0	
	Clyffe Pypard	1	10	0	
	Ogbourne	15	0	0	
	Luckington	5	0	0	
72b	Barford St Martin	3	0	0	
74b	Ratfyn	1	10	0	
	Dorset				
75	Child Okeford	10	0	0	
	Puddletown	73	0	0	The third penny of all the shire of Dorset pertained to this manor
	Charborough	9	0	0	
	Ibberton	10	0	0	
	Fleet	7	0	0	
75b	Chaldon	13	0	0	
	Loders	33	0	0	
78b	Bincombe	12	0	0	
	Stour	8	0	0	Harold seized this manor unjustly from Shaftesbury Abbey
82b	Tolpuddle	10	0	0	
83	Okeford Fitzpaine	16	0	0	
80	Islington	(1	0	0)	Eadnoth held it through (*per*) Earl Harold, who had taken it from a certain cleric
75b	Melcombe	(16	0	0)	Goda *comitissa* held it: Harold had taken it unjustly from St Mary's, Shaftesbury
	Somerset				
86b	Dulverton	11	10	0	
	Old Cleeve	23	0	0	Includes the third penny of 5 hundreds
	Capton	1	2	6	
	North Curry	23	0	0	
87	Congresbury	28	15	0	
	Henstridge	23	0	0	

Land to Earl Harold (*cont.*):

Ref. (fos.)	Location	Value £	s.	d.	Notes
88b	Lullington	4	0	0	
89b	Banwell	30	0	0	
92	Preston Bowyer	1	10	0	
97	Nether Stowey		12	0	
	Devonshire				
101	Bridestowe	3	0	0	
	Black Torrington	18	0	0	
	Holesworthy	12	0	0	
	Shebbear	18	0	0	
	Tavistock	24	0	0	
	High Bickington	4	0	0	
	Molland (W. Anstey)	24	0	0	Includes the third penny of 3 hundreds
	Morebath	7	0	0	
	Alphington	6	0	0	
	Topsham	6	0	0	
	Moretonhampstead	12	0	0	Includes the third penny of the hundred
	Colaton Raleigh	8	0	0	
	Broadhempston	2	0	0	
	Spitchwick	3	0	0	
	King's Nympton	18	0	0	
102	Fremington	12	0	0	
104	Dennington	2	0	0	
	Yarcombe	3	0	0	
	Cornwall				
120	Helston	8	0	0	
	Towan	5	0	0	
120b	Nancenuke	5	0	0	
120	Kilkhampton	18	0	0	
	Blisland	6	0	0	
	Pendrim	3	0	0	
	Caradon	7	0	0	
	Climsom	6	0	0	
	Callington	6	0	0	
	Roseworthy	4	0	0	
	Penheale	5	0	0	
	Winnianton	(20	10	0)	This land was assessed at 15 hides. 11 were held by

Ref. (fos.)	Location	Value £	s.	d.	Notes
					seventeen thegns who could not sell their land away from Harold
121	Trecknow		7	6	Harold seized the land unjustly from St Peter's
121b	Treglasta	8	0	0	
122	Halton	2	0	0	
123	Philleigh		10	0	
	Middlesex				
128b	Harmondsworth	25	0	0	
129	Feltham	4	13	4	
128b			(10	0)	Godwine, the man of Earl Harold, held it but could not sell
129	East Bedfont		(10	0)	Gouti, a housecarl of Earl Harold, held it and could sell
130	West Bedfont	(6	0	0)	Beorhtram, the man of Harold, held it
130b		(10	0	0)	Algar, the man of Harold, held it
	Hertfordshire				
132	Hertford				Eighteen burgesses were the men of Earl Harold and Earl Leofwine
	Wymondley				Valued in Hitchen. It had belonged to the demesne of Chatteris, but Harold took it and placed it in Hitchen three years before King Edward's death
133	Hitchen	100	0	0	Of the value, £60 was from Hitchen and £40 from the sokemen who were attached to it
138	Amwell	18	0	0	
132b	King's Walden	(2	0	0)	Leofgifu held it from Earl Harold
	King's Walden	(8	0	0)	A widow, the man of Asgeir, held it *TRE* from Earl Harold and could sell

Land to Earl Harold (*cont.*):

Ref. (fos.)	Location	Value £	s.	d.	Notes
132b	Temple Deansley	(10	0	0)	Two sokemen held this from Earl Harold as two manors, which they could sell
	Great Offley	(5	4	0)	Five sokemen held this from Earl Harold and could sell
133	Wellbury	(3	0	0)	Leofgifu held it from Earl Harold
	Wain Wood	(1	10	0)	Godwine, the man of Earl Harold, held it and could sell
	Wain Wood		(16	0)	Eadmund, the man of Earl Harold, held it and could sell
	Hexton		(3	4)	A sokeman, the man of the Abbot of St Albans, held it and could sell. Harold placed this land in Hitchen wrongly, and by force
134b	Eckington		(15	0)	A man of Earl Harold held it and could sell
	Rye	(1	10	0)	Swein, the man of Earl Harold, held it
136b	Berkhamstead	(24	0	0)	Eadmær, a thegn of Harold, held it
137	Reed	(4	0	0)	Alweard, the man of Earl Harold, held it
	Anstey	(15	0	0)	Alweard, a thegn of Harold, held it
	Cornbury		(5	0)	Alweard, the man of Earl Harold, held it and could sell
137b	Wakeley		(5	0)	Alweard, the man of Earl Harold, held it and could sell
	Cockhampstead	(7	0	0)	Gauti, a thegn of Harold, held it and could sell
	Berkesdon	(5	0	0)	Alweard, the man of Earl Harold, held it and could sell
138	Westmill	(20	0	0)	Aki, a thegn of Earl Harold, held it and could sell
138b	Hertingfordbury	(10	0	0)	Alwin, a thegn of Earl Harold, held it and could sell

Ref. (fos.)	Location	Value £	s.	d.	Notes
139	Munden	(8	0	0)	Leofwine, the man of Earl Harold, held it and could sell
140	Langley	(1	10	0)	Swein, the man of Earl Harold, held it and could sell
	Lilley	(7	0	0)	Leofgifu held it from Earl Harold
	Hailey	(4	0	0)	Wulfwine, the man of Earl Harold, held it
	Eastwick	(4	0	0)	Wulfwine, the man of Earl Harold, held it and could sell
140b	Wymondley	(3	0	0)	Swein, the man of Earl Harold, held it and could sell
	Graveley	(2	0	0)	Swein, the man of Earl Harold, held it and could sell
141	Sacombe	(2	0	0)	Leofwine, the man of Earl Harold, held it and could sell
141b	Reed	(5	0	0)	Sigeræd, the man of Earl Harold, held it and could sell
	Barley		(15	0)	A man of Earl Harold held it and could sell
	Wyddial	(2	10	0)	Sigeræd, the man of Earl Harold, held it and could sell
142	Bramfield	(5	0	0)	Aki, the thegn of Earl Harold, held it and could sell
142b	Hoddesdon	(6	0	0)	Leofwine, the man of Earl Harold, held it and could sell
	Buckinghamshire				
143b	Risborough	10	0	0	
	Swanbourne	1	10	0	
	Upton (in Slough)	15	0	0	
144	Wooburn	12	0	0	
148b	Ellesborough	9	0	0	
144	Buckland		(5	0)	Leofric, the man of Earl Harold, held it and could sell
	Chesham	(1	10	0)	A sokeman of Earl Harold held it
	Taplow	(9	0	0)	Asgautr, a man of Earl Harold, held it
146	Wing	(32	0	0)	Eadweard Cilt, the man of Earl Harold, held it and could sell

Land to Earl Harold (*cont.*):

Ref. (fos.)	Location	Value £	s.	d.	Notes
146	Hardwick	(2	0	0)	Sæward, the man of Earl Harold, held it
	Burston		(5	0)	Siweard, the man of Earl Harold, held it
	Ickford	(7	0	0)	Ulf, the man of Earl Harold, held it
	Horsenden	(3	10	0)	Two sokemen of Earl Harold held it
146b	Swanbourne	(1	10	0)	Almar, the man of Earl Harold, held it
	Wavendon	(2	0	0)	Beorhtwine, the man of Harold, held it
148b	Ditton	(2	0	0)	Sigeræd, the man of Earl Harold, held it and could sell
	Stoke Poges	(6	0	0)	Sigeræd, the man of Earl Harold, held it and could sell
150	Chearsley	(1	2	0)	Halfdan, the man of Earl Harold, held it and could sell
	Saunderton	(6	0	0)	Alric, the man of Harold, held it and could sell
150b	Mursley Hundred	(1	0	0)	Sweinic, the man of Earl Harold, held it and could sell
151b	Twyford	(2	0	0)	A man of Earl Harold held it and could sell
	Charndon	(9	0	0)	Eingar, the man of Earl Harold, held it and could sell
152	Wolverton	(10	0	0)	A man of Earl Harold held it and could sell
	Shenley Brook End	(2	0	0)	Morcar, the man of Earl Harold, held it and could sell
152b	Datchett	(6	0	0)	Siweard, the man of Earl Harold, held it
	Boveney	(3	0	0)	Siweard, the man of Earl Harold, held it
	Oxfordshire				
154b	Langford	18	0	0	
	Shipton under Wychwood	10	0	0	

Ref. (fos.)	Location	Value £	s.	d.	Notes
157	Crowmarsh	6	0	0	
	Churchill	10	0	0	
160b	Shipton under Wychwood	2	0	0	
	Gloucestershire				
162b	Winchcombe	2	0	0	The earl's third penny of the burgh
163	Alveston	12	0	0	
164	Ness	7	0	0	
166b	Chipping Campden	30	0	0	
168	Bromsberrow	8	0	0	
164	Ashton under Hill	(30	0	0)	Thorbert, a thegn of Earl Harold, held it
	Hempsted	(3	0	0)	Eadric Lang, a thegn of Harold, held it
	Barrington	(7	0	0)	Tofi Widnesci, a housecarl of Earl Harold, held it
165	Oldland	(4	0	0)	Alwig, the man of Harold, held it
	Stoke Gifford	(2	0	0)	Ealdred, the man of Earl Harold, held it and could sell
167b	Oxenhall	(2	0	0)	Thurkill held it from Earl Harold
168b	Rodmarton	(1	10	0)	Leofwine held it from Earl Harold
	Brimpsfield	(12	0	0)	Duns held it from Earl Harold
169	Kempsford	(30	0	0)	Osgod held it from Earl Harold
169b	Weston Subedge	(2	10	0)	A man of Earl Harold held it
	Worcestershire				
174	Inkberrow	12	0	0	Harold held it unjustly and King William restored it to the Bishop of Hereford
	Herefordshire				
176	Hereford	6	0	0	The earl's third penny from the burgh. Harold also had twenty-seven burgesses there
179b	Much Marcle	30	0	0	
	Cleeve and Wilton	9	10	0	

Land to Earl Harold (*cont.*):

Ref. (fos.)	Location	Value £	s.	d.	Notes
181	Elvastone	1	10	0	Lay in Archenfield
	Old Radnor				Waste
	Mateurdin				Waste
	Eardisley				Waste
	Chickward				Waste
	Welso and five other vills				Waste
181b	Llanwarne				Harold held it unjustly from the Bishop of Hereford
	Easton Bishop	4	0	0	
182	Coddington	2	5	0	Harold held it unjustly from the Bishop of Hereford
	Hampton Bishop	5	0	0	Harold held it unjustly from the Bishop of Hereford
	Sugwas	1	3	0	Harold held it unjustly from the Bishop of Hereford
182b	Collington and Bridge Sollers	4	0	0	Harold held them unjustly from the Bishop of Hereford
183	Willersley and Winforton				Waste
183	Monnington on Wye	3	0	0	
185b	Rushock				Waste
186	Burghill	20	0	0	Includes the third penny of 2 hundreds. This manor and Hope Sollers
	Hope Sollers	8	0	0	were held by Godwine and Harold in 1051; during their exile they were given to Osbern, the uncle of Alfred of Marlborough
	Monnington in Vowchurch				Waste
	Breadwardine				Waste
	Eaton in Foy	2	10	0	
	Pembridge (Leominster)	16	0	0	Godwine and Harold took it from St Guthlac's
	Strettford	1	10	0	
	Much Cowarne	25	0	0	Includes the third penny of 3 hundreds

Ref. (fos.)	Location	Value £	s.	d.	Notes
186b	Clehanger				Waste
	Dorstone	2	10	0	
	Titley				Waste
187	Middlewood (in Clifford)				Waste
	Ailey				Waste
	Eardisley				Waste
	Chickward				Waste
187b	*Mateurdin*				Waste
	Curdeslege				Waste
182	Colwall	(3	0	0)	Harold held it unjustly, and Thurmod from him
	Hazle	(1	5	0)	Harold held this unjustly, and Godric from him
184	Yarkhill	(2	10	0)	Arkil held it from Earl Harold
	Castle Frome	(3	10	0)	Beorhtmær held it from Earl Harold
	Lyde	(1	0	0)	Thurkill held it from Earl Harold
184b	Little Marcle	(5	0	0)	Thurkill held it from Earl Harold
	Evesbatch	(1	8	0)	Elmar, Ælfric, and Thurkill held this land as three manors from Earl Harold, and could sell
	Birley	(1	10	0)	Seric, a thegn of Earl Harold held it. It did not pay geld
	Mansell	(7	0	0)	Elflæd held it from Earl Harold
	Lyonshall	(3	0	0)	Thurkill held it from Earl Harold
185b	Stretton Grandiston	(9	0	0)	Thurkill held it from Earl Harold
	Whitwick	(1	0	0)	Thurkill held it from Earl Harold
	Ashperton	(5	10	0)	Wulfwig, the man of Earl Harold, held it and could sell
186b	Ashperton	(1	0	0)	Earnwig, a thegn of Earl Harold, held it and could sell
	Cambridgeshire				
190	Shelford	4	0	0	

Land to Earl Harold (*cont.*):

Ref. (fos.)	Location	Value £	s.	d.	Notes
196	Bottisham	12	16	0	
202	Kirtling	18	0	0	
	Carlton	2	0	0	
190	Hinxton	(4	0	0)	Siweard held it from Earl Harold
190b	Childerley	(5	0	0)	Siweard, the man of Harold, held it
193	Sawston	(6	0	0)	Ordgar held it under Harold
195b	Dullingham		(15	0)	Vikingr, the man of Harold, held it
196	Barrington		(10	0)	Aki, the man of Earl Harold, held it and could sell
	Orwell		(2	0)	Aki, the man of Harold, held it
196b	Camps	(2	0	0)	Lefsig, the man of Harold, held it
197b	Westley Waterless		(1	4)	Two sokemen of Harold held it
	Carlton		(8	0)	Two sokemen of Harold held it
198	Weston Colville		(5	0)	Two sokemen of Harold held it; they could not sell
	Shelford		(5	0)	Two sokemen of Harold held it; they could not sell
200	Harston	(6	0	0)	Ordgar, the man of Earl Harold, held it and could sell
202	Westley Waterless	(1	0	0)	Two men of Harold held it but they could not sell
	Huntingdonshire				
207	Hail Weston	(6	0	0)	Wulfwine Chit held it: he was the man of Earl Harold (208)
	Bedfordshire				
212b	Stagsden	(1	13	4)	A man of Earl Harold held it and could sell
216	Shirdon		(2	0)	Alwin, the man of Earl Harold, held it and could sell
216b	Riseley	(1	0	0)	Homdei, the man of Earl Harold, held it and could sell
217	Oakley	(1	0	0)	Godwine, the man of Earl Harold, held it and could sell

Ref. (fos.)	Location	Value £	s.	d.	Notes
	Bromham		(10	0)	Godwine, the man of Earl Harold, held it and could sell
	Leicestershire				
237	Barrow upon Soar, Theddingworth, and Kegworth	40	0	0	
	Staffordshire				
246	King's Bromley	5	0	0	
	Shropshire				
257	Whitchurch	8	0	0	
	Cheshire				
265b	Marbury (nr. Nantwich)	1	3	0	A berewick of Whitchurch, Salop.
	Nottinghamshire				
282b	Sutton Bonnington	2	0	0	
	Bonnington	1	0	0	
	Rutland				
293b	Ashwell	5	0	0	
	Yorkshire				
298b	Yorkshire				Earl Harold had *sac*, *soc*, toll, and team
305	Flamborough	24	0	0	
	Catton	28	0	0	
317	Rothwell	5	0	0	
321	Conisborough	18	0	0	
323b	Cleeton	32	0	0	
325	Wilsthorpe				Waste
	Lincolnshire				
336	Lincoln				Earl Harold had three manses in the town
337	Lincolnshire				Earl Harold had *sac* and *soc*
349	Grantham	40	0	0	Plus half a mark of gold. It did not pay geld
	West Halton	19	0	0	
	Barnetby le Wold	14	0	0	
349b	Waddington	100	0	0	

Land to Earl Harold (*cont.*):

Ref. (fos.)	Location	Value £	s.	d.	Notes
349b	Ashwell (Rutland)	5	0	0	
	Fulletby	2	0	0	
	Tathwell	15	0	0	
351b	Carlton Scroop	6	0	0	
377	Long Bennington				Pertains to Carlton Scroop
vol. ii	*Essex*				
1b	Benfleet	8	0	0	
	Witham	10	0	0	
2	Hatfield Broad Oak	36	0	0	
2b	Havering-atte-Bower	36	0	0	
4b	Stanway	22	0	0	
5	Woolston	1	0	0	
	Fingrith	4	0	0	
	Writtle	10	0	0	And ten night's farm
6	Brightlingsea				Two night's farm
	Lawford				Two night's farm
7	Newport				Two night's farm
	Ricling	8	0	0	
14b	Feering	22	0	0	
15	Ockendon	4	0	0	
15b	Waltham Holy Cross	36	0	0	
26	Writtle	1	5	0	
26b	Nuttley	10	0	0	
27	Witham	1	0	0	
	Rivenhall	3	0	0	
31	St Lawrence	5	0	0	
32b	Frinton	3	0	0	
55	Ryes		10	0	Belongs to Hatfield
63	Thurrock	12	0	0	
84	Nutley	7	0	0	
85	Leyton	4	0	0	
90b	Chigwell	8	0	0	Harold held it from King Edward
95	Witham	1	0	0	
106b	Colchester				Harold had three houses *ad ferigens*
26b	Gravesend		(10	0)	Harold held it, and Ingelric from him

Ref. (fos.)	Location	Value £	s.	d.	Notes
54b	*Ateleia*	(1	0	0)	Gauti held it from Harold
55	Roding	(4	0	0)	Vidi held it from Earl Harold
59	Leighs	(4	0	0)	Asgeir the Staller gave it to Harold, and Harold gave it to a housecarl named Skalpi
61	Shellow Bowells	(4	0	0)	Wulfric, a freeman, held it from Harold
75	Plunkers Green		(5	0)	Wulfric the priest held it from Harold
101	Bollington	(4	0	0)	Godwine, a freeman, held it from Harold
	Norfolk				
109b	Massingham	2	0	0	
	Southmere	7	0	0	
111	Fakenham	8	0	0	
113	Walsingham				Valued with Fakenham
114b	Cawston	30	0	0	
	Taverham				Valued with Cawston
144	*Clareia*		6	0	
196b	Blickling	6	0	0	
	Marsham	6	0	0	
235b	Necton				Six night's farm
	Carbrooke and Acre				Berewicks of Necton
236b	Wretham				Berewick of Necton
110	Caston, Breckles, and Griston	(2	13	0)	Twelve freemen of Harold held it
113b	Martham		(2	0)	A freeman commended to Harold held it
115	Wickmere, Martham, Blickling, and Saxlingham				Thirty freemen commended to Harold held it. Valued with Cawston
116	Norwich				Thirty-two burgesses commended to Harold, of whom one could not separate himself from his lord
127	Roudham	(1	0	0)	A freeman held it under Harold
129b	Winfarthing	(2	0	0)	Algar, a freeman of Harold, held it
145b	Flockthorpe		(5	0)	A sokeman of Harold held it
	Bale		(3	0)	A freeman of Harold held it

Land to Earl Harold (*cont.*):

Ref. (fos.)	Location	Value £	s.	d.	Notes
146	Field Dalling		(2	0)	A sokeman of Harold held it
146b	Somerton	(5	0	0)	Ælfric, the man of Harold, held it
147	Briningham		(10	0)	Thorbern, a freeman commended to Harold, held it
148	Saxthorpe	(1	0	0)	A freeman of Harold held it
150b	Dunston		(8	0)	A freeman of Harold held it
151	Massingham	(2	10	0)	Twenty sokemen of Harold held it
158	Itteringham		(3	0)	A freeman of Harold held it
	Wickmere		(5	0)	A freewoman of Harold held it
	Little Barningham		(13	4)	Two freemen of Harold held it
158b	Brampton		(3	0)	The sokemen of Harold held it
	Irmingland		(10	0)	A sokeman of Harold held it
161b	Massingham		(15	0)	Ælflæd, a freewoman held it; she was commended to Tovi, the *antecessor* of William Warenne, but Harold had the soke
162b	Colveston		(8	0)	A freeman of Harold held it
	Munford		(10	0)	A freeman of Harold held it
163	Cranwich	(3	0	0)	A freeman of Harold held it
167	Yelverton				A freeman commended to Harold held it
171	Trunch		(10	0)	A freeman of Harold held it
172b	North Barsham				Two freemen of Harold held land which pertained to Fakenham
181b	Hales	(1	0	0)	Æthelstan, a thegn of Harold, held it
183b	Titchwell		(13	4)	Tofi, a freeman, held it under Harold
184	Hempton		(5	0)	A freeman of Harold held it
184b	Suffield	(2	0	0)	Two freemen of Harold held it
185	Aldborough		(15	0)	Four freemen of Harold held it
186b	Broome		(10	0)	Toka, a freeman commended to Harold, held it
	Erpingham and Thorpe		(14	0)	Four freemen of Harold held it

Ref. (fos.)	Location	Value £	s.	d.	Notes
	Alby	(1	0	0)	Osferth held it as a manor under Harold
187	*Torp*		(4	0)	A freeman of Harold held it
190	Bexwell		(2	8)	A freeman held it under Harold
197b	Saxlingham	(1	0	0)	Harold held two freemen here
198	Blakeney	(2	0	0)	Eadric held it under King Edward, freely from Harold
	Briningham	(2	10	0)	Four freemen of Harold held it
	Melton Constable	(1	10	0)	Four freemen of Harold held it
235b	Fransham, Dunham, Ickburgh, and Breckles				Valued with Necton. Nineteen of Harold's sokemen held it
236	Acre				Valued with Necton. Thorbern held this land under Harold
239b	Tunstall	(2	0	0)	Escule the man of Harold held it
241b	Stratton Strawless	(2	0	0)	Nineteen of Harold's sokemen held it
	Hevingham	(1	10	0)	Twenty-nine of Harold's sokemen held it
242b	Blakeney		(5	0)	Toka held it under Harold
244	Tunstead	(5	0	0)	Ælfhere, a thegn of Harold, held it
244b	Shernbourne	(2	0	0)	Sixteen freemen whom Harold held
245b	Hillington	(4	0	0)	Godric held it under Harold
250	Wheatacre	(1	10	0)	A freeman of Harold held it
252b	Wellingham	(1	0	0)	A freeman of Harold held it
253	Chedgrave	(1	10	0)	Leofric, a freeman commended to Harold held it
257b	Gunthorpe		(10	0)	A freeman of Harold held it
258b	Sandringham	(1	0	0)	A freeman commended to Harold held it
	Saxlingham		(16	0)	Leofwold, a freeman commended to Harold, held it
260b	Erpingham		(10	0)	Bundi, a freeman commended to Harold, held it
261	Edgefield	(1	10	0)	Bundi, a freeman commended to Harold, held it
	Stody	(1	10	0)	A freeman commended to Harold held it

Land to Earl Harold (*cont.*):

Ref. (fos.)	Location	Value £	s.	d.	Notes
261b	Booton		(10	0)	A sokeman of Harold held it
263	Osmondiston	(2	0	0)	Algar held it under Harold
264b	Holkham	(1	6	8)	Two freemen commended to Harold held it
268	*Wanelund*	(2	10	0)	Ælfric, a thegn of Harold, held it
	Scoulton	(2	10	0)	A freeman held it under Harold
277b	Somerton				A freeman of Harold held it
278b	Shernbourne		(6	8)	A freeman of Harold held it
279	Weybourne	(7	0	0)	Twelve and a half freemen commended to Harold held it
	Woodbastwick		(2	0)	Four freemen commended to Harold held it
	Suffolk				
286b	Harkstead	6	0	0	A berewick of Brightlingsea, Essex
287	Bergholt	24	0	0	Includes the third penny of $1\frac{1}{2}$ hundreds. 210 sokemen were attached to this manor
292	Bucklesham	(3	0	0)	Thirty freemen commended to Harold held it
	Alston		(2	8)	A freeman commended to Harold held it
	Grimston		(3	4)	Ælfric, a freeman commended to Harold, held it
300	Grundisburgh		(10	0)	A freeman commended to Harold held it
305b	Henley			(8)	A freeman commended to Stanwine held it under Harold
	Henley			(8)	A freeman commended to Stanwine held it under Harold
313	Peasenhall		(12	0)	Stanwine held it. He was commended first to Eadric then to Harold
320	Eye	(1	0	0)	Swartric, a freeman commended to Harold, held it
323b	Braiseworth		(5	0)	Beorhtmær Bubba, a freeman of Harold, held it

Ref. (fos.)	Location	Value £	s.	d.	Notes
332	Heveningham	(2	0	0)	Stanwine, a freeman commended to Harold, held it
336b	Battisford		(1	8)	Godric, commended to Harold, held it
339	Bruisyard	(1	0	0)	Wulfric, commended to Harold, held it
342b	Stratton		(5	0)	A freeman of Harold held it
341b	Langer		(1	8)	Ælfnoth, a man of Harold, held it
343	Norton	(1	14	0)	Godwine the priest, a freeman of Harold, held it
345	Swefling		(15	0)	Wulfric, a freeman, held it under Harold
346	Culpho		(10	0)	Godric, a freeman, held it under Harold
346b	Clopton	(2	0	0)	Wulfric, a freeman commended to Harold, held it
347	Otley	(5	0	0)	Ælfric, a freeman, held it under Harold
348	Wickham Skeith		(3	0)	One whole and three half freemen commended to Harold held it
	Wickham Skeith	(5	0	0)	Ælflæd, commended to Harold, held it
351	Stonham	(5	0	0)	Ælflæd, commended to Harold, held it
351b	Wilisham	(4	0	0)	Ælflæd, a freewoman commended to Harold, held it
350	Waldingfield	(1	10	0)	Wulfmær, a thegn of Harold, held it
	Stonham	(5	0	0)	Wulfmær, a thegn commended to Harold, held it
373	Seckford	(4	0	0)	Ælfric the son of Wulfgeat, the man of Harold, held it
377b	Wenham	(3	0	0)	Tuneman, a thegn of King Edward, who was commended to Harold, held it
381	Freckenham	(12	0	0)	Orth, a thegn of Harold's, held it
402b	Beyton	(3	0	0)	Godric, a thegn commended to Harold, held it

Land to Earl Harold (*cont.*):

Ref. (fos.)	Location	Value £	s.	d.	Notes
404b	Henley	(4	0	0)	Tepechin, a freeman commended to Harold, held it
406b	Crettingham	(5	0	0)	Ælfric, a freeman, held it from Harold
407	Crettingham		(19	0)	Nine freemen commended to Harold held it
412	Letheringham	(1	0	0)	Halfdan, a freeman commended to Harold, held it
	Shadingfield		(10	0)	Halfdan, a freeman commended to Harold, held it
419b	*Cercesfort*	(3	0	0)	Skalpi, a thegn of Harold, held it
423b	Burgh (Walton)		(3	0)	Godric, commended to one himself commended to Harold, held it
	Tuddenham (nr. Ipswich)			(4)	A freeman commended to Harold held it
425b	*Barchestuna*	(1	0	0)	Tepechin, a freeman commended to Harold, held it
426b	Bacton	(8	0	0)	Leofwine, a freeman of Harold, held it
	Cavendish	(1	0	0)	Ælfwold, a freeman of Harold, held it
428	Haughton	(4	0	0)	Uhtræd held it under Harold
428b	Newton (nr. Sudbury)	(2	0	0)	Uhtræd held it under Harold
	Bedingfield	(1	10	0)	Ælfric held it under Harold
429	Framlingham		(15	0)	Beorhtmær, a freeman, held it under Harold
432	Layham	(3	10	0)	Ælfnoth held it from Harold
	Sotherton	(2	0	0)	Rudda, a freeman commended to Harold, held it
435b	Bures		(5	0)	Two freemen held it under Harold and could sell
441	Grundisburgh		(16	0)	Godric, a freeman of Harold, held it
	Chippenhall		(10	0)	A freeman held it under Harold
441b	Grundisburgh				Three half freemen commended to Harold held it

Ref. (fos.)	Location	Value £	s.	d.	Notes
443	Martley	(2	0	0)	Beorhtmær, commended to Harold, held it
444	Easton Bavants	(2	0	0)	Ælfric the son of Wulfgeat, commended to Harold, held it
	Chediston		(4	0)	Godric, a freeman of Harold, held it
	Easton Bavants		(8	0)	Osketel and Godric, freemen of Harold, held it

LAND ASSIGNED TO EARL TOSTIG

vol. i	*Sussex*				
24	Fishbourne	6	0	0	
	Hampshire				
39	Holdenhurst	44	0	0	
	Ringwood	24	0	0	
47	Polhampton	12	0	0	
48	Winkton	10	0	0	Earl Tostig held it *in alodium* from King Edward
52	Brook (IOW)	7	0	0	
	Compton	6	0	0	
	Afton (IOW)	10	0	0	
	Freshwater (IOW)	16	0	0	
53b	Thorley (IOW)	8	0	0	
39b	Nunwell	(3	0	0)	Wulfgeat held it from Earl Tostig, but it was not *in alodium*
50b	Arnewood	(1	10	0)	Siweard held it from Earl Tostig
	Freshwater (IOW)	(2	0	0)	A reeve of Tostig held it in the manor of Freshwater
	Berkshire				
60	Hanney	10	0	0	
	Wiltshire				
65	Corsham	30	0	0	
71b	Maiden Bradley	12	0	0	
	Somerset				
86b	Winsford	10	10	0	

Land to Earl Tostig (*cont.*):

Ref. (fos.)	Location	Value £	s.	d.	Notes
	Hertfordshire				
133	Bayford	20	0	0	Earl Tostig held this manor but King Edward had it *in dominio* on the day on which he was alive and dead
	Buckinghamshire				
143b	Haddenham	40	0	0	
147	Brickhill	10	0	0	
	Fawley	6	0	0	
144	Weston Turville	(1	10	0)	A man of Earl Tostig held it
145b	Crafton	(4	0	0)	Blæchemann, the man of Earl Tostig, held it but could not sell
145b	Brickhill	(4	0	0)	Blæcheman the man of Earl Tostig held it and could sell
148	Caversfield (Oxon.)	(5	0	0)	Edward, the man of Tostig, held it and could sell
148b	Marston		(5	8)	Beorhtwine, the man of Earl Tostig, held it and could sell
152	Aston Sandford	(5	0	0)	Sorting, a man of Earl Tostig, held it
	Oxfordshire				
154b	Bloxham and Adderbury	56	0	0	Earl Eadwine held it *TRE*, but the entry also speaks of events 'in the time of Earl Tostig'
157b	Stoke Lynn	10	0	0	
	Gloucestershire				
168b	Eastleach	12	0	0	
166b	Driffield	(8	0	0)	Ecglaf held it from Earl Tostig
	Herefordshire				
184	Halmond's Frome	3	0	0	Tostig held it from Queen Eadgyth
	Cambridgeshire				
202	Tadlow	(2	0	0)	Thurkill, a priest of Earl Tostig, held it
	Trumpington	(5	0	0)	Normann held it from Earl Tostig and could sell

Ref. (fos.)	Location	Value £	s.	d.	Notes
	Huntingdonshire				
205b	Buckworth	10	0	0	
206	Cotton	2	0	0	
208					Elgar held land from Earl Tostig and later Earl Waltheof
	Bedfordshire				
217b	Potton		2	0	
	Potton	13	0	0	This manor was held by King Edward *TRE*, but it had been Earl Tostig's
	Cockayne Hatley	6	0	0	
	Everton	5	0	0	
	Chalton	12	0	0	This manor was held by King Edward *TRE*, but it had been Earl Tostig's
213b	Eastwick	(1	0	0)	Leodmær, a man of Earl Tostig, held it
214	Clophill	(8	0	0)	Two thegns, the men of Earl Tostig, held it
216b	Little Staughton		(12	0)	Stori the man of Tostig held it
	Beeston	(1	0	0)	Godwine the man of Earl Tostig held it and could sell
	Wootton	(10	15	0)	Almar the man of Tostig held it
	Shelton (in Marston Moretaine)	(2	5	0)	Almar the man of Tostig held it; it was a member of Wootton
217	Houghton Conquest	(2	0	0)	Leofsige the man of Tostig held it but could not sell
217b	Cardington	(2	0	0)	Azelin the man of Tostig held it but could not sell
	Harrowden	(2	0	0)	Azelin the man of Tostig held it but could not sell
218b	Postgrove		(10	0)	Oswig the man of Tostig held it and could sell
	Northamptonshire				
225	Pottersbury	6	0	0	
226b	Warden Hundred	5	0	0	
228	Towcester Hundred	6	0	0	
	Nottinghamshire				
280	Nottingham				Unvalued: assessed at 1 carucate

Land to Earl Tostig (*cont.*):

Ref. (fos.)	Location	Value £	s.	d.	Notes
281b	Bothamshall	8	0	0	Tostig had soke in Kirton, Lincs.
286	Bingham	10	0	0	
	Yorkshire				
299	Falsgrave	56	0	0	
	Hemingborough	2	0	0	
301b	Preston				Waste
	Halton (Lancs.)				Waste
	Whittington (Lancs.)				Waste
	Millom (Cumberland)				Waste
307b	Hexthorpe	18	0	0	
323b	Burstwick	56	0	0	
332	Grindleton				Unvalued: assessed at 4 carucates
	Beetham (Westmorland)				Unvalued: assessed at 6 carucates

LAND ASSIGNED TO EARL GYRTH

Ref. (fos.)	Location	Value £	s.	d.	Notes
vol. i	*Sussex*				
25b	Merston	5	0	0	Gyrth held it from King Edward
28	Washington	50	0	0	
28b	Coombe	12	0	0	
	Hampshire				
47b	Hartley Maudit	8	0	0	
	Berkshire				
61	Eaton Hastings	10	0	0	Gyrth held it from King Edward *in alodium*
59b	Chaddleworth	(7	0	0)	A freeman held it from Gyrth
	Hertfordshire				
138	Alswick	(8	0	0)	Almar the man of Earl Gyrth held it and could sell
138b	Ware				Unvalued. A sokeman of Gyrth held half a hide

Ref. (fos.)	Location	Value £	s.	d.	Notes
141b	Barley	(1	10	0)	A man of Gyrth held it
	Berkesdon		(5	0)	A man of Earl Gyrth held it and could sell
	Cambridgeshire				
197b	Clopton	2	0	0	
	Croydon	2	0	0	
	Wimpole	5	0	0	
202	Whittlesford	15	0	0	
198	Whittlesford		(2	8)	A man of Earl Gyrth held it and could not sell
	Shelford		(12	0)	Three sokemen held it from Gyrth and could not sell it
200b	Hatley		(5	0)	A sokeman of Gyrth held it
202	Babraham		(4	0)	Leofmær held it from Gyrth, but could not sell it
	Bedfordshire				
217	Kempston	30	0	0	
217b	Shelton (in Marston Moretaine)		(10	0)	Godwine, a man of Gyrth, held it and could sell
vol. ii	*Essex*				
10b	Warley	6	0	0	
	Norfolk				
132	Aylsham	12	0	0	
144b	Costessey	20	0	0	
145	Wramplingham	1	0	0	
193b	Sedgeford	16	0	0	
194	Langham	8	0	0	
210	Brooke	10	0	0	
257	Great Ryborough	4	0	0	
115b	Ormesby	10	0	0	Gyrth held it. 1 acre was held from Ramsey
113b	Martham		(2	0)	One freeman commended to Earl Gyrth held it
	Clippesby		(2	6)	A freeman commended to Earl Gyrth held it. It was always in Ormesby
116	Runham		(4	0)	Four freemen of Gyrth held it: it returned 4*s*. to Ormesby

Land to Earl Gyrth (*cont.*):

Ref. (fos.)	Location	Value £	s.	d.	Notes
116	Gillingham				Two freemen of Gyrth held it; it is valued with Gorleston (Suffolk)
128	Morston		(3	6)	A freeman of Gyrth held it: it lay in Stiffkey
129	South Walsham				Not valued. 1 carucate was held by one freeman of Gyrth's.
133	Crackford				1 carucate was held by one freeman of Gyrth. Valued in Aylsham
	Itteringham				A free man commended to Earl Gyrth held 1 carucate, valued in Aylsham
	East Tuddenham				Ten sokemen of Gyrth held 42 acres, valued in Costessey
145b	*Appetorp*				Three sokemen of Gyrth held 54 acres, valued in Costessey
147b	Attlebridge		(4	0)	Three freemen held it under Gyrth
150b	Flordon				A freeman of Gyrth held 7 acres, valued in Costessey
153	Hapton		(4	0)	A freeman of Gyrth held it
158b	Tuttington		(1	8)	Two freemen of Gyrth held it
173	East Winch	(2	0	0)	A freeman of Gyrth held it
180	Thrigby		(1	4)	A freeman of Gyrth held it
184	Felbrigg	(2	0	0)	Two freemen and eight sokemen of Gyrth held it
185b	Stoke Holy Cross		(5	0)	A freeman commended to Gyrth held it
186	Seething		(10	0)	A freeman held it under Gyrth
186b	Mundham		(5	0)	A freeman of Godwine held it under Gyrth
	Mundham		(5	0)	Three freemen of the same Godwine held it under Gyrth
187	Palling	(1	0	0)	A freeman of Gyrth held it
190b	East Winch	(2	0	0)	A freeman of Gyrth held it
197	Ormesby		(8	0)	Two freemen of Gyrth held it
199	Plumstead		(10	0)	Godwine, a freeman of Gyrth, held it

Ref. (fos.)	Location	Value £	s.	d.	Notes
200	Catton (in Postwick)		(1	3)	A freeman commended to Gyrth held it
200b	Witton (nr. Norwich)		(1	4)	A freeman half commended to Earl Gyrth held it
202b	South Walsham		(10	0)	A freeman of Gyrth held it
203b	Helhoughton				One freeman commended to Gyrth had 80 acres
210	Shotesham				Sixteen freemen commended to Earl Gyrth held 1 carucate; valued in Brooke
	Poringland				A freeman of Gyrth held 30 acres: valued in Brooke
223b	North or Southreppes		(2	0)	A freeman of Gyrth held it
225	Stokesby		(10	0)	Eadgifu, a free 'man' of Gyrth, held it
242	Warham		(16	0)	Gyrth had two freemen there
	Topcroft	(6	0	0)	Godwine, a freeman commended to Gyrth, held it
255	Baconsthorpe (nr. Holt)	(1	10	0)	Wulfric, a freeman of Gyrth, held it
255b	Loddon	(1	0	0)	Wulfric, a freeman, held it under Gyrth
264b	Holkham	(2	0	0)	A freeman of Gyrth held it
267	Kelling	(1	0	0)	Wester, a freeman of Gyrth, held it
269	Plumstead		(10	0)	Tofi, a freeman of Gyrth, held it
270b	Witton (nr. Norwich)		(15	0)	Two freemen of Gyrth held it
217b	Oxnead	(1	0	0)	Æthelwig, a freeman, held it under Gyrth
	Gnatingdon		(10	0)	Godwine, a freeman, held it under Gyrth and under Ralph, and *TRW*
	Suffolk				
283	Gorleston	10	0	0	Includes 6 berewicks, fishermen at Yarmouth, and a quarter of the market at Beccles. Also thirty-two freemen with 138 acres

Land to Earl Gyrth (*cont.*):

Ref. (fos.)	Location	Value £	s.	d.	Notes
287b	Bentley and Shotley	9	0	0	
438	Ipswich	5	0	0	The third penny of the burgh, plus the value of a grange of 2 carucates
282	Hemingstone		(5	0)	Alwin, a freemen commended to Gyrth, held it
282b	Worlingham				Ælfsige, a freeman commended to Gyrth, held it
	Weston		(6	8)	Alric, a freeman commended to Gyrth, held it
	Weston		(2	0)	Sprotwulf, a freeman commended to Gyrth, held it
	Worlingham				Ulf, a freeman commended to Gyrth, held 40 acres
283	Mutford	(3	0	0)	Earl Gyrth held it and Wulfsige under him
	Mutford				Twelve freeman commended to Gyrth held 3 carucates, valued above
283b	Lound	(1	0	0)	A freeman of Gyrth held land worth 10*s*., and under him four freemen held land worth the same
	Lound		(10	0)	Wulfsige, a freeman commended to Gyrth, held it
	Corton	(1	0	0)	The same man, commended to Gyrth, held half of it, and fifteen freemen held the other half under him
	Flixton	(1	10	0)	Hakon, a freeman commended to Gyrth, held it
284	Hopton		(5	0)	Sigeric, commended to Gyrth, held it
	Hopton		(5	0)	Thorgar, a freeman commended to Gyrth, held it
	Fritton	(1	0	0)	Godwine, a freeman of Gyrth, held it
	Somerleyton	(1	0	0)	Ulf, a freeman commended to Gyrth, held it

Ref. (fos.)	Location	Value £	s.	d.	Notes
293	Rushmere St Andrew		(5	0)	Eleven freemen commended to Gyrth held it
300b	Ilketshall	(2	0	0)	Wulfsige, a freeman commended to Gyrth, held it
301b	Worlingham		(1	0)	A freeman commended to Gyrth held it
302	Gisleham		(8	0)	A freeman commended to Gyrth held it
	Rushmere (in Lowestoft)		(5	0)	A freeman commended to Gyrth held it. It also owed 300 herrings
302b	Pakefield		(5	0)	A freeman commended to Gyrth held it
301b	Kessingland		(2	8)	A freeman commended to Gyrth held it
305b	Westerfield		(10	0)	Wulfgeat, a freeman commended to Gyrth, held it
315b	Rushmere St Andrew	(1	0	0)	Wulfgeat, a freeman commended to Gyrth, held it
335	Barsham		(10	0)	Ten freemen commended to Gyrth held it
	Barsham		(5	0)	Leofstan the priest, a freeman commended to Gyrth, held it
335b	Shadingfield		(10	0)	Godwine, son of Tuka, commended to Gyrth, held it
347	*Grenewic*	(2	0	0)	A freeman commended to Gyrth held it
347b	Newbourne		(1	4)	A freeman commended to Gyrth held it
377	Burstall		(2	8)	A freeman commended to Gyrth held it
381	Barsham		(8	0)	Ten freemen held this, of whom eight and a half were commended to Ælfric and Gyrth (see Burstall, below)
395	Burstall		(8	0)	Ælfric Stari, commended to Gyrth, held it
	Kirkton		(10	0)	Thuri, a freeman, held it from Gyrth
407	Worlingham		(1	0)	Five and a half freemen

Land to Earl Gyrth (*cont.*):

Ref. (fos.)	Location	Value £	s.	d.	Notes
					commended to Gyrth held it. It also owed 1,000 herrings
407b	Hornes		(3	0)	A freeman commended to Gyrth held it. It also owed 300 herrings
420	*Turchelstuna* and Brantham	(2	10	8)	Grim, a freeman commended to Gyrth, held it
422b	Akenham		(16	0)	Godwine, a freeman, held it under Gyrth
432	Stuston	(3	0	0)	Wulfsige, a freeman commended to Gyrth, held it
442	Rushmere St Andrew		(10	0)	Brunwin, a freeman commended to Gyrth, held it
442b	Akenham		(6	0)	Sunwin, a freeman commended to Gyrth, held it
445	Somerleyton		(2	0)	Ælfwold, a freeman commended to Gyrth, held it
	Caldecotan		(10	0)	Bundi, a freeman commended to Gyrth, held it

LAND ASSIGNED TO EARL LEOFWINE

vol. i	*Kent*				
7	Nashenden	3	0	0	
7b	Milton (nr. Gravesend)	4	0	0	
	Luddesdown	6	0	0	
	Burham	10	0	0	
	Peckham	12	0	0	
	Leeds	16	0	0	
8	Sutton Valence	12	0	0	
9	Beckley		(10	0)	Wulfwine held it from Earl Leofwine
	Cooling	(2	0	0)	Wulfwine held it from Earl Leofwine

Ref. (fos.)	Location	Value £	s.	d.	Notes
	Sussex				
18b	Eyelid		4	0	It did not pay geld
			(4	0)	Leofwine held it from Earl Leofwine. It did not pay geld

[Elsewhere in Sussex land worth £56 was held by a man, or men, called Leofwine, but there is no indication as to which, if any, of these entries refer to Earl Leofwine.]

Ref. (fos.)	Location	Value £	s.	d.	Notes
	Surrey				
31b	Gatton	6	0	0	
	Cuddington	11	0	0	
	Dorset				
77	Rampisham	10	0	0	
	Somerset				
87b	Combe (Abbas or Temple)	10	0	0	
	Devonshire				
101	Beaford	8	0	0	
	Pinhoe	6	0	0	
	Kilmington	7	0	0	
	Whitford	11	0	0	
	Langford (Ugborough)	11	0	0	
	Middlesex				
127	Harrow	60	0	0	May have been leased from Canterbury
127	Elthorne Hundred		(14	0)	Thorbert the man of Earl Leofwine held it but could not sell it away from Harrow
129b	Ickenham	(1	10	0)	A sokeman of Leofwine held it
130	East Bedfont		(6	8)	A sokeman of Leofwine held it
	Elthorne Hundred	(1	0	0)	Thorbert the man of Earl Leofwine held it and could sell
130b	Charlton	(2	10	0)	A man of Leofwine held it
130b	Spelthorne Hundred		(4	0)	Alwine, a man of Leofwine, held it and could sell

Land to Earl Leofwine (*cont.*):

Ref. (fos.)	Location	Value £	s.	d.	Notes
130b	Elthorne Hundred	(1	0	0)	Leofric, a man of Leofwine, held it and could sell
	Hertfordshire				
134	Puttenham	4	0	0	
132	Hertford				Eighteen burgesses were the men of Harold and Leofwine
134	Libury	(1	0	0)	Two sokemen, the men of Leofwine, held it and could sell
134b	Libury		(10	0)	A sokeman, the man of Leofwine, held it and could sell
	Buckland	(10	0	0)	Sæhild, Leofwine's man, held it and could sell
	Redbourn		(10	0)	Alwin *Venator*, the man of Leofwine, held it and could sell
136b	Shenley	(2	0	0)	A freeman, the man of Leofwine, held it and could sell
140	Windridge	(2	10	0)	Almar, the man of Leofwine, held it and could sell
	Willian	(12	0	0)	Leofric, one of Leofric's housecarls, held it and could sell
142b	Sacombe		(1	5)	A man of Leofwine held it
	Buckinghamshire				
143b	Halton	8	0	0	
144	Weston Turville	7	10	0	
	Chalfont	5	10	0	
	Dilehurst	6	0	0	Earl Leofwine held it *in dominio*
144b	Leckhampstead	8	0	0	
	Dunton	5	0	0	
143	Buckingham		(1	4)	Two burgesses, the men of Leofwine
144	Hartwell	(1	12	0)	A man of Leofwine held it
	Bourton	(1	5	0)	A man of Leofwine held it and could sell
	Horsendon		(5	0)	A man of Leofwine held it and could sell
	Horsendon		(5	0)	Godwine, the man of Leofwine, held it and could sell

Ref. (fos.)	Location	Value £	s.	d.	Notes
	Chesham	(1	10	0)	A sokeman, the man of Leofwine, held it and could sell
144b	Saunderton	(6	0	0)	A man of Leofwine held it and could sell
	Radnage	(3	0	0)	Fridebert, the man of Leofwine, held it
	Ilmer	(5	0	0)	Godwine, the man of Leofwine, held it and could sell
	Lenborough	(4	0	0)	Wiglaf, the man of Leofwine, held it and could sell
	Preston Bissett	(4	0	0)	Wiglaf, the man of Leofwine, held it and could sell
145	Barston Hartshorn	(3	0	0)	Wiglaf, the man of Leofwine, held it and could sell
	Addington	(3	0	0)	Godwine, the man of Leofwine, held it and could sell
	Lathbury	(1	0	0)	Sigeric, the man of Leofwine, held it and could sell
	Gayhurst	(8	0	0)	Sigeric, the man of Leofwine, held it and could sell
146	Burston		(10	0)	A thegn of Leofwine held it
147	Pitstone	(2	0	0)	Thorfinn, the man of Leofwine, held it and could sell
150b	Hardmead		(2	0)	Wulfgrim, the man of Leofwine, held it and could sell
151	Marston	(5	0	0)	Thorgot, the man of Leofwine, held it and could sell
152	Helsthorpe	(1	0	0)	A man of Leofwine held it
152b	Datchett	(6	0	0)	Saulf, a man of Leofwine, held it
vol. ii	*Essex*				
30b	Stanford Rivers	24	0	0	
	Laver	16	0	0	

LAND ASSIGNED TO GYTHA, EARL GODWINE'S WIFE

Ref. (fos.)	Location	Value £	s.	d.	Notes
vol. i	*Sussex*				
23	Binderton	5	0	0	
23	Harting	80	0	0	Gytha held it from King Edward
23	Trotton	3	0	0	Gytha held it from King Edward
24	Mundham	8	0	0	Gytha held it from Earl Godwine
27	Westmeston	7	0	0	Gytha held it and under her the villeins; there is not a hall there
28b	Woodmancote	3	10	0	
24	Marden	(2	10	0)	Leofsige held it from Gytha
	Surrey				
34	Oxted	16	0	0	
	Hampshire				
38b	Over Wallop	30	0	0	Gytha held it from Earl Godwine
39b	Wroxhall (IOW)	27	0	0	Gytha held it from Earl Godwine *in alodium*
	Berkshire				
59b	Chaddleworth	(7	0	0)	A freeman held it from Gytha
	Wiltshire				
65	Rushall	32	10	0	
	Aldbourne	60	0	0	
	Coombe Bissett	24	0	0	
	Dorset				
78b	Frampton	40	0	0	
	Somerset				
86b	Brampton Regis	27	12	0	
87	Queen Camel	23	0	0	Assessed at 15 hides, but pays geld for $8\frac{1}{2}$

Ref. (fos.)	Location	£	s.	d.	Notes
	Coker	19	12	0	Assessed at 15 hides, but pays geld for seven
	Devonshire				
100b	South Tawton	48	0	0	
	Ash (in South Tawton)	1	10	0	
	Hartland	24	0	0	
	Little Torrington	2	0	0	
	Witheridge		5	0	
	Woodbury	18	0	0	
	Chillington	24	0	0	
	Sherford (Kingsbridge)	3	0	0	
	Tiverton	18	0	0	
101	Worlington	24	0	0	
104	Otterton	10	0	0	
	Cornwall				
123b	Poundstock	1	0	0	
	St Gennys	1	0	0	
	Gloucestershire				
164	Woodchester	7	0	0	Earl Godwine bought this from Azur and gave it to his wife

Family of Godwine	Total value of land held					
	By subject			From subject or by his/her men		
	£	s.	d.	£	s.	d.
Earl Godwine	723	15	0	351	12	6
Earl Harold	2,846	14	4	836	5	8
Earl Tostig	491	12	0	59	19	0
Earl Gyrth	250	0	0	83	16	0
Earl Leofwine	287	4	0	98	11	0
Gytha (*comitissa*)	587	19	0	9	12	0
TOTAL	5,187	4	4	1,428	12	6

LAND ASSIGNED TO EARL ÆLFGAR

Ref. (fos.)	Location	Value £	s.	d.	Notes
vol. i	*Middlesex*				
130	Isleworth	80	0	0	
	Hampton	40	0	0	
	Hertfordshire				
133	Ley Green	(1	6	8)	Three of Earl Ælfgar's freemen held it, but could not sell outside Hitchen
133b	Much Hadham	(1	0	0)	A sokeman of Earl Ælfgar held it
	Patmore	(4	0	0)	Alweard, the man of Ælfgar, held it and could sell
134b	Hodenhoe		(15	0)	A man of Earl Ælfgar held it and could sell
139	Newsells	(1	16	0)	A man of Earl Ælfgar held it and could sell
140	Wallington	(5	0	0)	Eadric, the man of Ælfgar, held it and could sell
141b	Luffenhall		(10	0)	Alweard, the man of Ælfgar, held it and could sell
	Wyddial	(3	0	0)	Alweard, the man of Ælfgar, held it
	Hodenhoe	(1	5	0)	Two sokemen of Ælfgar held it and could sell
	Wakeley		(15	0)	Eadric, the man of Ælfgar, held it and could sell
	Berkesdon		(2	6)	A sokeman of Earl Ælfgar held it and could sell
	Barley		(15	0)	Three sokemen of Earl Ælfgar held it and could sell
	Barkway		(6	8)	A sokeman of Earl Ælfgar held it and could sell
142	Anstey	(1	0	0)	Alweard the man of Ælfgar held it and could sell
	Buckinghamshire				
152b	Marlow	25	0	0	
	Hambleden	16	0	0	

Ref. (fos.)	Location	Value £	s.	d.	Notes
151b	Turville	(7	0	0)	Thorbert the man of Ælfgar held it and could sell
	Oxfordshire				
154	Oxford	10	0	0	The earl's third penny from the burgh
	Oxford		13	10	From 20 dwellings which had to keep the wall repaired
160	Broadwell	25	0	0	Ælfgar held it freely
	Worcestershire				
176	Lindon	(2	0	0)	Ælfweard, a thegn of Earl Ælfgar, held it
	Alton	(2	0	0)	Godric, a thegn of Earl Ælfgar, held it and could sell
	Herefordshire				
176	[location not identified]		(15	0)	Ludrie the man of Ælfgar held it and could sell
	Cambridgeshire				
190	Litlington	22	0	0	
193	Dullingham	15	0	0	
196	Eltisley	13	0	0	
	Carlton	8	0	0	
190	Babraham	(1	10	0)	Wulfwine the man of Ælfgar held it but could not sell
193	Morden	(2	10	0)	Goda held it under Earl Ælfgar
	Morden	(1	10	0)	Goda held it under Earl Ælfgar
	Shingay	(14	0	0)	Goda held it under Earl Ælfgar
	Abington Pigotts		(13	4)	Goda held it under Earl Ælfgar
193b	Meldreth	(8	0	0)	Goda held it under Earl Ælfgar
	Melbourn		(5	0)	Goda held it under Earl Ælfgar
194b	Kingston		(2	0)	Alwit the man of Ælfgar held it and could sell
195	Fordham	(1	0	0)	A sokeman of Ælfgar held it and could sell
196b	Barrington	(3	0	0)	Four of Ælfgar's sokemen held it but could not sell
197b	Carlton		(2	0)	A sokeman of Ælfgar held it but could not sell

Land to Earl Ælfgar (*cont.*):

Ref. (fos.)	Location	Value £	s.	d.	Notes
197b	Dullingham	(1	0	0)	Eight sokemen held it from Ælfgar
198	Carlton		(2	0)	A sokeman of Ælfgar held it but could not sell
	Weston Colville		(10	0)	Thorgar the man of Ælfgar held it and could sell
	Hinxton		(10	0)	Estred held it under Ælfgar and could sell
	Ickleton	(1	5	0)	Estred held it under Ælfgar and could sell
	Duxford	(1	5	0)	A sokeman of Ælfgar held it but could not sell
	Shelford		(12	0)	Alsige the man of Ælfgar held it and could sell
	Morden		(10	0)	Winterled held it from Ælfgar but could not sell
	Littlington		(6	0)	Alwig the man of Ælfgar held it and could sell
	Abington Pigotts	(2	8	0)	Two sokemen of Ælfgar held it and could sell
198b	Bassingbourne	(2	0	0)	Two sokemen of Ælfgar held it and could sell
	Melbourn	(2	0	0)	Sigeræd the man of Ælfgar held it and could sell
	Shepreth		(10	0)	A sokeman of Ælfgar held it and could sell
	Whitwell		(5	0)	A sokeman of Ælfgar held it and could sell
	Eversden		(8	0)	A sokeman of Ælfgar held it and could sell
198	Caxton	(2	0	0)	Four sokemen of Ælfgar held it
	Wendy		(5	0)	Goda, commended to Ælfgar, held it and could sell
200	Meldreth	(2	0	0)	Five sokemen of Ælfgar held it and could sell
	Eversden	(2	0	0)	Seven sokemen of Ælfgar held it and could sell
	Hinxton	(1	0	0)	A sokeman of Ælfgar held it but could not sell

Ref. (fos.)	Location	Value £	s.	d.	Notes
	Morden	(1	10	0)	Two sokemen of Ælfgar held it but could not sell
200b	Kingston	(6	0	0)	Four sokemen of Ælfgar held it but could not sell
201	Bourne	(1	0	0)	A man of Ælfgar held it
201b	Fulbourn	(4	0	0)	Leofric the man of Ælfgar held it and could sell
	Teversham	(1	10	0)	Two of Ælfgar's sokemen held it
202	Babraham	(1	6	8)	Godgifu held it under Ælfgar and could sell
	Grantchester	(3	0	0)	A sokeman of Ælfgar held it and could sell
	Gamlingay	(2	0	0)	A man of Ælfgar held it and could sell
	Croxton	(6	0	0)	Three men of Ælfgar held it and could sell
	Huntingdonshire				
203b	Gransden	40	0	0	
	Bedfordshire				
213	Milton Bryant	(8	0	0)	Auti, a housecarl of Earl Ælfgar, held it and could sell
	Northamptonshire				
220	Weekley	3	0	0	
	King's Cliffe	7	0	0	
222	Boughton (in Weekley)		5	4	
	Scaldwell		16	0	
	East Farndon		10	0	
	Warwickshire				
239b	Myton	3	0	0	
241b	Marston (in Wolston)		10	0	
244	Aston Cantlow	5	0	0	
	Ipsley (Worcs.)	1	10	0	

Land to Earl Ælfgar (*cont.*):

Ref. (fos.)	Location	Value £	s.	d.	Notes
	Staffordshire				
246	Alrewas	10	0	0	
	Sandon	6	0	0	
246b	Chartley	5	0	0	
	Wolstanton	5	0	0	
	Penkull	6	0	0	
	Rocester	4	0	0	
	Crakemarsh		10	0	
	Uttoxeter	7	0	0	
	Barton under Needlewood	6	0	0	
	Leek	4	0	0	
	Rugley	1	0	0	
	Mayfield	2	0	0	
	Mere	4	0	0	
	Cannock				Not valued
	Elford	11	0	0	
	Kinver	5	0	0	
	Pattingham	3	0	0	
	Clifton Campville	11	0	0	
	Drayton Bassett	4	0	0	
	Hopwas	2	0	0	
	Harlaston	6	0	0	
247b	Meaford		13	0	Earl Ælfgar gave this land and the next to St Remigius's
248	Rideware		5	0	
	Kingsnordley (Salop)	8	0	0	
	Claverley (Salop)	7	10	0	
	Alveley (Salop)	6	0	0	
	Sheriff Hales (Salop)	8	0	0	
248b	Worfield	3	0	0	
249b	Sedgely	10	0	0	
	Penn	1	10	0	
	Amblecote		(10	0)	Two men held it from Ælfgar
	Derbyshire				
272b	Walton upon Trent and Rosliston	6	0	0	
	Newton Solney	5	0	0	

Ref. (fos.)	Location	Value £	s.	d.	Notes
	Bretby				
	Repton	17	0	0	
273	Weston upon Trent	8	5	0	
	Cotton in the Elms	2	0	0	Burton Abbey held it *TRW*
	Nottinghamshire				
281b	Upper Boughton and Thorpe in the Glebe	5	0	0	
292b	Willoughby in the Wolds				Not valued: 3 ploughs were held by two of Ælfgar's sokemen
	Lincolnshire				
338	Tydd St Mary	8	0	0	
	Lutton	8	0	0	
	Gedney	25	0	0	
	Fleet	4	0	0	
348b	Holbeach and Whaplode				Not valued: *TRW* they were berewicks of Addlethorpe
351b	Spalding	23	2	8	Includes profits from a market
vol. ii	*Essex*				
3b	Great Chesterford	24	0	0	
	Shelford	12	0	0	
4	Finchingfield	9	0	0	
	Wethersfield	20	0	0	
21b	Felsted	20	0	0	
	Beddow	17	0	0	Value is for *TRW*; *TRE* it rendered a night's farm
36b	Dunmow	1	0	0	
98b	Gestingthorpe	10	0	0	
96b	Felsted	(1	10	0)	Wulfsige held it under Ælfgar
102b	Bardfield				1 hide and 1 virgate, unvalued, were held here from Ælfgar
	Norfolk				
194b	Beighton	(6	0	0)	Sold to the Bishop of East Anglia *TRE*
195	Hemsby	(26	0	0)	Bought by Ailwig from Earl Ælfgar, but Stigand seized it and gave it to his brother

Land to Earl Ælfgar (*cont.*):

Ref. (fos.)	Location	Value £	s.	d.	Notes
	Suffolk				
289b	Badmondisfield	7	0	0	
421b	Bures	1	0	0	
438b	Denston	3	0	0	A berewick of Badmondisfield
289b	Badmondisfield	(2	0	0)	Twelve freemen, commended to Ælfric, held it
348b	Thurston	(2	0	0)	Ætmar, a thegn of Ælfgar, held it
355	Tuddenham	(2	0	0)	Leofric, a freeman commended to Ælfgar, held it
373	Eleigh		(5	0)	Three freemen, commended to Ælfgar, held it
394	*Facheduna*		(5	0)	A freeman, commended to Ælfgar, held it
395b	Burstall	(0	3	0)	Leofric, commended to Ælfgar, held it

LAND ASSIGNED TO EARL EADWINE

Ref. (fos.)	Location	Value £	s.	d.	Notes
	Buckinghamshire				
147b	Lamport	(2	0	0)	Swein Swart, the man of Earl Eadwine, held it
148b	Marston	(3	0	0)	Leofric, the man of Earl Eadwine, held it
	Oxfordshire				
154b	Bloxham and Adderbury	56	0	0	Includes the soke of 2 hundreds
	Worcestershire				
172	Bromsgrove	18	0	0	Value is the farm of the manor
	Worcester	8	0	0	
172b	Droitwich	24	0	0	$51\frac{1}{2}$ salt houses
177	Dudley	4	0	0	
172	Grafton, Cooksey Green, Willingwick, Chadwick	(6	13	0)	Earngeat, Beorhtræd, Alwin, Ælfwold, and Frane, five of Eadwine's thegns, held it. It belonged to Bromsgrove and they could not sell

Ref. (fos.)	Location	Value £	s.	d.	Notes
	Willingwick		(5	o)	Wulfwine, a thegn of Earl Eadwine, held it
176b	Shelsley	(2	o	o)	Sigmund, a thegn of Eadwine, held it but could not sell
177b	Bentley and Pauncefoot	(1	10	o)	Leofric held it from Earl Eadwine
	Herefordshire				
180b	Suckley (Worcs.)	10	o	o	
	Feckenham (Worcs.)	(14	o	o)	Five thegns held it from Eadwine
	Warwickshire				
238	Brailes	17	10	o	
	Coton	17	o	o	
	Sutton Coldfield	4	o	o	
241b	Myton	5	o	o	
	Myton		5	o	
243	Budbrooke	8	o	o	
	Aston (in Birmingham)	4	o	o	
	Erdington	1	o	o	
244	Ulverley	10	o	o	
	Staffordshire				
248b	Bradley (nr. Stafford)	7	o	o	
249b	Rickerscote	1	o	o	
	Monteville		10	o	
	Shropshire				
252b	Emstrey	5	o	o	
253b	Ford	9	o	o	
	Ellesmere	10	o	o	
	High Ercall	20	o	o	
	Wellington	20	o	o	
	Donnington	20	o	o	
	Ditton Priors	10	o	o	
254	Church Stretton	13	o	o	
	Stottesdon	20	o	o	
256	Crudington	3	13	4	
	Doddington		16	o	
257	Chelmarsh	6	o	o	

Land to Earl Eadwine (*cont.*):

Ref. (fos.)	Location	Value £	s.	d.	Notes
257b	Wykey				Waste
	Longford	9	0	0	
	Pilson		8	0	
	Cheshire				
263b	Weaverham	10	0	0	
	Frodsham	7	0	0	
	Eaton (nr. Chester)	10	0	0	
	Eastham	24	0	0	
	Hadlow				Waste
	Macclesfield	10	0	0	
264	Adlington	8	0	0	
	Upton (nr. Chester)	3	0	0	
	Bettisfield (Wales)	18	0	0	
	Iscoyd (Wales)	6	4	0	
	Worthebury		16	0	
	Malpas	11	4	0	
	Tilston	6	0	0	
	Christleton	6	0	0	
266b	Farndon	2	0	0	
	Harwarden	2	0	0	
267	Alpraham	1	0	0	
268	Nantwich	7	0	0	The earl's third penny
268b	Radington (Wales)				Waste
	Dodleston	2	0	0	
269	Rhuddlan (Wales)				Waste
	Bistre				Waste; it did not pay geld
	Derbyshire				
274	Doveridge	8	0	0	
275	Wyaston	3	0	0	
	Yorkshire				
298b	Yorkshire				Earls Eadwine and Morkær had *sac* and *soc* over the land of Ingold
299	Northallerton				'Now it is waste'; assessed at 85 carucates
301b	Bolton (in Craven)				'Now it is waste'; assessed at 6 carucates

Ref. (fos.)	Location	Value £	s.	d.	Notes
307	Hutton	8	0	0	
309	Gilling	56	0	0	
310b	Catterick	8	0	0	
313	Askam Bryan	3	0	0	
315	Kippax and Ledston	16	0	0	
319	Laughton en le Morthen and Throapham	24	0	0	
	Lincolnshire				
338	Kirton in Lindsey	24	0	0	

LAND ASSIGNED TO EARL MORKÆR

vol. i	*Herefordshire*			
179	Kingsland	6	0	0
	Northamptonshire			
219b	Casterton (Rutland)	6	0	0
225b	Weston	5	0	0
	Leicestershire			
230	Croxton Kerrial, Knipton, and Harston	10	0	0
	Broughton Astley	3	0	0
234b	Saltby	9	0	0
	Staffordshire			
248b	Rolleston	10	0	0
	Shropshire			
253b	Ness	3	0	0
	Tong	11		
254b	Cound	4	7	0
255b	The Rea		2	8
	Worthen	10	0	0
256b	Idshall and Shifnall	15	0	0
	Caysham	8	0	0
259	Sutton Maddock	2	0	0

Land to Earl Morkær (*cont.*):

Ref. (fos.)	Location	Value £	s.	d.	Notes
	Cheshire				
265b	Acton	10	0	0	This manor had its pleas in the lord's hall
267	Wheelock				Waste
	Derbyshire				
278	Alfreton	1	0	0	
	Nottinghamshire				
281b	*Neubold*	4	0	0	
285	Gunthorpe	15	0	0	
286b	Elton	4	0	0	
287	*Neubold*	4	0	0	
	Yorkshire				
298b	Yorkshire				Eadwine and Morkær had *sac* and *soc* over the land of Ingold
299	Easingwold	32	0	0	
	Pickering	88	0	0	
	Market Weighton and Shipton	30	0	0	
	Warter	40	0	0	
299b	Great Driffield	40	0	0	
	Beswick	1	0	0	
	Pocklington	56	0	0	
	Bridlington	32	0	0	
	Burton Agnes	24	0	0	
304b	Welton	20	0	0	
323b	Kilnsea	56	0	0	
	Withernsea	56	0	0	
	Mappleton	56	0	0	
	Hornsea	56	0	0	
	Easington	32	0	0	
	Lincolnshire				
336	Lincoln				Morkær had one house with *sac* and *soc*
337	Lincolnshire				Morkær had *sac* and *soc* in the county
	Torksey	6	0	0	The earl's third penny of the burgh

Ref. (fos.)	Location	Value £	s.	d.	Notes
337b	Kirkby la Thorpe and Evedon	4	0	0	
	South Kyme	2	0	0	
	Boothby Graffoe	20	0	0	
	Wellingore	30	0	0	
338	Bassingham	25	0	0	
338b	Caistor and Hundon	30	0	0	
340	Skillington	4	0	0*	
360	Barrow in Humber	32	0	0	
340	Skillington	4	0	0*	
357b	Great Coates	1	10	0	
	Healing	2	0	0	
358b	Sempringham	2	0	0*	
360b	Stroxton	6	0	0*	
	Stoke Rochford		10	0*	
	North Stoke				Not valued: assessed at 10 bovates
	Carlton le Moorland	10	0	0*	
	Bowthorpe	3	0	0	
	Bytham	19	0	0*	
362b	Burton Coggles	1	0	0	
364b	Bourne	5	0	0	
366b	Stapleford	7	0	0	

* These lands were mentioned in the will of Ulf and Madselin (Dorothy Whitelock, *Anglo-Saxon Wills* (Cambridge, 1930) no. 39.

LANDS ASSIGNED TO GODGIFU, THE WIFE OF EARL LEOFRIC

vol. i	*Worcestershire*			
177b	Belbroughton	4	0	0
	Leicestershire			
231b	Norton-juxte-Twycross		5	0
	Appleby	1	0	0
	Bilstone		5	0
	Warwickshire			
239b	Alspath	2	0	0
	Atherstone	2	0	0

Land to Godgifu (*cont.*):

Ref. (fos.)	Location	Value £	s.	d.	Notes
239b	Harshill and Ansley	4	0	0	
	Kingsbury	6	0	0	
	Ansty and Foleshill	4	0	0	
	Coventry	12	0	0	
241	Newton (nr. Rugby)		10	0	
244	Salford	4	0	0	
	Staffordshire				
247b	Branston	3	0	0	
248b	Cauldon				Waste: assessed at one virgate
249b	Penn	1	0	0	
250	Moseley		8	0	
	Essington	1	0	0	
	Shropshire				
254	Chetton	5	0	0	
256	Sutton (nr. Drayton)	1	5	0	
257	Highley		15	0	
257b	Chetwynd	1	5	0	
258b	Little Drayton		8	0	
	Derbyshire				
273	Appleby				Leased from Burton by Godgifu. Burton held it *TRW*
	Nottinghamshire				
280b	Newark Wapentake				Godgifu had *sac* and *soc* and the earl's third penny from the wapentake
283b	Newark	50	0	0	
284	Fledborough	8	0	0	
	Stokeham	1	0	0	
	Lancashire				
269b	Melling (nr. Liverpool)		5	4	

LAND ASSIGNED TO ÆLFGIFU, THE WIFE OF ÆLFGAR

Ref. (fos.)	Location	Value £	s.	d.	Notes
vol. i.	*Hertfordshire*				
134b	Kimpton	15	0	0	
	Northamptonshire				
222	Warkton	7	0	0	
	Leicestershire				
231b	Aylestone	5	10	0	
	Castle Donington	5	0	0	
	Nottinghamshire				
280b	Nottinghamshire				Ælfgifu *comitissa* had *sac* and *sac*
vol. ii	*Suffolk*				
286b	Sudbury	18	0	0	
	Cornard	10	0	0	
373b	Brandeston	5	0	0	
287	Groton				Four sokemen belonged to Cornard, and held 200 acres
373b	Brandeston				Three freemen commended to Ælfgifu held 24 acres and could sell

LAND ASSIGNED TO EARL LEOFRIC

Ref. (fos.)	Location	Value £	s.	d.	Notes
vol. i	*Warwickshire*				
239	Austrey	2	0	0	Earl Leofric gave it to Burton Abbey
238b	Alveston	(4	0	0)	Beorhtwine's two sons held it from Earl Leofric. They did not know if Beorhtwine held it from Leofric or the bishop
239	Rudge (Salop)	(3	0	0)	Eadric held it freely from Leofric
243b	*Optone*	(3	10	0)	Three of Leofric's men held it freely
	Shropshire				
252b	Eyton on Severn	21	0	0	

Land to Ælfgifu (*cont.*):

Ref. (fos.)	Location	Value £ s. d.	Notes
259b	Minton and Whittingslow		Assessed at 4 hides, and valued with the manor of Church Strettor., held by Earl Eadwine *TRE*

Family of Leofric	Total value of land held					
	By subject			From subject or by his/her men		
	£	s.	d.	£	s.	d.
Earl Ælfgar	714	3	2	128	2	10
Earl Eadwine	611	10	8	31	3	0
Earl Morkær	968	9	0	None		
Godgifu, wife of Leofric	111	6	4	None		
Ælfgifu, wife of Ælfgar	65	10	0	None		
Earl Leofric	23	0	0	12	5	0
TOTAL	2,493	19	2	171	10	10

LAND ASSIGNED TO EARL SIWEARD

Ref. (fos.)	Location	Value £	s.	d.	Notes
vol. i	*Derbyshire*				
273b	Markeston	4	0	0	Includes three berewicks, assessed at 4 carucates, which were waste
	Yorkshire				
305	Whitby	112	0	0	
	South Loftus	48	0	0	
	West Acklam and Barwick	48	0	0	

LAND ASSIGNED TO EARL WALTHEOF

Ref. (fos.)	Location	Value £	s.	d.	Notes
vol. i	*Middlesex*				
130b	Tottenham	26	0	0	
	Hertfordshire				
137b	Polehanger (Beds)	(1	0	0)	Ælfric, the man of Earl Waltheof, held it and could sell
	Buckinghamshire				
145	Tyringham	(3	0	0)	A man of Earl Waltheof held it and could sell
	Cambridgeshire				
193b	Croydon		(10	0)	Almar the man of Earl Waltheof held it and could sell
	Kingston		(2	0)	Almar the man of Earl Waltheof held it and could sell
	Arrington	(2	0	0)	A sokeman of Waltheof held it
197	Conington	(1	0	0)	A man of Waltheof held it
	Boxworth	(3	0	0)	Leofsige the man of Earl Waltheof held it and could sell
	Swavesey	(1	0	0)	Leofsige the man of Earl Waltheof held it and could sell
197b	Kingston			(8)	Almar the man of Earl Waltheof held it and could sell
198b	Orwell	(1	15	0)	A sokeman, the man of Earl Waltheof, held it and could sell
	Wratworth	(2	5	0)	A sokeman, the man of Earl Waltheof, held it and could sell
200b	Comberton		(9	0)	A sokeman, the man of Earl Waltheof, held it and could sell
201b	Cottenham		(1	6)	A man of Earl Waltheof held it and could sell
	Barton	(8	0	0)	Four of Waltheof's sokemen held it, of whom two could sell and two could not
201b	Longstanton		(2	0)	Hoch the man of Earl Waltheof held it and could not sell
202	Grantchester	(5	0	0)	Three of Earl Waltheof's men held it and could sell

Land to Earl Waltheof (*cont.*):

Ref. (fos.)	Location	Value £	s.	d.	Notes
202	Dry Drayton	(3	0	0)	Sagar the man of Waltheof held it and could sell
	Caldecote	(1	10	0)	Sigar the man of Waltheof held it and could sell
	Croxton	(2	0	0)	A man of Waltheof held it and could sell
	Westwick	(1	0	0)	Godmann the man of Waltheof held it and could sell
	Landbeach	(1	15	0)	A sokeman, the man of Waltheof, held it and could sell
	Trumpington		(10	0)	A sokeman, the man of Waltheof, held it and could not sell
	Papworth Hundred	(1	0	0)	Huscarl held it from Waltheof and could sell
	Northstow Hundred	(2	0	0)	Four men of Waltheof held it and could sell
202b	Oakington	(4	0	0)	Godwine the man of Waltheof held it and could sell
	Over	(2	0	0)	Godwine the man of Waltheof held it and could sell
	Dry Drayton	(1	0	0)	A man of Waltheof held it and could sell
	Childerley	(8	0	0)	A man of Waltheof held it and could sell
	Oakington	(4	0	0)	Siward the man of Waltheof held it and could sell
	Comberton		(10	0)	A man of Waltheof held it and could sell
	Comberton		(10	0)	A man of Waltheof held it and could sell
	Huntingdonshire				
207	Diddington	2	0	0	
203b	Leighton Bromswold	(20	0	0)	Thurkill held it. Waltheof gave this manor to St Mary's, Lincoln, in alms
	Bedfordshire				
210b	Kinwick	4	0	0	Waltheof and his wife gave this manor to St Edmund's in alms

Ref. (fos.)	Location	Value £	s.	d.	Notes
213	Apsley Guise	(10	0	0)	Leofgifu, commended to Waltheof, held it and could sell
216	Totternhoe	(8	0	0)	Leofwine the man of Waltheof held it
217b	Southill	(3	0	0)	Tuffa the man of Waltheof held it and could sell
	Northamptonshire				
228	Ryhall and Belmesthorpe	6	0	0	
	Ashley		5	4	
	Sutton Bassett		10	8	
	Weston by Welland	1	1	4	
	Dingley		10	8	
	Brampton Ash		5	4	
228b	Yardley Hastings	12	0	0	Includes nine members, and the profits of 2 hundreds
	Daventry	3	10	0	
228	Chadstone	(1	0	0)	Ulf the man of Waltheof held it
	Leicestershire				
233	Haughton on the Hill	1	0	0	
236	Oadby	2	0	0	
	Peatling Magna				Not valued: assessed at 4 carucates
	Cosby	1	10	0	
	Frolesworth	2	0	0	
	Sharnford		2	8	
	Willoughby Waterless	1	10	0	
	Heather		1	4	
	Derbyshire				
274b	Brailsford	3	0	0	
275	Osmaston (nr. Ashford)	2	0	0	
	Rutland				
293b	Market Overton	12	0	0	
	Whissendene	8	0	0	
	Exton	8	0	0	
	Yorkshire				
298	Heworth		10	0	

Land to Earl Waltheof (*cont.*):

Ref. (fos.)	Location	Value £	s.	d.	Notes
305b	Newsham (in Amotherby)				Waste *TRW*
	Cawton				Waste *TRW*
	Sackleton				Waste *TRW*
	Barton le Street	1	0	0	
	Fadmoor		10	0	
	Eston	2	0	0	
306	Terrington		10	0	
	Crambe		10	0	
	Whitwell on the Hill	3	0	0	
	North Kilvington				Waste *TRW*
307	Howsham	4	0	0	
	Kirkham	3	0	0	
	Barthorpe				Waste *TRW*
308b	Cundhall	4	0	0	
320	Hallam	5	6	8	Includes 19 berewicks. Value was recorded as 'eight marks of silver'
vol. ii	*Essex*				
92	Walthamstow	15	0	0	

Family of Siweard	Total value of land held: By subject £	s.	d.	From subject or by his/her men £	s.	d.
Earl Siweard	212	0	0	None		
Waltheof	136	13	0	83	18	8
TOTAL	348	13	0	83	18	8

LAND ASSIGNED TO EARL RALPH

Ref. (fos.)	Location	Value £	s.	d.	Notes
vol. i	*Berkshire*				
61	Wooley	10	0	0	Earl Ralph held it from King Edward

Ref. (fos.)	Location	Value £	s.	d.	Notes
	Buckinghamshire				
152b	Ixhill Hundred	(2	0	0)	Saulf the man of Ralph held it and could sell
	Gloucestershire				
169	Sudeley and Toddington	40	0	0	
	Northamptonshire				
226b	Burton Latimer	2	0	0	
	Leicestershire				
231	Great Easton	6	0	0	
232	Wigston Magna	8	0	0	
	Stockerston	8	0	0	
234	Welham		3	0	
236	Lutterworth	7	0	0	
	Misterton	1	0	0	
	Catthorpe	1	0	0	
	Warwickshire				
244	Chilvers Coton	2	0	0	
	Lincolnshire				
337	Lincolnshire				Earl Ralph had *sac* and *soc* in the county

LAND ASSIGNED TO GYTHA, WIFE OF EARL RALPH

Ref. (fos.)	Location	Value £	s.	d.	Notes
vol. i	*Buckinghamshire*				
148	Adstock	8	0	0	
	Haversham	7	0	0	
	Stoke Goldington	4	0	0	
	Northamptonshire				
225b	Higham Ferrers	10	0	0	Gytha held it with *sac* and *soc*
	Nobottle and 5 other vills	5	0	0	Gytha held it freely with *sac* and *soc*
	Duston	2	0	0	Gytha held it with *sac* and *soc*
	Naseby	1	0	0	Gytha held it with *sac* and *soc*
	Courteenhall	4	0	0	Gytha held it with *sac* and *soc*
	Blisworth	3	0	0	Gytha held it with *sac* and *soc*
226	Catesby	2	0	0	Gytha held it freely
	Guilsborough		6	0	Gytha held it freely

Land to Gytha (*cont.*):

Ref. (fos.)	Location	Value £	s.	d.	Notes
226	Blakesley		10	0	Gytha held it freely
	Courteenhall		6	0	Gytha held it freely
	Mollington (Oxon)	4	0	0	Gytha held it freely

LAND ASSIGNED TO HAROLD, THE SON OF EARL RALPH

vol. i	*Middlesex*				
129b	Ebury	12	0	0	Harold the son of Earl Ralph held it, but Queen Eadgyth had charge of him and the manor on the day King Edward was alive and dead
	Worcestershire				
177	Droitwich	2	0	0	Includes twenty burgesses
	Warwickshire				
238	Warwick				Harold had two houses
244	Dassett	16	0	0	

Family of Ralph	Total value of land held					
	By subject			From subject or by his/her men		
	£	s.	d.	£	s.	d.
Earl Ralph	85	3	0	2	0	0
Gytha, Ralph's wife	55	2	0	None		
Harold, Ralph's son	30	0	0	None		
TOTAL	170	5	0	2	0	0

APPENDIX II

Non-Earlish Lay Estates Valued at over £40

LAND ASSIGNED TO ÆLFRIC CAMP

Ref. (fos.)	Location	Value £	s.	d.	Notes
vol. i	*Berkshire*				
61b	Losfield	4	0	0	Ælfric held it from King Edward
	Cambridgeshire				
196b	Duxford		5	0	Ælfric held it from King Edward and could sell
	Fowlmere	12	0	0	Ælfric held it from King Edward
	Babraham		3	4	Ælfric held it and could sell
197b	Sawston	8	0	0	Ælfric held it from King Edward
	Pampisford			(6)	Burro the man of Ælfric Camp held it and could sell
	Bedfordshire				
212	Southill		4	0	Ælfric held it and could sell
vol. ii	*Essex*				
66	Wivenhoe	2	0	0	
67b	Tendring	11	0	0	
69b	Barn Hall	1	10	0	Ælfric Camp, a freeman, held it
70b	Ramsey	12	0	0	
	Witelbroc		10	0	
83	Delham	12	0	0	
83b	Bradfield	7	0	0	
	Suffolk				
403b	Layham	6	0	0	
378	Raydon		(5	0)	Smeri, a freeman commended to Ælfric Camp, held it

Land to Ælfric Camp (*cont.*):

Ref. (fos.)	Location	Value £ s. d.	Notes
421b	*Linhou*		Wulfric Camp held 30 acres under Ælfric Camp
448	Cornard	(1 0 0)	Two freemen under commendation to Ælfric, held it

Ælfric Camp	Total value of land held	
	By subject £ s. d.	From subject or by his men £ s. d.
	76 12 4	None

LAND ASSIGNED TO ÆLFRIC, GODING'S SON

vol. i	*Hertfordshire*		
147	Chilton	8 0 0	Ælfric, King Edward's thegn, held it
	Easington	3 0 0	Ælfric, King Edward's thegn, held it and could sell
	Dorton	5 0 0	Ælfric, King Edward's thegn, held it and could sell
	Pollicott	3 10 0	
147b	Akeley	3 0 0	Ælfric held it and could sell
	Maids Moreton	1 10 0	
	Beachampton	4 10 0	Ælfric, the man and thegn of King Edward, held it and could sell
	Bourton	1 0 0	Ælfric, King Edward's thegn, held it
	Hillesden	8 0 0	Ælfric, King Edward's thegn, held it and could sell
	Woolstone	4 0 0	Ælfric held it and could sell
148	Great Linford	4 0 0	Ælfric held it and could sell
146b	Hillesden	(1 10 0)	Leofwine the man of Ælfric held it and could sell
	Loughton	(1 0 0)	Almar the man of Ælfric held it and could sell

Ref. (fos.)	Location	Value £ s. d.	Notes
	Great Linford	(2 0 0)	Two of Ælfric's men held it and could sell
	Weston Underwood		A man of Ælfric held it and could sell
	Lavendon	(4 0 0)	A man of Ælfric held it and could sell
	Wootton on the Green	(1 10 0)	Five of Ælfric's men held it and could sell
147b	Maids Moreton	(1 0 0)	Wulfric the man of Ælfric held it
	Lenborough	(2 0 0)	Tovi the man of Ælfric held it and could sell
148	Hardmead	(2 0 0)	A man of Ælfric held it and could sell
	Broughton (nr. Mousloe)	(4 0 0)	Oswi the man of Ælfric held it and could sell
	Bedfordshire		
211	Woburn	15 0 0	Ælfric, King Edward's thegn, held it

Ælfric, Goding's son	Total value of land held	
	By subject £ s. d.	From subject or by his men £ s. d.
	60 10 0	19 0 0

LAND ASSIGNED TO ÆLFSTAN OF BOSCOMBE

vol. i	*Hampshire*		
47	Silchester	5 0 0	Ælfstan held it from King Edward *in alodium*
	Berkshire		
61	Padworth	2 10 0	Ælfstan held it from King Edward
	Wiltshire		
67	Bremhill	6 0	Leased by the Abbot of Malmesbury to Ælfstan *TRE*

Land to Ælfstan of Boscombe (*cont.*):

Ref. (fos.)	Location	Value £	s.	d.	Notes
71b	Littleton Panell	10	0	0	Ælfstan held it. It was thegnland of the Church of Salisbury *TRE*
	Ditteridge	1	10	0	1 hide and 3 virgates, of which 1 hide was leased from Malmesbury
	Durnford	24	0	0	
	Compton Bassett	5	0	0	
	Beversbrook	1	10	0	
	Charlton (Berks.)	5	0	0	
	Grafton	3	0	0	
	Boscombe	10	0	0	
	Cholderton	5	0	0	
	Hilmarton	7	0	0	
	Codford	4	0	0	
	Leckham	6	0	0	
	Sevington	6	0	0	
	Getone		5	0	
	Dorset				
80b	Thorton	2	0	0	
	Wynford Eagle	12	0	0	
	Chilfrome	3	0	0	
	Crichel	10	0	0	
	Elworth	3	0	0	
	Somerset				
96b	Whatley (in Winsham)		10	0	
	Hinton St George	12	0	0	
	Yeovilton	9	0	0	
	Laverton	7	0	0	
	Laverton	6	0	0	
	Yeovil	8	0	0	
	Chilton Cantelo		10	0	
	Hertfordshire				
138b	Graveley		2	0	
	Welwyn		3	0	This lay in Weston
	Welwyn	2	0	0	This lay in Weston

Ref. (fos.)	Location	Value £	s.	d.	Notes
	Weston	30	0	0	Ælfstan a thegn of King Edward held it
	Clothall		3	0	This lay in Weston
139	Great Offley	15	0	0	Ælfstan a thegn of King Edward held it
138b	Welwyn	(2	0	0)	Ælfgyth a man of Ælfstan held this and could sell. It lay in Weston
	Hinxworth		(6	0)	A sokeman of Ælfstan held it
	Gloucestershire				
166b	Wyegate	3	0	0	
	Duntisbourne	10	0	0	
167	Badgeworth	15	0	0	
169	Frampton Cotterell	8	0	0	
	Bedfordshire				
211b	Sundon	20	0	0	Ælfstan of Boscombe, a thegn of King Edward, held it
212	Edworth	10	0	0	
	Arlesey	7	0	0	
	Campton		(5	0)	Alwin the man of Ælfstan held it and could sell
	Streatley	(2	0	0)	Godwine the man of Ælfstan held it and could sell
	Millow		(10	0)	Godmar the man of Ælfstan held it and could sell

Ælfstan of Boscombe	Total value of land held					
	By subject			From subject or by his men		
	£	s.	d.	£	s.	d.
	289	9	0	3	1	0

LAND ASSIGNED TO ÆLFWEALD

vol. i	*Dorset*			
80b	Gillingham	3	0	0

Land to Ælfweald (*cont.*):

Ref. (fos.)	Location	Value £	s.	d.	Notes
	Somerset				
97b	Pitcombe	8	0	0	
	North Cadbury	20	0	0	
	Maperton	8	0	0	
	Wenstrow	3	0	0	
	Dunkerton	5	0	0	
	Cheriton	2	0	0	
96b	Cheriton	4	0	0	This land was leased by Ælfweald from the Abbot of Cerne Abbey for his life only, and was to return on his death
	Gloucestershire				
169b	Tortworth	7	0	0	

Ælfweald	Total value of land held					
	By subject £	s.	d.	From subject or by his men £	s.	d.
	60	0	0	None		

LAND ASSIGNED TO ÆLFWEALD OF STEVINGTON

vol. i	*Bedfordshire*				
211	Stevington	30	0	0	Ælfweald a thegn of King Edward held it and could sell
	Pavenham	4	0	0	Ælfweald a thegn of King Edward held it and could sell
	Turvey	1	0	0	Ælfweald a thegn of King Edward held it and could sell
	Odell	8	0	0	Ælfweald a thegn of King Edward held it and could sell
	Sharnbrook	4	0	0	Ælfweald a thegn of King Edward held it and could sell
	Bromham		5	0	Ælfweald a thegn of King Edward held it and could sell

Ref. (fos.)	Location	Value £	s.	d.	Notes
209b	Turvey	(2	0	0)	One of Ælfweald of Stevington's men held it and could sell

Ælfweald of Stevington	Total value of land held					
	By subject			From subject or by his men		
	£	s.	d.	£	s.	d.
	47	5	0	2	0	0

LAND ASSIGNED TO 'ÆLFWINE', SHERIFF OF GLOUCESTER

[The name given in Domesday Book is Alwin, which could represent either Ælfwine or Æthelwine, and there is no evidence to prove which was intended. Furthermore, the name is a particularly common one, and it is entirely possible that this man held land elsewhere in Gloucestershire and beyond.]

Ref.	Location	£	s.	d.	Notes
vol. i	*Gloucestershire*				
167	Cirencester	5	0	0	
	Caldicott	3	0	0	
	Aylworth		6	0	
	Farmcote	10	0	0	
	Guiting Power	16	0	0	King Edward held it and leased it to Alwine his Sheriff so that he might have it for his lifetime; however, he did not give it as a gift, as the county testifies
	Castlett	2	0	0	
	Taynton	6	0	0	
	Little Barrington	2	0	0	
	Westbury Hundred				Half a hide of land and half a fishery, which Alwine the Sheriff held and gave to his wife. It belonged to the king's farm of Westbury
168	Dodington	3	0	0	

Land to Ælfwine (*cont.*):

Ref. (fos.)	Location	Value £	s.	d.	Notes
168b	Aylworth	2	0	0	
169b	Sezincote	2	0	0	
170	Sezincote	2	10	0	

'Ælfwine'	Total value of land held	
	By subject £ s. d.	From subject or by his men £ s. d.
	53 16 0	None

LAND ASSIGNED TO ÆTHELFRITH AND ÆLMAR

[There is no direct evidence that these men were brothers, but there is a certain amount of indirect evidence. Both men were the *antecessors* of Roger Arundel; they held almost exactly the same amount of land (Æthelfrith and 40 hides, Ælmar 39½) which suggests a possible division between brothers; and they had the estate of Piddletrenthide between them. For these reasons, their land has been considered to be a single estate.]

1. Æthelfrith

Ref.	Location	£	s.	d.	Notes
vol. i	*Dorset*				
77b	Piddletrenthide	15	0	0	30 hides held by Æthelfrith and Ælmar as two manors, which they could not separate from St Peter's, Winchester. The full value was £30
82b	Chelborough	2	10	0	5 hides
	Langton Long Blandford	4	0	0	5 hides
	Worth Maltravers	16	7	6	Æthelfrith held it from King Edward; 16½ hides
	Somerset				
94b	Beckington	10	0	0	10 hides
	Marston Bigot	6	0	0	3½ hides

Ref. (fos.)	Location	Value £	s.	d.	Notes
2.	Ælmar				
vol. i	*Dorset*				
77b	Piddletrenthide	15	0	0	30 hides held by Æthelfrith and Ælmar as two manors, which they could not separate from St Peter's, Winchester. The full value was £30
82b	Bexington	4	0	0	9½ hides
	Powerstock	4	0	0	6 hides
	Wraxhall	4	0	0	
	Somerset				
94b	Halse	5	0	0	4 hides
	Whitelackington	12	0	0	10 hides

Æthelfrith and Ælmar	Total value of land held	
	By subjects £ s. d.	From subjects or by their men £ s. d.
	89 17 6	None

LAND ASSIGNED TO ÆTHELGYTH, THURSTAN'S WIFE

		£	s.	d.	
vol. ii	*Essex*				
30b	Onger	5	0	0	
69b	Wimbish	12	0	0	
69	Dunmow	8	0	0	
71	Henham	12	0	0	
	Ashdon	6	0	0	
	Pentlow	10	0	0	
69	Dunmow	(1	0	0)	A sokeman of Æthelgyth held it
	Norfolk				
250b	Fincham	2	10	0	
	Barton Bendish	4	0	0	
	Shouldham	7	0	0	
251	Shouldham Thorpe	2	0	0	
	Wiggenhall	6	0	0	
	Boughton	2	0	0	

Land to Æthelgyth (*cont.*):

Ref. (fos.)	Location	Value £	s.	d.	Notes
252	Bradenham	6	0	0	
	Merton	5	0	0	
	Wilby	2	0	0	
263	Mildenhall (Suffolk)	5	0	0	
	Suffolk				
413b	Kedington	6	0	0	
415b	Shimpling	10	0	0	Æthelgyth held it from King Edward
413b	Poslingford	(1	11	0)	Two freemen commended to Æthelgyth held it
	Kedington	(2	0	0)	Twenty-four freemen commended to Æthelgyth held it
415b	Shimpling		(10	0)	A freeman held it under Æthelgyth

Æthelgyth	Total value of land held					
	By subject			From subject or by her men		
	£	s.	d.	£	s.	d.
	110	10	0	5	1	0

LAND ASSIGNED TO ÆTHELMAR MELC

vol. ii	*Essex*				
20b	Easter	8	0	0	Æthelmar, King Edward's thegn, held it
32	Tolleshunt	2	0	0	
33b	Elmdon	16	0	0	Æthelmar, King Edward's thegn held it
71	Langford		15	0	Æthelmar held it *ad censum* from St Paul's
71b	Tolleshunt	3	0	0	
72	Hatfield Peverel	16	0	0	

Ref. (fos.)	Location	Value £	s.	d.	Notes
	Terling	8	0	0	Æthelmar, King Edward's thegn held it
73b	Hazleigh	1	0	0	Æthelmar, a freeman held it
90	Horndon	3	0	0	Æthelmar, a freeman held it
	Thurrock	6	0	0	
107	Colchester				Æthelmar Melc had six houses: one was outside the walls, and one *ad collensum*

Æthelmar Melc	Total value of land held			
	By subject £	s.	d.	From subject or by his men £ s. d.
	63	0	0	None

LAND ASSIGNED TO ÆTHELNOTH CILT

Ref.	Location	£	s.	d.	Notes
vol. i	*Kent*				
1	Kent				Æthelnoth Cilt had *sac* and *soc* in Kent and Canterbury
2	Merclesham and Hwakhurst				Æthelnoth took these lands from St Martin's, with Earl Harold's support, and with inadequate compensation
6	Addington	4	0	0	Leofstan was said to have held it from King Edward, but after Leofstan's death it reverted to Æthelnoth
7	Eccles	3	0	0	
8	Chart Sutton	12	0	0	
8b	West Farleigh	7	0	0	Æthelnoth held it from King Edward
	Pimp's Court	1	0	0	Æthelnoth held it from King Edward
	Boxley	25	0	0	
9b	Easole	9	0	0	Æthelnoth held it from King Edward

Land to Æthelnoth Cilt (*cont.*):

Ref. (fos.)	Location	Value £	s.	d.	Notes
10b	Bilsington	10	0	0	
6b	Foots Cray	(4	0	0)	Alwin held it from Æthelnoth
7	Allington (Maidstone)	(5	0	0)	Wulfric held it from Æthelnoth
7b	Offham	(5	0	0)	Wulfric held it from Æthelnoth
8b	Bensted	(2	0	0)	Godric held it from Æthelnoth
	Sussex				
17b	Alciston	58	0	0	Includes £10 from the manor of Banstead, 31b
	Surrey				
31	Bramley	40	0	0	
	Hampshire				
46	Monk Sherbourne	25	0	0	
	Buckinghamshire				
144b	Westbury	3	0	0	Æthelnoth, King Edward's thegn, held it
145	Chetwode	3	0	0	Æthelnoth, King Edward's thegn, held it and could sell
	Tingewick	10	0	0	
	Oxfordshire				
155b	Stanton Harcourt	30	0	0	
	Tew	20	0	0	

Æthelnoth Cilt	Total value of land held					
	By subject			From subject or by his men		
	£	s.	d.	£	s.	d.
	260	0	0	20	0	0

LAND ASSIGNED TO ÆTHELRIC, MÆRGEAT'S SON

Ref.	Location	£	s.	d.	Notes
vol. i	*Warwickshire*				
242b	Wolvey	2	0	0	Æthelric held it freely
	Whitacre		10	0	Æthelric held it freely

Ref. (fos.)	Location	Value £	s.	d.	Notes
	Leicestershire				
234	Gilmorton		10	0	Æthelric held it and was a freeman
	Shenton		1	0	
	Kilworth		6	0	
	Gumley		1	0	
	Shancton		1	0	
	Thorpe Langton		4	0	
	Husbands Bosworth		4	0	
	Husbands Bosworth	1	0	0	
	Kibworth	2	0	0	
	Newton Harcourt	1	10	0	
	Lincolnshire				
337	Lincolnshire				Æthelric had *sac* and *soc* in the county
346	Doddington	20	0	0	Æthelric gave this to St Peter's, Westminster
363	Helpringham	3	0	0	
	Caythorpe	30	0	0	
	Stenning	1	0	0	
370	Haddington	1	0	0	Pertains to Doddington
	South Hykeham	2	0	0	Pertains to Doddington
	Skellingthorpe	2	0	0	Pertains to Doddington
	North Hykeham	1	0	0	Pertains to Doddington
vol. ii	*Essex*				
14b	Kelvedon Hatch	2	0	0	Æthelric fought in a naval battle against William. He fell sick on his return and gave this manor to St Peter's

Æthelric	Total value of land held	
	By subject £ s. d.	From subject or by his men £ s. d.
	67 17 0	None

LAND ASSIGNED TO ÆTHELSIGE (*ANTECESSOR* OF WALTER OF DOUAI)

Ref. (fos.)	Location	Value £	s.	d.	Notes
vol. i	*Somerset*				
95	Bratton Seymour	7	0	0	
	Wincanton	3	10	0	
	Castle Cary	16	0	0	
	Barrow	5	0	0	
95b	Adber (Dorset)	0	15	0	
	Devonshire				
111b	Dunsford	2	0	0	
112	Luppitt	1	0	0	
	Ottery	4	0	0	
	Greenway	1	10	0	
	Heathfield (in Honiton)	2	0	0	
	Ottery	4	0	0	
117	Lowley		10	0	
	Doddiscombleigh	2	0	0	

Æthelsige	Total value of land held	
	By subject £ s. d.	From subject or by his/her men £ s. d.
	49 5 0	None

LAND ASSIGNED TO ÆTHELSTAN, GODRAM'S SON

Ref. (fos.)	Location	Value £	s.	d.	Notes
vol. i	*Lincolnshire*				
337	Lincolnshire				Æthelstan, Godram's son, had *sac* and *soc* in the county
367	Rippingale	4	0	0	
	Pointon	1	0	0	
	Scottlethorpe	1	0	0	
367b	Swarby	2	0	0	
	Welby	2	0	0	

Ref. (fos.)	Location	Value £	s.	d.	Notes
	Wyberton	3	0	0	
	Frampton	3	10	0	
	Burton Coggles	6	0	0	
	Wrangle				Waste. *Wastus est propter fluxis maris*
	Fishtoft	8	0	0	
	Bicker	1	0	0	
368	Drayton		5	0	
	Houghton	4	0	0	
	Holbeach and Whaplode	5	0	0	
	Spalding	2	0	0	
	Boothby Pagnall and Old Somerby	1	0	0	
377b					Count Alan claimed that Æthelstan did not have Bicker or Drayton *TRE*

Æthelstan	Total value of land held			
	By subject £	s.	d.	From subject or by his/her men £ s. d.
	44	15	0	None

LAND ASSIGNED TO ÆTHELWIG
(*ANTECESSOR* OF ALFRED OF SPAIN)

vol. i	*Wiltshire*				
73	Yatesbury	3	0	0	
	Dorset				
82b	Turnworth	6	0	0	
	Somerset				
97	Woolmersdon	1	10	0	
	Woolmersdon		10	0	The reeve of the king's manor of South Peret leased this land to Æthelwig

Land to Æthelwig (*cont.*):

Ref. (fos.)	Location	Value £	s.	d.	Notes
97	East Bower	5	0	0	To this manor was added 1 virgate of the king's farm from South Peret
	Huntworth		5	0	
	Stringston	2	10	0	
	Spaxton	2	10	0	
	Marshmills	3	0	0	
	Alfoxton	1	0	0	
	Rodhuish		2	0	
	Stawley	5	0	0	
	Isle Brewers	1	0	0	
	Preston Bowyer	1	10	0	
	Spaxton	3	0	0	
	Monksilver	3	0	0	
97b	Goathurst	3	10	0	
	Merridge	1	0	0	
	Quantock	1	0	0	
	Hillfarrance	3	0	0	
	Luckington	6	0	0	
	Oakley	2	10	0	This manor was added to the royal manor of Mantock
	Devon				
115b	Arlington	8	0	0	
	Orway	1	10	0	

Æthelwig	Total value of land held			
	By subject £	s.	d.	From subject or by his/her men £ s. d.
	65	7	0	None

LAND ASSIGNED TO ASBIORN BIGGA

vol. i	Location	Notes
	Kent	
1	Kent	Asbiorn Bigga did not have to pay relief on alloidal lands

Ref. (fos.)	Location	Value £	s.	d.	Notes
2	Canterbury				Asbiorn had *sac* and *soc* in Canterbury
	Canterbury		11	2	Asbiorn had eleven houses there
7	Keston	2	0	0	Asbiorn held it from King Edward
	Ditton	5	0	0	Asbiorn held it from King Edward
7b	Birling	12	0	0	Asbiorn held it from King Edward
8	Thurnham	10	0	0	Asbiorn held it from King Edward
	Fairbourne	1	10	0	Asbiorn held it from King Edward
10b	Pivington	8	0	0	Asbiorn held it from King Edward
13	Postling	10	0	0	Asbiorn held it from King Edward
12	Garrington	(4	0	0)	Eadric held it from Asbiorn Bigga

Asbiorn Bigga	Total value of land held					
	By subject			From subject or by his/her men		
	£	s.	d.	£	s.	d.
	49	1	2	4	0	0

LAND ASSIGNED TO ASGEIR THE STALLER

Ref.	Location	£	s.	d.
vol. i	*Berkshire*			
62	Lambourn	20	0	0
	Hurley	12	0	0
	Streatley	20	0	0
	Middlesex			
129b	Northolt	12	0	0
	Edmonton	40	0	0
	Enfield	50	0	0

Land to Asgeir the Staller (*cont.*):

Ref. (fos.)	Location	Value £	s.	d.	Notes
129b	Greenford		(3	0)	Azur the man of Asgeir held it but could not sell
	Greenford	(1	0	0)	A man of Asgeir held it but could not sell
	Ickenham	(1	0	0)	A man of Asgeir held it but could not sell
	Hertfordshire				
132	Hertford				Asgeir had seven houses
139b	Shenley	8	0	0	
140	Sawbridgeworth	60	0	0	
132b	King's Walden	(7	0	0)	A widow, the woman of Asgeir held it
133b	Much Hadham		(15	0)	Eadric the man of Asgeir held it and could sell
	Pelham	(5	0	0)	Two brothers, the men of Asgeir held it and could sell
	Pelham	(2	10	0)	Ælfred the men of Asgeir held it and could sell
	Pelham	(1	10	0)	A man of Asgeir held it
134	Hixham	(3	0	0)	Wulfwig the man of Asgeir held it and could sell
	Wickham		(3	4)	A sokeman of Asgeir held it and could sell
134b	Libury	(3	0	0)	Almar held it of the king's soke; he was the man of Asgeir
137	Eckington	(2	0	0)	Godgyth the man of Asgeir held it and could sell
	Eckington		(3	0)	Godgyth the man of Asgeir held it and could sell
	Beauchamps	(2	0	0)	Godgyth the man of Asgeir held it and could sell
137b	Hormead	(5	0	0)	Wulfweard the man of Asgeir held it and could sell
	Bozen	(4	0	0)	Nine of Asgeir's sokemen held it and could sell
	Hoddesdon	(2	0	0)	Godgyth the man of Asgeir held it and could sell
	Braughing	(10	0	0)	A thegn of Asgeir held it but he could not sell

Ref. (fos.)	Location	Value £	s.	d.	Notes
138	Hyde Hall	(1	0	0)	Ælfred the man of Asgeir held it and could sell
138b	Hormead		(5	0)	Wulfweard the man of Asgeir held it
139b	Theobald Street		(6	8)	Two of Asgeir's sokemen held it
	Digswell	(4	0	0)	Thorkell the man of Asgeir held it and could sell
	Wallington		(10	0)	Eadred the man of Asgeir held it and could sell
	Ashwell		(10	0)	Godgifu the 'man' of Asgeir held it but could not sell
	Hainstone	(4	0	0)	Wulfric the man of Asgeir held it and could sell
	Barkway	(6	0	0)	Two of Asgeir's man held it and could sell
	Hare Street		(5	0)	Ælfred the man of Asgeir held it and could sell
	Bozen	(2	0	0)	Four sokemen held it of the soke of Asgeir and could sell
	Stiuicesworde	(2	0	0)	Burgi the man of Asgeir held it and could sell
	Hoddesdon	(2	0	0)	Godgyth the man of Asgeir held it and could sell
	Brickendon		(10	0)	Oswig the man of Asgeir held it and could sell
	Bengeo	(4	0	0)	Thorkell the man of Asgeir held it
	Stanstead Abbots		(2	0)	A sokeman of Asgeir held it
140	Thorley	(10	0	0)	Godgyth the man of Asgeir held it, but the Bishop of London claimed to have bought it
	Wickham	(2	0	0)	Two of Asgeir's sokemen held it and could sell
	Hexton	(2	0	0)	Alric the man of Asgeir held it and could sell
142	Brakway	(2	0	0)	Two sokemen of Asgeir held it and could sell
	Hormead	(2	10	0)	Wulfwine the man of Asgeir held it

Land to Asgeir the Staller (*cont.*):

Ref. (fos.)	Location	Value £	s.	d.	Notes
142	Wormley	(3	0	0)	Wulfweard the man of Asgeir held it
	Buckinghamshire				
143	Monks Risborough	(16	0	0)	Asgeir held it from Christ Church but could not sell
149b	Ivinghoe Aston	(3	0	0)	Asgeir held this land in demesne
147b	Leckhampstead	(1	10	0)	Swartin a man of Asgeir held it and could not sell
	Maids Moreton	(1	0	0)	Eadric the man of Asgeir held it and could sell
148	Moulsoe	(1	4	0)	Ulf the man of Asgeir held it
149b	Waldridge		(15	0)	Doding the man of Asgeir held it and could sell
	Claydon	(5	0	0)	Swein the man of Asgeir held it and could not sell
	Quarrendon	(6	0	0)	Swein the man of Asgeir held it and could not sell
	Swanbourne	(1	10	0)	Swein the man of Asgeir held it and could not sell
	Leckhampstead	(1	10	0)	Swartin the man of Asgeir held it but could not sell
149b	*Lamau* Hundred	(2	0	0)	Ulf the man of Asgeir held it and could sell
151	Marlow	(4	0	0)	Godric the man of Asgeir held it and could sell
	Oxfordshire				
160	Wendlebury	5	0	0	
	Kingham	12	0	0	No holder is recorded *TRE*, but these
	Rycote		5	0	Two manors make up all the land which Asgeir's successor, Geoffrey de Mandeville, had in the county
	Cambridgeshire				
194b	Whaddon	(8	0	0)	Leofwig the man of Asgeir held it and could sell

Ref. (fos.)	Location	Value £	s.	d.	Notes
196	Grantchester	(2	0	0)	A sokeman of Asgeir held it and could sell
196b	Barrington	(2	0	0)	Three sokemen of Asgeir held it and could sell
197	Fulbourn	(3	0	0)	Alsige the man of Asgeir held it and could sell
	Sawston	(5	0	0)	Sigar the man of Asgeir held it and could sell
	Thriplow	(2	0	0)	Sigar the man of Asgeir held it and could sell
	Foxton	(4	0	0)	Sigar the man of Asgeir held it and could sell
	Chippenham	(12	0	0)	Ordgar, King Edward's sheriff and the man of Asgeir, held it
	Morden	(2	0	0)	Godwine the man of Asgeir held it and could sell
	Haslingfield	(6	0	0)	Sigar the man of Asgeir held it and could sell
	Shepreth	(1	3	0)	Sigar held it from Asgeir and could sell
	Orwell		(10	0)	Sigar held it from Asgeir and could sell
198b	Croydon	(1	0	0)	Ælfric the man of Asgeir held it and could sell
	Whaddon		(2	0)	Danemund the man of Asgeir held it and could sell
200	Tadlow	(1	10	0)	Godric the man of Asgeir held it and could sell
200b	Haslingfield		(15	0)	A sokeman of Asgeir held it and could sell
	Harlton	(1	0	0)	Godman held it under Asgeir and could sell
201	Bourn	(2	0	0)	A man of Asgeir held it and could sell
	Bedfordshire				
209b	Biscott	(3	0	0)	Eadwine the man of Asgeir held it and could sell
	Northamptonshire				
227	Aynho	6	0	0	
	Croughton		3	0	Asgeir held it freely

Land to Asgeir the Staller (*cont.*):

Ref. (fos.)	Location	Value £	s.	d.	Notes
227b	Hinton	2	0	0	
	Easton in the Hill	6	0	0	
	Flore		5	0	
	Silverstone		10	0	
	Culworth	3	0	0	
227	Croughton	(1	10	0)	Swartlin held it from Asgeir but could not sell
	Warwickshire				
243b	Long Compton	15	0	0	
vol. ii	*Essex*				
58	Waltham	50	0	0	
59	Leighs	4	0	0	Asgeir gave this land to Harold
60	Notley	5	0	0	
	Ridley	1	10	0	
	Hallingbury	2	0	0	
	Matching		10	0	
	High Easter	20	0	0	
	High Easter	(6	0	0)	Held by eight sokemen. Ely claimed both lands at High Easter, although admitting that Asgeir held both at the time of the Conquest
61	Bigods	7	0	0	
	Dunmow	5	0	0	
	Shellow Bowells	2	0	0	
61b	Roding	5	0	0	
	Dunmow	1	0	0	
	Canfield	2	0	0	
	Roding	3	0	0	
62	Saffron Walden	36	0	0	
63	*Weneswic*	4	0	0	
61b	Roding	(2	0	0)	Two freemen held this, of whom one gave his soke to Asgeir
62	Dunmow		(7	0)	A sokeman of Asgeir held it
	Roding		(10	0)	Asgeir held it, and Leofgyth, a freewoman, held it under Asgeir

Ref. (fos.)	Location	Value £	s.	d.	Notes
62b	Birchanger	(1	0	0)	A sokeman of Asgeir held it
	Plegdon	(1	1	0)	A sokeman of Asgeir held it
	Norfolk				
149b	Shelfhanger	(1	0	0)	A freeman of Asgeir held it
248	East Ruston	(2	0	0)	Asgeir held it under Asgeir Staller
	Suffolk				
411	Holton St Mary	3	0	0	
	Raydon	8	0	0	
395	*Toft*		(5	0)	Alwin, a freeman commended to Asgeir, held it
411b	Raydon		(5	0)	Edwin and Beorhtmær, freemen commended to Asgeir, held it
440	Ixworth	(3	0	0)	Ketel held it under commendation to Asgeir

Asgeir the Staller	Total value of land held	
	By subject £ s. d.	From subject or by his/her men £ s. d.
	447 13 0	205 10 0

LAND ASSIGNED TO THE BROTHERS ASGAUTR, BEORHTRIC, AND EDMUND

[Asgautr (*antecessor* of William Leofric), Beorhtric (*antecessor* of Thurstan fitz Rolf), and Edmund (*antecessor* of Roger Lacy) are assumed to be related because of their joint tenure at Childrey and Coleshill in Berkshire. Each man held manors of approximately equal size at Childrey. At Coleshill, each of the three men held eight hides of land valued at £7, including a third of a mill; in addition, a further hide recorded in Wiltshire, but relating to Coleshill, was held jointly by their Norman successors.]

vol. i	*Hampshire*				
47b	Newton Valence	15	0	0	Beorhtric held this from King Edward *in alodium*

Land to Asgautr, Beorhtric, and Edmund (*cont.*):

Ref. (fos.)	Location	Value £	s.	d.	Notes
	Berkshire				
59b	Coleshill	7	0	0	Edmund held it from King Edward *in alodium*
61	Coleshill	7	0	0	Asgautr held it from King Edward *in alodium*
	Childrey	9	0	0	Asgautr, a freeman, held it
	Oldstone	12	0	0	Asgautr held it from King Edward *in alodium*
62b	Enborne	2	0	0	Edmund, a thegn of King Edward, held it *in alodium*
	Childrey	8	10	0	Edmund, a freeman, held it
63	Coleshill	7	0	0	Beorhtric held it from King Edward *in alodium*
	Upton	13	0	0	Beorhtric, a freeman, held it
	Childrey	10	0	0	Beorhtric, a freeman, held it
	Sparsholt	1	10	0	Beorhtric, a freeman, held it
	Wiltshire				
72b	Coleshill	4	0	0	Roger Lacy, Thurstan fitz Rolf, and William Leofric held one hide in Coleshill. Three thegns held it *TRE*
	Buckinghamshire				
144	Taplow	8	0	0	Asgautr, a man of Earl Harold, held it
151	Little Kimble	6	0	0	Beorhtric, King Edward's thegn, held it
	Gloucestershire				
167b	Leckhampton	2	0	0	Asgautr held it
	Hailes	2	0	0	Asgautr held it
	Wittington	5	0	0	Asgautr held it
	Shipton Oliffe	2	0	0	Asgautr held it
	Lower Turkdean	4	0	0	Asgautr held it
168	Stratton	8	0	0	Edmund held it
169	Kempsford	30	0	0	Asgautr held it from Earl Harold
169b	Oakley	2	10	0	Beorhtric held it from King Edward

Ref. (fos.)	Location	Value £	s.	d.	Notes
	Herefordshire				
185b	Alvington (Gloucs.)	1	0	0	Beorhtric held it. The manor also returned renders in honey and iron
	Little Mercle	3	0	0	Beorhtric held it from Earl Harold
vol. ii	*Essex*				
93	*Scilceham*	6	0	0	Asgautr, a freeman, held it

	Total value of land held: By subject £ s. d.	From subject or by their men £ s. d.
Asgautr	88 6 8	None
Beorhtric	60 6 8	None
Edmund	26 16 8	None
TOTAL	175 10 0	None

LAND ASSIGNED TO ASKELL OF WARE

Ref. (fos.)	Location	£	s.	d.	Notes
vol. i	*Hertfordshire*				
138b	Ware	50	0	0	
133b	Pelham	(10	0	0)	Two thegns, the men of Askell of Ware, held it and could sell
138	Westmill		(15	0)	A freeman of Askell held it and could sell
138b	Stanstead	(5	0	0)	Four freemen of Askell held it and could sell
141	Sacombe	(1	0	0)	A freewoman of Askell held it. She could sell 4 of the 5 virgates. The 5th had been given in pledge to Ælfmar of Bennington for 10*s*.
	Wallington	(1	10	0)	Wulfmær the man of Askell held it and could sell
141b	Sacombe		(15	0)	Two of Askell's men held it and could sell

Land to Askell (*cont.*):

Ref. (fos.)	Location	Value £	s.	d.	Notes
	Bedfordshire				
212b	Keysoe	5	0	0	Askell, King Edward's thegn, held it
	Putnoe	2	0	0	Askell, King Edward's thegn, held it
	Chainelle	7	0	0	Askell, King Edward's thegn, held it
213	Willington	6	0	0	Askell, King Edward's thegn, held it
	Stotfold	20	0	0	Askell, King Edward's thegn, held it
	Streatley	5	0	0	Askell, King Edward's thegn, held it
	Wyboston		2	0	
218	Hockliffe	12	0	0	Askell held it and could sell
	Henlow	1	10	0	A berewick of Stotfold
213	Maulden		(12	0)	Goda the man of Askell held it and could sell
213b	Goldington	(3	0	0)	Almar the man of Askell held it and could sell
	Holme		(5	0)	A sokeman held it under Askell and could sell
218b	Henlow	(1	8	0)	Two sokemen of Askell held it and could sell

Askell of Ware	Total value of land held					
	By subject			From subject or by his men		
	£	s.	d.	£	s.	d.
	108	12	0	24	5	0

[Askell's successor in Bedfordshire, Hugh Beauchamp, held a considerable number of sokemen who had no recorded *TRE*. A proportion of these—perhaps most of them—may have been the men of Askell of Ware.]

LAND ASSIGNED TO AZUR, THORED'S SON

Ref. (fos.)	Location	Value £	s.	d.	Notes
vol. i	*Wiltshire*				
69	Elcombe	27	0	0	
	Stratford Tony	20	0	0	
	Gussage St Michael	40	0	0	
	Buckinghamshire				
143b	Biddlesden	2	0	0	
	Oxfordshire				
157b	Iffley	5	0	0	Azur held it freely
	Minster Lovell	10	0	0	No named tenant *TRE*, but it is the only other manor held in Oxfordshire by Aubrey de Vere, Azur's successor
	Northamptonshire				
224	Halse, Syresham, and Brackley	12	0	0	Azur held these freely

Azur, Thored's son	Total value of land held	
	By subject £ s. d.	From subject or by his men £ s. d.
	116 0 0	None

LAND ASSIGNED TO AZUR, TOTI'S SON

Ref. (fos.)	Location	Value £	s.	d.	Notes
vol. i	*Middlesex*				
130	Stanwell	14	0	0	Azur, one of King Edward's housecarls, held it and could sell
	East Bedfont	5	0	0	A berewick of Stanwell
	East Bedfont	(1	0	0)	Three of Azur's sokemen held it and could sell
	West Bedfont	(1	10	0)	Two of Azur's sokemen held it but could not sell

Land to Azur, Toti's son (*cont.*):

Ref. (fos.)	Location	Value £	s.	d.	Notes
130	Hatton	(1	10	0)	Two of Azur's sokemen held it but could not sell
	Buckinghamshire				
143	Buckingham				Six burgesses were Azur's men
149b	Shalstone	3	0	0	Azur held it and could sell
	Water Stratford	7	0	0	
151	Nashway	2	10	0	Azur, Toti's son, the man of Queen Eadgyth, held it and could sell
151b	Radclive	6	0	0	Azur held it and could sell
	Thornton	8	0	0	Azur held it and could sell
152b	Quainton	2	10	0	Azur, Toti's son, a housecarl of King Edward, held it
	Woughton on the Green	5	0	0	
144b	Marston	(1	0	0)	A man of Azur held it and could sell
	Beachendon		(2	6)	A man of Azur held it and could sell
147b	Maids Moreton		(2	6)	Sæward, a man of Azur, held it and could sell
150	Beachendon		(12	6)	A man of Azur held it and could sell
151b	Beachampton		(10	0)	Leofric the man of Azur held it and could sell
152b	Woughton on the Green	(1	0	0)	A thegn, the man of Azur, held it and could sell
	Warwickshire				
244	Leamington Hastings	10	0	0	Azur held it freely
	Haseley	1	0	0	Azur held it freely
	Northamptonshire				
255	Wicken	2	0	0	

Azur, Toti's son	Total value of land held					
	By subject			From subject or by his men		
	£	s.	d.	£	s.	d.
	66	0	0	7	6	0

LAND ASSIGNED TO AZUR

Ref. (fos.)	Location	Value £	s.	d.	Notes
vol. i	*Sussex*				
19b	Eckington		6	0	Azur, a freeman held it; it was not gelded
19b			10	0	Azur, a freeman held it
21	Dean	7	0	0	
21b	Taring Neville	8	0	0	Azur held it from Earl Godwine
	Hartfield Hundred		10	0	Azur held it *sicut alodium*
22b	Bevendean				Valued with Taring Neville; Azur held Bevendean from King Edward
23	Cocking	15	0	0	Azur held it from King Edward
24b	Toddington	3	0	0	Azur held it from King Edward
	West Chiltington	1	10	0	Azur held it from King Edward
	Lyminster		10	0	
	Greatham	6	0	0	Azur held it from Kind Edward
25	Slindon	20	0	0	Azur, a freeman held it
25b	Binsted Hundred		8	0	Azur, a freeman held it
	Binsted Hundred	1	10	0	Azur, a freeman held it
26b	Bevendean	5	0	0	Azur held it from King Edward
	Esmerwic	2	0	0	Azur held it from King Edward
	Hangleton	10	0	0	Azur held it from King Edward. The manor lay in Kingston by Sea
27	Keymer	14	0	0	Azur held it from King Edward
	Clayton	10	0	0	Azur held it from King Edward
27b	Barcombe	12	0	0	Azur held it from Earl Godwine
	Moustone	1	0	0	Azur held it from King Edward at the manor of Ovingdean
28	Shoreham	25	0	0	Azur held it from King Edward
	Wiston	12	0	0	Azur held it from Earl Godwine
28b	Shermanbury	1	4	0	Azur held it from Earl Harold
	Kingston by Sea	15	0	0	Azur held this manor from Earl Harold. Part of it lay in the Rape of William Warenne (see Hangleton, above)
26b	Ovingdean	(1	0	0)	Morkær held it from Azur
27	Perching	(3	0	0)	Azur held it from the king, and two men from Azur
	Wickham				Alwin held it from Azur

Land to Azur (*cont.*):

Ref. (fos.)	Location	Value £	s.	d.	Notes
28b	Woolfly		(5	0)	Alwin held it from Azur
	Morely		(10	0)	Alweard held it from Azur
	Wantley	(2	0	0)	Beorhtmær held it from Azur, and Azur from Earl Harold
	Sakeham		(10	0)	Beorhtwine held it from Azur
29	Cokeham	(1	0	0)	Beorhtmær held it from Azur
	Surrey				
34	Henley	6	0	0	Azur held it and after his death gave it to Chertsey for his soul, in the time of King William
34b	Tillingdown	8	0	0	Azur held it from King Edward
	Beddington	10	0	0	Azur held it from King Edward
35	Woodmansterne	10	0	0	Azur held it from King Edward
35b	Albury	10	0	0	Azur held it from King Edward
35b	Effingham	4	0	0	Azur held it from King Edward. He bought another hide there *TRE*
36	Walton on Thames	8	0	0	Azur held it from King Edward
	Hambledon	5	0	0	Azur held it from King Edward
	Hampshire				
45b	Upton Grey	10	0	0	Azur held it from King Edward *in alodium*
	Littleton (in Kimpton)	5	0	0	Azur held it from King Edward *in alodium*
	Clanville	1	10	0	Azur held it from King Edward *in alodium*
	Wiltshire				
69b	Chitterne	20	0	0	
	Rockley	2	0	0	
	Langford	1	0	0	
	Gloucestershire				
164	Woodchester	7	0	0	Earl Godwine bought this manor from Azur

Azur	Total value of land held					
	By subject			From subject or by his men		
	£	*s.*	*d.*	£	*s.*	*d.*
	271	8	0	8	5	0

LAND ASSIGNED TO BALDWIN, HERLUIN'S SON

Ref. (fos.)	Location	Value £	*s.*	*d.*	Notes
vol. i	*Berkshire*				
61	Hodcott	6	0	0	Baldwin held it from King Edward
	Yattendon	7	0	0	Baldwin held it from King Edward *in alodium*
	Ilsley	7	0	0	Baldwin held it from King Edward
61b	Pangbourne	6	0	0	Baldwin held it from King Edward
	Sulham	1	0	0	Baldwin held it from King Edward
	Wiltshire				
69b	North Wraxhall	5	0	0	
	Buckinghamshire				
148b	Ellesborough	1	0	0	Baldwin the man of Stigand held it
	Hampden	5	0	0	Baldwin the man of Stigand held it
	Hampden	1	6	0	
149	Chichley	2	0	0	
144b	Stowe	(3	0	0)	Thorgills the man of Baldwin held it
146b	Woughton on the Green		(2	6)	A man of Baldwin held it
149	Hardmead		(13	4)	Three brothers, of whom two were the men of Baldwin, held it

Land to Baldwin (*cont.*):

Ref. (fos.)	Location	Value £	s.	d.	Notes
	Gloucestershire				
162	Gloucester				Baldwin had one house
163	Bradley Hundred	12	0	0	
168	Childs Wickham (Worcs.)	12	0	0	
169	Quinton (Warwicks.)	7	0	0	
	Weston on Avon (Warwicks.)	7	0	0	
	Northamptonshire				
224b	Welton	1	0	0	Baldwin held it freely
	Newbottle (nr. Brackley)	4	0	0	Baldwin held it with *sac* and *soc*
	Woodford Halse	2	0	0	Baldwin held it freely
224b	Charlton on Otmoor (Oxon)	8	0	0	Baldwin held it freely
	Sibford (Oxon)	4	10	0	
	Staverton		(15	0)	Leofric held it from Baldwin
	Thorpe Lubbenham		(1	0)	Alwin held it from Baldwin
	Leicestershire				
232		1	0	0	
	Warwickshire				
240b	Tachbrook	3	0	0	Baldwin held it freely
242	Marston (in Lea Marston)	10	0	0	Baldwin held it freely
	Pillerton	10	0	0	Baldwin held it freely
	Lapworth		10	0	Baldwin held it freely
	Thurlaston	2	0	0	Baldwin held it freely
	Eatingdon	1	0	0	Baldwin held it freely
	Rowington	5	0	0	Baldwin held it freely
	Billesley	5	0	0	Baldwin held it freely
	Whitacre		2	0	Baldwin held it freely

Baldwin	Total value of land held					
	By subject			From subject or by his men		
	£	s.	d.	£	s.	d.
	136	8	0	4	6	0

LAND ASSIGNED TO BEORHTMÆR

Ref. (fos.)	Location	Value £	s.	d.	Notes
vol. i	*Devon*				
105b	Chichacott		15	0	
	Dunterton	1	0	0	
106	Highampton	3	0	0	
	Ashmansworthy		10	0	
	Sedborough				
106b	Kenn	12	0	0	
	Shirwell	2	0	0	
	Heanton Punchardon	4	0	0	
	Charles	2	0	0	
107	Langford (in Cullompton)	2	0	0	
	Combe Sackville	1	0	0	
	Lincombe	2	0	0	
	Ashford (nr. Barnstaple)	1	0	0	
107b	Clifford	1	0	0	
	Melhuish	1	0	0	
108	Chulmleigh	12	0	0	
	Selake		5	0	
108b	Englebourne		15	0	
	Cornwall				
121b	Brannel	8	0	0	
121b	Rillaton	30	0	0	
122	Torwell	2	0	0	
	Trematon	10	0	0	
	Tregantle	1	0	0	
	Tremoan		10	0	
	Trehawke		5	0	
	Gear	1	5	0	
122b	Lantivet		2	0	
123	Arrallas	1	0	0	
	Trewoon		10	0	
	Trenant (in Fowley)	1	0	0	
	Worthyvale	4	0	0	
123b	Moreton		10	0	
124	Treluggan (in Landrake)		10	0	

Land to Beorhtmær (*cont.*):

Ref. (fos.)	Location	Value £	s.	d.	Notes
124	Treveniel	1	0	0	
125	Tredwen		15	0	

Beorhtmær	Total value of land held			
	By subject			From subject or by his men
	£	s.	d.	£ s. d.
	109	2	0	None

[In other counties in the West Country 'Beorhtmær' was said to hold land valued at £72, which was held by a number of tenants-in-chief in 1086. Some or all of this land might have been held by the man who held the above estate.]

LAND ASSIGNED TO BEORHTRIC, ÆLFGAR'S SON

vol. i	*Hampshire*			
39b	Knighton	1	0	0
	Wiltshire			
68b	Deverill	15	0	0
	Dorset			
75b	Frome St Quentin	12	0	0
	Cranbourne	24	0	0
	Ashmore	15	0	0
77b	Boveridge	5	0	0
79	Dewlish	23	0	0
79b	Tarrant	11	0	0
83	Tarrant	2	0	0
	Tyneham	3	0	0
	Devonshire			
101	Northlew	9	0	0
	Halwill	3	10	0
	Clovelly	6	0	0

Ref. (fos.)	Location	Value £	s.	d.	Notes
	Bideford	1	5	0	
	Littleham (nr. Bideford)	3	0	0	
	Langtree	7	5	0	
	Iddesleigh	14	0	0	
101b	Winkleigh	30	0	0	
	Ashreigny	7	0	0	
	High Bickington	12	0	0	
	Morchard Bishop	4	0	0	
	Holcombe Burnell	8	15	0	
	Halberton	27	0	0	
	Ashprington	4	0	0	
104	Northam	12	0	0	
	Umberleigh	10	0	0	
113	Sampford Peverell	5	0	0	
101	Iddesleigh	(1	0	0)	Alwar held it from Beorhtric but could not sell it
	Cornwall				
120	Connerton	12	0	0	7 hides gelded as 3
120b	Coswarth	3	0	0	1 hide 3 virgates gelded as 1 virgate
	Binnerton	10	0	0	8 hides gelded as 4
	Trevalga	4	0	0	1 hide gelded as half a hide
	Carwogie		17	6	
	Gloucestershire				
163b	Thornbury	50	0	0	
	Sodbury	16	10	0	
	Avening	27	0	0	
	Fairford	38	0	0	
	Tewkesbury	100	0	0	
164	Modesgate	4	0	0	
166b	Woolaston	1	0	0	
163b	Ashton under Hill (Worcs.)	(2	0	0)	A thegn held it*
	Kemworth (Worcs.)	(8	0	0)	Let held it*
	Boddington	(2	0	0)	Pertains to Kemerton*
	Wincot (Warwicks.)	(2	0	0)	A thegn held it*
	Alderton and Dixton	(11	0	0)	Dunning held it*
	Twining	(1	15	0)	A thegn held it*

Land to Beorhtric (*cont.*):

Ref. (fos.)	Location	Value £	s.	d.	Notes
163b	Stoke Orchard	(3	0	0)	Harmer and Alwin held it*

* Of these manors it was said that Beorhtric had the lands of these thegns completely under his power *TRE*. The holders of these lands had put themselves and their lands into his power.

Ref. (fos.)	Location	Value £	s.	d.	Notes
	Worcestershire				
173	Bushley	2	0	0	
	Barley		15	0	Beorhtric held both lands from the Bishop of Worcester, who claimed that Beorhtric paid an annual farm for them, and paid the soke that was due to the king to the bishop. But Beorhtric stated that he paid 3 marks of gold for the land, and held it freely, owing no service for it to any man (180b)
	Herefordshire				
180b	Hanley and Forthampton	15	0	0	

	Total value of land held					
Beorhtric, Ælfgar's son	By subject £	s.	d.	From subject or by his men £	s.	d.
	559	17	6	30	15	0

LAND ASSIGNED TO BEORHTRIC THE MAN OF QUEEN EADGYTH

Ref.	Location	£	s.	d.	Notes
vol. i	*Hertfordshire*				
136b	Wiggington	3	0	0	Beorhtric the man of Queen Eadgyth held it
137b	Tiscot	(2	0	0)	Two of Beorhtric's sokemen held it

Ref. (fos.)	Location	Value £	s.	d.	Notes
	Buckinghamshire				
149	Wycombe	12	0	0	Beorhtric held it from Queen Eadgyth
149b	Marshworth	20	0	0	Beorhtric, a thegn of King Edward, held it
150	Waddesdon	30	0	0	Beorhtric the man of Queen Eadgyth held it
	Wingrave	5	0	0	Beorhtric the man of Queen Eadgyth held it and could sell
150b	Chesham	12	0	0	Beorhtric the man of Queen Eadgyth held it
144b	Beachendon		(2	6)	A man of Beorhtric held it and could sell
146	Wingrave	(1	0	0)	Ordmær the man of Beorhtric held it and could sell
	Drayton Beauchamp	(1	0	0)	A widow held it from Beorhtric and could sell
148b	Marston	(1	0	0)	Alwig the man of Beorhtric held it and could sell
148b	Littlecote	(1	10	0)	Two men of Beorhtric held it and could sell
	Swanbourne		(2	0)	Oswing the man of Beorhtric held it and could sell
	Hollingdon		(8	0)	Four of Beorhtric's sokemen held it and could sell
150	Aston Sandford		(15	0)	Wulfric and Coleman, men of Beorhtric, held it and could sell
	Sortelai		(10	0)	Two thegns, the men of Beorhtric, held it and could sell
	Soulbury	(1	0	0)	Almar the man of Beorhtric held it but could not sell
	Beachendon		(12	6)	A man of Beorhtric held it and could sell
	Marston	(1	0	0)	A man of Beorhtric held it and could sell
	Wingrave		(10	0)	Lemar, a man of Beorhtric, held it and could sell
	Wingrave	(2	0	0)	Almar the man of Beorhtric held it and could sell
	Littlecote	(1	5	0)	Herch, a man of Beorhtric, held it and could sell

Land to Beorhtric (*cont.*):

Ref. (fos.)	Location	Value £	s.	d.	Notes
150	Burston	(1	0	0)	Oswulf the man of Beorhtric held it and could sell
	Pitstone	(2	0	0)	Lepsi the man of Beorhtric held it and could sell
	Pitstone	(1	0	0)	Lepsi the man of Beorhtric held it and could sell
150b	Horton		(13	4)	Lepsi the man of Beorhtric held it and could sell
	Brook		(10	0)	Odo, a man of Beorhtric, held it and could sell
	Oxfordshire				
159b	Somerton	1	0	0	
	Wainhill		10	0	
	Bedfordshire				
212	Clapham	12	0	0	Ramsey claims that the land had been '*ad victum monachorum*', and that Beorhtric held it from the abbey. The hundred supports this claim
	Thurleigh		(10	0)	Leofric, a man of Beorhtric, held it and could sell
215b	Milton Ernest	(1	5	0)	Two sokemen, men of Beorhtric, held it and could sell
	Worcestershire				
176b	Stanford on Teme	1	0	0	Beorhtric, a thegn of Queen Eadgyth, held it

Beorhtric, Eadgyth's man	Total value of land held					
	By subject			From subject or by his men		
	£	s.	d.	£	s.	d.
	100	10	0	21	13	4

LAND ASSIGNED TO BEORHTRIC (*ANTECESSOR* OF ODO FITZ GAMELIN)

Ref. (fos.)	Location	Value £	s.	d.	Notes
vol. i	*Devon*				
112	Shapcombe	1	0	0	This lay in Broadhembury
116b	Delley		10	0	
	Great Torrington	24	0	0	
	Broadhembury	11	0	0	
	Plymtree	5	0	0	
	Dart Raffe	1	0	0	
	Little Wear		10	0	

Beorhtric, *antec.* of Odo fitz Gamelin	Total value of land held					
	By subject			From subject or by his men		
	£	s.	d.	£	s.	d.
	43	0	0	None		

LAND ASSIGNED TO BEORHTSIGE CILT

vol. i	*Kent*				
1b	Aylesford Last				Beorhtsige Cilt had *sac* and *soc* in Aylesford Last
6	Lullingstone	3	0	0	Beorhtsige Cilt held it from King Edward
6b	Plumstead	10	0	0	Beorhtisge Cilt held it from King Edward
	Seal	30	0	0	Beorhtsige Cilt held it from King Edward
	Greenwich	4	0	0	
6	Horton Kirby	(4	0	0)	Godel held it from Beorhtsige and could sell
	Sussex				
20b	Itford	4	0	0	Beorhtsige held it from King Edward; he could go where he would

Land to Beohtsige Cilt (*cont.*):

Ref. (fos.)	Location	Value £	*s.*	*d.*	Notes
24b	North Stoke	20	0	0	Beorhtsige held it from King Edward
29	Thakeham	14	0	0	Beorhtsige held it from King Edward
	Surrey				
31b	Hatcham	2	0	0	Beorhtsige held it from King Edward
35	Stoke d'Abernon	4	0	0	Beorhtsige Cilt held it from King Edward
36	Compton	8	0	0	Beorhtsige held it from King Edward
	West Horsley	8	0	0	Beorhtsige held it from King Edward

Beorhtsige Cilt	Total value of land held					
	By subject			From subject or by his men		
	£	*s.*	*d.*	£	*s.*	*d.*
	107	0	0	4	0	0

LAND ASSIGNED TO BUNDI THE STALLER

Ref.	Location	£	*s.*	*d.*	Notes
vol. i	*Hampshire*				
48	Church Oakley		15	0	Bundi held it *in alodium* from King Edward
	Stratfield	15	0	0	Bundi held it *in alodium* from King Edward
	South Warnborough	12	0	0	Bundi held it from King Edward
	Berkshire				
60	Ashridge	12	0	0	Bundi held it from King Edward
60b	Bisham	8	0	0	Bundi held it from King Edward
	Burghfield	(1	0	0)	An *alodarius* who served Bundi held it

Ref. (fos.)	Location	Value £	s.	d.	Notes
	Wiltshire				
72b	Fisherton de la Mere	25	0	0	
	Dorset				
83	Compton Valence	20	0	0	
85	Broadwindsor	20	0	0	
	Somerset				
92b	Sutton Montis	5	0	0	
	Buckinghamshire				
151	Grendon Underwood	7	0	0	Bundi *constabularius* held it and could sell
	Shipton Lea	5	0	0	
146b	Marsh Gibbon		(9	0)	A man of Bundi the Staller held it and could sell
148b	Hoggeston	(4	0	0)	Almar the man of Bundi the Staller held it
	Oxfordshire				
157b	Sibford Ferris	10	0	0	
	Fifield	5	0	0	
	Dean and Chalford	7	0	0	Bundi held these lands freely
	Gloucestershire				
166b	Allaston	1	0	0	Henry Ferrers claims this because Bundi held it *TRE*
	Northamptonshire				
225	Titchmarsh	3	0	0	Bundi held it freely
	Ecton	3	0	0	
vol. ii	*Essex*				
57	Steeple	3	0	0	Bundi, a freeman, held it
	Woodham Ferrers	20	0	0	

Bundi the Staller	Total value of land held					
	By subject £	s.	d.	From subject or by his men £	s.	d.
	181	15	0	5	9	0

LAND ASSIGNED TO BUNDI (*ANTECESSOR* OF HUGH DE MONTFORT)

Ref. (fos.)	Location	Value £	s.	d.	Notes
vol. ii	*Norfolk*				
197b	Gateley			6	
233	Raynham		10	0	
237	Bodney	5	0	0	Not assessed for geld
	Langford	6	0	0	Not assessed for geld
	South Creake	2	0	0	
	Burnham	4	0	0	
237b	Raynham	8	0	0	
	Roughton	1	0	0	Bundi, a freeman, held it
	Beeston Regis	1	0	0	Bundi, a freeman, held it
238	West Binley	8	0	0	
	Ilsington and Middleton	5	0	0	
239	*Lavendic* Hundred	5	10	0	Bundi, a freeman, held it
	Bodham	1	0	0	
258	Walsingham Magna	1	10	0	Bund, a thegn, held it

	Total value of land held					
	By subject			From subject or by his/her men		
	£	s.	d.	£	s.	d.
Bundi, *antec.* of Hugh de Montfort	48	10	6	None		

LAND ASSIGNED TO BURGERÆD AND HIS SONS

1. Burgeræd

Ref. (fos.)	Location	Value £	s.	d.	Notes
vol. i	*Buckinghamshire*				
145b	Olney	12	0	0	
	Lavendon				One of Burgeræd's men held it and could sell
	Lavendon	(1	0	0)	Wulfric the man of Burgeræd held it and could sell

Ref. (fos.)	Location	Value £	s.	d.	Notes
	Lavendon	(1	0	0)	Two of Burgeræd's thegns helf it
	Weston Underwood	(6	0	0)	The thegns, the men of Burgeræd, held it and could sell
	Bedfordshire				
209b	Knotting	3	0	0	
	Melchbourne	6	0	0	
	Yelden	4	0	0	
210	Riseley	1	13	8	Burgeræd held it in demesne
209b	Yelden	(4	0	0)	A sokeman of Burgeræd held it and could sell
210	Dean	(2	0	0)	Six of Burgeræd's men held it
	Shelton (Swineshead)	(4	0	0)	Wulfgifu held it under Burgeræd but could not sell
	Little Staughton		(5	0)	Four of Burgeræd's sokemen held it
	Riseley	(3	6	8)	Six of Burgeræd's men held it and could sell
	Newton Bromswold		(1	4)	Alwin the man of Burgeræd held it
	Sharnbrook		(15	0)	Alwin the man of Burgeræd held it
	Sharnbrook	(3	0	0)	Seven of Burgeræd's sokemen held it and could sell
	Sharnbrook	(1	0	0)	Ælfric the man of Burgeræd held it and could sell
	Rushden (Northants.)		(10	0)	Ælfric the man of Burgeræd held it
215	Wymington		(10	0)	Leofric the man of Burgeræd held it
218	Milton Bryant	(4	0	0)	Godwine the man of Burgeræd held it
	Northamptonshire				
220b	Raunds	3	0	0	Burgeræd held it with *sac* and *soc*
	Denford	5	0	0	Burgeræd held it freely with *sac* and *soc*
	Wadenhoe	4	0	0	Burgeræd held it with *sac* and *soc*

Land to Burgeræd (*cont.*):

Ref. (fos.)	Location	Value £	s.	d.	Notes
220b	Burton Latimer	1	0	0	Burgeræd held it with *sac* and *soc*
	Isham	1	0	0	Burgeræd held it with *sac* and *soc*
	Clipston		10	0	Burgeræd held it with *sac* and *soc*
	Edgecote	4	0	0	Burgeræd held it with *sac* and *soc*
	Finedon		5	0	
	Hackleton		1	4	
	Woodford (nr. Denford)		10	0	Burgeræd held it but the *soc* pertained to Peterborough
	Thrapston		1	0	Burgeraed held it freely
225b	Rushton, Irchester, Raund	(6	0	0)	Twelve sokemen held it and were men of Burgeræd

2. Eadwine

Ref. (fos.)	Location	Value £	s.	d.	Notes
vol. i	*Somerset*				
87b	Exton	6	0	0	
	Middlesex				
130b	Kensington	10	0	0	Eadwine, a thegn of King Edward, held it
	Buckinghamshire				
145	Oving	7	0	0	Eadwine, a thegn of King Edward, held it and could sell
145b	Lathbury	3	0	0	Eadwine, a thegn of King Edward, held it
	Sherington	6	0	0	
	Marston		(3	4)	Leofric the man of Eadwine held it and could sell
	Sherington	(1	0	0)	Alwin, a man of Eadwine, held it
	Northamptonshire				
220b	Harrowden	5	0	0	
	Stanion		2	0	Eadwine held it freely
221	Heyford (Oxon)	6	0	0	Eadwine held it freely
	Shelswell (Oxon)	5	0	0	

Ref. (fos.)	Location	Value £	s.	d.	Notes
	Croughton		(10	0)	Ælfric, the man of Burgeræd's son, held it but could not sell
3. Ulf					
	Buckinghamshire				
146b	Marsh Gibbon	8	0	0	

Burgeræd and sons	Total value of land held					
	By subjects			From subjects or by their men		
	£	s.	d.	£	s.	d.
	100	8	4	26	19	4

LAND ASSIGNED TO CYPPING

Ref.	Location	£	s.	d.	Notes
vol. i	*Hampshire*				
38b	Stanswood	10	0	0	Cypping held it from King Edward
39b	Stenbury and Whippingham (IOW)	12	0	0	Cypping held these as two manors
46b	Otterbourne	8	0	0	Cypping held it from the Church of Winchester and could not sell
	Headbourne Worthy	25	0	0	Cypping held this from King Edward . . . this manor was sold from the Church with the agreement that the manor with all its revenues should return to St Peter's after three lives
	Barton Stacey	3	0	0	Cypping held it from King Edward *in paragio*
	Shirely	5	0	0	Cypping held it from King Edward *in paragio*
	Botley	10	0	0	Cypping held it from King Edward
47	North Baddesley	10	0	0	Cypping held it from King Edward

Land to Cypping (*cont.*):

Ref. (fos.)	Location	Value £	s.	d.	Notes
47	Knowle	3	0	0	Cypping held it from King Edward
	Swampton	1	5	0	Cypping held it from the bishop and the monks. This land belonged to the monastery and was granted to him for his lifetime only; it was to return there after Cypping's death
	Titchfield Hundred		5	0	Cypping held it from King Edward
	Somborne Hundred	7	0	0	Cypping held it from King Edward
	Preston Candover	8	0	0	Cypping held it from Earl Harold *in alodium*
	Silchester	5	0	0	Cypping held it from Earl Harold *in alodium*
	Stratfield Mortimer (Berks.)	9	0	0	
51	*Achelie*	2	10	0	Cypping held it *in paragio*
51b	*Achelie*	2	0	0	
52	Southampton				Cypping had three houses
	Hadley (IOW)	3	0	0	Cypping held it from King Edward
	Berkshire				
62b	Stratifield Mortimer	9	0	0	Cypping held it *in paragio* with Eadwine (the total value of the manor was £18)

Cypping	Total value of land held	
	By subject £ s. d.	From subject or by his men £ s. d.
	136 10 0	None

LAND ASSIGNED TO DUNNA (*ANTECESSOR* OF OSBERN GIFFARD)

Ref. (fos.)	Location	Value £	*s.*	*d.*	Notes
vol. i	*Wiltshire*				
*72*b	Winterbourne	7	0	0	
	Middleton	1	0	0	
	Tytherton	4	0	0	
	Somerset				
98	Great Elm	3	0	0	
	Woodborough	1	10	0	
	Gloucestershire				
168b	Rockhampton	6	0	0	
	Stoke Giffard	6	0	0	
	Brimpsfield	12	0	0	Dunna held it from Earl Harold

Dunna	Total value of land held	
	By subject £ *s.* *d.*	From subject or by his men £ *s.* *d.*
	40 10 0	None

LAND ASSIGNED TO EADGIFU THE FAIR

Ref. (fos.)	Location	Value £	*s.*	*d.*	Notes
vol. i	*Hertfordshire*				
134	Bishop's Stortford	10	0	0	
137	Munden	16	0	0	
	Wakeley	1	0	0	
	Cheshunt	30	0	0	
134	Wickham		(3	4)	A sokeman of Eadgifu held it
137	Clothall	(1	0	0)	Osgot the man of Eadgifu held it
	Wallington	(2	0	0)	Two sokemen of Eadgifu held it and could sell
	Reed	(3	0	0)	Leofwine the priest, the man of Eadgifu, held it and could sell

Land to Eadgifu (*cont.*):

Ref. (fos.)	Location	Value £	s.	d.	Notes
137	Reed	(3	0	0)	Thorbern, a man of Eadgifu, held it and could sell
	Wormley	(3	0	0)	Alsige, a man of Eadgifu, held it and could sell
	Bengeo		(5	0)	Snerri, a man of Eadgifu, held it and could sell
140b	Wallington				A man of Eadgifu held it and could sell
141b	Berkesdon		(3	4)	A sokeman of Eadgifu held it
	Buckinghamshire				
146b	Mentmore	14	0	0	
148b	Hoggeston		(5	0)	A man of Eadgifu the Fair held it
152	Soulbury	(2	0	0)	Alwin the man of Eadgifu the Fair held it and could sell
	Yardley Hundred	(1	0	0)	Alwin the man of Eadgifu the Fair held it and could sell
	Cambridgeshire				
189b	Exning	56	0	0	
193b	Cherry Hinton	12	0	0	
	Horseheath	5	0	0	
	West Wickham	8	0	0	
	Barham	12	0	0	
194	Linton	15	0	0	
	Little Linton	5	0	0	
	Abington	10	0	0	
	Duxford	7	0	0	
	Fowlmere	1	5	0	
	Wendy	8	0	0	
	Bassingbourne	26	0	0	
194b	Whaddon	6	0	0	
	Wetherley Hundred	5	0	0	Income from two mills
	Haslingfield		8	0	
	Wimpole	8	0	0	
	Toft	2	0	0	A berewick of Swavesey
195	Swavesey	18	0	0	
	Waterbeach	3	0	0	
	Dry Drayton	3	0	0	

Ref. (fos.)	Location	Value £	s.	d.	Notes
	Ditton	7	0	0	
	Swaffham	1	0	0	
195b	Wicken	6	0	0	
	Borough Green	10	0	0	
193b	Fulbourn	(15	0	0)	Godwine Cilt the man of Eadgifu held it but could not sell
	Teversham		(10	0)	Five men held from Eadgifu but could not sell
	Horseheath		(5	0)	Godwine the man of Eadgifu held it but could not sell
	Barham		(4	0)	A sokeman held under Eadgifu
194	Babraham	(2	10	0)	Six sokemen held under Eadgifu but could not sell
	Babraham	(1	0	0)	Alric the priest held it under Eadgifu but could not sell
	Pampisford	(1	10	0)	Almar held it under Eadgifu and could sell
	Harston	(1	5	0)	Four sokemen held it from Eadgifu
	Shelford	(2	0	0)	Six sokemen held it under Eadgifu and could sell
	Hatley	(3	0	0)	Almar held it under Eadgifu and could sell
	Croydon		(15	0)	Godgifu held it under Eadgifu and could sell
	Croydon		(5	0)	Leofgifu held it under Eadgifu and could sell
	Wendy	(2	0	0)	Six sokemen held it under Eadgifu and could sell
194b	Whaddon	(2	0	0)	Held from Eadgifu and could be sold
	Whaddon		(2	0)	A sokeman held it under Eadgifu
	Meldreth	(1	10	0)	Colswein held it under Eadgifu and could sell
	Melbourne	(2	0	0)	Colswein held it under Eadgifu and could sell
	Grantchester	(1	0	0)	Gogan the man of Eadgifu held it but could not sell

Land to Eadgifu (*cont.*):

Ref. (fos.)	Location	Value £	s.	d.	Notes
194b	Haslingfield	(1	2	0)	Ealdred held it under Eadgifu but could not sell
	Haslingfield		(2	0)	Merwine held it from Eadgifu and could sell
	Orwell	(1	10	0)	Thorbern held it under Eadgifu
	Wratworth		(10	0)	A sokeman held it under Eadgifu and could sell
	Whitwell	(1	0	0)	Godwi held it under Eadgifu and could sell
	Arrington	(1	0	0)	Leofgifu held it under Eadgifu and could sell
	Eversden	(1	0	0)	Two sokemen held it under Eadgifu and could sell
195	Bourn	(5	0	0)	Almar the man of Eadgifu held it and could sell
	Caldecote	(1	10	0)	Almar the man of Eadgifu held it and could sell
	Longston	(1	10	0)	Almar the man of Eadgifu held it and could sell
	Hatley		(2	4)	Almar the man of Eadgifu held it and could sell
	Papworth	(9	0	0)	Goda held it under Eadgifu and could sell
	Boxworth		(18	8)	Two sokemen held it under Eadgifu and could sell
	Fen Drayton	(1	7	0)	Five sokemen held it under Eadgifu
	Willingham		(3	0)	Oswulf the man of Eadgifu held it and could sell
	Long Stanton	(5	0	0)	Twelve sokemen held it under Eadgifu and could sell
	Cheveley	(2	0	0)	Herulf the man of Eadgifu held it and could sell
	Swaffham	(1	0	0)	Six sokemen held it under Eadgifu
	Swaffham	(1	0	0)	Wulfwig the man of Eadgifu held it
195b	Wilbraham	(10	0	0)	Ordmær the man of Eadgifu held it and could sell

Ref. (fos.)	Location	Value £	s.	d.	Notes
	Swaffham	(2	0	0)	Grimbold the man of Eadgifu held it but could not sell
	Badlingham	(5	0	0)	Ordmær held it under Eadgifu and could sell
	Exning	(3	0	0)	Alsige the man of Eadgifu held it and could sell
	Burwell	(6	0	0)	Two sokemen held it under Eadgifu and could sell
	Burwell	(2	0	0)	Eadwine held it under Eadgifu and could sell
	Fordham	(1	5	0)	Two sokemen, the men of Eadgifu, held it
	Soham	(6	0	0)	Alsige held it under Eadgifu and could sell
	Stetchworth		(10	0)	Grim the man of Eadgifu held it but could not sell
	Westley Waterless	(1	0	0)	Seven sokemen held it from Eadgifu but could not sell
	Weston Colville	(3	0	0)	Godwine Cilt held it from Eadgifu but could not sell
	West Wratting	(1	0	0)	Two sokemen of Eadgifu held it but could not sell
	Balsham				Leofgeat held it under Eadgifu but could not sell
196b	Whaddon		(15	0)	Sageva held it under Eadgifu and could sell
198	Duxford	(1	5	0)	A sokeman of Eadgifu held it but could not sell
198b	Kingston		(2	0)	Goding Thorbert the man of Eadgifu held it and could sell
	Caldecote	(1	12	0)	Two sokemen held it under Eadgifu
199	Dry Drayton	(1	10	0)	Four sokemen of Eadgifu held it and could sell
199b	Abington				A priest of Eadgifu held it
200	Barton	(1	0	0)	A sokeman of Eadgifu held it and could sell
	Eversden	(2	0	0)	A sokeman of Eadgifu held it and could sell
200b	Morden		(5	0)	A sokeman of Eadgifu held it and could sell

Land to Eadgifu (*cont.*):

Ref. (fos.)	Location	Value £	s.	d.	Notes
201	Rampton		(10	0)	A sokeman of Eadgifu held it and could sell
	Lolworth		(13	4)	Two sokemen of Eadgifu held it and could sell
201b	Fulbourn	(2	0	0)	Three of Eadgifu's men held it
195b	Dullingham		(11	0)	Horulf the man of Eadgifu held it
vol. ii	Essex				
7b	Sampford	20	0	0	
	Willingale	3	0	0	
	Canfield	3	0	0	
35b	Roding		5	0	
	Stevington		2	0	
	Finchingfield	(5	0	0)	Three freemen held it under Eadgifu
	Steeple Hampstead		(2	0)	A sokeman held it under Eadgifu
	Suffolk				
286	Norton	10	0	0	This land belonged to the demesne of St Edmund, and was to return there on Eadgifu's death
	Thurlow	9	0	0	
295	*Beria*	2	0	0	
430b	Harkstead	10	0	0	
431	Gusford	3	0	0	
284b	Tostock		(13	4)	Thirty-six freemen commended to Eadgifu held it
285	Saxham		(10	0)	Six freemen commended to Eadgifu held it
	Blakenham		(12	4)	Five freemen commended to Eadgifu held it
	Langhedena, Ofton, Badley, Darmsden, Sharpstone, and Ashbocking	(4	10	2)	Eight freemen and a sokeman held this. *Sac* and *soc* and commendation belonged to Eadgifu in Norton

Ref. (fos.)	Location	Value £	s.	d.	Notes
295	Wenham	(3	0	0)	Ansgot, commended to Eadgifu, held it
	Holbrook	(1	0	0)	Godman, commended to Eadgifu, held it
295b	Dodnash		(15	0)	Eadwine, commended to Eadgifu, held it
	Brantham		(13	4)	Eadwine held it in Eadgifu's soke
	Woolverstone	(1	0	0)	Thurstan, commended to Eadgifu, held it
	Bentley		(5	4)	Thurstan, commended to Eadgifu, held it
	Pannington		(8	0)	Thurstan, commended to Eadgifu, held it
	Wherstead		(5	0)	Thurstan, commended to Eadgifu, held it
	Kalweton		(5	4)	Thurstan, commended to Eadgifu, held it
296	Boynton		(8	0)	Wulfstan, a freeman of Eadgifu, held it
397	Hunston		(6	0)	Seven freemen commended to Eadgifu held it
	Thurlow	(1	0	0)	Five freemen commended to Eadgifu held it
397	Thurlow		(4	4)	Two sokemen of Eadgifu held it
410	Beyton		(5	0)	A freeman of Eadgifu held it

Eadgifu the Fair	Total value of land held					
	By subject			From subject or by her men		
	£	s.	d.	£	s.	d.
	366	0	0	160	4	0

LAND ASSIGNED TO EADMÆR ATRE

Ref. (fos.)	Location	Value £	s.	d.	Notes
vol. i	*Dorset*				
79b	Sydling	4	0	0	
	Gussage All Saints	15	0	0	
	Blandford St Mary	10	0	0	
	Bestwall	1	10	0	
	East Stoke	2	10	0	
80	Wootton	5	0	0	
	Somerset				
90b	Camerton	7	0	0	
72b	Chinnock	5	0	0	
	Odcombe	5	0	0	
	Devonshire				
104b	Buckland Brewer	7	10	0	
	East Putford	1	10	0	
105	Frizenham	1	0	0	
	Wedfield	0	10	0	
	Feniton	4	0	0	
	Cotleigh	1	0	0	
	Cornwood	2	0	0	
	Newton Ferrers	6	0	0	
	Middlesex				
129b	Stanmore	10	0	0	
	Hertfordshire				
136b	Berkhampstead	24	0	0	Eadmær, a thegn of Harold, held it
	Little Gaddesden	4	0	0	A berewick of Berkhampstead
137b	Tiscot	(1	0	0)	A man of Eadmær Atule held it
	Buckinghamshire				
146b	Bledlow	20	0	0	Eadmær Atule, a thegn of King Edward, held it
	Northamptonshire				
233	East Haddon	2	0	0	
	Ravensthorpe	0	5	0	

Ref. (fos.)	Location	Value £	s.	d.	Notes
	Brampton	3	0	0	
	Alderton	1	0	0	

Eadmær Atre	Total value of land held					
	By subject £	s.	d.	From subject or by his men £	s.	d.
	142	15	0	1	0	0

LAND ASSIGNED TO EADNOTH THE STALLER AND HEARDING, HIS SON

1.	Eadnoth the Staller				
vol. i	*Hampshire*				
41	Freefolk	16	0	0	Eadnoth held it from the Bishop of Winchester, and could not sell
	Berkshire				
58b	Shippon	3	6	8	
60	Drayton	2	10	0	Eadnoth held it from Harold but could not sell
	Wiltshire				
68b	Roughmoor	2	10	0	
	Wilsford (nr. Amesbury)	2	0	0	
	Hartham	2	0	0	
	Burcombe	3	0	0	
	Cadenham	1	10	0	
	Somerset				
91b	Tatton	2	0	0	
	Aller (Sampford Brett)	2	0	0	
	Henstridge	4	10	0	
91b	Sampford Brett	3	0	0	This manor was not attributed to Eadnoth *TRE*, but was the

Land to Eadnoth and Hearding (*cont.*):

Ref. (fos.)	Location	Value £	s.	d.	Notes
					only other manor in this shire which was held by Earl Hugh, whose other manors in Somerset had all been held by Eadnoth *TRE*
	Gloucestershire				
164	Ampney	20	0	0	Assessed at 15 hides, but 5 were remitted by the king, so it answered for only 10
2.	Hearding				
vol. i	*Wiltshire*				
67b	Beechingstoke	3	0	0	Hearding held it from Salisbury for his life only
68b	Winterslow	8	0	0	
69	Compton (in Enford)	10	0	0	
	Durrington	3	0	0	
	Winterslow	1	0	0	
	Ablington	4	0	0	
	Chitterne	4	0	0	
	Tytherington	1	0	0	
74	Knighton	11	0	0	
	Figheldean	9	0	0	
	Ogbourne	4	0	0	
	Dorset				
82b	Bredy	3	0	0	
	Somerset				
90b	Cranmore	4	0	0	Hearding held it from Glastonbury but could not sell
	Leicestershire				
231b	Knaptoft	1	0	0	
	Sapcote		2	0	
	Hinkley	6	0	0	
	Sibson	3	0	0	
	Shenton		1	0	

Ref. (fos.)	Location	Value £	s.	d.	Notes
	Shearsby		15	0	
	Croft		5	8	
	Broughton Astley and Sutton in the Elms				Waste
	Fenny Drayton	1	10	0	
	Bitteswell		10	0	
	Swinford		2	0	
	Walton (nr. Kimcote)		10	0	
	Theddingworth	2	10	0	
	Little Thorpe		10	0	
	Wanlip		10	0	
	Shoby	1	0	0	
	Walton in the Wolds		2	8	Hearding held all these lands in Leicestershire with his men
	Warwickshire				
239b	Smeeton	2	0	0	Hearding, a freeman, held it
	Nuneaton	4	0	0	
	Radway	1	0	0	

Family the Fair	Total value of land held	
	By subjects £ s. d.	From subjects or by their men £ s. d.
	154 15 0	None

LAND ASSIGNED TO EADRIC OF LAXFIELD

vol. ii	*Norfolk*				
133b	Happisburgh	7	0	0	
135	Eaton	4	0	0	
144b	Palgrave		10	0	
153b	Kilverstone	3	0	0	
155	Horsford	3	0	0	Eadric, a freeman, held it

Land to Eadric of Laxfield (*cont.*):

Ref. (fos.)	Location	Value £	s.	d.	Notes
155b	Horsham	5	10	0	Eadric, a freeman, held it
156	Dilham	1	10	0	
178	Hockham	4	0	0	Eadric, a thegn, held it
179b	Sutton (nr. Stalham)	4	10	0	
125	Redenhall	(3	0	0)	A freeman commended to Eadric held it
125b	Redenhall	(1	0	0)	A freeman commended to Eadric held it
133b	Happisburgh		(2	6)	A freeman commended to Eadric held it
134b	Runham		(10	0)	Two of Eadric's freemen held it
148	Hickling	(2	0	0)	Godric, a freeman of Eadric, held it
148b	Ingham	(5	0	0)	Eadric, a man of Eadric, held it
	Waxham		(10	0)	A freeman of Eadric held it
	Ingham	(1	4	0)	Eadric, the man of Eadric of Laxfield, held it
150b	Earlham		(8	0)	A freeman of Eadric held it
154	Saxlingham	(1	10	0)	Two and a half sokemen of Eadric held it
	Shotesham		(5	4)	Ulfketel, a man commended to Eadric, held it
	Shotford		(10	0)	A freeman commended to Eadric held it
	Gissing		(8	0)	Alstan, a freeman commended to Eadric, held it
	Burston		(8	0)	Aculf, a freeman commended to Eadric, held it
154b	Thorpe Parva		(10	0)	Eadric, a sokeman, held it under Eadric the *antecessor* of Malet
	Burston		(8	0)	Morther, a freeman of Eadric, held it
	Frenze		(10	0)	Eadric held it under Eadric
	Roydon (nr. Diss)		(2	6)	A freeman commended to Eadric held it

Ref. (fos.)	Location	Value £	s.	d.	Notes
	Shimpling		(1	4)	Two freemen commended to Eadric held it
155	Semere		(8	0)	A freeman commended to Eadric held it
	Gissing		(1	0)	Half a freeman commended to Eadric held it
	Woodton	(1	0	0)	Ulfketel, a freeman commended to Eadric, held it
	Fritton		(8	0)	A freeman commended to Eadric held it
	Burgh St Margaret		(1	4)	Ulfketel, a freeman commended to Eadric, held it
174b	Bastwick		(0	8)	A freewoman of Eadric held it
176b	Osmondiston	(2	10	0)	Algar held it under Eadric
178	Sutton (nr. Stalham)	(2	0	0)	Fifty-four freemen commended to Eadric were attached to Eadric manor
182	Haddiscoe		(10	0)	A sokeman of Eadric held it
184	Roughton				A freeman of Eadric held it but could not sell
186	Poringland		(1	0)	A freeman of Eadric held it
187	Smallburgh		(3	4)	A freeman commended to Eadric held it
247	Bessingham	(1	0	0)	A freeman commended to Eadric held it
260	Fritton	(1	5	0)	Ulfketel, a freeman of Eadric, held it
263	Hethel	(1	0	0)	Algar held it under Eadric
	Suffolk				
306	*Brutge*		14	8	
307b	*Chiletuna*	8	0	0	
	Rendham	3	10	0	Berewick of *Chiletuna*
311	Huntingfield	8	0	0	
311b	Leiston	16	0	0	
	Leiston	1	0	0	
	Dunwich	50	0	0	And 8,000 herrings
312b	Sibton		3	0	

Land to Eadric of Laxfield (*cont.*):

Ref. (fos.)	Location	Value £	s.	d.	Notes
313b	Darsham		8	0	
314	Holton		3	4	
316	Snape	6	0	0	
	Aldeburgh		2	0	
	Stickingland		6	8	
316b	Farnham	1	0	0	
317	Hollesley	5	0	0	
317b	*Culeslea*	3	0	0	Berewick of Hollesley
	Bawdsey	1	5	0	Berewick of Hollesley
319b	Byng	1	0	0	Berewick of Staverton
	Eye	15	0	0	
325	Staverton	6	0	0	
328	Dennington	14	0	0	
	Tannington	14	0	0	
328b	Laxfield	15	0	0	
	Badingham	15	0	0	
	Stradbroke	14	0	0	
282b	Darsham		(10	0)	Alfwin the priest, commended to Eadric, held it
	Stickingland	(1	5	0)	Alfwin the priest commended to Eadric, held it
283	Kessingland		(2	0)	Osfert, a freeman commended to Eadric, held it
292	Morston		(2	0)	Wulfwine, a freeman commended to Eadric, held it
	Grimston		(3	4)	Beorhtnoth, a freeman commended to Eadric, held it
	Thorpe (Trimley)		(2	8)	Brumer, a freeman commended to Eadric, held it
293b	Kettleburgh	(5	0	0)	Eadric Grim, half commended to Eadric and half to Ely, held it
296	Wantisden		(10	0)	Sixteen freemen, half commended to Eadric, half to Ely, held it
296b	Blaxhall		(3	4)	Eadric Grim, half commended to Eadric and half to Ely, held it
	Carlton		(1	6)	Stain, a freeman commended to Eadric, held it

Ref. (fos.)	Location	Value £	s.	d.	Notes
	Carlton	(3	0	0)	Eadric Grim, half commended to Eadric and half to Ely, held it
	Carlton		(2	0)	Alfric, a freeman commended to Eadric, held it
297	Glemham		(1	3)	A freeman under commendation to Eadric held it
	Great Glemham		(1	3)	Almar, a freeman commended to Eadric held it
	Great Glemham		(1	3)	Godric, a freeman under commendation to Eadric held it
	Great Glemham		(1	3)	Hunepot, a freeman commended to Eadric, held it
	Great Glemham		(10	0)	Spearhavoc, a freeman commended to Eadric, held it
	Great Glemham		(2	6)	Two freemen called Leofric, commended to Eadric, held it
	Great Glemham		(2	6)	Two freemen called Wulfmær held it and were commended to Eadric
	Bruisyard		(10	0)	Starling, a freeman half commended to Eadric and half to Ely, held it
297b	Swefling		(2	0)	Dot, a freeman commended to Eadric, held it
	Swefling		(5	0)	Osmund, a freeman commended to Eadric, held it
	Swefling		(2	0)	Alfric, a freeman commended to Eadric, held it
	Swefling	(1	10	0)	Four and a half freemen commended to Eadric, and a half subcommended to Eadric, held it
	Rendham		(7	0)	Ostula, a freeman commended to Eadric, held it
	Rendham	(1	0	0)	Nine freemen commended to Eadric held it
298	Benhall		(5	0)	Nine freemen commended to Eadric held it
299b	Middleton		(1	4)	Grim, commended to Eadric the son of Ingold, held it

Land to Eadric of Laxfield (*cont.*):

Ref. (fos.)	Location	Value £	s.	d.	Notes
299b	Middleton		(1	4)	Kenric, a freeman, the man of Eadric, held it
	Middleton		(10	0)	Munnulf, half commended to Eadric and half to Ailmer, held it
302b	Framlingham	(2	0	0)	Munnulf, half commended to Eadric and half to Ailmer, held it
303b	Debenham		(2	0)	Wulfgeat, a freeman commended to Eadric, held it
304b	Creeting St Peter	(1	0	0)	Leofwine, a freeman commended to Eadric, held it
	Creeting		(3	4)	A freeman commended to Eadric held it
	Creeting		(2	0)	A freeman, the man of one himself commended to Eadric, held it
	Creeting		(2	0)	A man of Eadric held it
	Coddenham		(1	8)	A freeman commended to Eadric held it
	Olden		(2	8)	A freeman commended to Eadric held it
	Olden			(10)	A freeman commended to Eadric held it
305	Debenham		(10	0)	Eadric, commended to Eadric the predecessor of Malet, held it
	Debenham		(10	0)	Six freemen commended to the above Eadric held it
	Barham		(6	8)	Beorhtwold, a freeman commended to Eadric, held it
305b	Winston		(2	0)	Two freemen commended to one himself commended to Eadric held it
	Debenham			(4)	Half a freeman commended to one himself commended to Eadric held it
	Manwic		(5	0)	A freeman commended to Eadric held it

Ref. (fos.)	Location	Value £	s.	d.	Notes
306	Ashfield		(5	0)	Three freemen commended to Eadric held it
	Thorpe Ashfield			(10)	A freeman commended to Eadric held it
	Thorpe Ashfield		(1	4)	A freeman subcommended to Eadric held it
	Westerfield		(2	0)	A freeman commended to Eadric held it
	Thorpe Ashfield		(1	8)	A freeman subcommended to Eadric held it
	Parham	(1	15	0)	Alnod, a freeman half commended to Eadric, held it
306b	*Brutge*		(4	0)	Five freemen commended to Eadric held it
	Blaxhall		(10	0)	Six freemen commended to Eadric held it
	Blaxhall		(5	0)	Three freemen commended to Eadric held it
	Wantisden	(1	10	0)	Twenty-two freemen commended to Eadric held it
	Parham		(7	0)	Earnulf, a freeman commended to Eadric, held it
	Parham		(6	8)	Blachesune, a freeman commended to Eadric, held it
	Parham		(2	0)	Two freemen commended to Eadric held it
	Parham		(7	0)	Two freemen commended to Eadric held it
307	Blaxhall		(2	4)	A freeman half commended to Eadric and half to Ely held it
	Blaxhall			(6)	A freeman commended to Eadric held it
	Blaxhall		(3	0)	A freeman commended to Eadric held it
	Blaxhall			(2)	A freeman commended to Eadric held it
	Blaxhall		(2	0)	A freeman half commended to Eadric and half to Ely held it
	Blaxhall		(1	4)	Two freemen held it; one and a half were commended to Eadric and half to Ely

Land to Eadric of Laxfield (*cont.*):

Ref. (fos.)	Location	Value £ s. d.	Notes
307	Wantisden	(7)	Alflet held it under commendation to Eadric
	Parham	(2 0)	A freeman commended to Eadric held it
307b	*Chiletuna*	(1 10 0)	Sixteen and a half freemen commended to Eadric held it
	Cransford	(1 0 0)	Cus, a freeman commended to Eadric, held it
308	Swefling	(10 0)	Ten freemen commended to Eadric held it
	Swefling	(10)	Beorhtnoth, a freeman commended to Eadric, held it
	Swefling	(1 0 0)	Osbern, a freeman commended to Eadric, held it
	Great Glemham	(10 0)	Hunepot, a freeman commended to Eadric, held it
308b	Great Glemham	(1 0 0)	Wulfmær, a freeman commended to Eadric, held it
	Stratford St Andrew	(1 0 0)	Hunepot, a freeman commended to Eadric, held it
	Benhall	(10 0)	Six freemen commended to Eadric held it
	Farnhan	(1 1 0)	Two freemen commended to Eadric held it
	Swefling	(8 0)	Ailwi commended to Eadric held it
309	Cransford	(2 0)	A freeman commended to Eadric held it
	Benhall	(6 10)	Six freemen commended to Eadric held it
	Great Glemham	(1 0)	A freeman commended to Eadric held it
	Wyverstone	(1 0 0)	Ailwi commended to Eadric held it
	Wyverstone	(5 0)	Alfric held it. He was commended one-sixth to Eadric and five-sixths to Achi
309b	Wyverstone	(3 0)	A man half commended to Eadric and half to Ely held it

Ref. (fos.)	Location	Value £	s.	d.	Notes
	Wyverstone			(6)	Alflet held it under commendation to Eadric
	Westhorpe		(10	0)	Leofric, a freeman commended to Eadric, held it
	Westhorpe		(5	2)	Five freemen commended to Eadric held it
	Cotton		(6	4)	Five freemen commended to Eadric held it
	Rickinghall Superior	(1	0	0)	Britfelda, a freewoman commended to Eadric, held it
310	Brome		(5	0)	Wulfmær, a freeman commended to Eadric, held it
	Brome		(2	0)	Five freemen commended to Eadric held it
	Oakley		(10	0)	Godman, a freeman commended to Eadric, held it
	Thrandeston		(2	0)	Godman, a freeman commended to Eadric, held it
	Thrandeston		(1	0)	A freeman commended to Eadric held it
	Bedingfield		(5	0)	A freeman commended to Eadric held it
310b	Denham		(5	0)	Four freemen commended to Eadric held it
	Kelsale		(5	0)	A freeman commended to Eadric held it
	Aldringham		(3	4)	A freeman commended to Eadric held it
	Bedingfield		(10	0)	Six freemen commended to Eadric held it
	Darsham		(18	8)	Eadric, a freeman commended to Eadric of Laxfield, held it, and six freemen under him
	Fordley		(14	0)	The same Eadric, and six men under him, held it
311	Huntingfield	(2	8	0)	Twenty-five freemen of Eadric of Laxfield held it
	Linstead	(1	0	0)	Wulfric, a freeman commended to Eadric, held it

Land to Eadric of Laxfield (*cont.*):

Ref. (fos.)	Location	Value £	s.	d.	Notes
311b	Leiston	(4	0	0)	Forty-seven freemen held it and were attached to Eadric manor of Leiston
312	Stickingland		(1	0)	Half a freeman commended to Eadric held it
313	Sibton		(10	0)	Blæchemann, a freeman commended to Eadric, held it
	Darsham		(10	0)	Blæchemann, a freeman commended to Eadric, held it
	Peasenhall		(12	0)	Stanwine, a freeman commended to Eadric, (and sometime to Harold) held it
313b	Stickingland		(10	0)	The above Stanwine held it
	Westleton		(8	0)	A freeman commended to Eadric held it
	South Cove		(3	0)	Two freemen commended to Eadric, himself commended to Malet's predecessor, held it
313	Peasenhall		(2	0)	Almar, a freeman commended to Eadric held it
313b	*Wrabetuna*		(1	6)	Two freemen commended to Eadric held it
	Hopetuna		(3	0)	Two freemen commended to Eadric held it
314	Darsham		(0	8)	A freeman commended to Eadric held it
	Peasenhall		(0	8)	A freeman commended to Eadric held it
	Stratton	(1	0	0)	Wulfmær, a freeman, held it from Eadric
314b	Stratton		(4	0)	Leofwine, Brun's son, commended to Eadric, held it
	Stratton	(3	0	0)	Twelve freemen commended to Eadric held it
	Mycelgeta		(1	0)	Lustwine, a freeman commended to Eadric, held it
315	Lesser Waldringfield		(2	0)	A sokeman held it under Eadric
	Rushmere St Andrew		(10	0)	Three freemen commended to Eadric held it

Ref. (fos.)	Location	£	s.	d.	Notes
	Hopestuna		(2	8)	A freeman held it under Eadric
	Kesgrave		(1	4)	Oslac, a freeman commended to Eadric, held it
	Hasketon		(3	0)	Two freemen commended to Eadric held it
315b	Burgh (Woodbridge)		(1	11)	Wulfwine the priest, a freeman commended to Eadric, held it
	Burgh (Woodbridge)		(4	0)	Two freemen commended to Eadric held it
	Tuddenham		(2	0)	A freeman commended to Eadric held it
	Grundisburgh		(1	0)	Two sokemen commended to Eadric held it
	Hasketon		(1	0)	A freeman commended to Eadric held it
	Clopton		(7	4)	Two freemen commended to Eadric held it
316	Aldeburgh		(5	0)	Archill, a freeman commended to Eadric, held it
	Snape	(1	3	0)	Twenty-five freemen commended to Eadric held it
	Snape	(1	0	0)	Twenty-one freemen commended to Eadric held it
	Cransford		(10	0)	Godric the priest, commended to Eadric, held it
	Boyton		(5	0)	A freeman commended to Eadric held it
	Boyton		(5	0)	Eight freemen commended to Eadric held it
316b	Boyton		(16	0)	Twelve freemen commended to Eadric held it
	Farnham		(5	0)	Nine freemen commended to Eadric held it
	Rushmere (Friston)		(7	0)	Eight freemen commended to Eadric held it
	Boyton		(4	0)	A freeman commended to Eadric held it
	Sternfield	(1	0	0)	Fifteen freemen commended to Eadric held it
	Sudbourne	(2	2	0)	Thirteen freemen commended to Eadric held it

Land to Eadric of Laxfield (*cont.*):

Ref. (fos.)	Location	Value £	s.	d.	Notes
317	Burgh		(1	0)	A freeman commended to Eadric held it
317b	*Culeslea*		(1	4)	Two freemen commended to Eadric held it
	Bawdsey		(10	0)	Seventeen freemen commended to Eadric held it
	Alderton	(2	0	0)	Thirty-one freemen commended to Eadric held it
	Bawdsey		(12	0)	Twelve and a half freemen commended to Eadric held it
318	Alderton		(6	0)	Three freemen commended to Eadric held it
	Sutton		(2	0)	Godwine, a half freeman commended to Eadric, held it
	Sutton	(2	1	8)	Six freemen commended to Eadric held it
318b	*Laneburc*		(11	0)	Six freemen commended to Eadric held it
	Wilford		(16	0)	A sokeman commended to Eadric held it
	Melton		(15	0)	Two freemen commended to Eadric held it
	Ramsholt		(2	0)	Five freemen commended to Eadric held it
	Boyton	(3	0	0)	Stanwine commended to Eadric held it
319	Charsfield	(1	10	0)	Twenty-four freemen commended to Eadric held it
	Bromswell		(4	0)	Four and a half freemen commended to Eadric held it
	Capel St Andrew	(3	0	0)	Twenty-four freemen commended to Eadric held it
319b	Byng and Loudham	(2	10	0)	Thirty-two freemen commended to Eadric held it
	Bromswell		(16	0)	Sixteen freemen commended to Eadric held it
320	Eye	(1	0	0)	Wulfric, a freeman commended to Eadric, held it

Ref. (fos.)	Location	Value £	s.	d.	Notes
	Occold		(10	0)	Five freemen commended to Eadric held it
320b	Braiseworth		(10	0)	Seven freemen commended to Eadric held it
	Thornham Parva		(1	8)	Two and a half freemen commended to Eadric held it
	Aspall		(5	0)	Beorhtmær, a freeman commended to Eadric, held it
	Yaxley		(1	0)	Alnod, a freeman half commended to Eadric, held it
	Gislingham		(2	0)	Stubbard, a freeman commended to Eadric, held it
	Gislingham		(2	0)	Stannard, a freeman commended to Eadric, held it
	Thornham Parva		(1	0)	Stannard, a freeman commended to Eadric, held it
	Mellis		(10	0)	Fulchard, a freeman half commended to Eadric, held it
	Thrandeston		(5	0)	Alweard, a freeman commended to Eadric, held it
321	Thrandeston		(2	2)	Two freemen commended to Eadric held it
	Brome			(8)	Two freemen commended to Eadric held it
	Aspall			(6)	A freeman commended to Eadric held it
	Knetishall			(6)	A freeman commended to Eadric held it
324	Stokerland		(1	8)	Two freemen commended to Eadric held it
	Shottisham	(1	0	0)	Osmund, a freeman commended to Eadric, held it
	Shottisham		(17	0)	Nineteen freemen commended to Eadric held it
	Ufford		(10	0)	Almar, a freeman half commended to Eadric and half to Ely, held it
324b	Alderton		(1	0)	A freeman commended to Eadric held it
	Ufford		(1	0)	A freeman commended to Eadric held it

Land to Eadric of Laxfield (*cont.*):

Ref. (fos.)	Location	Value £	s.	d.	Notes
324b	Boulge			(6)	One and a half freemen commended to Eadric held it
	Bredfield		(3	4)	Two freemen commended to Eadric held it
	Sutton		(10	4)	Five freemen commended to Eadric held it
	Byng		(7	0)	Godric, a freeman commended to Eadric, held it
	Loudham	(1	0	0)	Morewine, a freeman half commended to Eadric and half to Ely, held it
	Bromswell		(1	4)	A freeman commended to Eadric held it
	Hundeshost		(2	4)	Two freemen commended to Eadric held it
	Harpole	(1	0	0)	Hunepot held it under Eadric
325	Harpole		(5	0)	Bondi, a freeman half commended to Eadric, held it
	Wilford			(4)	A freeman commended to Eadric held it
	Staverton		(10	0)	Thirteen freemen commended to Eadric held it
	Kettleburgh		(10	0)	A freeman commended to Eadric held it
325b	Monewden	(2	0	0)	A freeman commended to Eadric held it
	Woodbridge		(5	8)	A freeman commended to Eadric held it
	Framlingham		(2	0)	Thorketel, a freeman commended to Eadric, held it
	Framlingham		(13	4)	A sokeman commended to Eadric held it
	Dallinghoo		(2	8)	A freeman half commended to Eadric and half to Ely held it
	Framlingham			(8)	A freeman commended to Eadric held it
326	Keton	(1	0	0)	Beorhtmær commended to Eadric held it

Ref. (fos.)	Location	Value £	s.	d.	Notes
	Rendlesham		(12	0)	Eleven freemen commended to Eadric held it
	Kenton		(7	0)	Hunepot, a freeman commended to Eadric, held it
326b	Staverton		(12	4)	Three freemen commended to Eadric held it
	Marlsford		(12	8)	Seven freemen commended to Eadric held it
	Rossefella		(10	0)	Two freemen commended to Eadric held it
	Brodertuna			(8)	A freewoman commended to Eadric held it
	Campsey			(8)	The same freewoman held it
	Ash	(1	0	0)	Twelve freemen commended to Eadric held it
	Hacheston		(17	0)	Thirteen freemen commended to Eadric held it
	Kenton		(10	0)	Udebrun, a freeman commended to Eadric, held it
327	*Clachestorp*		(3	0)	Three and a half freemen commended to Eadric held it
	Soham		(2	0)	A sokeman commended to Eadric held it
	Gedgrave		(5	0)	A freeman commended to Eadric held it
	Woodbridge		(8	0)	Two freemen and one sokeman commended to Eadric held it
	Ash		(3	0)	A freeman commended to Eadric held it
	Dallinghoo	(1	1	0)	Four freemen commended to Eadric held it
327b	Buteley		(5	0)	Three and a half freemen commended to Eadric held it
	Martley		(8	0)	A freeman commended to Eadric held it
	Thiccebrom		(2	0)	A freeman commended to Eadric held it
	Walsham in the Willows		(10	0)	A freeman commended to Eadric held it
	Barsham		(3	0)	Ailwi, a freeman commended to Eadric, held it

Land to Eadric of Laxfield (*cont.*):

Ref. (fos.)	Location	Value £	s.	d.	Notes
328	Stanton		(16	0)	A freeman half commended to Eadric and half commended to St Edmund's held it
	Rickinghall Inferior		(5	0)	A freeman commended to Eadric held it
329	Chipenhall	(5	0	0)	Nine freemen commended to Eadric held it
	Horam and Wilby	(2	0	0)	Alfric, a freeman commended to Eadric, held it
329b	Weybread	(4	5	0)	Seven freemen commended to Eadric held it
	Mendham	(1	5	0)	A freeman commended to Eadric held it
	Horham		(12	0)	Three freemen commended to Eadric held it
	Chickering		(6	0)	Three freemen commended to Eadric held it
330	Chickering		(10	0)	A freeman commended to Eadric held it but Eadric had it in pledge for £3
	Beddingfield	(1	2	8)	A freeman commended to Eadric held it
332	Heveningham	(2	0	0)	Stanwine, commended to Eadric and then to Harold, held it
332b	Chediston		(2	4)	Leofwine, a freeman commended to Eadric, held it
333	Halesworth		(3	0)	Gunner, a freeman commended to Eadric, held it
	Thorpe (Aldingham)		(19	4)	Wulfmær, a freeman commended to Eadric, held it
333b	Holton		(12	0)	Ailwi, a freeman commended to Eadric, held it
334	Fordley		(3	0)	Two freemen half commended to Eadric held it
	Blaxhall		(2	6)	A freeman commended to Eadric held it
334b	Rendlesham		(2	8)	A freeman commended to Eadric held it

Ref. (fos.)	Location	Value £	s.	d.	Notes
	Cransford		(2	2)	A freeman commended to Eadric held it
	Sternfield		(6	0)	Three and a half freemen commended to Eadric held it
335	Thorrington and Middleton		(8	0)	Alveva, a freewoman half commended to Eadric and half to Norman, held it
336b	Baylham	(1	0	0)	Wulfric commended to Eadric held it
338b	Saxmundham		(1	3)	Wulfnoth, a freeman commended to Eadric, held it
343b	Loudham		(1	4)	Turnold, a freeman commended to Eadric, held it
344b	Benhall		(10	0)	Wulfnoth, a freeman commended to Eadric, held it
	Benhall		(1	10)	Beorhtmær, a freeman commended to Eadric, held it
345	Bruisyard		(5	6)	Beorhtmær, a freeman commended to Eadric, held it
	Rendham		(12	0)	Blachesunc, a freeman commended to Eadric, held it
	Great Glemham		(8	0)	Four freemen commended to Eadric held it
	Rendham		(3	0)	Three freemen commended to Eadric held it
348	Thrandeston		(3	4)	Three half freemen commended to Eadric held it
349b	Mendham	(2	0	0)	Two freemen commended to Eadric held it
354b	Darsham		(3	4)	Osmund, a freeman commended to Eadric, held it
373b	Charsfield		(8	0)	Three half freemen commended to Eadric held it
	Charsfield		(10	0)	Marculf, a freeman commended to Eadric, held it
374	Crowfield		(5	0)	Udebrun, a freeman commended to Eadric, held it
374b	Olden		(3	4)	A freeman commended to Eadric held it
	Stonham		(5	4)	Leofwine, a freeman commended to Eadric, held it

Land to Eadric of Laxfield (*cont.*):

Ref. (fos.)	Location	Value £	s.	d.	Notes
375b	Helmingham	(1	10	0)	Durand commended to Eadric held it
376	Helmingham		(5	0)	Blæchemann, a freeman commended half to Eadric and half to Saxo, held it
379b	Chickering		(1	4)	A freewoman commended to Eadric held it
380b	Elmham		(10	0)	Ailwi, a freeman commended to Eadric, held it
388	Ufford		(10	0)	Almar, a freeman half commended to Eadric and half to Ely, held it
388b	Loudham	(4	0	0)	Fifteen freemen commended to Eadric held it
399	Wrentham	(2	0	0)	Thorkell, a freeman commended to Eadric, held it
400	Middleton	(2	0	0)	Alfric, a freeman commended to Eadric, held it
	Thorrington	(3	0	0)	Alfric, a freeman commended to Eadric, held it
403b	Great Glemham	(2	0	0)	Wulfric, a freeman half commended to Eadric and half to Ely, held it
407	Cretingham		(2	0)	A freeman commended to Eadric held it
407b	Kesingland		(5	0)	A freeman commended to Eadric held it
411	Creeting St Peter		(3	0)	A freeman commended to Eadric held it
417b	Clopton	(3	0	0)	Eadric Grim, half commended to Eadric and half to Ely, held it
	Debach		(3	0)	Eadric Grim, half commended to Eadric and half to Ely, held it
422	Stonham Aspall	(1	0	0)	Almar, a freeman commended to Eadric held it
424	Hemley		(1	0)	Hardwine, a freeman half commended to Eadric and half to Norman, held it

Ref. (fos.)	Location	Value £	s.	d.	Notes
424b	Hapsley		(6	0)	A man half commended to Eadric held it
429	Bedingfield			(8)	A freeman half commended to Eadric held it
430	Blaxhall		(1	8)	Godric, a freeman half commended to Eadric and half to Ely, held it
	Great Glemham	(2	0	0)	Starling commended to Eadric held it
	Stratford St Andrew	(2	0	0)	The above Starling held it
432b	Creeting St Peter	(5	0	0)	Alfric, a freeman commended to Eadric, held it
433	Otley	(5	0	0)	Leofleda, a freewoman commended to Eadric, held it
434b	Westhorpe	(1	0	0)	Wulfric Hagana, commended to Ely and Eadric, held it but could not sell
438	Horham		(6	8)	A freeman commended to Eadric held it
	Stonham	(1	0	0)	Alfric, a freeman commended to Eadric, held it
440b	Hemingstone	(1	0	0)	Wulfmær commended to Eadric held it
441	*Brutge*	(1	0	0)	Eadric commended to Eadric of Laxfield held it
	Colston		(10	0)	A freeman commended to Eadric held it
	Petthaugh	(3	0	0)	Beorhtwold, a freeman commended to Eadric, held it
	Ashfield		(10	0)	Godman, a freeman commended to Eadric, held it
441b	Grundisburgh		(5	0)	Brun, a freeman commended to Eadric, held it
442	Little Bealings		(1	0)	A sokeman commended to Eadric held it
	Tuddenham	(1	0	0)	Beorhtmær commended to Eadric held it
442b	Bredfield	(1	0	0)	Swartling, a freeman commended to Eadric, held it
	Thistleton		(8	0)	Frana, a freeman commended to Eadric, held it

Land to Eadric of Laxfield (*cont.*):

Ref. (fos.)	Location	Value £	s.	d.	Notes
443	Otley	(1	0	0)	Lustwine commended to Eadric held it
	Bredfield		(2	0)	A freeman commended to one himself commended to Eadric held it
	Sutton		(10	0)	A freeman commended to Eadric held it
	Wickham Market		(10	0)	Atsur, a freeman commended to Eadric, held it
	Sutton		(10	0)	Atsur, a freeman commended to Eadric, held it
	Harpole		(3	0)	Weneling, a freeman half commended to Eadric and half to Ely, held it
443b	Potsford	(1	0	0)	Weneling, a freeman half commended to Eadric and half to Ely, held it
	Campsey		(10	0)	Swartling, a freeman commended to Eadric, held it
	Campsey		(8	0)	Twelve freemen commended to Eadric held it
	Campsey	(1	0	0)	A freeman commended to Eadric held it
	Rendlesham	(1	0	0)	Godgifu, a freewoman half commended to Eadric and half to Ely, held it
444	Cransford	(1	0	0)	Atsur, commended to Eadric, held it
	Dallinghoo		(1	0)	Two freemen commended to Eadric held it
	Glevering		(8	0)	Beorhtmær commended to Eadric held it

	Total value of land held					
	By subject			From subject or by his men		
	£	s.	d.	£	s.	d.
Eadric of Laxfield	191	11	8	224	10	1

LAND ASSIGNED TO EADRIC THE WILD

Ref. (fos.)	Location	Value £	s.	d.	Notes
vol. i	*Herefordshire*				
183b	Burrington	2	0	0	
	Staunton on Arrow		12	0	
	Kinnersley				Waste. Assessed at 1 hide; Eadric could sell
	Shropshire				
253b	Lydham	10	0	0	
	Loppington	3	0	0	
	Great Berwick	1	10	0	
254	Siefton	6	0	0	
	Culmington	4	0	0	
254b	Kenley	1	10	0	Eadric, a freeman, held it
	Halston				Waste. Assessed at 7 hides
255	Melverley				Waste. Assessed at 1 hide
	Middleton Scriven		13	0	
	Wooton				Waste. Assessed at 2 hides
255b	Watnor	6	0	0	Eadric, a freeman, held it
	Loton		5	0	
	Yockleton	8	0	0	Eadric, a freeman, held it
	Hanwood		10	0	Eadric, a freeman, held it
	Wattleborough				Waste. Assessed at 2 hides
256	Middleton		4	0	
256b	Cressage	5	10	0	Eadric, a freeman, held it
	Weston under Redcastle	3	0	0	
257	Eudon St George	1	5	0	Eadric, a freeman, held it
	Walton Savage		10	0	Eadric, a freeman, held it
	Catesley		6	6	
	Overton	1	0	0	
	Bayston		10	0	Eadric held it of the Bishop of Hereford for one life
258	Pitchford		2	8	
	Hopesay	10	0	0	Eadric held it freely
	Clun	25	0	0	
	Hopton	2	0	0	Eadric held it freely
	Minton				Waste. Assessed at 1 hide
	Hope Bendrid				Waste. Assessed at 2 hides and 1 virgate

Land to Eadric the Wild (*cont.*):

Ref. (fos.)	Location	Value £	s.	d.	Notes
258b	Oxenbold		5	6	
	Harley		5	3	
	Alcaston	1	0	0	
	Chelmick		12	0	Eadric held it freely
	Hope Boulder	1	5	0	
	Shawbury		6	0	
259	Cantlop	1	0	0	Eadric held it freely
259b	Acton Scott		10	0	
260	Ackhill				Waste. Assessed at 3 hides
	Adforton		8	0	
	Lingen (Heref.)				Waste. Assessed at 3 virgates

	Total value of land held					
	By subject			From subject or by his men		
	£	s.	d.	£	s.	d.
Eadric the Wild	100	7	7	None		

LAND ASSIGNED TO EADRIC OF ELMHAM

vol. i	*Kent*				
9b	Elmham	30	0	0	Eadric held it from King Edward
11	Temple Ewell	12	0	0	Eadric held it from King Edward
	Westcliffe	8	0	0	Eadric held it from King Edward
	Tickenhurst	4	0	0	Eadric held it from King Edward
13b	Newington (nr. Folkestone)	12	0	0	Eadric held it from King Edward

Eadric of Elmham	Total value of land held	
	By subject £ s. d.	From subject or by his men £ s. d.
	66 0 0	None

LAND ASSIGNED TO EADRIC (*ANTECESSOR* OF ARNULF OF HESDIN)

Ref. (fos.)	Location	Value £	s.	d.	Notes
vol. i	*Hampshire*				
43	Linkenholt	5	0	0	Eadric held it from King Edward
46b	Combe (Berks.)	6	0	0	Eadric held it from King Edward
	Wiltshire				
70	Winterbourne	1	0	0	
	Etchilhampton	2	0	0	Eadric's wife held it in 1086
	Calstone Wellington	4	0	0	Eadric's wife held it in 1086
	Dorset				
80b	Kingston Magna	4	0	0	
	Somerset				
98	Weston (nr. Bath)	8	0	0	
	Tickenham	2	0	0	
	Rodden	4	0	0	
	Gloucestershire				
169	Oldbury on the Hill	10	0	0	
	Great Badminton	10	0	0	
	Acton Turville	5	0	0	
	Hanham	2	0	0	

Eadric, *antec.* of Arnulf	Total value of land held	
	By subject £ s. d.	From subject or by his men £ s. d.
	63 0 0	None

LAND ASSIGNED TO EADWEARD CILT

Ref. (fos.)	Location	Value £	s.	d.	Notes
vol. i	*Hertfordshire*				
146	Wing	32	0	0	Eadweard Cilt the man of Earl Harold held it and could sell
	Crafton	6	0	0	Eadweard held it and could sell
147b	Singleborough	4	0	0	Eadweard Cilt, King Edward's thegn, held it
	Whaddon (nr. Bletchley)	8	0	0	Eadweard Cilt, King Edward's thegn, held it
	Woolstone	3	0	0	Eadweard, King Edward's thegn, held it
	Newton Longville	10	0	0	
148	Broughton (nr. Moulsoe)	10	0	0	Eadweard, King Edward's thegn, held it
	Moulsoe	(2	0	0)	Algar the man of Eadweard Cilt held it
	Northamptonshire				
228b	Bisbrooke (Rutland)	1	0	0	Eadweard held it with *sac* and *soc*
	Tickencote (Rutland)	1	10	0	
	Horne (Rutland)	1	0	0	
	Glaston (Rutland)	2	0	0	Eadweard held it with *sac* and *soc*
	Lincolnshire				
336b	Stamford				Eadweard Cilt had fourteen houses there
340	Witham				Eadweard had a third of a church there
360b	Bytham	6	0	0	
	Witham	6	0	0	
367	Binbrook	2	0	0	

Eadweard Cilt	Total value of land held					
	By subject £	s.	d.	From subject or by his men £	s.	d.
	92	10	0	2	0	0

LAND ASSIGNED TO EARNESIGE

Ref. (fos.)	Location	Value £	s.	d.	Notes
vol. i	*Gloucestershire*				
167	Swell	2	0	0	
167b	Painswick	20	0	0	He could go where he would
168	Swell	8	0	0	
168b	Frampton on Severn	5	0	0	
169b	Eyford	4	0	0	
	Aston Somerville (Worcs.)	6	0	0	
	Siddington	10	0	0	
	Miserden	5	0	0	
	Worcestershire				
176	Astley	10	0	0	

Earnesige	Total value of land held	
	By subject £ s. d.	From subject or by his men £ s. d.
	70 0 0	None

LAND ASSIGNED TO ENGELRIC

Ref. (fos.)	Location	Value £	s.	d.	Notes
vol. i	*Hertfordshire*				
137	Tring	25	0	0	
136b	Gubblecote	(1	10	0)	Eddeva held it from Engelric but could not sell it from Tring
	Pendley	(2	0	0)	Eddeva the nun held it from Engelric but could not sell it from Tring
	Wiggington	(3	0	0)	Godwine held it from Engelric but could not sell it from Tring
	Oxfordshire				
159b	Newnham Murren	12	0	0	

Land to Engelric (*cont.*):

Ref. (fos.)	Location	Value £	s.	d.	Notes
vol. ii	*Essex*				
26b	Orsett	1	0	0	Engelric held it from the Bishop of London
	Gravesend		10	0	Harold held it and Engelric from him
27b	Langhoe	17	0	0	
	Suffolk				
303b	Finborough	2	10	0	
404b	Buxhall	2	0	0	
404	Finborough		(1	0)	A freeman commended to Engelric held it

Engelric	Total value of land held					
	By subject			From subject or by his men		
	£	s.	d.	£	s.	d.
	60	0	0	6	11	0

LAND ASSIGNED TO GAUTI, EARL HAROLD'S HOUSECARL

Ref. (fos.)	Location	£	s.	d.	Notes
vol. i	*Middlesex*				
129	East Bedfont	1	0	0	Gauti, a housecarl of Earl Harold
	Feltham	5	0	0	Two thegns, one Earl Harold's man [perhaps, but not certainly, Gauti]
	Hertfordshire				
137b	Cockhamstead	7	0	0	Gauti, a thegn of Earl Harold
vol. ii	*Essex*				
20b	Hutton	5	0	0	Gauti, a freeman, held it
54b	*Ateleia*	1	0	0	Gauti held it from Earl Harold
55b	Little Wigborough	7	0	0	Gauti, a freeman held it

Ref. (fos.)	Location	Value £	s.	d.	Notes
	Stambourne and Toppesfield	12	0	0	
	Suffolk				
381	Freckenham	12	0	0	'Orth' held it [see Fleming, *Kings and Lords*, 88 n. 139, for this identification]

Gauti	Total value of land held					
	By subject			From subject or by his men		
	£	s.	d.	£	s.	d.
	50	0	0	None		

LAND ASSIGNED TO GODRIC THE SHERIFF

Ref.	Location	£	s.	d.	Notes
vol. i	*Berkshire*				
58	Reading				Godric held a house *ad hospitum*
60b	Bagshot (Wilts.)	1	10	0	It was of the king's farm; Godric held it from King Edward
	Sparsholt	2	0	0	Godric, a freeman, held it
	Fyfield	10	0	0	Godric held it of the Abbot of Abingdon and could not sell
	Fyfield	6	0	0	Godric held it from King Edward. The king reduced its assessment from 10 to 5 hides
	Hendred	5	0	0	Godric held it from King Edward
	Woolhampton	6	0	0	Godric held it from King Edward. It had belonged to the king's farm, and Edward gave it to Godric
	Wiltshire				
72	Standen (Berks.)	5	0	0	
	Clyffe Pypard	4	0	0	

Land to Godric (*cont.*):

Ref. (fos.)	Location	Value £	s.	d.	Notes
	Buckinghamshire				
144	Weston Turville	2	10	0	
144b	Shalstone	2	10	0	
144	Weston Turville	(2	10	0)	Two of Godric's men held it and could sell
152	Amersham	(1	0	0)	Ælfric, the man of Godric, held it and could sell
	Bedfordshire				
213	Riseley		(8	0)	Wenot the man of Godric held it and could sell

Godric the sheriff	Total value of land held					
	By subject			From subject or by his men		
	£	s.	d.	£	s.	d.
	44	10	0	3	18	0

LAND ASSIGNED TO GODWINE THE PRIEST

Ref.	Location	£	s.	d.	Notes
vol. i	*Sussex*				
17b	East Lavington	10	0	0	Godwine the priest held it in alms
23	Lavant	8	0	0	Godwine held it from Earl Godwine
27	Saddlescombe	15	0	0	Godwine the priest held it from Earl Godwine
	Plumpton	25	0	0	Godwine the priest held it from Earl Godwine
	Hampshire				
43	Farringdon	15	0	0	Godwine the priest held it. It pertained to the church at Bosham

Godwine the Priest	Total value of land held	
	By subject	From subject or by his men
	£ s. d.	£ s. d.
	73 0 0	None

LAND ASSIGNED TO GODWINE
(*ANTECESSOR* OF EUDO DAPIFER)

Ref. (fos.)	Location	Value £	s.	d.	Notes
vol. ii	*Essex*				
49	Harlow	2	0	0	
49b	Munden	10	0	0	
51	Weeley	8	0	0	
	Suffolk				
402b	Eriswell	10	0	0	Godwine, King Edward's thegn, held it
	Chamberlain's Hall	12	0	0	A berewick of Eriswell

Godwine (*antec.* of Eudo Dapifer)	Total value of land held	
	By subject	From subject or by his men
	£ s. d.	£ s. d.
	42 0 0	None

LAND ASSIGNED TO GODWINE AND AZUR, SON OF SUALEVA

[The connection between Godwine and Azur is not stated in Domesday, but is presumed because of the entry on f. 377, and because Azur was listed as a holder of *sac* and *soc* in Lincolnshire. Azur, with land worth £3, can hardly have been the lord of Godwine, who had land worth £37: it seems more likely that Godwine was Azur's father, or at least, Azur's immediate predecessor to the land.

Land to Godwine and Azur (*cont.*):

As we know from references to Earl Godwine, men and women who were dead before 1066 were still recorded as landholders on occasion.]

Ref. (fos.)	Location	Value £	s.	d.	Notes
vol. i	*Nottinghamshire*				
337	Nottinghamshire				Azur, son of Sualeva, had *sac* and *soc* and toll and team in Nottinghamshire
291b	Bradmore	3	0	0	Azur held it
	Lincolnshire				
337	Lincolnshire				Azur, son of Sualeva, had *sac* and *soc* and toll and team in Lincolnshire
368	Welbourne	16	0	0	Godwine held it
	Barrowby	12	0	0	Godwine held it. Includes soke in Ingoldsby
	Sedgebrook	9	0	0	Godwine held it
377	Ingoldsby				Robert Malet (predecessor to Godwine and Azur) claims soke over 4 bovates of land which Gilbert of Ghent has, and the Wapentake states that it should be Robert's through his predecessor Azur

Godwine and Azur	Total value of land held	
	By subject £ s. d.	From subjects or by their men £ s. d.
	40 0 0	None

LAND ASSIGNED TO GUTHMUND

Ref. (fos.)	Location	Value £	s.	d.	Notes
vol. ii	*Essex*				
32	Tollesbury	4	0	0	Guthmund, a freeman, held it
52b	Kelvedon	4	0	0	Guthmund, King Edward's thegn, held it

Ref. (fos.)	Location	Value £	s.	d.	Notes
53	Purleigh	8	0	0	Guthmund, a freeman, held it
	Latchingdon	7	0	0	
53b	Rayne	6	0	0	
	Markshall	2	0	0	
54	Bensted	8	0	0	
	Suffolk				
406	Nacton	3	10	0	Guthmund held it from Ely, could not sell, and it reverted to Ely on his death
408	Great Livermere	2	0	0	Guthmund held it under Ely but could not sell
	Stanstead	6	0	0	Guthmund, a thegn, held it
408b	Haughley	16	0	0	Guthmund held it from King Edward
410b	Occold	3	0	0	Guthmund held it from Wulfric his brother (the Abbot of Ely)
403b	Finborough	(4	0	0)	Leofsune, commended to Guthmund held it
404	Finborough	(1	0	0)	Two freemen commended to Guthmund held it
405	Wattisfield		(3	0)	Two freemen commended to Guthmund held it
406	*Brihtoluestuna*, Levington, *Culuerdestuna*, *Isteuertuna*, and Bixley	(4	10	0)	thirty freemen commended to Guthmund held it
408	Gislingham		(2	0)	A freewoman commended to Guthmund held it
	Great Livermere		(13	0)	Three men commended to Guthmund held it
408b	Dagworth	(2	5	0)	Seven freemen commended to Guthmund held it
409	Wetherden	(2	10	0)	Seventeen freemen commended to Guthmund held it
	Eruestuna	(1	0	0)	Ten freemen commended to Guthmund held it
	Torp	(1	10	0)	Sixteen freemen commended to Guthmund held it
	Ulutuna		(12	0)	Three freemen commended to Guthmund held it

Land to Guthmund (*cont.*):

Ref. (fos.)	Location	Value £	s.	d.	Notes
410	Darmsden		(2	7)	Wulfric, a freeman commended to Guthmund, held it
410b	Occold		(10	0)	Eight freemen commended to Guthmund were attached to the manor
427	Dagworth and *Waledena*	(1	0	0)	A freeman, half commended to Guthmund and half to Teri, held it

Guthmund	Total value of land held					
	By subject			From subject or by his men		
	£	s.	d.	£	s.	d.
	72	10	0	19	7	7

LAND ASSIGNED TO HROLF, SCELDEWARE'S SON

vol. i	*Leicestershire*				
236	Burton on the Wolds		1	6	
	Nottinghamshire				
291b	Owthorpe	1	10	0	
	Lincolnshire				
337	Lincolnshire				Hrolf had *sac* and *soc* and toll and team in the county
342b	Rasen	1	0	0	
	Tealby	1	0	0	
	Hainton	2	0	0	
343b	Owmby (nr. Fillingham)		7	6	
344	Messingham	2	0	0	
	Wyham	1	10	0	
345b	Yawthorpe		12	0	
346	Manton	12	0	0	
	Hibaldstow	6	0	0	

Ref. (fos.)	Location	Value £	s.	d.	Notes
347	Fulstow	2	0	0	
357b	Thoresway	2	0	0	
358	South Gadeby	1	10	0	
	Kelstern		15	0	
360	Keelby	2	0	0	
	Weelsby	6	0	0	
360b	Stainton le Vale	2	10	0	
365	Nettleton	4	0	0	
	Searby		10	0	
	Ewerby	2	0	0	
	Linwood	1	10	0	
	Rothwell	2	0	0	
	Navenby	1	12	0	
	Great Cotes	3	0	0	

Hrolf	Total value of land held					
	By subject			From subject or by his men		
	£	s.	d.	£	s.	d.
	59	8	0	None		

LAND ASSIGNED TO INGWARE

Ref. (fos.)	Location	Value £	s.	d.	Notes
vol. i	*Cambridgeshire*				
196	Duxford	7	0	0	Ingware held it from King Edward and could sell
201b	Gamlingay		10	0	Ingware, King Edward's thegn, held it and could sell
	Huntingdonshire				
207	Everton	10	0	0	
vol. ii	*Essex*				
22b	Burstead	20	0	0	
33	Chrishall	15	0	0	
80	Roydon	6	0	0	
80b	Thorpehall	4	0	0	
81	Baythorn	7	0	0	
	St Lawrence	1	0	0	
	Fouchers	8	0	0	

Land to Ingware (*cont.*):

Ref. (fos.)	Location	Value £ s. d.	Notes
	Suffolk		
308b	South Elmham	(4 0 0)	Alwin, a freeman commended to Ingware the thegn, held it

Ingware	Total value of land held	
	By subject £ s. d.	From subject or by his men £ s. d.
	78 10 0	4 0 0

LAND ASSIGNED TO JOHN THE DANE

[John was the *antecessor* of Matthew of Mortagne. Matthew also held a further £15's worth of land at Shipton Moyne which had been held by Strang the Dane, and, in Somerset, land worth £2 at Cheveley which had been held by Thorkell the Dane. It is possible that either or both were related to John.]

Ref.	Location	Value £ s. d.	Notes
vol. i	*Dorset*		
82b	Milborne St Andrew	5 0 0	
	Owermoigne	15 0 0	
	Somerset		
89b	Yatton	15 0 0	
98	Clevedon	2 0 0	John the Dane [*Liber Exoniensis* f. 450]
	Gloucestershire		
170	Shipton Moyne	5 0 0	

John the Dane	Total value of land held	
	By subject £ s. d.	From subject or by his men £ s. d.
	42 0 0	None

LAND ASSIGNED TO KARL

Ref. (fos.)	Location	Value £	s.	d.	Notes
vol. i	*Sussex*				
21b	Hartfield	4	0	0	Karl held it *sicut alodium*
22b	Barkham		7	0	Karl held it from King Edward; it did not pay geld
28	Wappingthorne	5	0	0	Karl held it from King Edward
	Surrey				
36b	Send	20	0	0	Karl held it from King Edward
	Hampshire				
47b	Shipton Bellinger	6	0	0	Karl held it from King Edward *in alodium*
	Eastrop	4	0	0	Karl held it from King Edward and could go where he would
	Berkshire				
63	Speen	8	0	0	Karl held it from King Edward *in alodium*
	Wiltshire				
70	Allington (All Cannings)	6	0	0	
	Teffont Evias	6	0	0	
	Crofton	7	0	0	
	Newton Tony	10	0	0	
	Winterbourne		10	0	
	Lydiard Tregoze	10	0	0	
70b	Swindon		12	0	
	Moredon	5	0	0	
	Widhill	2	0	0	
	Upton Scudamore	8	0	0	
	Norton Bavant	24	0	0	
	Rockley	8	0	0	
	Fifield Bavant	4	0	0	
	Lacock		10	0	
	Somerset				
97b	Chelwood	5	0	0	

Land to Karl (*cont.*):

Karl	Total value of land held	
	By subject	From subject or by his men
	£ *s.* *d.*	£ *s.* *d.*
	143 19 0	None

LAND ASSIGNED TO KETILL ALDER

Ref. (fos.)	Location	Value £	*s.*	*d.*	Notes
vol. ii	*Essex*				
75b	Fratting	2	0	0	
	Norfolk				
223	Harling	1	10	0	Ketill, a freeman, held it
230b	Barton Bendish	3	0	0	Ketill, a freeman, held it
233	Walsingham	6	0	0	
	Alia Walsingham	4	0	0	
	Stiffkey	4	0	0	
233b	Whitwell	4	0	0	
234	Witchingham	1	0	0	
	Scottow	1	0	0	
243b	Hainford	5	0	0	Ketill held it under Stigand
254	Walsingham	3	0	0	Ketill, a thegn of Stigand, held it
254b	Great Melton	6	0	0	
	Mettingham	1	10	0	
254	East Carlton	(1	0	0)	Godric, a freeman of Ketill, held it
	Suffolk				
416b	Onehouse	2	0	0	Ketill, King Edward's thegn, held it
	Rushford		15	0	Ketill, a freeman and thegn, held it
	Rushford		(5	0)	Four freemen commended to Ketill held it
436	Onehouse		(10	0)	Ten freemen commended to Ketill held it

Ketill Alder	Total value of land held					
	By subject			From subject or by his men		
	£	*s.*	*d.*	£	*s.*	*d.*
	45	15	0	1	15	0

LAND ASSIGNED TO LEOFNOTH, SON OF OSMUND

Ref. (fos.)	Location	Value £	*s.*	*d.*	Notes
vol. i	*Bedfordshire*				
215b	Totternhoe	16	0	0	Leofnoth, a thegn of King Edward, held it and could sell
	Turvey	2	0	0	Leofnoth, a thegn of King Edward, held it and could sell
	Odell	10	0	0	Leofnoth, a thegn of King Edward, held it
	Podington	2	10	0	Leofnoth, a thegn of King Edward, held it
	Thurleigh	4	0	0	Leofnoth, a thegn of King Edward, held it
216	Segenhoe	16	0	0	Leofnoth, a thegn of King Edward, held it
	Silsoe	11	0	0	Leofnoth, a thegn of King Edward, held it
215b	Wymington	(4	0	0)	Lent the man of Leofnoth held it
	Thurleigh		(5	0)	Ordric the man of Leofnoth held it and could sell
	Northamptonshire				
222b	Litchborough	2	0	0	Leofnoth held it freely
223b	Croughton	1	0	0	Leofnoth held it freely as a berewick of Evenly
	Syresham	1	0	0	Leofnoth held it freely
224	Berkswell (Warwicks.)	2	0	0	Leofnoth held it freely
226b	Pipewell		4	0	
	Cottebrooke		10	0	
	Hanging Houghton		4	0	

Land to Leofnoth (*cont.*):

Ref. (fos.)	Location	Value £	s.	d.	Notes
226b	Lamport	4	0	0	
	Wythemail	2	0	0	
	Pitsford	3	10	0	
	Horton		10	0	
	Evenly	2	0	0	
	Canons Ashby	2	0	0	
	Evenly	1	10	0	
	Evenly	1	10	0	
	Cold Higham	2	0	0	
	Plumpton	2	0	0	
	[location not identified]	2	0	0	
	Astcote		15	0	
	Wootton	4	0	0	
	[location not identified]	2	0	0	All the entries from Pipewell to this entry were held freely by Leofnoth, who could sell
226b	Pattishall	10	0	0	
	Buckinghamshire				
151b	Ellesborough	10	0	0	Leofnoth the man of King Edward held it
146b	Wavendon		(5	0)	Chentis the man of Leofnoth, Osmund's son, held it and could sell

Leofnoth	Total value of land held: By subject £	s.	d.	From subject or by his men £	s.	d.
	117	13	0	4	10	0

LAND ASSIGNED TO THE BROTHERS LEOFNOTH AND LEOFRIC

Ref. (fos.)	Location	Value £	s.	d.	Notes
vol. i	*Staffordshire*				
250b	Kingsley		17	0	Leofric held it freely
	Bradley in the Moor		5	0	Leofric, a freeman, held it
	Kingsley		6	0	Leofric, a freeman, held it
	Derbyshire				
277	Eckington	7	0	0	Leofnoth held it
	Barlborough	6	0	0	Leofnoth held it
	Palterton	6	0	0	Leofnoth held it
	Duckmanton	4	0	0	Leofnoth held it
	Stretton	3	0	0	Leofnoth held it
	Harthill	1	0	0	Leofnoth held it
	Boulton	2	0	0	Leofnoth held it
	Kirk Langley	5	0	0	Leofnoth held it
	Ripley	4	0	0	Leofnoth held it
	Stretton		3	0	Leofric, Leofnoth's brother, held it
	Willington	2	0	0	Leofric held it
	Ashover	4	0	0	Leofnoth and Leofric held it as two manors
	Newton	4	0	0	Leofnoth and Leofric held it
	Crich	2	0	0	Leofnoth and Leofric held it as two manors
	Stoney Middleton				Waste. Leofnoth and his brother held it as two manors
	Hathersage	3	0	0	Leofnoth and Leofric held it as two manors
	Ballidon	3	0	0	Leofnoth and Leofric held it as two manors
277b	Clifton	2	0	0	Leofnoth and Leofric held it as two manors
	Warrington		5	0	Leofnoth held it
	Nottinghamshire				
280	Litchurch (Derbys.)				Leofric had a church there
289b	Bunny	4	0	0	Leofnoth held it
	Kirkby in Ashfield	4	0	0	Leofnoth held it
	Annesly	2	0	0	Leofnoth held it
	Cassall		16	0	Leofnoth held it

Land to Leofnoth and Leofric (*cont.*):

Ref. (fos.)	Location	Value £	s.	d.	Notes
289b	Barton in Fabis	6	0	0	Leofric held it
	Tevershall	3	0	0	Leofric held it
	Wansley		8	0	Leofric held it

Leofnoth and Leofric	Total value of land held					
	By subjects £	s.	d.	From subjects or by their men £	s.	d.
Leofnoth	49	1	0			
Leofric	12	19	0			
Jointly	18	0	0			
TOTAL	80	0	0	None		

LAND ASSIGNED TO MÆRLSWEIN THE SHERIFF

vol. i	*Somerset*				
86	Over Stratton	3	0	0	This was thegnland of the royal manor of South Peret
95	Bridgewater	5	0	0	
	Wembdon	3	0	0	
	Bawdrip	2	10	0	
	Brean	5	0	0	
96b	Stockland	5	0	0	
	Quantoxhead	11	0	0	
	Huish (in Nettlescombe)	3	0	0	
	Bagborough	2	10	0	
	Newhall		10	0	
	Devon				
113b	Dunchideok	3	0	0	
	Kerswell (in Broad Hembury)	2	0	0	
	Aller and Bulealler	3	0	0	
	Throwleigh	4	0	0	
	Chagford	3	0	0	

Ref. (fos.)	Location	Value £	s.	d.	Notes
	Ilsington	9	0	0	
	Ingsdon	9	0	0	
	Tiverton	2	0	0	
	Washfield		10	0	
	Edginswell		15	0	
	Cornwall				
121b	Trewirgie	5	0	0	
	Liskeard	8	0	0	
	Fawton	8	0	0	
122b	Trenderway		5	0	
	Trevisquite	1	10	0	
	Downinney	3	0	0	
124b	Veryan	5	0	0	
	Trewderet		15	0	
	Yorkshire				
289	York				One house held by Mærlswein
298b	Yorkshire				Mærlswein had *sac* and *soc* and toll and team in the county
313	Theakston, Newton Picot, Gatenby, and *Ounesbi*	6	0	0	Mærlswein held these as three manors
325b	Thorganby	1	0	0	
	Barlby				Waste. Assessed at 1 carucate
	Newton (in Wintringham)	4	0	0	
	Rudston	3	0	0	
	Nunnington	2	0	0	
	Newton upon Ouse and *Toresbi*	2	0	0	
	Drax, Little Airmyn, Camblesforth, and Barleigh	2	0	0	
	Ribston	1	0	0	
	Goldsborough	4	0	0	
326	Deighton	3	0	0	
	Ripley	1	0	0	
	Lincolnshire				
336	Lincoln				Mærlswein had one house in the city

Land to Mærlswein (*cont.*):

Ref. (fos.)	Location	Value £	s.	d.	Notes
337	Lincolnshire				Mærlswein had *sac* and *soc* in the shire
362b	Burton Coggles	10	0	0	
	Dunholme		10	0	
	Roxby	6	0	0	
	Rasen	16	0	0	
	Tealby	12	0	0	
	Witham on the Hill	1	0	0	
363	Irnham	12	0	0	
	Ashby de la Launde	4	0	0	
362b	Burton Coggles	(2	0	0)	Grimketill held it *TRE*
	Scrawby and Sturton	(3	0	0)	Grimketill held it *TRE*. Mærlswein's successor held both lands *TRW*
376					*TRE* Grimketill had *sac* and *soc* over his land, but in the year King Edward died he forfeited his land, which was given to Mærlswein the Sheriff to administer for the king [Grimketill's land may have been worth as much as £35, depending on whether other references to Grimketill in Lincolnshire should be included]

Mærlswein	Total value of land held	
	By subject £ s. d.	From subject or by his men £ s. d.
	214 0 0	None

[This total excludes the land of Grimketill.]

LAND ASSIGNED TO NORMANN

Ref. (fos.)	Location	Value £	s.	d.	Notes
vol. i	*Kent*				
1	Kent				Normann did not have to pay relief on alloidal land
8b	Nettlestead	8	0	0	Normann held it from King Edward
13b	Tiffenden		8	4	Normann held it from King Edward
	Swanton (in Bilsington)	1	5	4	Normann held it from King Edward
	Bonnington	4	0	0	Normann held it from King Edward
14	Mereworth	12	0	0	Normann held it from King Edward
	Blean	8	0	0	
	Sussex				
18	Frankwell	2	0	0	
18b	Dallington	2	0	0	Normann held it and could sell
19b	Henhurst Hundred	1	0	0	Normann, a freeman, held it
21	Wannock	5	10	0	Normann held it from King Edward
28	Annington	12	0	0	Normann held it from King Edward
	Surrey				
36b	Camberwell	12	0	0	

Normann	Total value of land held	
	By subject £ s. d.	From subject or by his men £ s. d.
	68 3 4	None

LAND ASSIGNED TO ORDWULF

Ref. (fos.)	Location	Value £	s.	d.	Notes
vol. i	*Somerset*				
92	Brushford	4	0	0	
	Devonshire				
104b	Wyke (in Shobrooke)		10	0	
	Shobrooke (nr. Crediton)	1	0	0	
	West Raddon	1	0	0	
	Alwington	1	10	0	
	Monkleigh	4	0	0	
	Frithelstock	8	0	0	
105	Alverdiscott	6	0	0	
	Bratton Fleming	8	0	0	
	Croyde	4	0	0	Ordulf's sister held 1 virgate of this land (out of a total of 1 hide) but could not separate it
	St Mary Church	1	0	0	
	Broadhempston	2	0	0	
	Harford	3	0	0	
	Bigbury	7	0	0	
	Bere Ferrers	3	0	0	
	Bratton Fleming		(15	0)	Two thegns, the men of Ordwulf, held it
	Modbury		(2	0)	Wado held it, but could not separate it from Ordwulf
	Cornwall				
121b	Moresk	5	0	0	
	Tehidy	8	0	0	

Ordwulf	Total value of land held					
	By subject			From subject or by his men		
	£	s.	d.	£	s.	d.
	67	0	0		17	0

LAND ASSIGNED TO ORM (*ANTECESSOR* OF HUGH FITZ BALDRIC)

Ref. (fos.)	Location	Value £	s.	d.	Notes
vol. i	*Yorkshire*				
327	Bagby	8	0	0	In addition, there were six attached berewicks at Kirby Knowle, Carlton Miniott, Islebeck Grange, Sutton under Whitestone Cliffe, Arden Hall, and Kepwick
327b	Crunkly Gill	3	0	0	Four berewicks: Danby, Lealholm, Great Broughton, and *Camisedale*
	Kirby Moorside	12	0	0	Fourteen berewicks: Walton, Hutton le Hole, Gillamoor, Hoveton, Kirby Moorside, Welburn, *Middelham*, Harome, Nawton, Great Barugh, Normanby, Misperton, Ryton, Marton, Little Barugh
	Holker				Not valued: also a berewick at Birkby Hall, in total 8 carucates
	Hovingham	12	0	0	Fifteen berewicks: Wath, Fryton, Howthorpe, Scackleton, *Hawade*, Coulton, Grimston, East Newton, East Ness, South Holme, Slingsby, Butterwick, Amotherby, Broughton, Newsham
327b	Laysthorpe Lodge				Not valued: 2 carucates
	Heslington	1	1	0	In 1086 valued with Thorpe Hill and Buttercrambe, and were held by Orm and Fulcher
328	Langton	12	0	0	Five berewicks: Kennythorpe, Burdale, Raisthorpe, Sherburn, and East Heslerton
	Bishop Thorpe	1	0	0	
	Crunkly Gill				Waste. 12 carucates, with Leaholm and Danby

Land to Orm (*cont.*):

Ref. (fos.)	Location	Value £	s.	d.	Notes
	Camisedale				Waste. 1 carucate
	Heworth		10	0	

Orm	Total value of land held			
	By subject £	s.	d.	From subject or by his men £ s. d.
	49	11	0	None

LAND ASSIGNED TO OSFRITH

Ref. (fos.)	Location	£	s.	d.	Notes
vol. i	*Devon*				
105b	Okehampton	10	0	0	
106	Kelly	3	0	0	
	Belstone	1	10	0	
107b	Drewsteignton	2	0	0	
	Spreyton	2	10	0	
108	Whiteway		10	0	
108b	East Prawle		10	0	
111b	Challonsleigh	1	0	0	
115	Yealmpstone		10	0	
	Cornwall				
124	Boconnoc	2	0	0	The same man held it in 1086
	Trenant (in Duloe)	3	0	0	The same man held it in 1086
	Glynn	2	0	0	The same man held it in 1086
	Bowithick		5	0	The same man held it in 1086
	Penhalt	1	0	0	The same man held it in 1086
	Penpont	5	0	0	The same man held it in 1086
	Lantyan	3	0	0	The same man held it in 1086
	Treslake	3	0	0	The same man held it in 1086

Osfrith	Total value of land held			
	By subject £	s.	d.	From subject or by his men £ s. d.
	40	15	0	None

LAND ASSIGNED TO OSMUND

Ref. (fos.)	Location	Value £	s.	d.	Notes
vol. i	*Surrey*				
34b	Burgham	8	0	0	Osmund held it from King Edward
	Worplesdon	10	0	0	Osmund held it from King Edward
	Loseley	2	0	0	Osmund held it from King Edward
	Hampshire				
44b	Penton	7	0	0	Osmund held it from King Edward *in alodium*
	Houghton	1	10	0	Osmund held it from King Edward
	Wiltshire				
68b	Castle Eaton	15	0	0	
	Milston	3	10	0	Osmund, a thegn, held these two manors *TRE*

Osmund	Total value of land held			
	By subject £	s.	d.	From subject or by his men £ s. d.
	53	0	0	None

LAND ASSIGNED TO OSWEARD OF NORTON

Ref. (fos.)	Location	Value £	s.	d.	Notes
vol. i	*Kent*				
1b	Aylesford Last				Osweard had *sac* and *soc* in the Last
7b	Harrietsham	10	0	0	Osweard held it from King Edward
8	Allington (Hollingbourn)	9	0	0	Osweard held it from King Edward
8b	Delce	5	0	0	Osweard held it from King Edward

Land to Osweard (*cont.*):

Ref. (fos.)	Location	Value £	s.	d.	Notes
9	Haven	2	10	0	Osweard held it from King Edward
	Tunstall	7	0	0	Osweard held it from King Edward
	Upchurch	6	0	0	
	Stuppington	1	10	0	
	Tonge	7	0	0	Of Tunstall, Upchurch, Stuppington, and Tonge, Osweard had 5 sulungs *ad gablum* and took three sulungs and one and a half jugungs from the royal villeins
10	Norton	8	0	0	Osweard held it from King Edward
	Hurst (in Chiham)		10	0	Osweard held it from King Edward
13b	Sellindge	8	0	0	Osweard held it from King Edward
	Sussex				
18	*Medehei*	4	0	0	Osweard held it from King Edward and could go with his lands where he would
20	Claverham		7	6	Osweard, a freeman, held it
21	Ratton	5	0	0	Osweard held it from King Edward
22	Claverham	2	0	0	Osweard held it from King Edward
	Chalvington	1	0	0	Osweard held it *sicut alodium*
20	Lordine		(14	0)	Wenestan held it from Osweard but could not go where he would with it
	Surrey				
33	Tooting		15	0	Osweard held it from King Edward and could sell
34	Walkingstead	20	0	0	Osweard held it from King Edward and could sell
36b	Addington	5	0	0	Osweard held it from King Edward and could sell

Ref. (fos.)	Location	Value £	s.	d.	Notes
vol. ii	*Essex*				
23b	Stambridge	6	0	0	

Osweard	Total value of land held					
	By subject £	s.	d.	From subject or by his men £	s.	d.
	108	12	6		14	0

LAND ASSIGNED TO OSWULF, FRANE'S SON

vol. i	*Hertfordshire*				
138	Miswell	8	0	0	Oswulf, King Edward's thegn, held it
	Barwyth (Beds.)	3	0	0	Oswulf, King Edward's thegn, held it
136b	Miswell		(10	0)	Wiga the man of Ordwulf held it and could sell
	Wiggington		(8	0)	Leofric the man of Oswulf held it and could sell
137	Tring	(3	0	0)	Two of Oswulf's sokemen held it and could sell
137b	Tiscot	(2	0	0)	Two of Oswulf's men held it and could sell
	Buckinghamshire				
149	Cheddington	5	0	0	Oswulf, King Edward's thegn, held it and could sell
	Clifton Reynes	6	0	0	Oswulf, King Edward's thegn, held it and could sell. Of these 4 hides Ælfric, the man of Oswulf, held 1 virgate and could sell

Land to Osweard (*cont.*):

Ref. (fos.)	Location	Value £ s. d.	Notes
	Bedfordshire		
215	Studham	8 0 0	Oswulf, King Edward's thegn, held it
	Oakley	4 10 0	Oswulf, King Edward's thegn, held it
	Turvey	3 10 0	
	Northamptonshire		
225	Stoke Albany	3 0 0	Oswulf held it freely
	Desborough	5 0	Oswulf held it freely
	Brampton Ash	10 0	Oswulf held it freely

Oswulf	Total value of land held	
	By subject £ s. d.	From subject or by his men £ s. d.
	41 15 0	None

LAND ASSIGNED TO RALPH THE STALLER

vol. i	*Cornwall*		
121b	Tybesta	12 0 0	
	Lincolnshire		
337	Lincolnshire		Ralph had *sac* and *soc*
	Colby (Boothby Raffoe)	2 0 0	
347	Waltham	20 0 0	
347b	Hough on the Hill	12 0 0	
	Brant Broughton	15 0 0	
	Fulbeck and Leadenham	30 0 0	
348	Longbennington	26 0 0	
	Drayton	30 0 0	
348b	Stoke Rochford	1 10 0	
vol. ii	*Norfolk*		
117b	Norwich		Ralph had 13 acres there

Ref. (fos.)	Location	Value £	s.	d.	Notes
119	Sporle	10	0	0	It was not gelded. It belonged to the king before Edward gave it to Ralph
128b	Acle	8	0	0	
	Halvergate	8	0	0	
144	Swaffham	8	0	0	It was not gelded and pertained to the demesne before Edward gave it to Ralph
147	Bylaugh	3	0	0	
149	Middleton (King's Lynn)	1	0	0	
194	Eccles (Attleborough)	5	0	0	
134b	Runham		(5	0)	A freeman of Ralph held it
	Mautby	(2	0	0)	Wistan, a freeman of Ralph, held it
148	Dilham		(8	0)	A sokeman of Ralph held it
	Suffolk				
293	Wisset	8	0	0	
	Wrabetuna		1	3	
409b	Thorney	3	0	0	Ralph had this in pledge from Toli
293	Bixley		(4	0)	A freeman commended to Ralph held it
	Tuddenham (Ipswich)			(8)	A freeman of Ralph held it
297b	Rendham		(5	0)	Hunepot, a freeman commended to Ralph, held it
295	Westerfield		(4	0)	Six freemen commended to Ralph held it
	Westerfield		(10	0)	Bar, a freeman commended to Ralph, held it
343b	Charsfield		(3	4)	A freeman commended to Ralph held it
365	Elmham		(7	0)	Godric, a freeman of Ralph, held it
411b	Debach		(1	0)	A freeman, commended to one himself commended to Ralph, held it

Land to Ralph (*cont.*):

Ref. (fos.)	Location	Value £ s. d.	Notes
431	Clopton	(3 0)	A freeman commended to Ralph held it

Ralph the Staller	Total value of land held	
	By subject £ s. d.	From subject or by his men £ s. d.
	200 11 3	2 11 0

LAND ASSIGNED TO ROBERT FITZ WYMARC

Ref.	Location	Value £ s. d.	Notes
vol. i	*Wiltshire*		
74b	Widhill	1 0 0	
	Somerset		
92b	Stoke Trister	3 0 0	
96b	Brewham	12 0 0	
	Brewham	(1 0 0)	Erbold held this from Robert but could not separate it from the manor
	Hertfordshire		
133b	Little Hadham	(2 0 0)	A sokeman of Robert held it
134	Wymondley	(10 0)	Alfgeat held it from Robert but could not sell
137b	Wymondley	(15 0)	Alfgeat held it under Robert but could not sell
141b	Ashwell	(1 10 0)	Uchtræd held it under Robert but could not sell
	Herefordshire		
186b	Thruxton		Waste. Assessed at 3 hides
187	Winnhall		Waste. Assessed at 3 hides
	Cambridgeshire		
197	Hateley	(1 10 0)	Almar the man of Robert held it and could sell
197b	Hateley	(1 0 0)	Two sokemen of Robert held it and could sell

Ref. (fos.)	Location	Value £	s.	d.	Notes
198b	Wratworth		(5	0)	A sokeman of Robert held it and could sell
	Whitwell		(10	0)	A sokeman of Robert held it and could sell
	Kingston			(6)	Wulfmær the man of Robert held it and could sell
199b	Papworth	(2	10	0)	Ornod the man of Robert held it and could sell
200b	Croydon	(2	0	0)	Elward the man of Robert held it and could sell
	Barrington		(5	0)	Ezi held it under Robert and could sell
	Whitwell		(10	0)	A sokeman of Robert held it
201	Hateley	(5	0	0)	Alward the man of Robert held it and could sell
	Huntingdonshire				
205b	Wareley	8	0	0	
	Eynesbury	24	0	0	
	Shropshire				
252	Bromfield				Waste. 10 hides. This land was given to Robert after Spirites was outlawed. Robert was to hold it *sicut canonici*, but he gave it to his son-in-law, and the canons appealed to Edward for its return
vol. ii	*Essex*				
43b	Eastwood	6	0	0	
45	Plumberow	1	0	0	
45b	Nevendon		10	0	
	Sutton	1	0	0	
46b	Mersea	10	0	0	
	Clavering	20	0	0	
47	Eiland	10	0	0	
48	Elmstead	9	0	0	

Land to Robert (*cont.*):

Ref. (fos.)	Location	Value £	s.	d.	Notes
43b	Rayleigh	10	0	0	These manors were not assigned a holder *TRE*, but *TRW* they were held by Robert's son, Swein
44	Wakering	9	0	0	
	Prittlewell	12	0	0	
	Canewdon	12	0	0	
45	Hockley	3	0	0	
23	Ramsden	(1	10	0)	A freeman of Robert held it
41	Berden	(1	10	0)	A sokeman of Robert held it
	Suffolk				
395b	Freston	8	0	0	
401	Stoke by Nayland	10	0	0	
	Withermarsh	10	0	0	
401b	Polstead	10	0	0	
	Naylands	6	0	0	
402	Pannington	2	0	0	
	Stratford St Mary	6	0	0	
	Freston		10	0	
295b	Wherstead	(1	0	0)	Edmund, a freeman of Robert, held it
	Bentley		(10	0)	The above Edmund held it
392b	Waldingfield	(2	10	0)	Two freemen commended to Robert held it
401	Stoke by Nayland	(1	10	0)	Twelve freemen commended to Eadric held it and could sell
401b	Aveley	(1	0	0)	Brungar commended to Robert held it
402	Ipswich				Forty-one burgesses were commended to Robert
	Wherstead		(10	0)	Toli, a freeman commended to Robert, held it
436b	Higham	(1	10	0)	Asseman commended to Robert held it
447b	Groton		(10	0)	A freeman commended to Robert held it
448	*Saibamas*	(1	0	0)	A freeman commended to Robert held it

	Total value of land held					
	By subject			From subject or by his men		
	£	s.	d.	£	s.	d.
Robert fitz Wymarc	204	0	0	34	15	6

LAND ASSIGNED TO SAXI

Ref. (fos.)	Location	Value £	s.	d.	Notes
vol. i	*Hampshire*				
38b	Upper Clatford	20	0	0	Saxi held it from King Edward
48b	*Clere*	7	0	0	Saxi held it from King Edward
49	Thruxton	13	0	0	
	Berkshire				
57	Swallowfield	7	0	0	Saxi held it from King Edward *in alodium*
	Shinfield	7	0	0	Saxi held it from King Edward *in alodium*

	Total value of land held	
Saxi	By subject £ s. d.	From subject or by his men £ s. d.
	54 0 0	None

LAND ASSIGNED TO SIGERÆD OF CHILHAM

Ref. (fos.)	Location	Value £	s.	d.	Notes
vol. i	*Kent*				
1	Kent				Sigeræd did not have to pay relief on allodial land in Kent
2	Canterbury				Sigeræd had *sac* and *soc* in Canterbury
9b	Wickambreaux	3	0	0	Sigeræd held it from Ælfred Bigga
10	Chilham	40	0	0	Sigeræd held it from King Edward
10b	Eastling	10	0	0	Sigeræd held it from King Edward
	Luddenham	10	0	0	Sigeræd held it from King Edward
	Pising and Pineham	1	0	0	Sigeræd held it and could sell
11b	Elmton	1	10	0	Sigeræd held it from King Edward

Sigeræd	Total value of land held	
	By subject £ s. d.	From subject or by his men £ s. d.
	65 10 0	None

LAND ASSIGNED TO SIWEARD BARN

Ref. (fos.)	Location	Value £	s.	d.	Notes
vol. i	*Berkshire*				
60b	Greenham	8	0	0	Siweard held it from King Edward *in alodium*
	Lockinge	10	0	0	Siweard held it from the king
	Stanford in the Vale	30	0	0	Siweard held it from King Edward, who reduced the assessment from 40 hides to 30
	Gloucestershire				
169	Lechlade	20	0	0	
	Warwickshire				
242	Grendon	2	0	0	
	Burton Hastings	4	0	0	
	Harbury	2	0	0	
	Derbyshire				
274	Brassington	6	0	0	
	Croxhall (Staffs.)	3	0	0	
	Catton	3	0	0	
	Cubley	5	0	0	
	Norbury and Roston	5	0	0	
	Duffield	9	0	0	
275b	Breadshall	4	0	0	
	Wormhill				Waste. Assessed at 4 carucates
	[location not identified]				Assessed at $\frac{2}{3}$ of a carucate
276	Moreley				Assessed at $\frac{2}{3}$ of a carucate
	Nottinghamshire				
280b	Nottinghamshire				Siweard Barn had *sac* and *soc*
291b	Leake	6	0	0	

Ref. (fos.)	Location	Value £	s.	d.	Notes
291b	Bonnington		6	0	
	Yorkshire				
326	Adlingfleet	4	0	0	
	Lincolnshire				
337	Lincolnshire				Siweard Barn had *sac* and *soc*
353b	Whitton	10	0	0	
369	Haxey	5	0	0	
vol. ii	*Norfolk*				
223b	Sheringham	4	0	0	
	Salthouse	2	0	0	

Siweard Barn	Total value of land held	
	By subject £ s. d.	From subject or by his men £ s. d.
	142 6 0	None

LAND ASSIGNED TO SIWEARD GROSSUS

vol. i	*Herefordshire*				
180b	Hollow Court (Worcs.)	4	0	0	Siweard, a kinsman of King Edward, held it
vol. i	*Shropshire*				
254	Montgomery				Waste. Siweard held 52.5 hides with Oslac and Azur, for hunting
	Marchamley	2	10	0	
	Stanton on Hine Heath	1	15	0	Siweard was free with this land
254b	Child's Ercall	2	5	0	
	Upton Magna	10	0	0	
	Weston Rhyn, Morton, Weston				Waste. Assessed at 12.5 hides

Land to Siweard Barn (*cont.*):

Ref. (fos.)	Location	Value £	s.	d.	Notes
	Cotton, West Felton, Osbaston, and Kynbaston				
255	Albright Hussey		15	0	Not assessed for geld
	Little Ness	3	0	0	
	Middle	6	0	0	
	Albright Hussey		14	0	
	Acton Reynold	4	0	0	
255b	Winsley		15	0	
	Bausley		2	0	
	Leighton		5	0	
256	Ratlinghope, Brompton				Waste. Assessed at 2.5 hides
	Walford		15	0	
257b	Grinshill		8	0	
258b	Oxenbold		5	6	Siweard held it freely
	Bouldon		4	0	Siweard held it freely
259b	Frodeley		10	0	The same man *TRW*
	Overs		3	0	The same man *TRW*
	Eyton				Waste. Assessed at 3 virgates: held with Wulfric as two manors
	Cheney Longville	1	0	0	The same man *TRW*
	Fennymere				Waste. Assessed as half a hide
260	Coreley	2	8	0	Siweard held this as two manors
	Letton				Waste. Assessed at 1.5 hides
260b	Cleobury North		12	0	
	Hopton Wafer		10	0	
	Stanton Lacy	24	0	0	
	Aldon	5	5	0	

Siweard Grossus	Total value of land held			
	By subject £	s.	d.	From subject or by his men £ s. d.
	72	1	0	None

LAND ASSIGNED TO SIWEARD OF MALDON

Ref. (fos.)	Location	Value £	s.	d.	Notes
vol. i	*Essex*				
18b	Tollesbury	1	5	0	Siweard held it from the Abbot of Barking. Rannulf Peverel held it from the abbot *TRW* and owed such service as Siweard had given
19	Rettendon	1	0	0	Siweard held it from Ely. Rannulf Peverel held it from *TRW* from King William. Further entry on fo. 75b
72b	Chickney	5	0	0	Siweard, a thegn of King Edward, held it
73	Willingale	5	0	0	
	Woodham	5	0	0	
	Maldon	12	0	0	
	Hazeleigh	4	0	0	
73b	Debden (nr. Newport)	24	0	0	
	Amberden	12	0	0	
74	Stebbing	10	0	0	
74b	Down	10	0	0	
	Stanesgate	10	0	0	
75b	St Osyth	9	0	0	
	Tolleshunt	5	0	0	
	Suffolk				
416	Icklington	4	0	0	Siweard held it under King Edward
	Acton	20	0	0	
416b	Assington	10	0	0	
	Acton, Waldingfield, *Honilega*, Manton, and Assington	(4	0	0)	Nineteen freemen held this land. Of these, all but one was commended to Siweard and only four could sell
355	Kentwell	(2	0	0)	Algar held it freely from Siweard
416b	Glemsford		(6	0)	Blacuin, commended to Siweard, held it

Siweard of Maldon	Total value of land held	
	By subject £ s. d.	From subject or by his men £ s. d.
	147 5 0	6 5 0

LAND ASSIGNED TO SIWEARD
(*ANTECESSOR* OF BALDWIN OF EXETER)

Ref. (fos.)	Location	Value £ s. d.	Notes
vol. i	*Somerset*		
93	Hemington	29 0 0	
	Devon		
108	Rose Ash	3 0 0	
	Creacombe	10 0	
	Rackenford	1 0 0	
	Wolborough	10 0	
	Rackenford	10 0	
	Chawleigh	10 0 0	

Siweard (*antec.* of Baldwin)	Total value of land held	
	By subject £ s. d.	From subject or by his men £ s. d.
	44 10 0	None

LAND ASSIGNED TO SPIRITES THE PRIEST

vol. i	*Kent*		
1b	St Margarets	1 0 0	Spirites held it *in prebenda*
	Hampshire		
49	Brockham	1 10 0	Spirites held it from King Edward *in alodium*

Ref. (fos.)	Location	Value £	s.	d.	Notes
	Wiltshire				
73	Stratton St Margaret	18	0	0	
	Chisenbury	13	0	0	
	Netheravon	3	0	0	
	Sutton Veny	4	0	0	
	Herefordshire				
183	Sutton	1	10	0	
	Thinghill	1	0	0	
	Little Cowarne	2	10	0	
	Avenbury	5	0	0	
	Shropshire				
252	Bromfield				Waste. Held by Spirites until he was outlawed, when it was given to Robert fitz Wymarc to hold *sicut canonicum*
258	Woolston	1	0	0	
260b	Winstanton	1	10	0	Spirites held it of St Almund *ad victum canonici*
	Clev		12	0	

Spirites	Total value of land held	
	By subject £ s. d.	From subject or by his men £ s. d.
	53 12 0	None

LAND ASSIGNED TO STORI (*ANTECESSOR* OF IVO TAILLEBOIS)

vol. i	*Lincolnshire*				
336	Lincoln				Stori had a house in the city
337	Lincolnshire				Stori had *sac* and *soc* in the county
350b	Belchford	15	0	0	

Land to Stori (*cont.*):

Ref. (fos.)	Location	Value £ s. d.	Notes
351	Bolingbroke	30 0 0	
366b	Hougham	1 0 0	

Stori	Total value of land held	
	By subject £ s. d.	From subject or by his men £ s. d.
	46 0 0	None

LAND ASSIGNED TO THORGAUTR LAG

Ref. (fos.)	Location	Value £ s. d.	Notes
vol. i	*Oxfordshire*		
159	Broughton (nr. Banbury)	16 0 0	
	Horley	2 10 0	
	Yorkshire		
298b	Yorkshire		Thorgautr Lag had *sac* and *soc* in the county
314	Naburn	0 10 0	
	North Dalton	4 0 0	
	Lincolnshire		
337	Lincolnshire		Thorgautr Lag had *sac* and *soc* in the county
352b	Ingleby	8 0 0	
	Aisthorpe	2 0 0	
	Bransby	3 0 0	
	Corringham	2 10 0	
353	Binbrook	7 0 0	
	Greatford	8 0 0	
	Auborn	5 0 0	

Thorgautr Lag	Total value of land held	
	By subject £ s. d.	From subject or by his men £ s. d.
	58 10 0	None

LAND ASSIGNED TO THORKELL WHITE AND HIS WIFE LEOFFLÆD

Ref. (fos.)	Location	Value £	s.	d.	Notes
1.	Thorkell White				
vol. i	*Gloucestershire*				
169	Brockworth	6	0	0	Thorkell held it from King Edward
	Herefordshire				
184	Lyde	1	0	0	Thorkell held it from Earl Harold
184b	Little Marcle	2	10	0	Thorkell held it from Earl Harold
	Canon Frome	3	10	0	
	Canon Frome	1	0	0	Ælmar, Ælfric, and Thorkell held from Earl Harold and could go where they would with their land
	Leadon	1	0	0	Thorkell held it and could go where he would with his land
	Leadon				Waste. Half a hide
	Lyonshall	3	0	0	Thorkell held it from Earl Harold
185b	Stretton Grandisdon	9	0	0	Thorkell held it from Earl Harold
	Whitwick	1	0	0	Thorkell held it from Earl Harold
187	Fownhope	12	0	0	Thorkell White held it
	Wellington	8	0	0	Thorkell White held it
	Credenhill	1	10	0	
187	*Bernoldune*				Waste. 2 hides
	Strangford				Alric held half a hide from Thorkell White for two sesters of honey
2.	Leofflæd, wife of Thorkell				
vol. i	*Herefordshire*				
180	Hatfield	4	0	0	
183	Bartestree	5	0	0	Leofflæd held it. Nigel *Medicus* held it of the land of St Guthlac

Land to Thorkell white and his wife Leofflæd (*cont.*):

Ref. (fos.)	Location	Value £	s.	d.	Notes
	Bowley	1	5	0	
	Sutton	3	0	0	
	Maund	2	0	0	Leofflæd held it from St Guthlac
187	Sutton	1	10	0	
	Beltrou				Waste. Half a hide
	Wluetone				Waste. 2 hides
	Wilmastone				Waste. 5 hides
	Alcamestune				Waste. 3 hides
	'One manor'	1	10	0	
	'One manor'		13	0	
	Lincumbe		9	0	

Thorkell and Leofflæd	Total value of land held	
	By subject £ s. d.	From subject or by their men £ s. d.
	68 17 0	None

LAND ASSIGNED TO THORKELL
(*ANTECESSOR* TO COUNTESS JUDITH)

vol. i	*Buckinghamshire*				
152b	Hollingdon	1	10	0	Thorkell held this land and could sell. The same man held *TRW*
	Huntingdonshire				
206b	Sawtry	10	0	0	
	Conington	9	0	0	Of the 9 hides held here, Thorkell held 6 from Thorney. On his death, all 9 were to go to Thorney
	Northamptonshire				
228	Fotheringay	8	0	0	Thorkell held it freely
	Harringworth	10	0	0	Thorkell held it freely
228b	East Farndon		2	8	Thorkell held it freely

Ref. (fos.)	Location	Value £	s.	d.	Notes
229	Lilford	8	0	0	Thorkell held it freely
	Leicestershire				
236b	Owston	2	10	0	Thorkell held it with *sac* and *soc*

Thorkell (*antec.* of Judith)	Total value of land held			
	By subject £	s.	d.	From subject or by his men £ s. d.
	49	2	8	None

LAND ASSIGNED TO TOKI, OTTA'S SON

vol. i	*Northamptonshire*				
227	Milton (nr. Northampton), Collingtree, and Rothersthorpe	4	0	0	Toki held it with *sac* and *soc*
	Leicestershire				
235b	Hallaton	3	0	0	
	Goadby	1	0	0	
	Keythorpe		5	0	
	Billesdon	2	15	0	
	Rolleston	1	0	0	Toki held these lands with *sac* and *soc*
	Derbyshire				
276b	Scropton	10	0	0	
	Alvaston	12	0	0	
	Ednaston	4	0	0	
	Eggington	8	0	0	
	Ockbrook	4	0	0	
280	Derby				Toki had a single house there
	Nottinghamshire				
280	Nottingham				Toki had twenty-one houses there

Land to Toki (*cont.*):

Ref. (fos.)	Location	Value £	s.	d.	Notes
280b	Nottinghamshire				Toki had *sac* and *soc* in the county
289	Laxton	9	0	0	
	North Muskham	5	0	0	
	Stoke Bardolph	5	10	0	
	Shelford	8	0	0	
	Yorkshire				
298b	Yorkshire				Toki had *sac* and *soc* in the county
319	Wadworth	7	0	0	Claimed by Geoffrey, Toki's successor *TRW* (fo. 373b)
326b	Branton in Cantley	8	0	0	
	Healaugh	8	0	0	
	Lincolnshire				
337	Lincolnshire				Toki had *sac* and *soc* in the county
369b	Ruskington	25	0	0	
	Westborough	15	0	0	
370	Wrawby	10	0	0	

Toki, Otta's son	Total value of land held	
	By subject £ s. d.	From subject or by his men £ s. d.
	150 10 0	None

LAND ASSIGNED TO TOKI (*ANTECESSOR* OF WILLIAM WARENNE)

Ref.	Location	£	s.	d.	Notes
vol. i	*Cambridgeshire*				
196b	Carlton	4	0	0	Toki, a thegn of King Edward, held it
	Weston Colville	10	0	0	Toki held it from Ely but could not sell
	West Wratting		5	0	
	West Wickham	5	0	0	

Ref. (fos.)	Location	Value £	s.	d.	Notes
196b	Trumpington	7	0	0	Toki held it from Ely but could not sell
	Kennet	12	0	0	
198	West Wratting		1	6	
vol. ii	*Norfolk*				
157b	Taverham	1	10	0	Toki, a freeman, held it
160	West Walton	17	10	0	
160b	Castle Acre	5	0	0	
161b	Harpley	3	0	0	
163	Heacham	3	0	0	
165	Gressenhall	2	0	0	
165b	Rougham	2	0	0	Toki, a freeman, held it
168	Sculthorpe	6	0	0	
	Barsham	4	0	0	
168b	Barsham	2	0	0	
	Fulmodeston	2	0	0	
169	Croxton (nr. Fakenham) and Burnham Thorpe	3	0	0	
	Rudham	8	0	0	
169b	Tattersett		10	0	
170	Briston		(16	0)	Fourteen of Toki's sokemen held it
	Suffolk				
398b	Depden	4	0	0	
399	Clopton	1	0	0	

Toki (*antec.* of William)	Total value of land held					
	By subject £	s.	d.	From subject or by his men £	s.	d.
	102	16	6		16	0

LAND ASSIGNED TO TOLI THE DANE

Ref. (fos.)	Location	Value £	s.	d.	Notes
vol. i	*Hampshire*				
47	*Somborne*	14	0	0	*Toli Dacus tenuit de Rege Edwardo*
	Deane	10	0	0	Toli held it from King Edward
	Wiltshire				
71b	Tollard Royal	1	0	0	
	Upton Scudamore		15	0	
	Dorset				
80b	Bradford Peverel	12	0	0	
	Lytchett Maltravers	9	0	0	
	Blandford St Mary	2	0	0	
	Swyre	9	0	0	
	Terente	4	0	0	
82	Stock Gaylard	2	10	0	Toli held this land in pledge of the land of Sherbourne
82	Stourton Caundle	3	0	0	
	Somerset				
92b	Shepton Montague	7	0	0	
	Devon				
111b	Whitestone		6	0	

Toli the Dane	Total value of land held	
	By subject £ s. d.	From subject or by his men £ s. d.
	74 11 0	None

LAND ASSIGNED TO TONNI

vol. i	*Berkshire*			
62	Rowbury Hundred	6	0	0
	Oxfordshire			
159b	Handborough	10	0	0

Ref. (fos.)	Location	Value £	*s.*	*d.*	Notes
	Northamptonshire				
227b	Kislingbury	4	0	0	
	Nether Heyford	0	10	0	
	Stowe	3	0	0	
	Empingham (Rutland)	5	0	0	
	Empingham	8	0	0	
	Easton		5	0	
	Yorkshire				
329b	Appleton Roebuck	1	6	8	
	Lincolnshire				
354b	Lusby	14	0	0	
355	Culverthorpe	18	0	0	
	Willoughby in the Marsh	4	0	0	
	Claxby (nr. Normanby le Wold)	8	0	0	
355b	Well	8	0	0	
	South Kyme	8	0	0	
375	Langton by Wragby				140 acres of woodland pasture

Tonni	Total value of land held					
	By subject			From subject or by his men		
	£	*s.*	*d.*	£	*s.*	*d.*
	93	1	8	None		

LAND ASSIGNED TO ULF FENISC

vol. i	*Buckinghamshire*				
149b	Edlesthorpe	14	0	0	Ulf, a thegn of king Edward, held it
	Horton (Ivinghoe)		(6	8)	A man of Ulf's held it but could not sell

Land to Ulf Fenisc (*cont.*):

Ref. (fos.)	Location	Value £	s.	d.	Notes
	Oxfordshire				
159b	Ewelme	6	0	0	
	Cambridgeshire				
197	Papworth		10	0	Ulf, a thegn of king Edward, held it
197b	Swavesey	1	0	0	
	Fen Drayton	1	0	0	
197	Elsworth		(6	8)	Two of Ulf's sokemen held it and could sell
197b	Connington	(1	10	0)	Eight of Ulf's sokemen held it
	Boxworth	(1	0	0)	Six of Ulf's sokemen held it
	Huntingdonshire				
203	Huntingdon				Ulf had eighteen burgesses there
207	Fen Stanton	17	0	0	
	Bedfordshire				
215	Edlesborough (Bucks.)	10	0	0	
	Northamptonshire				
227b	Wichford (Warwicks.)	10	0	0	Ulf held it freely
	Derbyshire				
277b	Ilkeston	8	0	0	
	Nottinghamshire				
280b	Nottinghamshire				Ulf had *sac* and *soc* over his own land, and did not give the third penny to the earl
290b	Roughton	1	0	0	
	Rufford	6	0	0	
	Kneeshall	8	0	0	
	Creilege	6	0	0	
	Kirklington	2	0	0	
	Normanton (in Southwell)		16	0	
	Ruddington	1	0	0	
	Whatton	20	0	0	
	Rutland				
293b	Burley	4	0	0	

Ref. (fos.)	Location	Value £	s.	d.	Notes
	Yorkshire				
298b	Yorkshire				Ulf Fenisc had *sac* and *soc*
324	Aldborough	40	0	0	
	Lissett	3	0	0	
	Beeford	20	0	0	
	North Frodingham	14	0	0	
324b	Brandesburton	6	0	0	
	Seaton	4	10	0	
	Long Riston		15	0	
	Lincolnshire				
336	Lincoln				Ulf had one house with *sac* and *soc*
337	Lincolnshire				Ulf had *sac* and *soc* in the county
354b	Scampton	6	0	0	
	Cherry Willingham	5	0	0	
	Appleby	2	10	0	
	Winteringham	10	0	0	
	Barton upon Humber	39	16	0	
	Bardney	20	0	0	
	Baumber	10	0	0	
	Edlington	10	0	0	
	Edenham	10	0	0	
355	Cranwell	5	0	0	
355b	Holme (in Beckingham)	10	0	0	
	Burley (Rutland)	4	0	0	Possible repetition of entry on fo. 293b
	Folkingham	50	0	0	
364b	Hacconby	1	0	0	
	Morton (nr. Hanthorpe)	2	0	0	
369	Belton (nr. Epworth)	3	10	0	
369b	Luddington		10	0	In the soke of Belton

Ulf Fenisc	Total value of land held					
	By subject			From subject or by his men		
	£	s.	d.	£	s.	d.
	393	17	0	3	3	4

LAND ASSIGNED TO ULF AND HALDEIN, THE SONS OF TOPE, AND THEIR MOTHER EADGIFU

Ref. (fos.)	Location	Value £	s.	d.	Notes
vol. i	*Leicestershire*				
231	Buckminster	4	0	0	Haldein held it with *sac* and *soc*
236	Hoby		2	0	Ulf held it with *sac* and *soc*
	Yorkshire				
324b	Ganstead	1	0	0	Haldein held it
	Bilton		10	0	Haldein held it
	Lincolnshire				
340	Lenton	4	0	0	Ulf held it. It was bought by the Archbishop of York, with Skillington (fo. 376b)
344	Bigby	2	10	0	Haldein held it
	Worlaby (nr. Elsham)	2	10	0	Haldein held it
	Grayingham	2	0	0	Haldein held it
344b	Keelby	1	10	0	Haldein held it
	Dunsby (nr. Hacconby)	3	0	0	Haldein held it
	Ringstone	3	0	0	Haldein held it
348b	Stenning	1	0	0	Haldein held it
360	Kettleby	2	0	0	Ulf held it
	Kirmington	2	0	0	Ulf held it
	Limber	2	0	0	Ulf held it
360b	North Ormaby	1	15	0	Ulf held it
	Witham Hundred	1	10	0	Ulf held it
	Normanby le wold	1	10	0	Ulf held it
	Stroxton	6	0	0	These lands (Stroxton to Skillington) were assigned in DB to Earl Morkær. In Ulf's will they were bequeathed freely, and they went to Ulf's successor, with the exception of Skillington. This last manor had been bought from Ulf by the Archbishop. Morkær's connection is unclear, but it is possible that Ulf acquired them after the Conquest
	Stoke Rochford		10	0	
	Carlton le Moorland	10	0	0	
	West Bytham	19	0	0	
340	Skillington	4	0	0	

Ref. (fos.)	Location	Value £	s.	d.	Notes
362	Melton Ross	6	0	0	Eadgifu, the mother of Ulf and Haldein, held it
	Messingham	3	0	0	Eadgifu held it
	Kettleby	2	0	0	Eadgifu held it
	Brocklesby	1	0	0	Eadgifu held it
362b	Grayingham	2	0	0	Eadgifu held it

Ulf, Haldein, and Eadgifu	Total value of land held					
	By subject			From subject or by their men		
	£	s.	d.	£	s.	d.
Ulf	14	17	0			
Haldein	21	0	0			
Eadgifu	14	0	0			
TOTAL	49	17	0	None		

[These figures exclude the land assigned to Morkær in Domesday, worth £39 10*s*. 0*d*.]

LAND ASSIGNED TO ULF (*ANTECESSOR* OF ROBERT DE TOSNY)

vol. i	*Buckinghamshire*				
149	Stone	5	0	0	Ulf, a housecarl of King Edward, held it
144	Stone	3	0	0	One of Ulf's men held it
	Gloucestershire				
168	Rissington	12	0	0	
	Horton	12	0	0	
	Sapperton	14	0	0	
	Cambridgeshire				
196b	Duxford	8	0	0	Ulf, King Edward's thegn, held it

Land to Ulf (antecessor of Robert De Tosny) (*cont.*):

Ref. (fos.)	Location	Value £	s.	d.	Notes
vol. ii	*Suffolk*				
429b	Bradley	6	0	0	Ulf, a thegn, held it
	Syleham	3	0	0	
	Syleham		(5	0)	Five freemen commended to Ulf held it

Ulf (*antec.* of Robert)	Total value of land held					
	By subject £	s.	d.	From subject or by his men £	s.	d.
	57	0	0	3	5	0

LAND ASSIGNED TO WIGOT OF WALLINGFORD

Ref. (fos.)	Location	Value £	s.	d.	Notes
vol. i	*Sussex*				
23b	Bepton	4	0	0	Wigot held it from King Edward
26b	Aldrington	4	0	0	Wigot held it from King Edward; it lay in Broadwater
28b	Broadwater	15	0	0	Wigot held it from King Edward
	Hampshire				
50b	Kingsclere	(2	0	0)	Alwin held this land under Wigot *ab tuitionem*
	Berkshire				
61b	*Lonchelei*				1 hide, valued with Gatehampton, Oxon.
62	Letcombe	15	0	0	
	Wiltshire				
71	Rodbourne Cheney	5	0	0	
	Manton	3	0	0	
	Devonshire				
102	Clyst St Mary	1	0	0	

Ref. (fos.)	Location	Value £	s.	d.	Notes
	Middlesex				
129	Harlington	8	0	0	
	Colham	10	0	0	
	Harmondsworth		(10	0)	Alwin the man of Wigot held it and could sell
	Dawley	(3	0	0)	Godwine Alfit, the man of Wigot, held it and could sell
	Buckinghamshire				
150	Shabbington	10	0	0	
	Quainton	8	0	0	
	Mursley Hundred		(10	0)	Ordwig the man of Wigot held it
	Oxfordshire				
158	Goring	10	0	0	
159	Gatehampton	4	0	0	
159	Chesterton	3	0	0	
	Cuxham	3	0	0	
	Gloucestershire				
169b	Brawn	2	0	0	
	Alderley	3	0	0	

Wigot	Total value of land held					
	By subject			From subject or by his men		
	£	s.	d.	£	s.	d.
	117	0	0	6	0	0

LAND ASSIGNED TO WIHTGAR, ÆLFRIC'S SON

Ref.	Location	£	s.	d.	Notes
vol. i	*Hertfordshire*				
140	Barley		(3	0)	Algar the man of Wihtgar held it and could sell
	Cokenach	(5	0	0)	Algar the man of Wihtgar held if and could sell

Land to Wihtgar (*cont.*):

Ref. (fos.)	Location	Value £	s.	d.	Notes
vol. ii	*Essex*				
38b	Thaxted	30	0	0	Wihtgar held it in demesne
	Dunmow	3	0	0	
39	Panfield	0	10	0	
40b	Bentley	2	0	0	
41	Bardfield	16	0	0	
	Sampford	12	0	0	
41b	Hempstead	12	0	0	
39	Yeldham	(3	0	0)	Eight sokemen held it under Wihtgar
	Wickham St Pauls	(1	10	0)	Two sokemen held it under Wihtgar
39b	Finchingfield		(10	0)	Two sokemen held it under Wihtgar
	Binsley	(1	0	0)	A sokeman held it under Wihtgar
	Ashton	(1	0	0)	Two sokemen held it under Wihtgar
	Finchingfield	(2	0	0)	Three sokemen held it under Wihtgar
	Bulmer	(1	2	2)	A sokeman held it under Wihtgar
	Howe	(1	10	0)	Three sokemen held it under Wihtgar
40b	Rodings	(3	0	0)	Coleman held it with *sac* and *soc* and could sell; however he was the man of Wihtgar
	Bromley	(2	0	0)	A man commended to Wihtgar held it
	Lexden Hundred		(12	0)	Wihtgar held three sokemen here
41	*Witesuuorda*		(3	0)	Algar held it under Wihtgar
41b	Bardfield	(1	0	0)	Two servants held it of Wihtgar but could not sell
101b	Pebmarsh, Alphamstone, Bumpstead, Saling, and Ovington	(1	10	0)	Six freemen, of whom Wihtgar had the commendation only

Ref. (fos.)	Location	Value £	s.	d.	Notes
	Suffolk				
389b	Clare	40	0	0	Wihtgar's father gave this to St John's, but it was to be held by Ælfric and his son for their lives. King William took it into his hands
	Hundon	30	0	0	
	Desning	30	0	0	
392	Barton Mills		3	0	Wihtgar held it in demesne
	Ipswich	5	0	0	This land was attached to a church which Wihtgar held
	Tuddenham	2	10	0	
349	Thurlston		(6	8)	Twelve and a half freemen commended to Ælfric, himself commended to Wihtgar, held it
	Thorpe Morieux	(3	0	0)	A freeman commended to Wihtgar held it
349b	Boxted	(3	0	0)	Five freemen commended to Wihtgar held it
351b	Tunstall		(2	6)	Edred, a freeman commended to Wihtgar, held it
352	Barham		(10	0)	Lustwine, half commended to Wihtgar and half to Ely, held it
	Coddenham		(4	0)	Godwine, a freeman commended to Wihtgar, held it
374	Creeting St Peter	(1	2	0)	Ælfric fitz Brun, commended to Whitgar, held it
377b	Ulverston		(10	0)	Ælfric, a freeman commended to Wihtgar, held it
390	Denston	(2	0	0)	A sokeman held it from Wihtgar
	Clopton	(1	0	0)	Two sokemen held it from Wihtgar
	Dalham	(2	0	0)	A sokeman held it from Wihtgar
390b	Denham	(3	0	0)	Two sokemen held it from Wihtgar
	Haweden	(2	0	0)	Two sokemen held it from Wihtgar

Land to Wihtgar (*cont.*):

Ref. (fos.)	Location	Value £	s.	d.	Notes
	Little Wratting	(1	0	0)	A sokeman held it from Wihtgar
	Stansfield	(1	0	0)	A sokeman held it from Wihtgar
	Hundon	(2	0	0)	Eleven sokemen held it from Wihtgar
	Farley		(1	2)	A sokeman held it from Wihtgar
	Brockley		(8	0)	A sokeman held it from Wihtgar
	Kedington		(1	8)	A freeman commended to Wihtgar held it
	Kedington		(5	0)	A sokeman held it from Wihtgar
	Boyton		(10	0)	A sokeman held it from Wihtgar
	Stoke by Clare		(6	2)	A sokeman held it from Wihtgar
	Wimundestuna		(10	0)	A sokeman held it from Wihtgar
	Bardwell		(5	0)	A freeman commended to Wihtgar held it
	Timworth		(10	0)	A freeman commended to Wihtgar held it
391b	Westley		(10	0)	Three freemen commended to Wihtgar held it
	Saxham		(3	0)	A sokeman held it from Wihtgar
	Horringer		(4	0)	A sokeman held it from Wihtgar
	Hawstead		(2	0)	Two freemen held it under Wihtgar and could sell
	Manston		(10	0)	A freeman held it under Wihtgar and could sell
	Rede	(1	10	0)	Seven freemen held it under Wihtgar
	Barton Mills		(5	0)	A sokeman held it under Wihtgar
392	Mildenhall		(5	0)	Two sokemen held but could not sell. It belonged to Desning

Ref. (fos.)	Location	Value £	s.	d.	Notes
392	Herringswell		(15	0)	A sokeman held this land and soke under Wihtgar, and half under St Edmund's
	Wangford		(10	0)	Four sokemen held it from Wihtgar
	Bures	(1	10	0)	Eighteen freemen held it from Wihtgar and could sell
	Bures	(1	10	0)	Four sokemen held it under Wihtgar but could not sell
	Cornard	(1	6	8)	Seven freemen commended to Wihtgar held it
392b	*Corsfella*	(3	0	0)	Seven freemen commended to Wihtgar held it
	Eleigh		(10	0)	Seven freemen commended to Wihtgar held it
	Little Waldingfield	(2	10	0)	Three freemen commended to Wihtgar held it
	Cavendish	(3	0	0)	Nine freemen commended to Wihtgar held it
	Hartest	(2	0	0)	Two freemen commended to Wihtgar held it
	Little Waldingfield	(1	5	0)	A freeman commended to Wihtgar held it
	Groton		(1	8)	Six freemen commended to Wihtgar held it
393b	Flowton	(4	0	0)	Godman, commended to Wihtgar, held it
395b	Stansfield		(8	0)	Eadric Spud, a freeman commended to Wihtgar, held it
	Stansfield		(10	0)	Crawa, a freeman commended to Wihtgar, held it and could sell
396	Wratting	(1	10	0)	Goda, a freeman commended to Wihtgar, held it and could sell
	Depden		(15	0)	Godwine, a freeman commended to Wihtgar, held it
	Depden		(15	0)	Blacuin, commended to Wihtgar, held it and could sell

Land to Wihtgar (*cont.*):

Ref. (fos.)	Location	Value £	s.	d.	Notes
396b	Poslingford		(8	0)	Eadric, a freeman commended to Wihtgar, held it and could sell
	Wratting	(2	10	0)	Ailbern, a freeman commended to Wihtgar, held it and could sell
	Beyton		(4	0)	Ainwar, a freeman commended to Wihtgar, held it and could sell
	Bradley		(17	6)	Two freemen commended to Wihtgar held it and could sell
	Chilbourne	(2	0	0)	Godwine, a freeman commended to Wihtgar, held it and could sell
	Clopton		(2	0)	Roc, a freeman commended to Wihtgar, held it
	Boyton		(1	4)	Wulfgar, a freeman commended to Wihtgar, held it and could sell
396b	Withersfield	(4	8	0)	Three freemen commended to Wihtgar, held it and could sell
	Withersfield		(8	0)	Wulfmær, a freeman commended to Wihtgar, held it and could sell
	Withersfield	(1	10	0)	Leofgeat, a freeman commended to Wihtgar, held it
397	Withersfield	(1	0	0)	Nine freemen commended to Wihtgar held it and could sell
	Thurlow		(10	0)	Ten freemen commended to Wihtgar held it and could sell
	Kedington	(1	0	0)	Ten freemen commended to Wihtgar held it and could sell
	Haverhill	(1	10	0)	Thirteen freemen commended to Wihtgar held it and could sell
	Stoke by Clare	(1	0	0)	Twenty-one freemen commended to Wihtgar held it and could sell
	Poslingford		(14	2)	Twenty-one freemen commended to Wihtgar held it and could sell

Ref. (fos.)	Location	Value £	s.	d.	Notes
397	Wickhambrook		(10	0)	A freeman commended to Wihtgar held it and could sell
	Stradishall	(1	0	0)	Sixteen freemen commended to Wihtgar held it and could sell
	Hawkedon		(13	4)	Eight freemen commended to Wihtgar held it and could sell
	Haverhill		(4	6)	Two freemen commended to Wihtgar held it and could sell
397b	*Wimundestuna*	(2	0	0)	Six freemen held it, of whom one could not sell from Wihtgar
	Kersey		(0	10)	A freeman commended to Wihtgar held it
	Whatfield		(10	0)	Three freemen commended to Wihtgar held it
	Stone Street		(4	0)	A freeman, half commended to Wihtgar and half to Ely, held it

Withgar	Total value of land held					
	By subject			From subject or by his men		
	£	s.	d.	£	s.	d.
	182	3	0	102	16	11

LAND ASSIGNED TO WULFGIFU OF BETTESLAU

vol. i	*Hampshire*				
38	Mapledurham	25	0	0	
39	Monxton	5	0	0	Wulfgifu held it *in alodium*
43	Laverstock	7	0	0	Wulfgifu held it from St Peter's, Winchester
45	Sherborne St John	10	0	0	Wulfgifu held it from King Edward and could sell
47b	Fyfield	5	0	0	Wulfgifu held it from King Edward *in alodium*

Land to Wulfgifu (*cont.*):

Ref. (fos.)	Location	Value £	*s.*	*d.*	Notes
50	Farleigh Wallop	8	0	0	Wulfgifu held it from King Edward
	Enham	1	10	0	
51b	Harbridge	4	10	0	
	Berkshire				
62b	Great Shefford	6	0	0	Wulfgifu held it from King Edward *in alodium*
63	Bagnor	4	0	0	Wulfgifu held it from King Edward *in alodium*
	Wiltshire				
74b	Clyffe Peppard	1	0	0	This land was held by Wibert, a king's thegn *TRW*: it was '*de terra Ulveva de Betteslau*'
	Dorset				
85	Bockhampton	3	0	0	
	Winterborne Monkton	6	0	0	
	Swanage	0	15	0	These three manors were held *TRE* by Wulfgifu, who could go with her land where she would
	Somerset				
91b	Loxton	5	0	0	
	Kingweston	6	0	0	

Wulfgifu	Total value of land held	
	By subject £ *s.* *d.*	From subject or by her men £ *s.* *d.*
	97 15 0	None

LAND ASSIGNED TO WULFMÆR OF EATON

vol. i	*Hertfordshire*	
132	Hertford	Wulfmær had a house there

Ref. (fos.)	Location	Value £	s.	d.	Notes
	Cambridgeshire				
197b	Gamlingay	18	0	0	
202b	Tadlow	2	0	0	Wulfmær, King Edward's thegn, held it
200b	Hateley		(7	6)	A sokeman of Wulfmær of Eaton held it
	Bedfordshire				
212	Eaton Socon	10	0	0	
	Sandy	10	0	0	Wulfmær, King Edward's thegn, held it
212b	Stanford	4	0	0	Wulfmær, King Edward's thegn, held it
	Clifton	6	0	0	
218	Cockayne Hateley	6	0	0	Wulfmær, King Edward's thegn, held it
	Stondon	4	0	0	Wulfmær, King Edward's thegn, held it
216b	Little Barford	3	0	0	Wulfmær, King Edward's thegn, held it
212	Tempsford	(3	0	0)	Three of Wulfmær's sokemen held it, of whom two could sell and one could not
212b	Beeston	(1	0	0)	Raven the man of Wulfmær held it
	Northill	(1	5	0)	Raven the man of Wulfmær held it and could sell
218	Wyboston	(1	10	0)	Ælfmar the man of Wulfmær held it and could sell
	Chicksands	(1	10	0)	Swetman the man of Wulfmær held it
vol. ii	*Essex*				
49	Lindsell	5	0	0	
50	Hawkwell	6	0	0	
	Shellow Bowells		10	0	Wulfmær, a freeman, held it
	Takeley	8	0	0	
50b	Theydon	2	0	0	
	Roding	8	0	0	
51b	Hawkwell	6	0	0	

Wulfmær	Total value of land held	
	By subject	From subject or by his men
	£ s. d.	£ s. d.
	98 10 0	8 12 6

LAND ASSIGNED TO WULFWEARD WHITE, HIS WIFE AND SON

Ref. (fos.)	Location	Value £	s.	d.	Notes
1.	Wulfweard White				
vol. i	*Kent*				
1b	Aylesford Last				Wulfweard White had *sac* and *soc*
9	Merston		10	0	Wulfweard held it from King Edward
11b	Waldershare	7	10	0	
	Hampshire				
43b	Hayling Island	15	0	0	Wulfweard White held it of Queen Eadgyth *in alodium*. But Winchester claimed that Wulfweard had only a life interest in the manor. See S 1476
	Berkshire				
62b	Newbury	9	0	0	Wulfweard held it from King Edward *in alodium*
63	Lambourn	3	0	0	Wulfweard held it from King Edward *in alodium*
	Wiltshire				
66	Potterne	3	10	0	Wulfweard held it from the Bishop of Salisbury. He had bought it, but it was to return on Wulfweard's death
70	Cholderton	1	5	0	
73	Winterbourne	2	0	0	

Ref. (fos.)	Location	Value £	s.	d.	Notes
	Dorset				
82	Silton	11	0	0	
	Silton		10	0	Wulfweard held this land in pawn from one of his reeves
	Silton	1	0	0	Wulfweard bought this land from the Bishop of Exeter
	Somerset				
87	Corton Denham	7	0	0	
	Whitcomb	4	0	0	
	Pitney	1	0	0	
	Mutford	3	0	0	
	Middlesex				
129	Kempton	6	0	0	Wulfweard White, a thegn of King Edward, held it and could sell
129b	Ruislip	30	0	0	
130	Kingsbury	6	0	0	
129	Ickenham	(2	10	0)	Two of Wulfweard's sokemen held it
130b	Ickenham	(2	0	0)	Ælfmær, the man of Wulfweard, held it
	Oxfordshire				
160	Chipping Norton	15	0	0	
	Gloucestershire				
169	Hatherop	9	0	0	
	Bedfordshire				
212	Toddington	30	0	0	
	Lincolnshire				
337b	Lincolnshire				Wulfweard White had *sac* and *soc* in the shire
367b	Butterswick (Freiston)	10	0	0	

Land to Wulfweard (*cont.*):

Ref. (fos.)	Location	Value £	s.	d.	Notes
2.	Eadgifu, Wulfweard's wife				
	Buckinghamshire				
145	Worminghall	7	0	0	Eadgifu, Wulfweard's wife, held it under Queen Eadgyth and could sell
145	Ludgershall	6	0	0	Eadgifu held it from King Edward
	Water Eaton	10	0	0	Eadgifu held it and could sell
	Little Linford	3	0	0	Eadgifu held it *TRE* and *TRW*
148b	Wichendon	12	0	0	Eadgifu held it from Queen Eadgyth
3.	Wulfweard Cilt, the son of Wulfweard White				
	Buckinghamshire				
145	Stewkley	4	0	0	
147	Addingrove	4	0	0	Wulfweard the man of Queen Eadgyth held it and could sell
153	*Sortelai*	3	0	0	Wulfweard the man of Queen Eadgyth held it. The Queen gave it to Alsige with Wulfweard's daugher
143	Buckingham		(6	6)	Three burgesses were the men of Wulfweard, Eadgifu's son
146b	Wroughton on the Green	(1	0	0)	A man of Wulfweard held it
149	Milton Keynes	(1	0	0)	Sawold the man of Wulfweard Cilt held it and could sell

Wulfweard, his wife and son	Total value of land held					
	By subject			From subject or by their men		
	£	s.	d.	£	s.	d.
	223	5	0	6	16	0

LAND ASSIGNED TO WULFWINE
(*ANTECESSOR* TO AUBREY DE VERE)

Ref. (fos.)	Location	Value £	s.	d.	Notes
vol. i	*Cambridgeshire*				
199b	Ashley	2	0	0	Wulfwine, a thegn of King Edward held it
	Saxon Street	7	0	0	
	Silverley	20	0	0	
	Wilbraham	10	0	0	
	Camps	12	0	0	
	Horseheath	3	0	0	
	Hildersham	8	0	0	
	Horseheath		(5	0)	Leodmær held it under Wulfwine but could not sell
	Barbraham		(1	8)	Godwine held it from Wulfwine but could not sell
vol. ii	*Essex*				
76	Canfield	6	0	0	
	Udechesale	3	0	0	
76b	Ugley	6	0	0	
	Hedingham	13	0	0	
77	Belchamp	14	0	0	
	Colne	10	0	0	
77b	Bentley	6	0	0	
	Dovercourt	6	0	0	
	Beaumont	5	0	0	
	Helions Bumpstead	5	0	0	
107	Colchester				Wulfwine had two houses there
77	Horsham	(1	0	0)	Two of Wulfwine's sokemen held it but could not sell

Wulfwine	Total value of land held					
	By subject			From subject or by his men		
	£	s.	d.	£	s.	d.
	141	0	0	1	6	8

LAND ASSIGNED TO WULFWYNN OF CRESLOW

Ref. (fos.)	Location	Value £	s.	d.	Notes
vol. i	*Berkshire*				
63	Hinton Waldrist	11	0	0	Wulfwynn held it and could sell
	Wiltshire				
69b	Chitterne	3	0	0	
	Poole Keynes (Glos.)	5	0	0	
	Winterbourne	8	0	0	
	Dorset				
80b	Canford Magna and Kinson (Hants.)	50	0	0	
	Middlesex				
130b	Chelsea	9	0	0	Wulfwynn the 'man' of King Edward held it and could sell
	Hertfordshire				
139	Great Gaddesden	25	0	0	Wulfwynn held it on the day King Edward was alive and dead, from St Albans. She could not sell it, and it was to return to the abbey on her death
	Buckinghamshire				
150	Aston Sanford	20	0	0	Wulfwynn the 'man' of King Edward held it and could sell
150b	Creslow	6	0	0	Wulfwynn held it and could sell
150	Aston Sanford	1	0	0	Almar the man of Wulfwynn held it and could sell
152	Helsthorpe	1	0	0	A thegn of Wulfwynn held it

	Total value of land held					
	By subject			From subject or by her men		
	£	s.	d.	£	s.	d.
Wulfwynn	137	0	0	2	0	0

APPENDIX III

Secondary Sources Concerning the Earls

The following secondary sources provide details of the careers of the earlish families, their involvement in the politics of Edward's reign and their activities as great landholders. Barlow and Freeman examine two politics of Edward's reign as a whole, while the other articles look at specific aspects of the period.

BARLOW, F., *Edward the Confessor* (London, 1970), esp. 88–93, 99–127, 206–12, 219–29, 237–55, 291–306.

CAMPBELL, M. W., 'Tostig Displaced', in *Annales de Normandie* 22 (1972).

—— 'Godwin, Edward and William', in *Traditio* 28 (1972).

—— 'Emma', in *Annales de Normandie* 23 (1973).

—— 'Anti-Norman Reaction in 1052', in *Medieval Studies* 38 (1976).

—— 'Godwin the Kingmaker', in *Canadian Journal of History* 13 (1978).

DAVIES, R. H., 'The Lands of Harold, Son of Godwine, and their Distribution by William I', unpublished MA dissertation (Cardiff, 1967).

FLEMING, R., 'Domesday Estates of the King and the Godwines: A Study in Late Saxon Politics', in *Speculum* 58 (1983).

FREEMAN, E. A., *The History of the Norman Conquest*, vols. i, ii, 2nd edn. (London 1870) iii–v, 1st edn. (London, 1869–75), esp. ii and iv.

GRIERSON, P., 'A Visit of Earl Harold to Flanders in 1056', *EHR* 51 (1936).

HILL, D., *An Atlas of Anglo-Saxon England* (Oxford, 1981), esp. maps 179–86.

OLESON, T. J., *The Witenagemot in the Reign of Edward the Confessor* (Oxford, 1955).

WILLIAMS, A., 'Land and Power in the Eleventh Century: The Estates of Harold Godwineson', in R. A. Brown (ed.), *Proceedings of the Battle Conference on Anglo-Saxon Studies 1980* (Woodbridge, 1982).

—— 'The King's Nephew: The Family and Career of Ralph, Earl of Hereford', in C. Harper-Bill, C. J. Holdsworth, and J. L. Nelson (eds.), *Studies in Medieval History Presented to R. Allen Brown* (Woodbridge, 1989).

BIBLIOGRAPHY

Primary Sources

The Anglo-Saxon Chronicle, trans G. N. Garmonsway (London, 1972).

Calendar of Manuscripts of the Dean and Chapter of Wells, Historical Manuscripts Commission Reports (1907).

Carmen de Haestingae Proelio, ed C. Martin and H. Muntz, Oxford Medieval Texts (Oxford, 1972).

Chronicon Monasterii de Abingdon, ed. J. Stevenson, Rolls Series (London, 1858).

Chronica Abbatiae Ramsiensis, ed. W. D. Macray, Rolls Series (London, 1886).

Chronica Monasterii de Tewkesbury, in *Monasticon Anglicanum*, ed. W. Dugdale (London, 1817–30).

Councils and Ecclesiastical Documents relating to Great Britain and Ireland, ed. A. W. Hadden and W. Stubbs (Oxford, 1871).

Gesta Abbatum Monasterii Sancti Albani, ed. H. T. Riley, Rolls Series (London, 1867).

Domesday Book, Records Commission (London, 1783–1816).

English Historical Documents, gen. ed. D. C. Douglas; i. *100–1042*, ed. D. Whitelock (London, 1955); ii. *1042–1135*, ed. G. W. Greenaway (London, 1953).

Exon Domesday, in *DB*, vol. iv.

The Chronicle of Florence of Worcester, trans T. Forester (London, 1854).

HARMER, F. E., *Anglo-Saxon Writs* (Manchester, 1952).

HARPER-BILL, C., and MORTIMER, R. (eds.), *Stoke by Clare Chartulary* (Woodbridge, 1982).

Hemingi Chartularium Ecclesiae Wigorniensis, ed. T. Hearne (Oxford, 1723).

Inquisitio comitatus Cantabrigiensis, ed. N. E. S. A. Hamilton (London, 1876).

Liber Eliensis, ed. E. O. Blake, Camden Society, 3rd series, 92 (1962).

LIEBERMANN, F., *Gesetze der Angelsachsen*, i. *Text und Ubersetzung* (Halle, 1903).

ORDERIC VITALIS, *Historia Ecclesiastica*, ed. M. Chibnall, Oxford Medieval Texts (Oxford, 1969–80).

Penitential of Archbishop Theodore, in *Councils and Ecclesiastical Documents Relating to Great Britain and Ireland*, ed. A. W. Hadden and W. Stubbs (London, 1871).

PELTERET, D. A. E., *Catalogue of English Post-Conquest Vernacular Documents* (Woodbridge, 1990).

The Pinchbeck Register, ed. Lord Francis Hervey (London, 1925).
Regesta Regum Anglo-Normannorum, i, ed. H. W. C. Davis (Oxford, 1913).
SAWYER, P. H., *Anglo-Saxon Charters: An Annotated List and Bibliography*, Royal Historical Society Guides and Handbooks, 8 (London, 1968).
Vita Edwardi Regis, ed. F. Barlow, Nelson's Medieval Texts (London, 1962).
WACE, *Roman de Rou*, in *Chroniques Anglo-Normandes* i, ed. F. Michel (Paris, 1836).
WHITELOCK, D., *Anglo-Saxon Wills* (Cambridge, 1930).
WILLIAM OF POITIERS, *Gesta Guillelmi*, ed. R. Foreville (Paris, 1952).

Secondary Sources

ABELS, R., 'Bookland and Fyrd Service in Late Saxon England', in R. A. Brown (ed.), *Anglo-Norman Studies, VII: Proceedings of the Battle Conference, 1984* (Woodbridge, 1985).
—— *Lordship and Military Obligation in Anglo-Saxon England* (London, 1988).
ALCOCK, L., *By South Cadbury is that Camelot* . . . (London, 1972).
BARLOW, F., Review of T. J. Oleson's *The Witenagemot in the Reign of Edward the Confessor*, in *Journal of Ecclesiastical History*, 7 (1956), 86–7.
—— *Edward the Confessor* (London, 1970).
—— *The English Church 1000–1066*, 2nd edn. (London, 1979).
BATES, D., *Normandy Before 1066* (London, 1982).
BERESFORD, G., 'Goltho Manor, Lincolnshire: The Buildings and their Surrounding Defences', in R. A. Brown (ed.), *Anglo-Norman Studies, IV: Proceedings of the Battle Conference, 1981* (Woodbridge, 1982).
BLAIR, J. (ed.), *Minsters and Parish Churches in Transition 950–1200* (Oxford, 1988).
—— *Early Medieval Surrey* (Stroud, 1991).
BLOCH, M., *Feudal Society* (London, 1978).
BROOKS, N. P., 'Anglo-Saxon Charters', in *Anglo-Saxon England*, 3 (1974).
—— 'Arms, Status and Warfare in Late Saxon England', in D. Hill (ed.), *Ethelred the Unready*, British Archaeological Reports, 59 (1978).
BROWN, R. A., *The Origins of English Feudalism* (London, 1973).
CAM, H., *Law Finders and Law Makers in Medieval England* (London, 1962).
CAMPBELL, J., 'Observations on Early English Government', in *Transactions of the Royal Historical Society*, 5th ser., 25 (1979).
—— 'Some Agents and Agencies of the late Anglo-Saxon State', in J. C. Holt (ed.), *Domesday Studies* (Woodbridge, 1987).
CAMPBELL, M. W., 'Tostig Displaced', in *Annales de Normandie*, 22 (1972).
—— 'Godwin, Edward and William', in *Traditio*, 28 (1972).
—— 'Emma', in *Annales de Normandie*, 23 (1973).
—— 'Anti-Norman Reaction in 1052', in *Medieval Studies*, 38 (1976).
—— 'Godwin the Kingmaker', in *Canadian Journal of History*, 13 (1978).

CORBETT, W. J., 'The Development of the Duchy of Normandy and the Norman Conquest of England', in *The Cambridge Medieval History* (Cambridge, 1930), vol. v, ch. 15.

DARBY, H. C., *Domesday England* (Cambridge, 1977).

—— *Domesday Gazetteer* (Cambridge, 1975).

—— *Domesday Geography of Eastern England*, 3rd edn. (Cambridge, 1971).

DARBY, H. C., and MAXWELL, I. S., *Domesday Geography of Northern England*, 2nd edn. (Cambridge, 1977).

DARBY, H. C., and TERRETT, I. C., *Domesday Geography of Midland England*, 2nd edn. (Cambridge, 1971).

DAVIES, R. H., 'The Lands of Harold, Son of Godwine, and their Distribution by William I', unpublished MA dissertation (Cardiff, 1967).

DODWELL, B., 'Free Peasantry of East Anglia in Domesday', in *Norfolk Archaeology*, 27 (1941).

—— 'East Anglian Commendation', in *EHR* 63 (1948).

DOUGLAS, D. C., *The Social Structure of Medieval East Anglia*, Oxford Studies in Social and Legal History 9 (1927).

—— *Feudal Documents of the Abbey of Bury St Edmunds*, British Academy, Records of the Social and Economic History of England and Wales, viii (1972).

—— 'Odo, Lanfranc and the Domesday Survey', in J. G. Edwards, V. H. Galbraith, and E. F. Jacob (eds.), *Historical Essays in Honour of James Tait* (Manchester, 1933).

DUBY, G., 'The Nobility in Eleventh- and Twelfth-Century Maconnais', in F. L. Cheyette (ed.), *Lordship and Community in Medieval Europe* (New York, 1968).

EYTON, R. W., *Antiquities of Shropshire* (1854).

FAWTIER, R., *The Capetian Kings of France* (London, 1960).

FELL, C., 'The Icelandic Version of the Anglo-Saxon Emigration to Byzantium', in *Anglo-Saxon England*, 3 (1974).

FINN, R. W., *An Introduction to Domesday Book* (Cambridge, 1961).

—— *Domesday Studies: The Liber Exoniensis* (London, 1964).

—— *Domesday Studies: The Eastern Counties* (London, 1967).

FLEMING, R., 'Domesday Estates of the King and the Godwines: A Study in Late Saxon Politics', in *Speculum*, 58 (1983).

—— *Kings and Lords in Conquest England* (Cambridge, 1991).

FREEMAN, E. A., *The History of the Norman Conquest*, i, ii, 2nd edn. (London, 1870); iii–v, 1st edn. (London, 1869–75), esp. vols. ii and iv.

GENICOT, L., 'Recent Research on the Medieval Nobility', in T. Reuter (ed.), *The Medieval Nobility* (Amsterdam, 1978).

GILLINGHAM, J., 'William the Bastard at War', in C. Harper-Bill, C. J. Holdsworth, and J. L. Nelson (eds.), *Studies in Medieval History Presented to R. Allen Brown* (Woodbridge, 1989).

GODFREY, J., 'The Defeated Anglo-Saxons Take Service with the Eastern Emperors', in R. A. Brown (ed.), *Proceedings of the Battle Conference on Anglo-Norman Studies, 1978* (Woodbridge, 1979).

GREEN J., 'The Sheriffs of William the Conqueror', in R. A. Brown (ed.), *Anglo-Norman Studies, V: Proceedings of the Battle Conference, 1982* (Woodbridge, 1983).

GRIERSON, P., 'A Visit of Earl Harold to Flanders in 1056', *EHR* 51 (1936).

HART, C. J. R., *Early Charters of Eastern England* (Leicester, 1966).

HARVEY, S., 'Domesday and its Predecessors', in *EHR* 86 (1971).

—— 'Taxation and the Ploughland in Domesday Book', in P. H. Sawyer (ed.), *Domesday Book: A Reassessment* (London, 1985).

HASE, P. H., 'The Mother Churches of Hampshire', in J. Blair (ed.), *Minsters and Parish Churches in Transition, 950–1200* (Oxford, 1988).

HILL, D. (ed.), *Ethelred the Unready*, British Archaeologocal Reports, 59 (1978).

—— *An Atlas of Anglo-Saxon England* (Oxford, 1981), esp. maps 179–86.

HOLLISTER, C. W., *Anglo-Saxon Military Institutions* (Oxford, 1962).

HOLT, J. C., 'Feudal Society and the Family in Early Medieval England, I', *TRHS* 32 (1982).

—— (ed.), *Domesday Studies* (Woodbridge, 1987).

HOOPER, N., 'Anglo-Saxon Warfare on the Eve of the Conquest: A Brief Survey', in R. A. Brown (ed.), *Proceedings of the Battle Conference on Anglo-Norman Studies, 1978* (Woodbridge, 1979).

—— 'The Housecarls of England in the Eleventh Century', in R. A. Brown (ed.), *Anglo-Norman Studies, VII: Proceedings of the Battle Conference, 1984* (Woodbridge, 1985).

KEYNES, S. D., *The Diplomas of Ethelred 'the Unready'* (Cambridge, 1980).

LEMARIGNIER, J., 'Political and Monastic Structures in France at the End of the Tenth and the Beginning of the Eleventh Century', in F. L. Cheyette (ed.), *Lordship and Community in Medieval Europe* (New York, 1968).

LENNARD, R. V., *Rural England 1086–1135* (Oxford, 1959).

LEYSER, K., 'The German Aristocracy from the Ninth to the Early Twelfth Century: A Historical and Cultural Sketch', in *Medieval Germany and its Neighbours, 900–1250* (London, 1982).

LIEBERMANN, F., *Gesetze der Angelsachsen*, i. *Text und Ubersetzung* (Halle, 1903).

MACK, K., 'The Stallers: Administrative Innovation in the Reign of King Edward the Confessor', in *Journal of Medieval History* (1986).

MAITLAND, F. W., *Domesday Book and Beyond* (Cambridge, 1921).

MASON, E., 'Change and Continuity in Eleventh-Century Mercia', in R. A. Brown (ed.), *Anglo-Norman Studies, XI: Proceedings of the Battle Conference, 1985* (Woodbridge, 1986).

MASON, J., 'The Rapes of Sussex', in *Sussex Archaeological Collections*, 102 (1964).

MacDonald, J., and Snooks, G., 'Were the Tax Assessments of Domesday England Artificial? The Case for Essex', in *Economic History Review*, 2nd ser., 39 (1985).
—— 'The Determinants of Manorial Income in Domesday England: The Evidence for Essex', in *Journal of Economic History*, 45 (1985).
Miller, E., *The Abbey and Bishopric of Ely* (Cambridge, 1951).
Morris, W. A., *The Medieval English Sheriff to 1300* (Manchester, 1927).
Mortimer, R., 'The Beginnings of the Honour of Clare', in R. A. Brown (ed.), *Proceedings of the Battle Conference on Anglo-Norman Studies, 1980* (Woodbridge, 1981).
Okasha, E., *A Handlist of Anglo-Saxon Non-Runic Inscriptions* (Cambridge, 1971).
Oleson, T. J., *The Witenagemot in the Reign of Edward the Confessor* (Oxford, 1955).
Pollock, F., and Maitland, F. W., *The History of English Law* (Cambridge, 1968).
Rahtz, P., *The Saxon and Medieval Palaces at Cheddar*, British Archaeological Reports, 65 (1979).
Reid, R. R., 'Barony and Thegnage', in *EHR* 35 (1920).
Reuter, T. (ed.), *The Medieval Nobility* (Amsterdam, 1978).
Reynolds, S., 'Eadric *Silvaticus* and the English Resistance', in *Bulletin of the Institute of Historical Research*, 54 (1981).
Roffe, D., 'From Thegnage to Barony', in M. Chibnall (ed.), *Anglo-Norman Studies, XII: Proceedings of the Battle Conference, 1989* (Woodbridge, 1990).
Round, J. H., 'Introduction to the Hertfordshire Domesday', in *VCH, Hertfordshire*, I (London, 1902).
Sawyer, P. H., '1066–1086: A Tenurial Revolution', in P. H. Sawyer (ed.), *Domesday Book: A Reassessment* (London, 1985).
—— (ed.), *Domesday Book: A Reassessment* (London, 1985).
Scarfe, N., *The Suffolk Landscape* (London, 1972).
Schmid, K., 'The Structure of the Nobility in the Earlier Middle Ages', in T. Reuter (ed.), *The Medieval Nobility* (Amsterdam, 1978).
Searle, E., 'Women and the Succession to the Norman Conquest', in R. A. Brown (ed.), *Proceedings of the Battle Conference on Anglo-Norman Studies, 1981* (Woodbridge, 1982).
Searle, W. G., *Onomasticon Anglo-Saxonicum* (Cambridge, 1897).
Stenton, F. M., *Anglo-Saxon England*, Oxford History of England, ii, 2nd edn. (Oxford, 1947).
Stephenson, C., 'Commendation and Related Problems in Domesday', in *EHR* 59 (1944).
Stephenson, W., 'Yorkshire Surveys and Other Documents of the Eleventh Century', in *EHR* 27 (1912).
Sylvester, D., 'Rural Settlement in Domesday Shropshire', in *Sociological Review*, 25 (1933).

TAYLOR, H. M., *Anglo-Saxon Architecture* (Cambridge, 1965–78).

TELLENBACH, G., 'From the Carolingian Imperial Nobility to the German Estates of the Imperial Princes', in T. Reuter (ed.), *The Medieval Nobility* (Amsterdam, 1978).

TENGVIK, G., *Old English Bynames* (Uppsala, 1938).

TURNER, G. J., 'Bookland and Folkland', in J. G. Edwards, V. H. Galbraith, and E. F. Jacob (eds.), *Historical Essays in Honour of James Tait* (Manchester, 1933).

VERCAUTEREN, F., 'A Kindred in Northern France', in T. Reuter (ed.), *The Medieval Nobility* (Amsterdam, 1978).

VON FEILITZEN, O., *The Pre-Conquest Personal Names of Domesday Book* (Uppsala, 1937).

WHITE, G. H., 'The Earldom of Norfolk', in H. A. Doubleday and H. de Walden (eds.), *The Complete Peerage* (London, 1936), ix.

WILLIAMS, A., 'Land and Power in the Eleventh Century: The Estates of Harold Godwineson', in R. A. Brown (ed.), *Proceedings of the Battle Conference on Anglo-Norman Studies, 1981* (Woodbridge, 1982).

—— '"Cockles Amongst the Wheat": Danes and English in the Western Midlands in the First Half of the Eleventh Century', *Midlands History*, 11 (1986).

—— 'A Vice-Comital Family in pre-Conquest Warwickshire', in R. A. Brown (ed.), *Anglo-Norman Studies, XI: Proceedings of the Battle Conference, 1988* (Woodbridge, 1989).

—— 'The King's Nephew: The Family and Career of Ralph, Earl of Hereford', in C. Harper-Bill, C. J. Holdsworth, and J. L. Nelson (eds.), *Studies in Medieval History Presented to R. Allen Brown* (Woodbridge, 1989).

INDEX